A Critical History of Classical Chinese Philosophy

By He Zhaowu & Peng Gang

新世界出版社
NEW WORLD PRESS

First Edition 2009

By He Zhaowu and Peng Gang

Edited by Li Shujuan and Xu Jingguo

Final copy-editing done by Ricky Jeffrey

ISBN 978-7-5104-0537-2

Published by

NEW WORLD PRESS

24 Baiwanzhuang Street, Beijing 100037, China

Distributed by

NEW WORLD PRESS

24 Baiwanzhuang Street, Beijing 100037, China

Tel: 86-10-68995968

Fax: 86-10-68998705

Website: www.newworld-press.com

E-mail: frank@nwp.com.cn

Printed in the People's Republic of China

Preface

Some years ago, I was asked by the publisher to prepare a book for Western readers on the history of philosophy in China. Ever since accepting this invitation, I have pondered how the work should be done and in what form it should be presented. On this topic there were innumerable works and papers in circulation. And foreign works (including those by Chinese scholars) in this field are already more than one might expect. So where should I begin my task and how should I deal with it?

Systematic theoretical thinking has existed in China for more than twenty-five centuries, since Confucius, undoubtedly one of the earliest and most brilliant thinkers of world civilization. The late Prof. Feng Youlan summarized it into two periods: the period of the philosophers, and that of the scholastics. I regard this division as one of Prof. Feng's keenest insights, though it was the same path taken by Western intellectual history. The antiquity of the West was an epoch of classical civilization, while in the Middle Ages all that was entitled learning was scholastic study, and all thought was brought forth in the form of scholastic exegesis. This mediaeval feature was the same both in China and the West. The sole difference lay merely in the fact that China was in need of a modern age. But when considering traditional thought, the classical age certainly played a more important role than the scholasticism of the middle ages. Hence it was more worthy of our concern.

As for research on the history of ideas in general or on philosophy in particular, it should as a rule consist of three integral parts: (1) the revision and reconstruction of the historical sources and facts; (2) the interpretation and explanation of the theories under investigation; and (3) the criticism and evaluation of the theories and thoughts of our predecessors. All works of the first category presuppose common agreement on the criterion for what is factual and real, while those of the second category presuppose common agreement on the criterion for what is logical and reasonable. But for what falls within the sphere of the third category, there is no commonly agreed criterion whatsoever; it is entirely the author's own product, and can by no means be substituted by that of anybody else. In view of the fact that in the first two categories so many works have already been produced by so many researchers, I am inclined to concentrate more on what falls into the third category. This is the reason why the present work is entitled *Classical Philosophy in China—A Critical History*.

On the occasion of its publication, I'd like to take this opportunity to express my gratitude to some unforgettable teachers and friends. I was already too late to attend the lectures of Liang Qichao, the teacher of my teachers' generation, but a series of his writings related to this field, especially his *Main Trends of Learning in Ancient China, History of Learning in China in the Last Three Centuries, A Survey of Learning of the Qing Period* and *Studies on the Occidental Philosophers*, had been served as the introductory primers to the youngsters of my generation. In my university days, Prof. Feng Youlan conducted the course on the history of Chinese philosophy, and his epoch-making book *History of Chinese Philosophy* was then the standard textbook. Although there were polemics over his viewpoints and interpretations among our schoolmates, the many merits, insights and scrutinizing inquiries in his book could never be denied. It was also then that Prof. Zhang Xiruo gave his lecture courses on the history of Western political theory and on modern Western political theory. It was his lectures that kindled my interest in the history of ideas. Later, in the 1950s, I joined Prof. Hou Wailu's team working on intellectual history. As his student and assistant, I learned from him that the history of ideas was a part of the whole course of history and could never be treated as a purely logical structure. He was indeed a genuine Marxist that at times made him incompatible with the then prevailing current of political exegesis. As for myself, I am forever unable to let the inherent power of the idea itself shrink into total oblivion, in spite of the fact that all ideas are of necessity conditioned by historical circumstances. I like Beethoven's music. Yet I may have no knowledge at all of Beethoven the man and his time. I may not even know that Beethoven composed this piece of music, and simply be enchanted by the piece itself. And that will do. So it is with the case of every theory and every idea. History is the mother of all theories and ideas, but once an idea was born into this world, it was instantly endowed with its own existence and life, independent of its mother. Accordingly a researcher ought to judge a theory by the merits and defects of that theory itself alone, irrespective of what its material background might be. In this regard, a researcher ought to be value-free, or to be neutral in his value judgment. Yet a researcher cannot avoid having his own sense of humanistic value. Otherwise, he would be a researcher of the natural world and not of the human. Herein dwells the duality of human history, which forever advances as though in a state of perpetual antinomy.

Mr. Peng Gang has been a helpful co-author of the present book, of which he drafted a part, and prepared the final copy of the whole manuscript. Ms. Zhou Kuijie, Ms. Zhang Haiou, Ms. Li Shujuan and Mr. Xu Jingguo of New World Press, and Mr. Ricky Jeffery have generously aided the publication of this book. It is only appropriate that in my prefatory words I thank them for their kindness.

He Zhaowu
2009, Beijing

Contents

Introduction

When compared with the philosophy of the West, philosophy in China has had its own distinct history. The present work aims at an exposition of the history of philosophy in China from a critical point of view. In this short introduction it is hoped that some preliminary remarks will help readers to approach the general historical background of Chinese culture and thought.

[I] Philosophy, History, History of Philosophy

The scope of the history of philosophy covers both philosophy and history; it deals with the history of the specific topic of philosophy. Everything in the world has its history. Human civilization has its history, and so does the philosophical thought of mankind. The locus of the development of philosophical thought is what we delineate as the history of philosophy. But the study of philosophy differentiates itself from the study of history in an essential aspect. Ordinarily in the study of history, people may (though not always) reach a unanimous conclusion. For example, in relation to the birth year of Confucius, people could eventually reach a unanimous conclusion, because—in accordance with common sense—Confucius had to have been born in a certain year (and not any other). Even in the event that there is no year generally accepted as the definite one, it is simply due to the fact that our present studies cannot as yet afford a conclusion. It by no way means that Confucius had no definite birth year at all. Therefore, sooner or later, we may at least reach a unanimous conclusion on an exact birth date for Confucius. For another example, Mencius once said that after Confucius had developed the book *Spring and Autumn Annals,*[①] all the rebellious elements were held in horror and astonishment. Some scholars citing these words as evidence argue that the book *Spring and Autumn Annals* was the work of Confucius, while others argue against this on other grounds.

Whether the book *Spring and Autumn Annals* was the work of Confucius is a question about a definite fact, on which people can and should reach a common consensus. Though we are not as yet able to give a definite assertion, nevertheless the question itself of whether Confucius ever produced such a book

① On the book *Spring and Autumn Annals*, see next chapter.

Spring and Autumn Annals still exists. Whether Confucius has written such a book or not is after all a matter of historical fact, and a historical fact is unalterable, once wrought. Common sense tells us, history consists of objective facts on which people may and should come to a definite conclusion. If a conclusion has not been reached, it is simply because we have not yet been able to perform sufficient investigation, not because such facts do not exist.

But in the study of philosophy, the case appears to be somewhat otherwise. Philosophy deals with theories and thoughts. On whether the theory or thoughts of someone are such and such, people may hold very different opinions and interpretations. The well-known Greek philosopher Socrates branded his own method of argument as that of midwifery, meaning that he merely hoped to induce his conclusions from the thinking of others. When someone was wrong in their thinking without knowing it, Socrates would come forth to help draw out wrong conclusions from that person's own theory. Thus one's own errors are shown without Socrates' (or any other's) assertion. Once when Socrates held a dialogue with someone who was proud of his own theory of running the state, Socrates did not touch on his political ideas, but only talked about that man's family life. Socrates induced him to admit that he was not on good terms with other members of his own family. Then Socrates asked: if you are not on good terms with the members of your family, how could you behave on good terms with your country and your people? This was for nothing else than to draw the wrong conclusion out from this person's own ways—that is, the theories you might preach do not matter—indeed, they are not even practicable in your own life. The above example helps to illustrate something true of any philosophical theory. A theory necessarily involves some subjective elements in our understanding or interpretation, which are in their nature very different from pure historical facts. Historical fact *per se* has nothing to do with subjective understanding or interpretation. Confucius was born exactly in the year in which he was born. Did he ever compose the book *Spring and Autumn Annals*? He did, if ever he did; he did not, if never. But the case is different with our understanding of the philosophical theories we may attribute to people. We may find in his theory what he himself has not consciously come to know or to acknowledge. In other words, the understanding of philosophy involves interpretation and intellectual reconstruction in the mind of the reader.

Now let us come back to the history of philosophy in China. When we study Confucius, we have to arrange Confucius' sayings into a theoretical system by ourselves. As a matter of fact, what Confucius has left to the present day is nothing more than a miscellany of fragmentary remarks, which Confucius himself had no idea how to synthesize into a systematic philosophical theory. It was left to the later ages to propound or to develop it. Hence we are confronted with the problem of how to recreate Confucius' ideas into a whole—a problem never encountered by Confucius himself.

Usually, in studying philosophies in history, we are accustomed to employing certain models and paradigms to comprehend these theories—for instance, by first dealing with his life and time, his ways of thinking, then his epistemology, his cosmology, his ontology, his ethics and his social and political ideas, etc. Indeed the philosopher himself while forming his ideas had no intention to comply with such well-regulated models. This kind of structure is forced upon him by us, not by himself. Though this procedure of manipulation should not be seen as an erroneous fabrication, it is at any rate far from what the philosophers of the past originally had in mind. That is to say, his philosophy is now in essence what we have constructed through our own understanding and analysis of his sayings. Hence, whether what we have perceived in him is exactly what he originally intended to mean, and whether it corresponds with the thoughts that were in his mind, will remain a perennial question. Here arises the question of how we interpret and explain others' thoughts; and herein lies the difference between philosophy and history. Or, we may as well put it in this way; in understanding the philosophy of others, there is necessarily an element of personal subjectivity—while historical fact in a certain sense might be taken as something objectively given.

It is often believed that the study of history is necessary because understanding the past will help us understand the present. Further, in a broader sense, to understand anything is in a considerable degree only to understand its past, i.e. to grasp some historical understanding of it. This is just as in the diagnosis of a patient by the doctor, who has to consult the patient's medical record to understand the history of his illness. From the viewpoint of historiography, understanding the past is for the sake of a better understanding of the present; from the viewpoint of philosophy, understanding the past is for the sake of enriching our present theoretical knowledge. While our present theoretical knowledge is enriched, it is at the same time improved and reformed. Without this function, philosophy would be valueless. Later generations can only make progress on the shoulders of the earlier.

[II] Studies of the History of Philosophy in China

Philosophy in China traces back to very ancient times, and the same with the study of its history. In the last chapter of the *Book of Zhuang Zi*, "The World" (*Tian Xia*), there is a treatise on all the philosophical schools of ancient China and their representatives, with criticism and evaluations of their theories and ideas. It is in reality a history of ancient philosophy, written by an ancient philosopher. Later in the Han period (about a century after the great unification of Qin), Sima Tan, the father of the great historian Sima Qian and himself the royal historian, wrote a treatise *On the Essentials of the Six Schools*. It is also a history of philosophy, criticizing respectively the six main philosophical schools of ancient times. After that, there were many successive works dealing with the topic, the most well-known being *The Eminent Ming Philosophers* (*Ming Ruo Xue An*) by Huang Zhongxi, the famous scholar of the early 17th century.

This work was followed by a series of similar ones, including *The Eminent Song and Yuan Philosophers* (*Song Yuan Xue An*) by Huang and his followers and *The Eminent Qing Philosophers* (*Qing Ruo Xue An*) by others. All of them were written in the traditional fashion and hence not in line with the modern academic discipline.

The study of the history of Chinese philosophy, as that study is understood in its modern sense, dates back to the first years of the 20th century. In 1902, Liang Qichao, the forerunner of the Chinese Enlightenment, published his *The Main Trends of the Academic Ideas in China* (*Lun Zhong Guo Xue Shu Si Xiang Bian Qian Zhi Da Shi*). Liang himself was the foremost pioneer and founder of modern historiography in China, and this thesis should be deservedly ranked as one of the earliest works on the history of philosophy in China in a more strict sense. It surpassed the traditional way of thinking and its sense of value by observing ancient philosophy through modern eyes. This again relates to the above-mentioned difference between philosophy and the study of history. In Liang's treatise, what he dealt with was the philosophy of ancient times, but he discussed it from a view which is wholly new and modern. Sometime later in the year 1906, Zhang Taiyan published his *An Exposition of the Ancient Philosophers* (*Zhu Zi Xue Lun Shuo*), *Zhu Zi* meaning the various ancient philosophers and their schools. Zhang dealt with the ancient philosophers of China as well, and also considered it through a modern perspective. One of the cardinal differences between the traditional discipline and the modern lies primarily in this: in the modern perspective each school is considered respectively upon an equal basis without discrimination, or, all philosophers are equal before the academic court; whereas in the eyes of the ancients, it is the idea of orthodoxy that reigns supreme, unorthodox philosophies being branded as heresies. For instance, the Neo-Confucians of the Song period regarded the Buddhist and the Taoist school (*Er Shi*) as heresies, presupposing that all schools of philosophy are not theoretically equal, and that the Confucianism should hold sole supremacy over all others. Soon after Liang and Zhang, Cai Yuanpei, who was then already the leader of modern learning in China, on the eve of the 1911 revolution published his work *History of Ethics in China* (*Zhong Guo Lun Li Xue Shi*), in which he also explored ancient philosophy from a modern view.

These three writers mentioned above drew back the curtain of the history of philosophy in its modern sense, but the most salient representative work in this field should be attributed to Hu Shih's *An Outline History of Philosophy in China* (*Zhong Guo Zhe Xue Shi Da Gang*). This book is of epoch-making significance in the field of the history of philosophy, and even in some way laid down the foundation of academic research in modern China at large. Here it should be noted that an academic work may be evaluated either by its own academic merit or by its historical significance. The value of a book can exist either in its own innovation or in its influence on society at large. The contributions of these masters all lie predominantly in their historical influence rather than in their academic merits. It was these persons who initiated a new current of thought, the historical significance of which we can never overestimate, no matter what credit we may attach to the academic value within them. They are the great torch-bearers of the enlightenment of modern China.

Hu's work belonged to the May Fourth Movement of 1919. A decade and a half later Feng Youlan's (also known as Fung Yulan) *A History of Chinese Philosophy* (*Zhong Guo Zhe Xue Shi*) appeared before the reading public (1930-1934). Feng was then lecturing the history of philosophy in Tsinghua University and his lectures were put in book form, which at once swayed the academic field, and which was generally acknowledged as a model work of scholarship at that time. Feng has a theoretical system and viewpoint of his own, which he made full use of in the interpretation of the ancient philosophers as he saw them. A fact in history can exist only in one way. Of a historical fact, it can be said that there should only be one assertion; but for a philosophical theory, it can never be ascertained which among the various interpretations has the right to assume exclusive priority. Different persons are each perfectly qualified to justify their own interpretations in their own fashion. There is an old Chinese proverb: "There is no final explanation of a poem," meaning that for any poem there can be no interpretation which is so definite and exact that it should be generally accepted. Even the author himself cannot give a final explanation. Similarly, it can also be said that there is no final explanation for a philosophical theory. For any given philosophical theory of bygone days, one may explain either in this way or that, and no explanation is entitled to be assumed as the only one. Many of Feng's viewpoints nowadays may seem unacceptable, especially after the year 1949 when China was proclaimed liberated. Yet as a witness to the intellectual history of an age, this work nevertheless still holds great value in that it reflected a typical norm of the understanding of the time.

Down to the forties of the 20th century, Marxist theory (then not yet so much sinicized as decades later) began to propagate and prevail in China in a large torrent, and among the Marxist camp of scholars Hou Wailu should rightly be counted as the foremost in the study of the history of philosophy. His monumental work, *A General Intellectual History of China* (*Zhong Guo Si Xiang Tong Shi*) in six volumes was drafted in the early forties and completed in the late fifties. Hou's way of research is an approach from the socio-economic base to the intellectual superstructure, and then conversely from the superstructure to the base—a typically Marxist approach. As an insight to the age, this work offers a complete summation of the Marxist research into the philosophy of China.[①] And since then, the study of intellectual history has become a hot topic in the fields of both historical and philosophical research. There are at the same time many scholars outside of China engaging in research work in this field, some of whom are foreign sinologists and some overseas Chinese emigrants, including the "contemporary New Confucians."

In the above paragraphs we have sketched briefly the history of the study of the history of philosophy in China. Now the Chinese people are entering into a new age which in many ways differs greatly from the time of the fifties to the seventies. A new historical stage is unavoidably bringing forth its new points of view, with which people would reflect the past anew. Why is it that history needs to be studied again and again? Roughly speaking, the historical literature we are in possession of is rather limited in quantity, but as our ideas are ever-changing, the pictures we reconstruct in our minds' eye are always changing correspondingly. This is the reason why the study of history should be subject to an ever-renewing process of scrutiny and reflection. For instance, in studying

① The author is obliged to confess that in his university years he twice attended two courses in Professor Feng's classes and from the mid-fifties to mid-eighties he served as Professor Hou's assistant for many years. However, the views expressed in this book are wholly his own.

the ancient history of China, the sources we rely on are from Sima Qian's *Records of the Historian*. Most probably, there are certain historical facts we can know no more than he did, but still we have to engage in further study. We should not and cannot remain in the same spot where he once stood, because we have our own ideas different to his. People today are not the people of his day. Different ideas have set them apart. Different ideas beget different problems, which in turn beget different answers. Consequently historical study is a process of reinterpretation and reconstruction. This is so not only with historical understanding, but also with other subjects. The solar system varies little from what it was a hundred years (or even a thousand years) ago, but scientists still continue to study it strenuously, because the scientific knowledge and ideas of today are greatly changed from what they were a hundred years ago, and the scientists today study the solar system from a position far ahead that of a hundred years ago.

Subsequently the results of present-day research are greatly at variance with those of bygone days.

[III] Chinese Philosophy vs. Philosophy in China

The question arising in the next turn is: what are the objects of study of the history of philosophy in China? Of course, they fall within the sphere of Chinese philosophy or philosophy in China. But the following should be discerned. As early as the beginning of the thirties, when Feng Youlan completed his *History of Chinese Philosophy*, Jin Yuelin wrote a critical report of it in which we read the commentary: when an author writes a book on the *History of British Physics*, what he deals with is in reality not the history of "British physics," but the history of "the physics in Britain;" because strictly speaking, there is only physics in Britain, but no such thing as British physics, just as there is no such thing as French physics, but only physics in France. These two terms connote two different ideas. Yet one may still go on to ask: granted that there is no such thing as British physics, but is there also no such thing as British philosophy? At any rate, philosophy is after all no kind of physics. Is there such a thing as Chinese philosophy? Does the term "the history of Chinese philosophy" denote the history of philosophy in China or the history of "Chinese philosophy"? The answer is not as simple as it might seem *prima facie*. Until his very last, Feng Youlan held that there is such a thing as Chinese philosophy, and he dealt only with history of that sort of philosophy; while others think otherwise, holding that it deals only with the history of philosophy in China. Personally I would prefer an eclectic position—a position somewhere between the two opposites. As an academic discipline, philosophy like all other disciplines deals with what is universal and universally valid. Mathematics is universal and universally valid. That 2 + 2 = 4 is universally acknowledged, no matter whether in Britain or in China. Then is there a history of mathematics in China? Yes, there is, but only in so far as it denotes the history of mathematics in China. Apart from the idea of mathematics in China, the term "Chinese mathematics" is altogether meaningless. For a further illustration, take the example of geometry. As late as the first years of the 17th century, there had still been no geometry in China. But this by no means demonstrates that the Chinese are incapable of geometrical knowledge, or that the caliber of the Chinese mind is by nature unsuited to the study of geometry, so that geometry is not part of Chinese mathematics, or even that it cannot be mastered by the Chinese. In history, the Chinese indeed were long ignorant of geometry, but this does not make geometry by nature inassimilable to Chinese mathematics. As to why China had had no geometry, it has to be attributed to the historical background, that is, one has to resort to causes which are not inborn in Chinese minds. A national character or mind is formed through the long course of historical development; it is by no means doomed inevitably and unalterably to be so. There is no pre-determined national character or national mind whatsoever. Although it might be admitted that people in one part of the world are considerably different from others, that is entirely caused by their historical conditions, not by their nature. Some writers stress that the Chinese are not good at close analysis, and they interpret this as the reason why philosophy in China took the way of poetic apprehension rather than that of logical analysis. Let the case be so; it in no way means that Chinese minds are inappropriate for logical speculation. It is merely caused by their surrounding historical conditions. One such condition is the relative stagnation of China's natural sciences. Once the conditions are made ready, Chinese minds can just as wisely practice the learning of geometry and logic.

Philosophy has its universal objects and universal methods which are common to and equally valid for all peoples, and in this sense there is no problem of "Chinese philosophy" whatsoever. This is also the Marxist view. Engels in his *Feuerbach and the End of the German Classical Philosophy* proposed that the basic problem of all philosophies is that of thinking in relation to existence. Those who take thinking as primary are the idealists and those who take matter as primary are the materialists. This is a universal judgment, a judgment universally valid for all people whenever and wherever, including those in Chinese philosophy. Philosophy has its object of inquiry, which is none other than the universal principles of thinking and of existence. They are equally valid and available to all persons, places and times.

For the inquiry into its object, philosophy has to employ certain ways of thinking, i.e. its methodology. To meet such needs, people are in the habit of using some sort of manipulation, such as the metaphysical method, the dialectical method, the analytic method, the intuitive method and so on. So far as the object of inquiry and their relevant method are by nature universal, the term "Chinese philosophy" can imply nothing more than "philosophy in China." Thus the history of Chinese philosophy can only mean the history of philosophy in China; just as there is nothing that may be rightfully called Chinese mathematics, except in the sense of "mathematics in China," although Chinese mathematics could and did assume some form of expression different from the West. In the West, a triangle is always denoted by A, B and C, while in the very first stage of its introduction into China it is denoted by *Jia*, *Yi* and *Bing* the first three symbols of the Ten Heavenly Stems (*Tian Gan*). But as far as geometry proper is concerned, there is no difference whatsoever between the Western and the Chinese. In reality the value of truth lies nowhere else than in its universal validity. If it did not, it would cease to be a truth. It is this universal validity that makes a truth what constitutes a truth and a principle what constitutes a principle.

Yet when viewed from another level, under the universality there co-exist unique particularities. Each nation has its own particularity closely connected with and conditioned by its own particular history. The history of each nation differs from that of others. In contrast to their commonality or universality, this difference makes up their respective particularity. For instance, any ruler or small group of rulers under no supervision or constraint whatsoever always tends to corrupt or be corrupted, and to do whatever they please by making power absolute. Such is the case with all nations in the history of mankind, and hence what Lord Acton said ("Power corrupts, absolute power corrupts absolutely") may be regarded as a universal truth. However, under different historical circumstances power corrupts in different ways, and a ruler may be much more constrained in certain conditions than in others, and the degree of corruption might be lesser than in other cases; and here is just where the particular quality lies. There is a prevailing term for this particularity in present-day China, "*guo qing*" (literally the national condition). Each nation has its own national condition which is of course worthy of being studied carefully and minutely, and which is one factor differentiating the humanities from the natural sciences. Natural sciences place more stress on what is universal, while humanistic or historical studies stress what belongs to humanity, and hence the unique idiosyncrasies. Universality and particularity exist on different levels: what reigns universally is universality, and all idiosyncrasies are secondary and subordinate to the more general universality. It is for this reason that uniqueness should never be emphasized to such a degree as to abrogate universality entirely, as though there is such a thing as "Chinese philosophy" independent of philosophy in general. Above all, Chinese philosophy is philosophy and is a part of and subject to the universal principle of philosophy. Only in this respect, it possesses its particularity which is characteristic of the Chinese. Universal principle, after all, takes primacy, and the particular is secondary. By the same token, the so-called (and often too much quoted) national condition or character is secondary too, and priority should be placed on what is universal.

If in certain times the national condition or characteristics would happen to clash or conflict with the main trend of history, making them incapable of tolerating each other, then, as a rule, it ought to be the former that should accommodate itself to the latter, and not vice versa. One may remember that only about a hundred years ago, many Westerners were of the then prevailing opinion that it was the Chinese national way or characteristic that all males would sport pony-tails and all females were bound up in lily feet, while they both were opium-smokers. In a certain sense, such an opinion may be regarded as well-grounded, for we have not as yet come to know any other people with the practice of having the feet of their young girls bound up into a lily shape. We may fairly ask,if this practice is the national way according to which the Chinese people should comport themselves. Surely not. It is absolutely not the so-called national way or characteristic which we should adapt ourselves to; in fact it is the national way or characteristic that should comply with the historical trend of civilization. A national characteristic is always in a course of being formed and reformed, and national practices of lily feet and opium-smoking can be and ought to be reformed and abolished. It is not doomed inevitably to be so. It was also about a hundred years ago that some of the eminent Chinese took the three cardinal guides and the five constant virtues (*san gang wu chang*)[①] as the national character inherent in Chinese culture. Is the principle "the sovereign guides the subjects" really so deep-rooted in the Chinese that it can never be changed, even at the price of slavery? After all is said and done, what

① The three cardinal guides are: sovereign guides subject, father guides son, and husband guides wife. The five constant virtues are: benevolence, righteousness, propriety, wisdom and fidelity.

is most fundamental and essential is still the universal current of the progress of humanity. In the event that the national condition is not in conformity with the universal current of progress, it is the former that must be reformed or recast or even thrown away in order to accommodate itself to the latter, and not the converse. About fifty years ago those opponents of Marxism in China strongly argued that Marxism does not fit the conditions of China. The issue here is whether our understanding of the national condition should be constructed in conformity with the truth, or the reverse; and the answer is too obvious. When the purported national condition contradicts the universal historical current or the simple truth, then it is the national condition that should have to be reformed or recast. What one should ask at the very start is not whether a truth conforms with the national condition, but just the opposite, i.e. whether the national condition conforms with the universal truth. Particularity should always make room for universality, and can never be independent of it. One cannot nullify universality on the excuse of particularity, or else there can be no universality of truth at all. Philosophical inquiry covers both what is universal and what is particular. Yet it should always be kept in mind that universality precedes and overrides the particular. Philosophy pays attention to the unique only in so far as it affects or relates to the validity of the universal. In general, we may well say that what is particular is historically accidental, and hence cannot be identified with the substance of what constitutes history proper. The inquiry of philosophy is primarily concerned with universal truth and then only as a corollary with the particular forms it assumes. Particularity makes up what should be called national character, which is itself accidental, that is to say, not doomed necessarily to be so, but is formed in the course of history, and which can be and has to be changed or reformed in the course of history.

[IV] The Origin of Philosophical Thought in China

In ancient times, there were, generally speaking, four great civilizations, i.e. the Egyptian, the Babylonian, the Chinese and the Indian. With respect to the times of their emergence, the Chinese was later than the Egyptian and the Babylonian, but earlier than the Indian. These four ancient civilizations are the earliest ancestors of today's global civilization. The ancient Egyptian and Babylonian civilizations vanished in ancient times. Not only did their states and regimes vanish, but also their peoples and civilizations. Indian civilization did not vanish, but survived intermittently with no unbroken tradition. Only the Chinese endured in a continuous line for more than forty centuries with an unbroken record of history. In this respect, Chinese culture might be fairly regarded as unique in the history of mankind.

The origin of Occidental civilization generally traces back to Greece and Rome. Yet not only did the Greek and Roman civilizations emerge far later than the Chinese, but even ended earlier as well. In contradistinction to this lies the peculiarity of the civilization of China. In the field of philosophy, what we have before us is mostly what was written more than two thousand years ago by the hands of the ancient philosophers such as Confucius and Mencius. Yet a Chinese reader finds no great difficulty in reading them. A Chinese reader with no specific classical training at all will readily comprehend the main topic of what the ancients say in their writings in its original form and text. But a Western reader with no specific training in ancient Greek language could hardly know what the ancient Greek philosophers said at all. What follows may afford a few illustrations.

In the beginning of his *Analects*, Confucius said: "Is it not pleasant to learn with constant perseverance and application? Is it not pleasant to have friends coming from distant quarters? Is he not a man of complete virtue who feels no discomposure though others may take no note of him?" Somewhat later, in the beginning of his book, Mencius gave a description of his own journey, "Mencius went to see King Hui of Liang, and the king said, 'Venerable Sir, since you have not counted it far to come here, a distance of a thousand *li* [a Chinese *li* = 1/2 kilometer], may I presume that you likewise bear counsels to profit my kingdom?' Mencius replied, 'Why must Your Majesty use that word "profit"? What I bring are counsels about benevolence and righteousness.'" About the same time that Mencius flourished and professed his way of achieving the salvation of the world, Master Zhuang is reported as lamenting over the illusory nature of "life." When once we have received the bodily form complete, its parts do not fail to perform their functions till the end comes. In conflict with things or in harmony with them, they pursue their course with the speed of a galloping horse which cannot be stopped; is this not deplorable? To be constantly toiling all the time of one's life, without seeing the fruit of one's labor; to be weary and worn out, without knowledge of where one is going; is it not lamentable? There is no significant and insurmountable difficulty whatsoever in comprehending these ideas. Thus, it seems that while the Westerners learn the ideas of their ancient philosophers only through a logical approach, the Chinese may well accept the wisdom of their ancient philosophers in their bones. While the modern Westerners philosophize in the vein of the logical reasonings of their ancestors, the Chinese embody in their flesh and blood the living aspirations of their ancient sages. The former are the intellectual followers of ancient Grcccc and Rome, whereas the latter are direct heirs both in their blood and in their ways of thinking. In this sense, the Chinese offer a unique example in the history of world philosophy.

Further, it is noteworthy that the idea of history has forever been extremely strong in the minds of the Chinese—a fact so saliently manifested in their historiographic tradition, and characterized in their emphatic historical sense. Different from many historical works which were flooded with myths and legends of so many other ancient peoples, the main historical writings in ancient China are mostly reliable historical facts, like those we find in Sima Qian's *Records of the Historian*. But when one turns to ancient Indian historical documents, one can hardly distinguish what are facts from what are not. "Fantastic things" and "spiritual beings" are among the topics which Confucius never took up. So strong is the idea of history among the Chinese that almost every reigning dynasty compiled a voluminous collection of the history of the foregoing dynasty. Thus not only has the civilization of China not broken off, but also her historical records were in the main preserved continuously down to the present day.

It is in general an integrated record of history, unlike other peoples' records which were often interrupted by irreparable breaks. It is of historical significance that China has kept up an unbroken line of historiography and historical records.

Such is the wealthy heritage of the historical culture of China. It may prove to be on the one hand an unparalleled merit which we may put to good use, and on the other an intellectual burden hard to throw away when it turns out to be an obstacle in the way of going ahead. Especially down to modern times when China more and more lagged behind the West, many Chinese intellectuals began to realize that the traditional Chinese culture of the former days had become ever more a hindrance to the progress (and even to the very survival) of their country; and the only way out seemed to be an abrupt and wholesale smashing of the traditional culture of China. Some went even so far as to demand a "total Westernization," at the price of a complete demolition of the traditional culture of China. Thus we come to witness the scene of the bitter struggle between the Westernizer camp and the Sinophile camp—a scene not uncommon in many other countries, such as in Russia (the Westernizers vs. the Slavophiles) and in Spain (the Hispanophobes vs. the Hispanophiles). For the moment I beg to say a few words about the turbulent and vehement demands for a thoroughgoing smashing of the traditional culture of China.

Here the issue is not whether it ought to be so, but whether it is possible to be so. What we have to take into account is whether it is possible for a people to completely segregate from or break up with her past and to trample it under her feet. Surely not. All human developments, spiritual as well as material, are based on foundations furnished by tradition, without which humans could only retrogress into a savage state of antiquity, a state below even that in which Robinson Crusoe found himself, for Robinson Crusoe strove his utmost to use all of the knowledge and technique which he had acquired from tradition in order to survive on the desolate island. To a great extent he owed his ability to survive to tradition. In the same way, a nation can never possibly cut off its bondage or links to its past. She can absorb, modify and make use of it, but she can by no means discard it entirely, just as a person can never be cut off from his own past completely, his past destined to become a part of what he is today. History cannot be broken up or cut off; and the tradition of culture, instead of being cut off, forever penetrates into the nuclei of the cultural organism of the present. Hence the question is not how to throw away the tradition, but how to make use of it so as to turn it to our benefit. Without it, a people can have no starting point for further progress. The civilization of mankind is a complex creation of the sum of various cultures, each constituting an irreplaceable part. In order to participate in the great family of world civilization, it is never required that a nation should give up all of her cultural heritage. Exactly on the contrary, a world civilization is not to be formed at the price of sacrificing the spiritual wealth of each individual nationality, but instead by a process of the full absorption of all the civilizations of all nations. An ideal society would never demand that everyone should annihilate his own individuality, but conversely it exacts of everyone the full expression of his talent and individuality. In the same way a world civilization draws on the individual culture of all peoples.

[V] The Background of Chinese Culture

Just as all ancient civilizations were closely connected with great rivers—Egypt with the Nile, Babylon with the Tigris and Euphrates, India with the Indus—ancient Chinese civilization originated at the basin of the middle Yellow River.

This was largely conditioned by the natural environment. In ancient times the northern and western parts of China were much more fertile than in later times, the change perhaps a result of the later large-scale destruction of forests leading to the sterilization of the arable land. The weather then was far warmer than it is now. Two instances suffice as illustrations. One is that there were lots of elephants then in northern China, and indeed the elephants were so many as to be often employed in waging battles. Another is that there were huge tracts of bamboo as found in many literary records. Now elephants only live in the subtropical zone, while bamboo thrives only south of the Yangtze River. This change in natural conditions might also be attributed to human factors, i.e. the ecological equilibrium was badly damaged by man-made disasters (and especially by wars).

The term "history" as we understand it here, refers to the history of human civilization. As a matter of fact, everything has its history; the planets, the plants, the animals, etc. all have their histories. But their histories are natural history, not human (or rather humanistic) history, for natural history is not produced by human motives or through human action. The human species has also had its own natural history. About three or four million years ago, our earliest ancestors emerged on earth (presumably in eastern Africa). In the late twenties of the 20th century there were found the relics of the *homo erectus pekinenses* southeast of Beijing, generally acknowledged by anthropologists as the forefathers of the present day Chinese. It was dated to as early as half a million years ago. But by then, the people lived in a state of nature and hence their history belongs to the category of natural history, rather than to that of the civilized history of mankind. What do we mean by the history of civilization? Civilization means that mankind has stepped out of their natural state by consciously improving themselves intellectually as well as materially.

Generally speaking, there are two signals which mark the threshold of civilization: written script and civil organization. Literally the written record signifies the beginning of civilization. The key qualification which made it possible for mankind to pass out of the state of nature into the state of civilization is the continuous process of the accumulation of knowledge and technique. Animals of any species other than mankind, clever as they may be, are never capable of accumulating their knowledge and technique. So the later generations start from the same basis, and are never able to surpass their predecessors. For instance, dogs are clever, but dogs of a foregoing generation are never capable of passing their knowledge and technique to the next generation, for whom it is necessary to start everything once more from the very beginning. They act according to their instincts, while human beings act according to their knowledge. This accumulation of knowledge has made human beings what they are, distinct from the animals' state of nature. Thus the art of writing must be acknowledged as the greatest vehicle by which knowledge is made capable of transmission from one person to another and from generation to generation. Without this process of accumulation, there would be no progress whatsoever. Hence, it goes without saying that any idea of a complete smashing of the cultural heritage of the foregoing ages is logically self-contradictory. Without the wealth accumulated by our forefathers, where can we find a place to build up our own civilization? The reason we have progressed further than our predecessors is just because we are standing on the shoulders of our predecessors, so that we are enabled to become wiser than they were. The more we make good in using their achievements, the better our own achievements will be. Knowledge is power, preached Francis Bacon. With the accumulation of knowledge ever increasing, human power constantly grows, which leads mankind on a road of continuous progress.

Another factor which led mankind out of the state of nature into civilization is the emergence of civil organization, or "the state." Before that time, human history was no more than the natural history of mankind, dominated not by humanistic principles but by natural principles. As we may fairly see, community life is found not only in mankind but also in animals, such as in bees and ants, some of them even with very strict organization. But theirs is still the history of nature and not of civilization. The civil community of human beings is not one of nature, but one of the will, that is, an action of volition and an artificial organization. It is man-made, not something by nature or of nature, and hence characteristically distinct from the life of animal communities. The civil state is a human (hence artificial) creation, not something evolved by nature. Through its creation man is endowed with a special force to guarantee the progress of civilization. But, of course, in cases when people enact it foully (instead of wisely), there might also be a retrogression in human civilization. It will depend on how much wisdom (or foolishness) mankind has in manipulating this machine.

These two signs of civilization could already be found in China more than three thousand years ago. Before that time, there were many legends about the ancient sage-kings. But what might be regarded as authentic history should be dated from the "three dynasties", Xia, Shang and Zhou.

Our knowledge of the Xia Dynasty is still far from being complete, especially since few underground excavations have been discovered to allow us an all-round picture of that time. But at least one point should be mentioned here, and that is, nearly all ancient sources referred to these three dynasties in notably definite tones. For instance, in Sima Qian's *Records of the Historian* there are very formal records of the chronology of each of the three dynasties. He narrated the names of all the kings in a long train of successive reigns in their genealogical and chronological order. This narration can hardly be identified as a mere fiction, fabricated by the historian Sima Qian or anybody else. Furthermore, with the help of the archaeological excavations, it may well be asserted that the ancient narration of the history of the Shang Dynasty is in the main authentic and reliable, in conformity with the record of Sima Qian's *Records of the Historian*. It might reasonably be accepted that the history of the Xia Dynasty was not a fabrication, but was roughly based on facts. There is no need for anybody to have fabricated an entire genealogy of the Xia Dynasty. There seems no ground to doubt the very existence of such a dynasty as the Xia (presumed to exist from the 21st to the 17th century B.C.), though we do not know enough about it.

As for the history of the Shang, we do know a great deal more. It was the large scale excavations of inscribed bone relics that helped greatly in verifying the credibility of the written records of Shang history (presumably 17th to 11th century B.C.) as found in ancient sources. Since that time onward, or from the Western Zhou Dynasty (11th century-771 B.C.) onward, we possess more and more accurate and detailed historical records. Roughly speaking, China has a recorded history of more than 3,000 years. The wealth of her historical records and documents is unparalleled in world history. There remains the need for a searching inquiry as to the relations between the "three dynasties," whether they replaced each other one by one successively as detailed by later ages' well-known viewpoint of a "great unification", or whether they were different independent regimes in simultaneous co-existence. We need not look at them with the ideas of the later ages, recognizing that these three dynasties held their reign in the course of time from the 21st to the 3rd century B.C.

Historians usually demarcate historical periods by the instruments people employ at different times, thus: the Stone Age, the Bronze Age and the Iron Age. As late as the Shang Dynasty, already bronze instruments and articles were widespread. The exquisite technique of bronze casting reached a high level of production. Bronze was made of copper by adding tin to it, which could be cast into instruments and weapons both extremely hard and sharp. The appearance of bronze greatly promoted production which in turn provided grounds for significant strides forward in Chinese civilization. Along with the considerable progress in productive force, a great proportion of the workers were liberated from their age–old routine labors and became engaged in other, more elaborate works. For survival, people are compelled, first of all, to meet the living necessities of their daily life. When, with the increase in productive capability, fewer hands were needed to meet this requirement, there arose then surplus labor. Surplus labor is comprised of those who are freed from the necessary labor. A proportion of those who are no longer compelled to do simple manual labor turn to other fields of activity, such as arts and literature, science and other fields of knowledge, governing and administration, craftsmanship and amusement, etc. These people constituted a governing class accompanied by their followers, who eat without engaging in labor. But it is just herein where the origin of civilization lies. In other words, it is only where there exist those who eat without "sweat on their faces," or "thorns and thistles" about them (Genesis 3:18-19) that human civilization began to thrive. Or we may as well say that human civilization is an alienation of mankind from God and nature. It began in the break with the state of nature.

Engels' *Origin of Family, Private Property and the State* asserts that the population of ancient Athens never exceeded 300,000, among whom the free men were no more than 1/10. And it is the adult males among these 30,000 free people – indeed a very small number, only around a few thousand – that nourished the civilization of the golden age of ancient Athens.

In the transition from the state of nature to the civil state, the key moment comes with the appearance of agriculture. Agriculture made it possible for mankind to lead a settled life and procure a permanently reliable source of subsistence. It in turn promoted other related sciences (astronomy, meteorology, land cultivation) and techniques, with the result that one's labor became enough to support more people in addition to oneself. Before the emergence of agriculture, all peoples were around the same starting level of civilization. But with the influence of agriculture, the histories of different civilized peoples diverged from one another, and each took its own way. From then on we saw the flourishing of various civilizations, each with its own languages and written scripts, as well as their ways of thinking, characteristic of their history. This is what is generally taken as the national character. But meanwhile we have to recognize that since national character is something formed in the long course of history, it is also subject to change, to the reformation and transformation brought about by history.

Therefore, there is nothing in a people's character that qualifies as a transcendental quality, supposedly unchangeable and unchanged. The so-called nation character is in a state of historically coming into being, is subject to change, and reforms historically. So it is also with any alleged national condition, which is also formed historically and hence is subject to change in history. In the state of nature, almost all peoples trod roughly similar paths, but after they crossed the threshold of civilization, each began to follow its own way.

What marks the characteristic feature of the Chinese way is the extraordinarily strong ties of blood lineage in the relations among people. At first, all people were bound by their bloodline, which in course of time was gradually diluted in different ways, whether peacefully or by war, and eventually the division of people by their blood relationship was accompanied by division according to geographical area. Most peoples differentiated among themselves no longer by their ancestry, but by the areas they inhabited. But never in the history of China was blood lineage so thoroughly broken up, that her society was forced to be reorganized along the regional lines as is found in the West. Of course, there is no further scope for us to scrutinize in detail why this is so.

Suffice to say that this is the cardinal fact without which many qualities of the Chinese would be hard for us to comprehend in the slightest. On the whole, the Chinese society is one which never got rid of the blood-hierarchy of her past, even down to the present day. This is most clearly shown in their ways of addressing one another, which reflect minutely and accurately the relations among people with respect to their lineage. For example, the term "uncle" must be discerned whether it is directed to the uncle on the father's side or on the mother's; and if on the father side, whether it indicates the elder or the younger brother of one's father, and, further, of which place in the order of birth. One cannot find such distinctions in the Western languages. Language is but a way of expressing social relationships. If little attention is paid to this aspect of address, it means that there is no corresponding importance in social life that makes it worth paying attention to. Consequently, there is no need for such linguistic terms. On the other hand, if there are such pressures in the reality of their daily life, it is destined to be reflected in language. Here it seems as though we may glimpse the secrets of the Chinese way through their very language.

Closely connected with blood lineage is the trend of "returning to the ancients," and the idea of ancestor-worship which has dominated the Chinese ideology since antiquity. Most ancient thinkers in China were obsessed with a reverie about the age of "before the three dynasties." This longing for "before the three dynasties" furnished them with the model of an ideal society. There had always been a strong psychic tendency to resort to a reactionism, i.e. to return to their ancestors from whose standard they had supposedly fallen ever lower and lower. The famous poet Tao Yuanming (365-427) eulogized his ideal personality as "a subject under the reign of Wu Huai and of Ge Tian," the two legendary ancient sage-kings. As late as the end of the 19th century Kang Youwei still preached a return to Confucius and Confucianism as his utopia. The ancient thinkers always held a sanctuary for the ancient sage-kings in their hearts.

Confucius longed for the restoration of the rites of Duke of Zhou (a sage of some 500 years before Confucius), and the Taoists too professed the primitive society to be their ideal. So it was with the Mohists and many other schools. It is certainly not the case that the ancient times were indeed so enchanting, with all later society falling from bad to worse. This tendency in Chinese thought may well be explained as a byproduct of the system of blood lineage. The cohesive force of the patriarchal clan system based on bloodline drew its origin from the archaic tradition of their ancestors. Similar phenomena can also be found in other peoples, such as the Jews, who after the fall of their country were still able to maintain their pedigree and solidarity by upholding their ancient texts and manners, their religion and their scriptures.

Historical tradition provided a foundation on which later civilizations were to be built, but at the same time it also formed a burden which later prevented civilizations from going ahead easily and lightly. That is why during modern times when the Chinese intellectuals began to learn about the West, they were always inclined to discard the traditional culture as a whole, because the burden looked too heavy to allow quick progress along the road to modernization.

Herein lies another significant feature distinguishing China from many other peoples, who in struggling for national independence and prosperity against foreign invaders first resort to their traditional culture as a powerful spiritual weapon. When the Greeks threw themselves into the struggle for independence against Turkish rule, they gave priority to the glorification and worship of their traditional culture, as an effective means to evoke nationalistic sentiment. It was then that Lord Byron while personally taking part in the Greek war of independence so passionately exalted "The Isles of Greece" in his *Don Juan*. Even Hitler in the days of his absolute rule tried to use the mythical heroes of German legends to inspire nationalistic feeling. Almost all peoples of the world in their effort to arouse their nationalism or patriotism are, as a rule, trying to develop their traditional culture to the greatest extent. Strange to say, it is only the modern Chinese intellectuals who were extremely patriotic in their struggles against foreign invasions while yet embracing an extremely disappointed, disrespectful and even hostile attitude towards their traditional culture. On the opposite side, the conservative Sinophiles were mostly those who, while berating the Westernizers' camp, still colluded with the foreign invaders. The fact that most of them went over to join the Japanese puppet regime before and during the Second World War is an astonishing example. It is in the camp of the Westernizing intellectuals that could be found those outstanding representatives who, in their earnest pursuit of the prosperity and strengthening of their country, yet remained radically against their age-old cultural tradition. This must be a phenomenon almost unique in history.

It may perhaps be traced to the fact that the Chinese cultural tradition is too heavy a load to permit any large-scale reformation. When people intend to reform it to meet the new age and the new world, it has to be shaken completely from its very root. So much so that in the May Fourth movement some went even so far as to say "throw all the thread-bound books (of the Chinese tradition) into the sewer." In the following pages we will try to illustrate that part of the cultural tradition of the Chinese which deals with their ways of thinking falling under what is generally classified as philosophy.

[VI] Philosophy and Philosophizing

The national characteristic as such is, to a rather great extent, something environmentally influenced, i.e. it is formed in the course of history; even if there were something innate in it, it would matter very little. Suffice to say that the way of thinking characteristic of a people is formed under concrete historical conditions and upon a concrete cultural background. A way of thinking may be analyzed into two parts: one is the contents of the thoughts, the other the mode of reasoning. The former may be identified as the philosophical viewpoint. For instance, Confucius' proposition "the benevolent love others" is a philosophical viewpoint. Besides, there is yet the latter to be considered, i.e. how does one philosophize, or what is the way by which one manipulates one's philosophical viewpoint. As the philosophical content varies in each people, so also do their respective ways of philosophizing. In studying the history of philosophy, one may either emphasize the former aspect, i.e. the concrete substance and propositions, or one may equally emphasize the latter, i.e. how these propositions are derived, rather than what they affirm.

A theist holds that God exists while an atheist holds otherwise. This is the difference in their basic propositions. But one may concentrate not so much on what they assert as on how they argue or defend their respective cases, i.e. how their propositions are derived. One might argue that the existence of a table must need a maker who made it; since the world exists, there must be a creator behind its existence, who can be no other than God himself. Thus the theist presupposes a mode of reasoning from the relation between creation and creator. Yet an atheist may as well presuppose that the universe as an entity needs no creator at all, cite claiming that it is not created but exists by itself. Some may be more interested in the former aspect (whether God exists or not), while others more interested in the latter (how these different propositions are reasoned and defended). Perhaps both sides may hold a claim to priority, and thus we should pay due respect to both of them.

As mentioned above, the importance of blood lineage has played a tremendously powerful role in the history of China since her earliest antiquity. Up to the present day this role still remains stronger than in many other nations. From this emerged the paramount function of the *patria potestas* in China. Hegel, though possessing little knowledge of Chinese culture, made an astute assessment when he said that liberty in China dwells only in a single person (the emperor), who embodies the spirit of liberty of the whole nation. For Hegel, history is the manifestation of liberty. In China, it was manifested only in a single person. The substance (of liberty) in China exists only in an individual personality, and the whole nation is but an enlarged embodiment of the moral union of a family. An individual belongs above all to the family as a mere member in it, and likewise he belongs to his enlarged family (the state). As a son, he is subordinate to his family as an organic appendage. Similarly in the state he is a subject of the sovereign-father (*jun-fu*) in the sense that he is born a "subject-son" (*zi-min*). The existence of a person is, first of all, not the existence of an individual, but that of a member of a greater life. Only through one's function in it does one own one's existence.

[VII] Some Features of the Chinese Culture

During the long course of their natural history, nearly all peoples originally led their lives in roughly the same way, from the maternal clan society to the paternal, and then to the emergence of the *patria potestas*. But once they stepped into the state of civilization (i.e. the civil state), each people took its own characteristic way of development. This very much resembles a human being who in his infancy is largely the same as other infants. But as he grows up, he is more and more possessed of his own distinct individuality. As the culture of China comes of age, it is strongly endowed with a patriarchal character which led to a nostalgic tendency, always wishing to revert back to the time of the ancients and antiquity. This tendency must be reckoned a hindrance to the progress of Chinese minds and ideas, since resorting to a return to antiquity is inherently unconducive to any profound intellectual innovation, with the result of being stuck to the stagnant routine of the age-old ways. This perhaps will help to explain partly why there has been no scientific revolution in China (nor its subsequent intellectual consequences) as we find in the history of the West. No matter how radical in substance, almost all intellectual innovations in the history of China are always launched as a rule under the dress of antiquarianism (such as the reforms of Wang Anshi in the 11th century and of Kang Youwei in the 19th century).

Together with this may be noted two other spectacular phenomena. One is the lack of democratic traditions, which can be readily observed in ancient Greece, such as election, ostracism etc. The reason for this might partly be that the *patria potestas* originating from the blood bondage had always been too strong. The other is the prevailing practice of ancestor-worship in China which largely took the place that religion had for other peoples. There is no ritual ancestor-worship in the Occident, and the Occidentals, without the worship of their ancestors, have then had to rely on some superhuman force (i.e. religion). The Chinese do not need belief in religion, the worship of ancestors being enough for this function. The family bound up by close blood ties is where their spiritual life starts from and returns to. The individual constitutes merely a part of its long ancestral tradition. Other peoples believe in some sort of omnipotent God and thus have had a class of priests who are in charge of the relationship between God and men. Only this class of priests possesses the knowledge as well as the esoteric doctrine of the secrets lying between heaven and man. Though there were priests in ancient China, they never formed a particular class as the sole mediator between heaven and man. The intellectuals in ancient China were simply common people, not belonging to a specific class which could monopolize all knowledge of the affairs between heaven and man. Perhaps this can be most obviously seen in the Confucian school.

The Confucian school, possessing the "rites" in their hands, may look very akin to a priest class, but they did not ultimately act as mediators between God and man in any sense of esoteric tradition. On the whole, in their respective intellectual developments, there are both similarities and dissimilarities between the Chinese tradition and the West.

At bottom, all peoples are by nature roughly the same, though they take different courses in their development. What forms into their differences constitutes their specific national characters; and what forms into their similarities constitutes the common road of cultural development of mankind. Most ancient peoples, when stepping from the uncivilized state into the civilized, assumed the political institution generally known as the city-state. The city-state of ancient Greece is well-known to all, and that of ancient China is basically the same. Originally there is always a clan or a group of clans who built up a wall to guard themselves against possible invaders from outside. It is an armed castle with its own political and military organization. In the course of time, it grows larger and becomes a kingdom holding far larger territory. During the Spring and Autumn Period (770-476 B.C.)[①] or the early Eastern Zhou Dynasty, there had been many small feudal states, but later on in the Era of the Warring States (475-221 B.C.) or the later Eastern Zhou Dynasty, they were incorporated into seven great powers. Eventually in the year 221 B.C. all of them were brought under the sole imperial sovereignty of the Qin Dynasty, and a great unification of the whole of China was realized. We may find similar processes of historical evolution in ancient Greece (from city-states to the unification of Alexander the Great) and ancient Rome (from city-states to the unification of Caesar and Augustus).

A certain kind of political formation will require a certain ideology. Thus, at the very beginning of their civilized history, all peoples believe in fetishism, i.e. the worship of natural phenomena (thunder, lightning, etc.) as the manifestation of supernatural power. As the city-states expanded and competed with one another more and more, the ruling classes increasingly needed the services of those who could provide theoretical weapons and tactical devices, with which the sovereigns might enforce their domination. These intellectuals were the earliest philosophers in China. In response to the violent turbulence of the society, there emerged various schools of theories and ideology. Thus began a period of cultural flourishing, known in Chinese history as the period of the Hundred Schools of Thought, or Philosophers and Hundred Schools (*Zhu Zi Bai Jia*).

[VIII] Periodization of the History of Ideas in China

Here we encounter one of the most surprising phenomena in the history of

① The period is named after the book *Spring and Autumn Annals*, since the book offers a chronology of the time.

the ancient world. In the time from the 6th to the 3rd centuries B.C., the Greek culture of the West culminated in her golden age, i.e. the age of Pericles and its following years which witnessed the glory of thc sophists, the great systematic philosophers, the tragedians and comedians as well as a long series of eminent scientists and artists. It was also the age of the great philosophers and the hundred schools of classical China. And it was the age of the splendor of classical Indian culture when, according to legend, there were then ninety-six heresies in existence. It was then that the great Indian religions of Buddhism and Jainism were rising to their ascendancy. It is indeed a remarkable historical phenomenon, or in the words of A. Toynbee a spectacular "historical contemporaneity," that the three great cultures of classical antiquity were synchronous. It was also at this time that natural sciences rapidly began to thrive. The advances of astronomy and the calendar, which were closely connected to the agricultural knowledge of the early peoples, enhanced the development of mathematics. The art and craft of metallurgy made them able to step into an entirely new historical age, the Bronze Age.

With the heightening of productive efficiency, the newfound comfort and leisure in day-to-day life provided the conditions for a part of people to engage in thinking and research. Then systematic theories were worked out in various fashions under different circumstances. Among them, the most spectacular event is the formulation of their views on the ways of heaven and of man, from which germinated what might be called philosophy in its embryonic form.

The period of the Philosophers and Hundred Schools in China came to an end with the unification of the Qin Dynasty, and hence it is often known as the pre-Qin period. In the history of the West, there might be marked two hightides in her intellectual life: the classical age and the modern age (i.e. since the Renaissance), each being also a time of philosophers and a hundred schools. What is unique in the history of Western culture is the emergence of the modern culture which is not to be found in any other. Why is it so? Bertrand Russell once offered an explanation to the effect that the advancement of sciences and ideas require certain social conditions, i.e., they should never be subject to any single authority, or in other words, the freedom of expression should always be kept inviolate. Why was the thought of the ancient classical times so lively? It is because they were nurtured in a surrounding in which many city-states mutually competed, and no single one of them was in a position to rule over the others. Such situations provided a base from which different theories and ideas could thrive. So also was the case with the Renaissance in Italy and then in Western Europe. Had there been a great unified empire holding supreme sovereignty over all, every theory and idea would have been rendered incapable of free development. A great unified empire has to have a particular unified ideology in support of the ruling power of the regime. Once the thoughts and ideas of all people are brought under the dictatorship of a sole authority, then there can be no philosophy or science whatsoever. Perhaps this helps to explain why China in her later ages did not tread the path the West has taken, because she has survived for two thousand years and more under an intellectual autocracy.

Evidently the great unification of the Qin Dynasty signified a vital turning point both in the history and the philosophy of China. From Qin down to the early 20th century, the basic political structure remained essentially unchanged. Correspondingly, the philosophy and ideas of China have undergone two periods, one the period of classical antiquity, the other that of the great unification under the supremacy of an imperial sovereignty. The former is the age of the Hundred Schools of Thought, while the latter the reign of intellectual orthodoxy or scholasticism. Before the Great Unification, each philosopher and his school professed their own ideas, but afterward all philosophies were oriented to the exegesis of the official doctrines. The history of China after the Qin Dynasty again in its turn may be conveniently divided into the earlier middle ages and the later. The earlier middle ages witnessed a long course of intellectual clashes and fusions. In the Qin Dynasty, it was the Legalist doctrine which was hallowed as the guiding principle. The early Han Dynasty sanctified the Taoist teaching of non-activity and later Confucianism became the sole orthodoxy. During the Southern and Northern Dynasties (4th-6th centuries) Buddhism was introduced into China and mixed with Taoism, formulating the metaphysics (xuan) which dominated the elite circle of Wei and Jin for a considerable time. In the earlier years of the Tang Dynasty (7th-8th centuries) the royal court maintained the co-existence of the three teachings (i.e. Confucianism, Buddhism and Taoism). Towards the later years of the Tang Dynasty (9th century), the Chan (or Zen) sect of Buddhism was extremely widespread. It was not until the mid-Song Dynasty (11th century) that Confucianism was finally established as the sole orthodoxy, which later in the Southern Song dynasty (13th century) was elaborated by Zhu Xi into a systematic theory, resembling what Thomas Aquinas in mediaeval Europe had done with his *Summa Theologica*. Ever since then the Confucian teaching as formulated by the Song philosophers, generally known as the learning of Tao (literally the learning of the Logos), or as Neo-Confucianism as the Westerners are accustomed to calling it, has been in vogue as the orthodoxy. As a matter of fact, the so-called Neo-Confucianism is but a medley of Confucianism, Buddhism and Taoism. Thus in the early middle ages, there succeeded a long series of rises and falls of various philosophical teachings. It was only in the later middle ages that the three main teachings (Confucian, Buddhist and Taoist) were mingled into one and given the name "the learning of Tao" (*dao xue*), occasionally called "the learning of Reason" (*li xue*). This term, "the learning of Reason," is not as accurate as "the learning of Tao," for there were two different schools within the camp of the learning of Tao, i.e. the school of the learning of Reason (*li xue*) and the school of the learning of Mind (*xin xue*). Thus "the learning of Reason" bears a double significance. In a broader sense, it denotes the very learning of Tao at large; but in a narrower sense, it denotes the school within the camp of the learning of Tao in contradistinction with the school of the learning of the Mind. Up to the end of imperial reign in China, the learning of Tao was hallowed as the unique orthodoxy of the official ideology.

The third epoch of the philosophical development in China started in modern times. It has to be borne in mind that at first it was the cannons of the gunboats sent by the Western countries that forced open the tightly-closed gates of China to the outside world. With the shaking of the reign of the celestial dynasty, the traditional orthodox ideology began to shatter. People suddenly discovered that the age-old ideological tradition could not continue to adjust and accommodate itself to the new situation, and they began to try to find new ideas and theories to meet the much changed reality. In the course of one century and a half, that is from the Opium War (First Anglo-Chinese War, 1840) up to the present day, the Chinese have been incessantly grappling with and elaborating new ideas and new theories, which are in both their essence and orientation fundamentally different from what had been conceived for the preceding two thousand years. Thus we have three distinct historical epochs before our eyes: the classical times of the philosophers and the hundred schools, the mediaeval times under the sovereign's orthodoxy, and lastly the modern times of the clashes between the East and the West.

Before the Opium War, during the Ming and Qing dynasties (14th-19th centuries), the sea coast was strictly guarded against any liaison with abroad. But since the door of China was knocked open by foreign invaders (or to use the then prevailing expression, since the sea traffic was opened), the history of China was confronted "with a great upheaval never seen in the past two thousand years" (in the words of Li Hongzhang, the famous royal viceroy in charge of foreign affairs). The politico-cultural model of a great unified empire was falling apart. After the Revolution of 1911, when Wang Guowei (the foremost scholar of the age) followed Luo Zhenyu in exile to Japan, Luo said to Wang that before the sea traffic was opened, "the Way [in China] was one," but after that time "the Way [in China] was split into two" (i.e. the Chinese vs. the Western). Here the crucial point involved is that China was forced to step into her modern stage by compulsion, not through a natural process of her own evolution. There was no trace whatever that she herself was already so mature or the historical conditions already so ripe as to bring her to the threshold of modern statehood. People may pick at will this event or that to identify the modern elements or seeds in her development as a vindication of the birth of capitalism, but after all nothing whatsoever can be cited as evidence that she was really beginning a process on the way to modernization. Her own conditions were not yet ripe for becoming a modern state. This is essentially different from the course of history in the West, which by traversing the process of geographical discoveries, the Renaissance and the Reformation and the primitive accumulation of capital, was moving step by step into the modern stage. It can hardly be asserted convincingly that, without the invasion of the foreign force, China would at that time have stepped into a modern stage all by herself.

As she was forced to enter into modernization, the cardinal issue would be how to arrange the relationship with foreign countries. Herein lies the most spectacular key to understanding the historical and intellectual peculiarities of modern China. Or in other words, it is just from the maladjustment of this relationship that all troubles arise. This maladjustment shows itself always in an oscillation between the two extremes of the left and the right. At first, it assumed an extremely conservative attitude from the position of the superiority of a celestial dynasty, looking down on everything foreign as barbarous. But soon this self-assumed superior celestial nation was repeatedly defeated by the barbarian foreigners. Then it turned from one extreme to the other, from arrogance to servility, deeply hurt by a sense of inferiority. Then many demanded a wholesale Westernization. Both extremes, the Sinophiles as well as the Westernizers, are the reflections of an abnormal mentality. Against such a background the spiritual life of a nation cannot thrive in a sound mode. Then again it turned to extreme nationalism directed against everything foreign, as we might see in the mass uprisings against foreigners in the year 1900 known by the name Yihe Tuan (the "Boxer Rebellion" as some Westerners are accustomed to calling it).

Embarrassed by such tossing and turning, it seems even up to today that many still fail to find an appropriate position to locate themselves. Sometimes they assume themselves to be superior, while everything in the West is in mortal decadence and corruption; but at other times they blindly admire everything of the West so much that they even take foreign names for indigenous things, as though foreign names might elevate the intrinsic value of their commodities. If we fail to grasp this key notion, we will miss one of the most significant threads running through the Chinese mentality in the turbulence of its modern intellectual history.

Chapter One: Confucius and the Confucian School

[I] Confucius and the Six Scriptures

From the earliest stages in the foundation of cultures, each people owes much to the great founders who had, so to say, laid down the orientation and characteristic features of later intellectual developments. We see Zoroaster in Persia, Buddha in India, Moses in Judea, Jesus throughout the West, and Confucius in China. Confucius is known the world over as the paramount founder of Chinese culture, and of the Chinese mentality across centuries.

Confucius lived in an age generally known as the Spring and Autumn Period (after the ancient chronicle of the same name), or as the Late or Eastern Zhou Dynasty. With the capital removed from Gao (now Xi'an) to Luoyi (now Luoyang) by King Ping of Zhou, the royal dynasty was in rapid decline. Considered along with the subsequent Warring States Period, ending in the unification of the whole land by the First Emperor of Qin, this age lasted about five centuries (8th-3rd centuries B.C.). It was a time of rapid development of Chinese cultural life, when the archaic culture set down by the old tradition was shattered. Rapid growth of a new culture means at the same time a swift decline in the old tradition; if what is archaic remained fully intact, there would be no development. Development is a metabolic process, with the emergence of what is new substituting what is out of date. The epoch of the Spring and Autumn and later of the Warring States witnessed a fast-paced transformation both in social and political life as well as in intellectual life. The old tradition had lasted from the Shang to the Western Zhou, about a thousand years (17th-8th centuries B.C.), and had already elaborated a semi-religious and semi-philosophical ideology. The sovereign on earth was identified as the representative of the sovereign in heaven, who was in reality but an enlargement of the *patria potestas* in the hierarchical society. But with the incessant complication of social life and the aggrandizement of the state, the patriarch of the clan in the old days now became the ruler of the state, though still *à la mode* of the patriarch of the old days. The old world order was now replaced by a throng of the newly emerged states.

To meet the requirements of this new situation, each nation busied itself with its own reformation. To launch a reformation means to recast the old institution into a new form. The old institution was one of semi-religious rule, patriarchal in nature. Now it evolved more and more into a political or civil state, its rulers no longer necessarily of the old blood-lineage nobility. There came to the fore new noble classes who got their power by dint of intrigues, *coup d'etat* and other devices. In the process of the redistribution of political power they were often able to seize the greatest part, because the changed circumstances needed a new nobility to enhance the new ruling order, which gave priority not to birth but to individual talent. Thus original theories and ideologies were required for the maintenance of this new rule. It was in this historical period that new ideas sprang up one after another with exuberance.

It was the time of classical culture in China, when the intellectual formation of the Chinese people came into its definite shape. It is known in history as the age of the Hundred Schools of Thought. The most significant among the so-called hundred schools might in fact have numbered no more than a dozen. In the *History of Han* compiled by the famous historian Ban Gu (in "The Chapter on Literary Writings"), it was recorded that there were then ten schools "among which only nine are worthy of study."[①] Of these notable schools, the earliest were the Confucians. Though the exact dates of Confucius' life are still an issue open to debate, it is presumed he lived from 550 to 479 B.C. Founders of all other schools emerged later than Confucius.

When an increasing rate of productivity frees the people from the sorrows and worry of struggling day-to-day merely for subsistence, they are enabled to muse on more abstract ideas about man and the world he lives in, and thus originated the earliest germs of philosophy. Before Confucius there had already existed primitive philosophical ideas and theories in various forms and fashions, but it was Confucius who deserves to be taken as the earliest philosopher in China, for it was he who first personally elaborated a philosophical theory,

① Ban Gu, *The History of Han*, "The Chapter on Literary Writings."

which was both the earliest and most influential in the history of China. Previously, philosophical ideas were the official theories formed through the long course of traditional customs, such as how to worship heaven, how to venerate ancestors, etc. There had been no individual philosopher who propounded a set of ideas of his own. Thus it seems appropriate here to get a brief review of the Chinese intellectual tradition prior to Confucius.

The traditional Chinese classics were generally classified under four headings: scripture, philosophy, history and literature (*Jing, Zi, Shi, Ji*). In the 18th century, Emperor Qianlong ordered that a complete collection of all books then in existence be prepared. They were named *The Complete Collection in Four Treasuries*, divided under the aforementioned four headings.

The scriptures included the ancient sacred books. Originally, there were six such: the *Book of Songs*, *Book of History*, *Book of Changes*, *Book of Rites*, *Spring and Autumn Annals* and *Book of Music*. In the course of time they increased gradually to thirteen scriptures. The texts of the scriptures, together with their exegesis and commentaries, formed the main body of the academic studies that were considered classical scholarship.

The second group of classical learning was gathered under "Zi," or "philosophers" and their writings. In this group are included not only philosophical works but also works of science, perhaps since science also aims to discover the secrets of the world. When wishing to study the ancient science of China, one should consult these books in the collection of "*Zi Bu*" (i.e. the section of the writings of the philosophers), for science is, properly speaking, the philosophy of nature, or natural philosophy. Ultimately, beside the sacred classics and Confucian teachings, all ideas and theories dealing with the nature of the world and man fall within the scope of the philosophers' works.

In the collection "*Shi*" are included all books dealing with the topic of history. As mentioned above, the Chinese people are the past masters on account of their profound historical sense. Each reigning dynasty as a rule was compelled to take up the work of compiling the history of the foregoing dynasty or dynasties as its sacred obligation. Thus there was preserved for us a complete collection of the history of all the foregoing ages. The well-known collection of the twenty-four or twenty-five histories afforded an uninterrupted and unbroken historical record from the earliest times to the last imperial dynasty in the early 20th century.

In the collection of literary works are included, for instance, the writings of the famous Song writer Su Shi (Su Dongpo) collected into the *Works of Su Dongpo*, or those of the famous Tang writer Han Yu (Han Changli) as the *Works of Han Changli*, etc.

The earliest scriptures in China have always been known as the "Six Scriptures," all being collections of the materials and knowledge relevant to some sacred tradition since antiquity. They provided the maxims for the thinking and practice of all people. Among these six scriptures, the *Book of Music* has long been lost since the burning of books by the edict of the First Emperor of Qin. But the real reason for its loss may more probably be due to the technical problem that there was then no practical method of musical notation, for the preservation of music is not possible solely through the records of words, as other scriptures might do. It has to resort to musical performance. But later generations could not master the performing art merely by reading the written records. There have of course been some excellent descriptions of musical performance in literary writings, such as the famous "Rime on the Harp" (or pipa, an ancient string instrument), in which the author Bai Juyi, the famous poet of the Tang period, employed refined and exquisite metaphors to describe the beauty of music. But after all it is a literary composition, which by no way can restore the musical feeling the audience would experience.

Of the other Five Scriptures in existence throughout the later ages, the *Book of Songs* is a selection of ancient poems, including both popular lyrics (some extremely beautiful and touching) and formal and ceremonial poems for the occasions of courtly banquets, diplomatic meetings, etc. The *Book of History* (literally, the *Book of Documents*) is a selection from the official archives and documents, such as international agreements, the oath before some military expedition, etc. The *Book of Changes* is the study of divination and prognostication. It is a popular practice in all ancient peoples to pray to gods for prophecy or oracle in front of the altar, as in the practice of the ancient Athenians before the Altar at Delphi. The sum of the theory and practice of ancient Chinese divination was systematically formulated into a set of symbols known as the Hexagrams. Various combinations of these hexagrams would symbolize different changes and signify esoteric statements on the natural and human world. In the course of time, some extremely fine ideas and principles were elaborated to accommodate all events, both natural and human. Thus we have the earliest unifying synthesis of nature and man. We may find in them the wisdom the ancients employed to probe, to observe and to deal with the world and their own lives. Of course, there are inevitably lots of forced or fabricated analogies, for the changes and variations of the world are too abundant to be covered and formulated in a few images or figures in the Hexagrams. In present day China when a well-regulated uniform reasoning process results in an impasse blocking further analysis, some people turn to seek a way out in the *Book of Changes*. Hence the fever for the *Book of Changes*, as a reaction to the former prevailing mode of thinking. Some went even so far as to deify this classic, as though it might encompass all philosophical thought.

Surely this is an exaggeration. No person nor any discipline of learning, either in ancient times or modern, can exhaust all the wonders and multiplicity of the world. There is no summit for knowledge; if there were any, there would be no room for further advancement of mankind. Any deification of any classic is unscientific and unreasonable in its approach. As for why it is that many are turning to the study of the *Book of Changes*, not only certain Chinese scholars but also foreign, and indeed not only the *Book of Changes* but also other classical works such as *Book of Lao Zi* and *Book of Zhuang Zi*, the reason is perhaps simply their hope of finding revelations from the ancients (the Chinese from the foreigners as well as the foreigners from the Chinese) to enrich and to inspire their own ideas. The constant renovation of intellectual culture stretches far beyond the capacity of any single mind. It has to rely on the achievements of, and to draw inspirations from, others, among the ancients as well as from abroad. This is only natural. And in this sense, all the intellectual products of bygone days are of use to the present day. But this is no ground to make the ancients into idols, as though all is already included in the works of the ancients (say, in the *Book of Changes*).

The *Book of Rites* is itself constituted by three works, and is hence generally known as the "Three Rites": the "Rites of Zhou" (composed by the ancient sage the Duke of Zhou, according to legend) which is rather simple in form, the "Yi Rites," and the "Record of Rites" being a complementary commentary. Rites properly speaking are the rules of human behaviors, especially those concerning social ceremonies and manners, e.g. how to offer sacrifices to gods and ancestors, or how to arrange the ceremony of a wedding or funeral. In a certain sense, it is the constitution regulating social orders and social lives, or the codification of the ruling order of a society embodying the values and ideology of the day.

Of the *Spring and Autumn Annals* there have long been different opinions. Some assert that it was written by Confucius himself. As early as the work of Mencius, there was already the statement, "Confucius completed the *Spring and Autumn Annals* and rebellious ministers and villainous sons were struck with terror."[①] Yet Mencius' statement is not necessarily authentic. There is still

① *Book of Mencius*, "The Duke Wen of Teng," pt. 2, trans. James Legge.

disagreement on the issue of whether Confucius personally wrote the book *Spring and Autumn Annals*. This book deals with the chronology in a very simple way by recording the historical events under the corresponding dates, with no narration of the process of the event itself. Hence Wang Anshi of the 11th century regarded it as only a contemporary account in fragments and not a genuine composition in the proper sense. A mere chronological record is in need of further comment and narration. Thus in later ages there appeared three prevailing versions of commentaries on the *Spring and Autumn Annals*: the *Gong Yang Commentaries*, the *Gu Liang Commentaries* and the *Zuo Commentaries*. These commentaries explain the text of the classics. The relation between the *Gong Yang* and the *Gu Liang Commentaries* has also been a topic of incessant argument, with no definite conclusion or general agreement. Of the three commentaries, the most popular is the *Zuo*, the authorship of which is often attributed to the ancient historian Zuo Qiuming, still a debated figure. Though the *Zuo Commentaries* is among the most widely circulated readers, the *Gong Yang Commentaries* also had profound influence on later ages.

These Five Scriptures date much earlier than Confucius himself and have long been held sacred. They articulated the norms of daily life and the thoughts of the ancient Chinese. The contribution of Confucius lies in his compilation and edition of the classics, such that he is known as the greatest sage. Confucius was a great educator who taught his pupils with classics, and the classics he compiled and edited became the sacred books of China. The Five Scriptures we have today are the works as revised and arranged by him. In this aspect, his importance is unparalleled, for the traditional classics so compiled and arranged by Confucius became thenceforth the vehicle of the culture of the Chinese people from generation to generation. People praised him with the eulogy, "His virtue dwells together with heaven and earth, his Way permeates the past and present; he compiled the six scriptures and established the standard for all later ages."

Besides the Five Scriptures, there are the Four Books (the *Analects*, the *Book of Mencius*, the *Great Learning* and the *Doctrine of the Mean*) all of which were later canonized as classics too. The *Analects* is the record of Confucius' sayings and actions, recorded by his direct disciples and disciples of the second and third generations. Since it is the record of his sayings, its authorship may be attributed to Confucius himself. Though it is recorded in the form of short paragraphs or axioms, it became in fact the most important among Chinese classics, far surpassing all others. Perhaps its place in the history of China can only be rivaled by the sayings of Chairman Mao in the sixties and seventies of last century.

The *Great Learning* and the *Doctrine of the Mean* were excerpts taken from the "Record of Rites" and became two independent scriptures. And lastly it was the *Book of Mencius* that assumed too the status of scripture from the Four Books. It is interesting to note that before the Song Dynasty (10th-13th centuries) Mencius was ranked only as one among the philosophers in ancient times with no specific distinction. It was not until the Song Dynasty that Mencius was honored and elevated to the position of the sage second only to Confucius. Ever since then Confucius and Mencius have always been mentioned together and the *Book of Mencius* was held as scripture.

[II] Historical Place of Chinese Scholasticism

For ease of illustration, the Chinese classics may be compared with those of Christianity. As a rule, each people possesses its own traditional scriptures. The poems, legends and history of the Jewish people were collected into a set of scriptures, the *Old Testament*, the importance of which roughly corresponds to the Five Scriptures in China. After Jesus Christ, his followers of the succeeding generations laid down the record of his teachings and activities, known as the *New Testament*. The first part of the *New Testament*—the Gospels—deals with the life and teachings of Jesus himself, and may be compared with the *Analects*. Then the "*Book of Acts*" deals with the activities of the apostles, followed by the records of the speeches, letters and activities of his followers of later generations, such as the books of Timothy, of Peter and of Paul, which roughly correspond to the *Great Learning*, the *Doctrine of the Mean* and the *Book of Mencius*. The place of the Four Books in China may be compared to the *New Testament* and that of the Five Scriptures to the *Old Testament*.

In the above comparison, there is again something further worthy of notice. In contrast to Christianity, Judaism venerates only the *Old Testament*, while Christianity acknowledges both the *Old Testament* and the *New Testament*. Etymologically, the term "Christ" means savior, and all those who profess Jesus to be the savior are Christians. But the Jewish people did not agree, and so they accept only the *Old Testament*. A similar phenomenon may be observed in the history of China. All philosophical schools in ancient China accepted the Five Scriptures (the *Old Testament* of China), but none (with the exception of the Confucian school) acknowledged the Four Books (the *New Testament* of China) nor the unique supremacy of Confucius and his school. For instance, many scholars confronted Mencius with disputes, such that, being told, "People all speak of you as being fond of disputing," Mencius himself was obliged to concede, "Indeed, I am not fond of disputing, but I am compelled to do it."[1] Or take Marxism as another example. The Second International acknowledged Marxism, but excluded Leninism, while the Third International acknowledged Leninism as the sole genuine interpretation of Marxism. There lies the theoretical divergence between the Second International and the Third. Great similarity might be found in the struggles among different schools and sects throughout the history of mankind, though not necessarily in their substance, but still in many aspects of their modes.

Later, to the Four Books and Five Scriptures were added two other books: the *Book of Filial Piety* and the *Encyclopedia of Etymology* (*Er Ya*). The former is a work of the Confucian school, written about the time of Western Han (206 B.C.-A.D. 25 B.C.). Each epoch in history had its own spirit and sense of value, and the Han period stressed filial piety above all virtues. The Han emperors after their death were as a rule revered with the posthumous honorary title *Xiao* (filial piety). Filial piety was even honored as the fundamental virtue from which all others were derived, such that if, for example, one did not show enough valor when fighting in battle, he was said to lack the virtue of filial piety. It seems rather strange that another book was at the same time included into the scriptures too, i.e. the *Encyclopedia of Etymology*, literally an ancient dictionary or a book on words. The reason may perhaps be that, for all learning, one has to first learn the words. This dictionary was thus admitted into the family of scriptures. From that time on, the traditional scriptures assumed their definite shape as thirteen scriptures: the *Book of Songs*, *Book of History*, *Book of Changes*, the three works of the *Book of Rites*, *Spring and Autumn Annals*, *Analects*, *Book of Mencius*, *Book of Filial Piety* and *Encyclopedia of Etymology* (the *Great Learning* and the *Doctrine of the Mean* being also included in the *Book of Rites*). At the end of the 18th century, the famous Confucian scholar Ruan Yuan (himself also a long-prominent governor) compiled a voluminous collection *The Royal Exegesis of the Scriptures* (*Huang Qing Jing Jie*), also known as *The Exegesis of the Thirteen Scriptures*, in which all the hitherto existing important exegeses and commentaries of the scriptures were compiled together. Each generation and each person had its/his own understanding of the scriptures, which always underwent a ceaseless process of comment and explanation. In the middle ages, all learning was subject and subordinate to the

① Ibid.

study of scriptures, which provided the start and the end point of all thought. All studies were brought into the field of the scriptures, and scholars served only to amplify the teachings found in them. Traditional scholarship in China was properly the study of the classics, and here again we might observe a striking similarity between China and Western Christendom. For all learning in the West during its Middle Ages accorded to the rules of theology or scholasticism. Academic discipline then consisted only of how to interpret Christian teaching, outside of which there was no learning worthy of the word. Scripture, named as it is, signifies the deification of the traditional ideology which was both a product of the ancient society and at the same time an indispensable support to it. It regulated people's ideas, maxims of behavior and social norms. The study of the Chinese Scriptures was in its essence the same as the scholasticism of Christendom. And it was in the hands of Confucius that the Scriptures in China assumed their definite shape. That is why the later ages honored him with the title "The Supreme Patriarchal Master" (*Da Cheng Zhi Sheng Xian Shi*). The word "Confucius" in the Western languages was a transliteration of "Master Kong." In the *Analects*, he was also simply addressed as the Master (Zi). It was he who above all others laid down the cultural and intellectual foundation for the subsequent ages. But down to modern times, he also became the most polemicized figure in history.

Confucius was never pleased with himself throughout his whole life. In the late 2nd century under the imperial power of the great unified Han Dynasty, Emperor Wu promulgated an edict by which Confucianism was honored as the supreme ideology, to the exclusion of all other schools. Later on, the title of "king holding no reign" was dedicated to Confucius, elevating him to the supreme level of a monarch. But during the Wei and Jin period (3rd century) with the introduction of Buddhism into China and the revival of Taoist ideas (under the name of metaphysics or "*xuan xue*," i.e. the study of the Logos), Confucianism maintained its place only within a tripartite coexistence. In the early Tang Dynasty (7th century) the royal house was Li and hence paid homage to Taoism, because its founder Lao Zi also came from a family of Li (his name being Li Er). The great poet of that time Du Fu in his verse once said, "The violet atmosphere [a symbol of the Taoists] from the east pervades the Han Pass [east to the royal capital]." The Han Pass is, according to legend, the place from which Lao Zi went west on the back of a blue ox. The verse hinted at how the royal house indulged Taoism. (Lao Zi was the acknowledged founder of Taoism and his prominence rivaled that of Confucius.)

It was not until the Neo-Confucians of the Song Dynasty (11th-13th centuries) that Confucius formally attained his supremacy. Ever since then his place became absolute and unshakable, earning his title, "Supreme Patriarchal Master." In a course of about two and a half millennia, Confucius' position always varied with the time. In the early twenties of the 20th century, during the high tide of the May Fourth Movement, the young intellectuals shouted the slogan, "Down with the Confucian Firm." During the Cultural Revolution of the sixties and seventies, the Red Guards launched a campaign of radical criticism directed at Confucius, destroying the Confucian temple in his native town. But today the current in the intellectual market seems much changed and what is called "contemporary New Confucianism" appears to be greatly in vogue.

Confucius' historical place has always varied, as with all historical personages. Take Napoleon who died almost two hundred years ago. His place in the history of France, of Europe and of the world at large has been under constant change. This serves to illustrate why history needs to be forever subject to revision and rewriting. Historical judgment is the product of our reconsideration, to which there is and there can be no final conclusion. Around 2,500 years after the death of Confucius, there still can be no last word passed on him. Our historical judgment depends on what effect a person has exercised on history, and it is just this historical effect which can have no end. What judgments we pass on Confucius depend on the effects he brought to the history down to our day. How people in the future will judge him will depend on the effects he might bring to the history to come. If Confucius was indeed so powerful, as some contemporary new Confucians emphatically assert, that the economic leap of the Far East ought to be attributed to Confucian teaching, and if mainland China now began to venerate Confucius again, with the direct outcome of this Confucius worship resulting in an economic growth of leaps and bounds; then the historical place of Confucius would be diametrically otherwise.

[III] His Life and His Time

Confucius was born in a declined noble family. It was said that his mother prayed on the hill of Ni and then begot him, so he was named Qiu (hill) or Zhong Ni. Maybe he was an illegitimate child. A declined noble was not much differentiated in his social status from the common people, and he once said of himself, "When I was young, my condition was low, and therefore I acquired my abilities in many types of [manual] labor."① Through all his life, he had not been content with his position. He was once the chief of justice of Lu, his native country. Lu was a small state of the time, in the south of the present Shandong Province. It was originally the fief of Bo Qin, the eldest heir of the Duke of Zhou, the founder of the feudal enfeoffment of the Western Zhou Dynasty, and hence preserved many of the Zhou institutions and cultural practices. The Duke of Zhou (Ji Dan by name) was forever the Confucius' ideal sage and Confucius even often dreamed of the Duke of Zhou. Retiring from his official post, he started his travels to many states hoping to realize his ideal. His ideal may be summed in the succinct term: "a benevolent government." But this ideal could be carried out only on the condition that he would be accepted by some benevolent sovereign who would be willing to realize it. A longtime tradition existed in Chinese history such that intellectuals had to go and seek the sponsorship of a patron who would like to support their ideals. Without this favor from some sovereign, nothing could be achieved. Therefore, they had to pay their homage to their sovereign without the least thought of realizing their ideals independently all by themselves. Unfortunately, never did any sovereign receive Confucius with compassion. When he traveled through the states Chen and Cai (in present Henan Province), he was even besieged, having no food to feed himself and his followers. In his old age, he retreated to his native place (Qufu in Lu) where he taught his disciples and died at the age of seventy-three. His disciples numbered three thousand, quite a considerable sum at the time, and it was he who first initiated the practice of private instruction without regard to students' backgrounds, breaking away from the tradition of education only under official patronage.

Confucius taught his disciples with six arts: the rites, music, archery, charioteering, reading and arithmetic. It was said there were seventy-two among his disciples who were well versed in these six arts. These arts conformed to the requirements of upper class life in antiquity. At first, education was the privilege of the nobility. It was Confucius who began to propagate learning and knowledge to the lower strata in the society and thus led to a new phase in public life, called by then "the hectic discussions among the intellectuals" (*Chu Shi Heng Yi*), on political and social issues. Thenceforth all other schools followed. Confucius himself once professed: "When right principles (Tao) prevail in the World, there will be no discussions among the common people."②

① *Analects*, bk.9 "Zi Han," trans. James Legge, with alterations by the author.

② *Analects*, bk.16 "Ji Shi," trans. James Legge, with alterations by the author.

As the world was then in tumult and disorder without right principles (Tao), so the common people without any social status swarmed forth to discuss politics. In this respect Confucius led the current of the time. It was he who started a downward movement of both knowledge and political participation from the hereditary nobility to the common people. In antiquity, learning lay within religion, and those who possessed knowledge were exclusively the priests who had the power to expound the esoteric preachings of gods, nature and man. China was no exception. Knowledge then belonged solely to officialdom, or as some were apt to say, "All philosophers came from royal officialdom." By the time of Confucius, learning began to be liberated from the monopoly of the nobility and to move downward into the commonalty. So Confucius professed of himself, "I engage in instruction with no distinction to status,"[①] and again: "I learn without satiety and instruct others without being wearied," "to all those who brought a bundle of dried fish for my teaching, I have never refused my instructions."[②] Once the commonalty possessed knowledge through learning, they were consequently inspired by the hope of carrying out their own ideals to reform society.

After Confucius, many schools and sects sprang up, all engaging in private instruction. Though a great educator as Confucius was, he nevertheless always despised manual labor, regarding it as something proper only for the lower class or the "small man" (*xiao ren*). Once his disciple Fan Chi requested to be taught husbandry, but the Master said, "I am not as good at that as an old husbandman is." Fan requested also to be taught gardening, and was answered, "I am not as good at that as an old gardener is." Fan Chi having gone out, the Master said "a small man indeed is Fan."[③] Such an attitude may well be found also in ancient Greece where the higher class engaged in political and intellectual activities, while the lower in manual labor. One of the basic ideas of Confucius is the division of mankind into two classes: one is the superior man (or gentleman), the other the small man (both in intellect and in virtue). And he taught his disciples: "Be a scholar (or intellectual) after the style of the superior man, and not after that of the mean (the small) man."[④] Yet, where does the demarcation line between a superior man and a small man lie? It implies a double or triple connotation for us to discern. In one aspect, it implies the difference in social status: those who engage in manual work are small men, and those who run

① *Analects*, bk.15 "Duke Ling of Wei," trans. James Legge, with alterations by the author.

② Ibid., bk.7 "Transmitting" (*Shu Er*), trans. James Legge, with alterations by the author.

③ Ibid., bk.13 "Zi Lu," trans. James Legge.

④ Ibid., bk.6 "Yong Ye," trans. James Legge.

the state are the superior men. But besides this, there is evidently still another connotation, i.e. its moral implications. Those of high morality are the superior men (or gentlemen), while those of lower morality are the small (or mean) men. Regarding this connotation, the *Analects* gave many explicit expressions. Yet still another connotation not so explicitly expressed was also implied in his mind, that those who are intellectually well equipped or cultivated are the superior men and those who are intellectually less equipped or cultivated are the small men. The ideal of Confucius is to cultivate the superior men, aiming more specifically at the perfection of one's ideas and actions. This ideal of his comes very near to the educational idea in modern Britain where the aim is to cultivate gentlemen. The term "gentlemen" often denotes persons of the upper class. But more than this, a gentleman has to be a man of good cultivation, his behavior gentle and polite, his morals elevated, being never vulgar or inappropriate. Of course, the gentlemen as conceived and nourished by Confucius should hold important positions in the social hierarchy. It is hoped that as social and political leaders they would guide the social manners and the policies of the state, and in this fashion the ideal of a "benevolent statecraft" would naturally come true.

[IV] Confucius and the Zhou Institutions

The epoch in which Confucius lived was one when "the rites were broken and the music collapsed."[①] The traditional social and political order (as embodied in the rites and music) was tottering before the impetus of the new one then arising. Confronting such a situation, all schools tried to save society by proposing their own ideas or carrying out their own ideals.

The center of the Western Zhou (11th-8th centuries B.C.) was located at Zhou Yuan (now Xi'an). When the royal dynasty was in decline, the capital was moved to Luoyi (now Luoyang) and was hence known as the Eastern Zhou (8th-3rd centuries B.C.), or the epoch of the Spring and Autumn (after the name of the ancient chronicle previously mentioned). By the beginning of the Western Zhou, the Zhou regime subjugated the Shang Dynasty (17th-11th centuries B.C.) and carried out a large-scale feudalization. The very term "feudalism" has long been rather misleading in later ages. In the traditional historical records the Zhou regime started a process of feudalization with the result that a throng of small feudal states appeared all over the land. But as the First Emperor of Qin brought

① Ibid., bk.7 "Transmitting" (*Shu Er*), trans. James Legge.

the whole land under a great unification, he "abrogated the feudal system and established in its stead the prefectural system." Since then the prefectural system replaced the feudal system and ruled over all China. Yet in modern times, especially with the introduction of Marxism into China, people have been apt to employ the term "feudal" in describing or defining the nature of traditional Chinese society. This term was borrowed from the Japanese translation and resulted in a greatly misleading error. If the First Emperor of Qin had already abrogated the feudal system, how could Chinese society always be identified with the feudal? Here is an anachronism. As in the conventional usage, the term "feudal" is employed to signify the long post-Qin history which in its nature is different from the pre-Qin epoch. Hence the same term conveys two clearly different meanings; the one is the ancient usage, the other the modern. After all, what then is feudalism? This will be left for further elucidation in the chapter dealing with the middle ages. It is sufficient to say here that the feudal system in the early Zhou was an armed colonization, not unlike the Barbarian invasion of the Roman Empire in the early years of the Migration Period. As Zhou defeated Shang and conquered the vast area of the east (the middle and lower part of the Yellow River Valley), the conquering nobles were enfeoffed as new rulers of the conquered lands, which became the hereditary fiefs of those feudal princes: kings, dukes, counts etc. Such political practices were known as "feudal." There were in later ages also such practices of feudalization, but often only nominally. For instance, in the early Ming Dynasty (14th century) there had taken place a feudalization on a grand scale, but with this reservation: "enfeoffment with no private ownership of the whole land, and no direct reign over the people." In fact, it was no more the feudalism in its original sense, because the feudal nobility no longer exercised ruling power over the land, and took no part in real political processes. The local political mechanisms ever since Qin had been run by the prefectures on behalf of the royal court, and appointed by the central government.

The institution of feudalism was elaborated by the Duke of Zhou, and according to legend the part of the *Book of Rites* relating to Zhou was composed by him. He was indeed a key figure in the establishment of the rule of Rites. His son Bo Qin was given the country Lu, where the Zhou rites were preserved mostly intact. Confucius, a native of Lu, was a great admirer of the Zhou rites. In a turbulent age, there are as a rule two groups of people: one group is prone to innovate, regarding all traditions of the old days as out of date and demanding a brand new system, while the other tends to be conservative, regarding all the present evils as the outcome of breaking the age-old rules, and the only way out as none other than a return to the good old days. Confucius should belong to the latter group, i.e. the conservatives. He was of the opinion that the age-old institutions as incorporated in the Zhou rites were among the best, and that by maintaining the Zhou rites the political and social order would be kept stable. Confucius himself did not write any work, as the *Analects* had it: "The Master said, 'A transmitter and not a maker, believing in and loving the ancients, I venture to compare myself with our old Peng.'"[1] Old Peng was believed to be an ancient sage of the Shang Dynasty (17th-11th centuries B.C.) who venerated the old ways and disseminated them. But as Confucius' sayings were recorded by his disciples in the book *Analects*, it may be fairly regarded as the earliest work of an individual in China's intellectual history. Before him there had been no personal works, all being the collection of the age-old traditions, such as the Six Scriptures. It may well be admitted that it was in him that individual work began to emerge, and with it individual thought, and so Confucius has to be deemed the earliest philosopher in China. The recording of the *Analects* must have occurred over a rather long time, because the letters and texts therein bear different intonations. Some of them, being very succinct, may be of an earlier origin; others are very detailed, and perhaps of a much later date.

People often entertain a certain habit of thinking, such that they take conservatives as belonging to the reactionary camp and all innovations as emanating from the progressives. The issue perhaps is not that simple, for in the tradition of each people there are inevitably things which are the crystals of the wisdom of the whole people tempered through ages, which ought not to be abruptly abrogated. Conversely there are bad innovations as well as good. Mr. Hitler's National Socialism was indeed an innovation, but certainly not a good one.[2] As professed by himself, Confucius was just "a transmitter and not a maker"; he explained and amplified what the ancients had already laid down, rather than innovating what might look new. This shows the conservative side of his thoughts. But after all, the thoughts of any man are predominantly his own intellectual product rather than a simple repetition of the ideas of others—they are more than anything else his own creation. Of the thoughts of the ancients, each one has his own understanding. Or let us say, we interpret others according to our own understanding. Though "a transmitter, not a maker" as Confucius was, he fashioned his own ideas through his exposition of the ancient classics. It is really a spectacular phenomenon that before him the time was

① Sir Hendersen, then the British ambassador to Germany, in his memoir *The Failure of a Mission*, spoke of Hitler's National Socialism as a "revolution."

② *Analects*, bk.7 "Transmitting" (*Shu Er*), trans. James Legge.

not yet ripe for the fermentation of different ideas, but soon after him various theories and schools all of a sudden flourished in their full vitality. As the first and the foremost founder of the most significant school, Confucius marked the beginning of the maturity of Chinese intellectual civilization.

In the time of archaic antiquity, all peoples stood roughly at the same level of culture. But once they reached their maturity, each would have its own way, which differentiated itself from others. Confucius must be identified as the key figure at the turning point of the Chinese mind from infancy to maturity. As the national character has been historically nurtured, Confucius fully deserves the title of the *pontifex maximus* of Chinese philosophy. It is not until as late as the early 20th century that this orthodoxy of the Confucian ideology was challenged by the Chinese intellectuals under the impact of the Western tide.

There are some basic elements in Confucianism which have played a profound role in the history of China. As stated above, in the age of antiquity in China there was no such democracy as was seen in ancient Greece. The ancient city-states afforded the most fertile soil for fostering ancient democracy. Yet the ancient city-states in China did not bring forth ancient democracy, such as the convention of a peoples' assembly in which citizens were called to discuss and to vote on political issues and even to adopt such measures as banishment. Why was it so? The reason, I suppose, might be found in the predominance of blood lineage in the Chinese way of living. In an extremely strong patriarchal society like China, the individual never participated in political and social activities as a free man independently, a fact diametrically opposed to the practice in the history of the Occident. In his *Lectures on the Philosophy of History* Hegel touched briefly upon this characteristic of Chinese history.

[V] The Essence of Confucius' Thought

Indeed, Confucius himself never intended to work out a complete philosophical system as did philosophers in later ages. Nevertheless, there was an apparent indication in the *Analects* to take "benevolence" (*ren*) as the core of all conduct and morality. It might be fairly asserted that the idea of benevolence forms the nucleus of his theory. Together with the idea of benevolence, his theory reflected yet another characteristic feature of Chinese culture, i.e. its practicality. One of the consequences is that in China there has never been any religion in the strict sense. In the *Analects* Confucius was described thus: "The subjects on which the Master [Confucius] did not speak were extraordinary things, feats of strength, disorder and spiritual beings."[①] He was too practically minded to ponder over things supernatural or impractical in daily usage. A superhuman God would be impractical, because He proves of no avail in our practical life whether He be there or not. Some historians are led to suppose that the contribution of Confucianism lies in its liberation of Chinese culture from the bondage of religion (the presupposition being that religion is a spiritual chain), while others consider Confucianism as itself a religion. The answer will depend on how we define the term religion. At any rate, there has never been any exclusive religious belief in China such as Judaism or Christianity in the West because the Chinese people never embraced belief in the otherworldly. What they are interested in is no other than this present world; and if they would hope for any eternal life, that would be no other than the very prolongation of the practical life in this world. They are not at all interested in anything outside of the practical life in this world. In this respect Confucius reflected most strikingly the Chinese mind. He never preached nor propagated any religion, nor did he ever believe in any. All his teachings are wholly concerned with practical conduct in daily life, and hence are thoroughly ethically orientated in their essence: i.e. what attitude one ought to adopt towards others. As to the other world, he held all rites and sacrifices as but a social custom; "he [Confucius] sacrificed to the dead, as if they were present. He sacrificed to the spirits as if the spirits were present,"[②] reported the *Analects*. He would not affirm the reality of anything otherworldly. Here lies the basic distinction between Confucius and all theists in the ancient world. For him, "the way of Heaven is far away while the way of man is near at hand," so his disciple once remarked, "The Master's discourses about Nature and the way of Heaven cannot be heard." When once a disciple asked about serving the spirits, Confucius replied: "While you are not able to serve men, how can you serve their spirits?" and still "While you do not know life, how can you know about death?"[③] Confucius was concerned only with what is practical in daily life but never with what is beyond, for the way of Heaven is beyond what can be known.

But viewed from the other perspective, such an overemphasized practicality also proved a serious shortcoming of Confucianism. In all that is concerned with what is the beyond, he had no interest at all. He took no care of what is beyond practical life, either religion or science. In an important respect, science and

① *Analects*, bk.3 "Eight Lines of Dancing" (Ba Yi), trans. James Legge.

② *Analects*, bk.1 "The Former Times" (*Xian Jin*), trans. James Legge.

③ *Book of Zhuang Zi*, "The World" (*Tian Xia*).

religion are consistent, i.e. both pursue the "infinite," the mystery of the very nature of the world or something behind and beyond daily life. Too much practicality would prevent people from engaging in such impractical pursuits. Every day we see the sun rising and falling, but what is behind this, and controls its movement? Such an inquiry belongs to the scientific spirit for which Confucius and his disciples would never show any care, because it has nothing to do with "benevolence," the supreme virtue. People toil and moil all day long. But what is it that lies behind the appearance of our day-to-day life? What is the ultimate end of life, for which people are striving consciously or unconsciously? Is the soul immortal? Such inquiries aim at the pursuit of what is infinite and are not related with any practical issue in daily life. They are in pursuit of truth which is not necessarily in close connection with life's practicalities. In a certain sense, both science and religion in their very essence are impractical. But Confucius concentrated all his concern solely on practical life and entertained no interest at all in what is beyond or behind the realm of our practical life. To understand the spirit of the Chinese culture, one has to go into the depth of this practicality which is so thoroughgoing from beginning to end and which permeates into their very marrows and bones. In so far as being expedient to their practical life, they are ready to accept any preaching or doctrine whatsoever (for instance, in the case when Hong Xiuquan professed himself to be the brother of Jesus and preached his doctrine on behalf of Jehovah and Jesus). And they are as ready to give it up whenever and wherever practical life compels them. They act only in accordance with what their practical life demands. In reality, in their heart of hearts they never believe any preaching or faith. Or rather, they may embrace any doctrine or belief, provided it will be of practical value to them. To a considerable degree, these features of the Chinese mind, so well expressed in Confucius' teachings, have played a regulative role in the orientation of the Chinese way of thinking. It helps to explain why religious and scientific ideas never got an upper hand in the intellectual history of China.

By the time of Confucius, "the rites collapsed and music was corrupted," the traditional mentality and social order were totally shattered, or in the words of Zhuang Zi, "the art of the Way comes to be rent and torn apart by the world."① Then sprouted forth various schools, each endeavoring to save the world with its own teaching. Among them, Confucianism must be conceded to be the most practical in character, and this must be taken as the reason that in the

① A famous figure in Lu Xun's novel *The True Story of Ah Q*, who is well-known for his customary self-deception.

long run it eventually became the dominant school in China. It accommodated most perfectly the characteristic practicality of the Chinese mind. A nation totally dominated by practicality can have no faith, either in religion or in science. Many people followed Hong Xiuquan not because they believed in his doctrine of his godhood as Jesus' brother, but because they would avoid starvation once they followed him. But later as Hong was no longer in a position to feed them, the belief he preached could no longer lead them. What matters here is not the theory of his doctrine, but the reality of the practical life. China is a nation too practical to be involved in any pure theoretical pursuit, religious, scientific or any other. I would like to cite here one of my personal experiences. It was in the early seventies when we were sent down to the cadres' school for manual labor. One day after we recited Lin Biao's preface to the *Quotations of Mao Zedong* as usual, we were summoned to the mess hall by the leaders of the Propaganda Team of Mao Zedong Thought. Just over our heads there hung high on the wall two posters in big characters, one reading, "Pledge our lives in defending Chairman Mao," the other, "Pledge our lives in defending vice chairman Lin." The leader then gave us a speech on how "Lin, the traitor" committed counterrevolutionary crimes. When we joined together again in small groups to condemn his crime, someone uttered that he dared hardly even to think that such things could ever happen. But after the meeting, I found this man (and indeed almost all of us who had once pledged our lives in defending Vice Chairman Lin) ate and slept as usual. One cannot help wonder whether his former pledge was sincere. To a true believer, such an incident in which the idol of his worship suddenly turned to be a traitor would break his nerves. Then, what should we say about this? In one respect, we may admit the nerves of the Chinese mind are so solid and sound as to be able to bear all impacts. They are so practical that they may shout "support" or "down with" any person or any doctrine, if it be expedient to do so. But in the other respect, such indifference may be identified with an apathetic insensitiveness, much of which had been discussed so searchingly in Lu Xun's analysis of the Chinese character. Perhaps one may trace it back to the Confucian practicality: What lies outside of the immediate practicality deserves no concern at all. Marx once mentioned that under capitalism everything becomes a matter of money, citing two examples: religious belief and love. Perhaps one may fairly say that in the Chinese tradition everything is considered a matter of practicality, hence all are evaluated by their function with regard to practicality. If one is to scrutinize the core of the philosophy of China, one has to keep in mind its practical side; otherwise one would be misled by the face value of its texts. Its real value always lay deeply hidden in its historical and cultural background.

It is generally acknowledged that the Confucian school represented the most prevailing and long-standing doctrine in the history of China. With the wealth of its exuberant theory and dogma, it could rival Buddhism and Christianity in its historical significance. But I cannot but entertain a certain doubt as to the prevailing opinion that the spirit of Chinese philosophy should be represented by the Confucian school. It would be an absurdity to single out one person or one idea as the sole representative of a people who exhibit so much manifold variety in the treasure of their cultural legacy. If Confucius could be identified as the representative of the Chinese spirit, why would it not be Lao Zi or even why not Ah Q?① Don't we find something in Lao Zi's or Ah Q's ideas which are also deep-rooted among the Chinese, even sometimes much more so than in some high-sounding teachings of Confucius? In the culture or in the ideas of a people, there is no such thing as the so-called sole representative. A culture is inevitably a complex entity in which all sorts of ideas have right of place. In the realm of the intellectual culture, there is and there can be no official representative, like there is when a nation sends its delegation to the United Nations. In attending an UN conference, each nation can have only one delegation headed by only one person who is the sole legal representative of his country. But in the realm of intellectual culture, there can be and ought to be no such representative. Certainly some persons or ideas influenced later ages much more than others. Yet this in no sense means that such persons or ideas can represent the Chinese spirit. Nor does it mean that those with lesser influence are of less value. As was mentioned above, Confucianism did not ascend to the throne of the supreme orthodoxy until the Song Dynasty. And even by that time, many other religions, sects, pagan cults, heresies and popular beliefs were still much in vogue side by side with the Confucian orthodoxy officially sanctioned by the royal court, and Confucianism had undergone its rises and falls. As to the "contemporary Confucianism," it should be borne in mind that this Confucian revival has been conditioned by extraordinary political circumstances. By the fifties of the 20th century, as the Kuomintang regime retreated to the island of Taiwan, it endeavored to confront Leninist (or rather Maoist) Marxism by resorting to the age-old tradition of Confucianism. A number of the Chinese intellectuals overseas were also trying to seek a way of strengthening themselves spiritually, but certainly without recourse to the Maoist Marxism of the mainland, and thus the only choice left would

① *Analects*, bk.18 "Wei Zi," trans. James Legge, with alterations by the author.

be none other than the cause of Confucianism. Since the Chinese character is one of practicality, we have to view this phenomenon very practically. These intellectuals have to earn their living abroad. Professing Confucianism would be a most convenient and ready-made means of subsistence for them. Over the past decades, with the rapid economic growth of "the four small dragons" (Korea, Taiwan, Hong Kong and Singapore), contemporary Confucians seem to have discovered a new inspiration in their arguments: since all the four areas belong to the cultural circle of Confucianism, Confucianism must have been the main stimulus for their economic development. Such an argument seems to me too far-fetched. Confucianism has existed in China for more than two thousand years. If it were indeed helpful to economic growth, then China ought to have become a modernized country much earlier by far than those in the West. Then why is it that her economic boom just reached its infancy only in recent times? There seems no reason to assert that the Confucian ideology played less of a role in the past than in recent times, so that we had to wait until today for its fruition. Moreover, how can we explain the fact of the economic development of other countries which have never been influenced by Confucianism?

For a long time in the past, many a Chinese scholar in their study of Chinese intellectual history has been inclined to stress the conflicts between different schools while neglecting the fact that they were at the same time influencing, absorbing and merging with one another. In reality, different schools were mutually both in confrontation and in fusion at the same time. We should pay due attention both to their conflicts and to their fusions, or we would lose sight of a complete grasp of the historical panorama. No theory in history could ever be something one hundred percent pure and unaffected; it certainly had to be influenced by others. One should keep this in mind when dealing with either the ancient or the modern thinkers. Confucius and Confucianism are no exception.

[VI] The Ideal of Confucius

Confucius' ideal was to mold a "superior man" or gentleman. A superior man exists in contrast and in contradiction with a "small man." By his social status a superior man is of a higher social rank, while the small man of the lower. By profession, a superior man is a mental worker, a small man a manual laborer. But the difference is more than this. The core of Confucius' teaching dwells in moral cultivation, hence the difference between the superior man and the small is imbued with a strong ethical hue. A superior man is one with a more perfect spirit and morality than a small man. So the implication of his idea bears a double significance, one in regard to social status, the other to moral cultivation. And it is obvious that Confucius laid his emphasis on the latter. The six arts which Confucius taught his disciples afforded the necessary knowledge which would meet the requirements of a Confucian gentleman. But manual labor or technique was outside of that requirement. Some of his contemporaries were said to reproach the great master: "His four limbs are unaccustomed to toil, he cannot distinguish the five kinds of grain. Who is [worthy to be] the master?"① Yet, this conforms exactly with the ideal of a superior man who ought not to care for such trifling things. What Confucius aimed at was to cultivate the good rulers of the state, like Plato demanded in his Republic, to carry out his ideas, or in his own terminology, to cultivate "a superior scholar" (*jun zi ru*) who was supposed "to carry out the good principles" (*xing dao*). Herein is implied a notion of the social division of labor which lasted for thousands of years to come, including both a division of social functions and a division of manual and mental labors. In ancient China, just as in ancient Greece, one of the main factors which impeded the smooth progress of the intellectual and scientific development was the mentality of the mental laborers, who always held a disdain for the manual laborers as the inferior (or "small man"). Confucius' reply to his disciple Fan Chi's question, as cited above, furnished an example.

Confucius traveled widely from country to country, hoping to encounter some prince under whose patronage he might carry out his ideal of a benevolent government. This reflected one of the main characteristics of the Chinese intellectuals, in sharp contrast with the Chinese peasantry. The Chinese intellectuals never intended to attain supreme power by themselves. They had to seek the patronage of someone in power, whereas the peasants were often rising up in arms to seize power, like Chen Sheng and Wu Guang, leaders of peasant uprisings in the early 2nd century B.C., who protested: "Is it really true that the princes and dignitaries are born noble?"② The peasantry dared to make an attempt at imperial power. The intellectuals never attempted that, they wanted only to become the tutors of the sovereigns under whose patronage they would reach a position to carry out their ideals. Therefore they had to attach themselves to the power of some sovereign, and were thereby deprived of their independence. This mentality was best expressed by the well-known lines of the

① Sima Qian, *Records of the Histonan*, bk.48 "Life of Chen She."

② Du Fu, *Works*, vol. 1, "Lines dedicated to Wei Ji."

famous 8th century poet Du Fu: "[I hope] to promote the sovereign to the height of Yao and Shun [the legendary sage-kings] and thereby to restore customs and manners to their antique purity."① Unfortunately, Confucius had not led a very successful life, and once he deeply lamented: "As to my failure to make progress of the right principles, I am now fully aware of it."② He knew well that there was no chance for him to carry out his principles. In his last years, he again lamented: "The phoenix does not come, the [Yellow] River sends forth no map; alas, it is all over with me!"③ According to ancient legend, in an age of the rule of the sage-king, the phoenix would come, the Yellow River would send forth the map and the Lo River the book. The tragedy all through his life was: "He knows the impracticable nature of the times, and yet is still engaged in them."④

Every philosopher has his utopia, and so it was with Confucius whose ideal was the rule of a benevolent government, an ideal which was severely criticized by Mao Zedong⑤ more than two thousand years later. Indeed, the term "benevolence" appeared with greatest frequency in the *Analects* and afforded the highest principle and the guiding idea in his theory. According to Ruan Yuan's (late 18th and early 19th centuries) explanation, benevolence etymologically signifies the companionship of two persons or rather an ideal of the interpersonal relationship. Herein dwells the most characteristic feature of Chinese thought. The philosophies in China, no matter what school they belonged to, have from throughout the earliest times been the philosophy of man. They dealt only with man without paying any attention either to nature or to the relationship between man and nature. Further, in the philosophy of man, it is not the individual but the interpersonal relationship which is given priority. It is an ethico-politico-centric world-view. In this respect, Confucius was by far the undisputed authority beyond doubt. This philosophical tendency shows its interest in collectivism as superior to individualism, an interest which contrasts sharply with the individualistic tendency of the West. For instance, take the case of Defoe's Robinson Crusoe, who survived shipwreck and great hardship by force of will on an isolated island. He was acknowledged as a hero for his bold deeds. But he would never become a hero in Chinese fiction. The Chinese approach is otherwise: it starts not from the individual but from the interpersonal (i.e. ethical) relationship. On the isolated island there is no relation except that between an isolated

① *Analects*, bk.18 "Wei Zi," trans. James Legge, with alterations by the author.

② Ibid., bk. 9 "Zi Han," trans. James Legge, with alterations by the author.

③ *Analects*, bk.14 "Xian Wen," trans. James Legge, with alterations by the author.

④ Cf. Mao Zedong, *Works*, vol. 4 "On the People's Democratic Dictatorship."

⑤ *Analects*, bk.6 "Yong Ye," trans. James Legge, with alterations by the author.

man and nature; therefore, there is no benevolence whatever, as the Chinese philosopher would stress. The idea of benevolence would then totally come to nothing.

There are manifold implications in the idea of benevolence. Confucius said, "Benevolent is he who loves others," and again: "The benevolent person, wishing to be established himself, seeks also to establish others; wishing to be enlarged himself, he seeks also to enlarge others."① In regard to this implication, benevolence might be identified as humanitarianism. Once, "the stable being burnt down, he asked, `Has any man been hurt?' He did not ask about the horses."② The story is a good example of the spirit of his humanitarianism. Benevolence is something innate in our nature, and one need not seek it outside of oneself. Thus, "The Master said: Is benevolence a thing remote? I wish to be benevolent, and lo! Benevolence is already at hand."③ Yet as the primary and cardinal virtue, benevolence comprises many concrete moral items. It is interesting to compare Confucian benevolence with Mencian obligation. Obligation (*yi*) is the main idea of Mencius with whom we shall deal in detail later. Their respective emphases bear some difference. What benevolence stresses is not an obligation coercive or imperative in nature, but a natural spontaneity of one's inner sentiment or emotion. From it emanate many concrete virtues. Once our cultivation is elevated, all kinds of virtues inherent in us will naturally follow and become manifest. Confucius described his own cultivation with these words: "At fifteen I had my mind bent on learning. At thirty, I stood firm. At forty, I had no doubts. At fifty, I knew the decrees of Heaven. At sixty, my ear was an obedient organ④ [for the reception of truth]. At seventy, I could follow what my heart desired, without transgressing what was right."⑤ Only after a long process of self-cultivation did Confucius reach the state of perfect maturity, and then the spontaneity of his inner self would naturally exist in conformity with the right principle. Such is benevolence in which all virtues consist, e.g., loyalty and filial piety. Hence Confucius said: "My doctrine is that of an all-pervading unity." Another asked Zeng (Sheng), saying, "What do his words

① Ibid., bk.10 "The Community" (*Xiang Dang*), trans. James Legge.

② Ibid., bk.7 "Transmitting" (*Shu Er*), trans. James Legge, with alterations by the author.

③ Here the original text reads, "er shun," literally "the ear is obedient"—an almost incomprehensible expression. Some have claimed it was a mis-copying of "*er yi shun*," meaning complaisance with the outside world.

④ *Analects*, bk.2 "On Governing" (*Wei Zheng*), trans. James Legge, with alterations by the author.

⑤ Ibid., bk.4 "In Neighborhood of Benevolence" (*Li Ren*), trans. James Legge, with alterations by the author.

mean?" Zeng replied: "The doctrine of our master is to be loyal and to forbear. This and nothing more."① This all-pervading unity is benevolence; all other virtues come out of it.

Hand in hand with benevolence is the idea of "rites." In truth, this idea of rites was so important in the Confucian teaching that it assumed the name of "the doctrine of rites" or "the doctrine of name" in later ages. Rites are the norms regulating the interpersonal relations which have to be observed by everyone. Rites are but the outward expressions of benevolence. In our inner heart it is benevolence, and when expressed outwardly it becomes the rites. Here an interpersonal relationship is presupposed. If Robinson Crusoe were the only person in the world, then there would be no room for either benevolence or any rite. It seems that in the depth of their hearts the Westerners' approach is always toward the individualistic. That is to say, in the last analysis, the individual is the atom or the monad by which a society or state is formed. But the Chinese tradition is just the reverse: the original point from which they start is not the individual but the interpersonal relationship. Or to use an expression from physics, it is not the atom which regulates the field but the field which regulates the atom. The ultimate substance is not the individual but the inter-individual relationship, which is prior as well as superior to the individual. The individual is nothing more than the bearer of an ethical relationship which alone is the supra-individual substance. Without this net of relationships, the individual can have no existence of his own. This is not only the peculiarity of the Confucian school but of the philosophy in China in general. From their very start, there was a marked difference between the Chinese and the Western way of thinking: whether the individual exists for the sake of community or conversely the community for the sake of the individual. Ever since Confucius, the mainstream of thought in China has regarded the individual as a means to fulfill ends which are in nature supra-individual.

This way of thinking when applied to the realm of politics becomes the exaction of the "rectification of names" (*zheng ming*). Once his disciple "Zi Lu said: 'The prince of Wei has been waiting for you, in order for you to administer the government. What will you consider the first thing to be done?' The Master replied: 'What is necessary is to rectify the names.' ... If names be not correct, language is not in accordance with the truth of things. If language be not in accordance with the truth of things, affairs cannot be carried on to success."②

① Ibid., bk.13 "Zi Lu," trans. James Legge.

② Ibid., bk.12 "Yan Yuan," trans. James Legge, with alterations by the author.

Here the rectification of names is at the same time both an ethical and a political exaction. It ensures "the prince is prince, the minister is minister, the father is father, the son is son",[1] that is to say, one should above all fulfill the requirements his social status exacts of him. Man is above all an instrument of his social relationship rather than an end in himself and by himself. Or in other words, an individual, above all, ought to be a means for some ethico-political norm unconditionally, a bearer of some supra-individual idea for which he is born. The value of life consists only in this and in nothing else. Hence Confucius strongly condemned "the prince not being prince, the minister not minister, the father not father, the son not son." The name (status) stipulates the substance of life. Therefore everyone should fulfill all the duties his social status exacts of him. From this is derived the term of Ming Jiao (the instruction or doctrine of definition) which ever since became a profound tradition of Chinese spiritual life. In modern times when Zeng Guofan raised an army against the Taiping Uprising, he promulgated a well-known war proclamation in which he called on all the nation to rise up to defend the Ming Jiao (the traditional culture) against the Taiping regime lest it be destroyed. Earlier in the first years of the Qing Dynasty, when the emperor was executing his literary inquisitions, once he ordered that a big board be hung on the front door of one among the persecuted with these words on it: "A criminal against the Ming Jiao," then the greatest possible charge of indictment. Ming Jiao is in its substance, of course, the basic teaching of Confucianism. But this signifies only one aspect of Confucius, i.e. his sober and even sanctimonious side. If we are to know the historical reality, we have yet to look at his other side.

Among his disciples, numbering as many as three thousand, there were seventy-two who were said to have become well versed in the six liberal arts: the "seventy-two outstanding personages." And among them Confucius most appreciated Yan Yuan (Yan Hui). He praised Yan much more than the others, a fact which might be taken as evidence that Yan by far came nearest to the teaching of Confucius. This Yan Yuan was in fact a fascinating figure, with a somewhat mystic and otherworldly temperament. Yan led a very hard life. Confucius praised him: "Admirable indeed was the virtue of Yan Hui. With a single bamboo dish of rice, a single gourd of drink, and living in his mean narrow lane, while others could not have endured such distress, he did not allow his joy to be affected. Admirable indeed was the virtue of Yan Hui."[2] And Confucius himself

① Ibid., bk.13 "Zi Lu," trans. James Legge.

② *Analects*, bk.6 "Yong Ye," trans. James Legge, with alterations by the author.

shared the same joy with Yan Hui: "With coarse rice to eat, with water to drink, and my bended arms for a pillow, I still have joy in the midst of these things."[①] We find another record in the *Analects* which is comparatively much longer than others and is hence considered by some scholars to be of a much later date, but of which there is no doubt that it records the truth of Confucius' life and thoughts. Confucius asked some of his disciples what were their ideals in life. After others had talked about their wishes, Zeng Dian said he would cherish the wish that "in the last month of spring, with the dress of the season all complete, along with five or six young men who have assumed caps [a sign showing a person has grown up] and six or seven boys, I would wash in the Yi River, enjoy the breeze among the rain-altars, and return home singing." At these words, "the Master heaved a sigh and said: 'I give my approval to [Zeng] Dian.'"[②] Here was disclosed a sort of pleasure of the ancient mystics which Confucius and Yan Hui and some others held in common, and which came very near to those we might find in the ancient Greek sects. Almost all ancient philosophical schools were evolved out of religion. In early antiquity, it was religion that governed the relationship between gods and men. Later with knowledge moving downwards from the priesthood to the common people, various sects and schools sprang up, each having its own ideals and approaches, its own spiritual qualities and interests which constituted its character. The Confucians had their specific spiritual qualities and interests, and so too with the Taoists and other schools. They were all pursuing their ideal of perfect living, not only in social and political life, but, what was more, in a spiritual satisfaction. That state of spiritual satisfaction was much appreciated by the Song Confucians, so that they urged scholars "to learn the pleasures wherein Confucius and Yan Hui indulged themselves." An epigram composed by the Song Confucians reads: "To learn the pleasure in this very learning, to enjoy the pleasure in this very learning; no learning is without this pleasure, and no pleasure is without this learning." The ultimate end of learning is but to arrive at a spiritual state of perfection. The Confucian school paid much attention to the practical side of life, i.e. the political and social activities, but at the same time they were possessed or obsessed by a transcendental nostalgia, or even a longing, for a mystic ecstasy. It is this aspect of the ancient Confucians which seems often neglected by many inquirers. Here we single out this fact emphatically in order that we might better locate Confucius in a position of a great master in antiquity, rather than that

① Ibid., bk.7 "Transmitting", trans. James Legge.

② Ibid., bk.10 "The Community," trans. James Legge, with alterations by the author.

of a venerable sage in a worldly sense. He was often sanctified to too great an extent by later generations to be properly understood as a human being and as a philosopher.

[VII] Benevolence—the Philosophy of Man

Ancient and mediaeval philosophers as a rule were not accustomed to expounding their own systematic theories explicitly and straightforwardly. Often they resorted to their exegesis of the classics whereby their own ideas were expounded. Outside of this, they rarely made their own independent innovations. But elevation of the notion of benevolence to an unprecedented height as the supreme virtue was indeed an innovation of Confucius himself. But after all, what does benevolence signify? It is roughly equivalent to humanness, that which holds the nature of humanity, and hence it is simultaneously both humanitarianism and humanism. Humanitarianism means the compassion of man to man, and humanism the antithesis of theism or divinity-worship. During the age of the reign of religion, everything was valued and measured by divinity. In ancient Greece it was Protagoras, the Sophist, who first proposed, "Man is the measure of all things." And in China it was Confucius who first definitely proposed the same idea. He discarded all preachings and reasonings based on divinity worship and upheld humanity (i.e. that which belongs to human beings) as the sole criterion in every matter. For the first time in the history of China, the place of man was formally established as primary, while that of divinity was withdrawn into the background.

Benevolence, though an attribute inborn in man, had to be nourished and cultivated by the education of rites, or propriety. The spiritual qualities thus acquired were called virtues. So far as interpersonal relationship is concerned, benevolence is that which springs from our inner heart, while rites are those which are required by external norms. Benevolence is considered the essential and primary, while all else is derivative and secondary, the universe at large and even the supernatural world included. Confucius spoke of his own efforts, "while respecting spiritual beings, to keep aloof from them."[①] In the same fashion, "he sacrificed to the dead, as if they were present,"[②] although he knew well they could not be present. The belief in gods and spirits was a common practice

① Ibid., bk.6 "Yong Ye," trans. James Legge.

② Ibid., bk.3, "Ba Yi," trans. James Legge.

among the ancients, but as a thoroughgoing humanist, Confucius spoke nothing of them, his interest being concentrated only on what is human. It should be admitted that this attitude of his was of much value in liberating people's minds from superstition. But as was mentioned above, such a practical spirit was also acquired at the price of abandoning that scrutinizing interest indispensable for searching into the deeper layers of the universe and human life. Too much practicality would prove unfavorable to the development of science or any theoretical speculations for knowledge's sake. All that falls outside of the sphere of practicality (e.g. Nature and the Way of Heaven), Confucius would not care for. What is the ultimate nature of Heaven and of man; all those were beyond the sphere of Confucius' study. In this sense, Confucius was only a preacher of good everyday living rather than an explorer of the mysteries of the world and life. Perhaps we may for the sake of convenience delineate all philosophers into two groups: one is in search of the ultimate truth of the world, the other in search of the wisdom of how to lead a good life. Surely Confucius belongs to the second group rather than to the first. As a high priest of a noble life, he is regarded as one of the greatest masters in the history of mankind. The doctrine of the Confucian school is one of the most practical. To a considerable degree, this peculiarity explains why China has had no science—no "modern" science, to be exact—nor religious beliefs. Both science and philosophy demand that our thinking should penetrate into the depths behind phenomena and our daily experiences, but Confucius persistently stuck to the level of practicality in daily life and never tried to probe what lay behind it. The famous saying of Zi Chan, the well-known statesman of Zheng: "The Way of Heaven is far off, but the Way of man is near at hand," formulated very succinctly the spirit of the Confucians. This seems to show that since their very beginning the philosophies in the West and in China took different approaches. The philosophy in the West from its start took the way of natural philosophy, that is to scrutinize the Way of Heaven or the ultimate mystery of the universe; while that in China took interpersonal relationship and conduct as its ultimate concern, a way leading to practicality in the actual ways of behavior in our daily life. In other words, the road of philosophy in the West is the road of the sophists (in the sense that "sophia" means intellectualism), while that in China is that of virtue (in the sense that virtue leads to humanism). If we follow Kant to divide reason into three parts: pure reason, practical reason, and reason of judgment, respectively in pursuit of truth, goodness and beauty; then it may be fairly said that the road of the Chinese is that of virtue or goodness. There have been those in the West who dedicated their lives to truth or to beauty, like some among the scientists and artists. But in China neither truth nor beauty can have any value of its own; they have to be subordinated to the rule of virtue in the service of a moral or ethico-political end. The sole function of the philosophers or scholars of China is but "to speak in the name of the ancient sages." The readers might well recall a popular spectacle existing since the founding of the People's Republic, in the yearly National Day parade. On the placard of the scientific workers were written the large characters with the meaning: "Science for the sake of serving the proletarian politics." Science and art (truth and beauty) for the sake of politics have long been a deep-rooted credo of the Chinese cultural tradition, that is to say, all values in the last analysis depend on their relations to virtue or to their positions in the ethico-political spectrum. The end of philosophy is not to probe the ultimate truth of world and life, but to serve ethico-political utility or expediency. In this fundamental orientation, the Chinese way of thinking differs from that of the West. Aristotle in his discourse on life and living took the attitude of a disinterested contemplation of world and life to be the ideal state of man. Goethe in the last part of his *Faust* described an old warder who found his spiritual sustenance on the lighthouse by watching the world from his tower every day, chanting these words: "Zum sehen geboren, zum schanen bestellt."① Many artists in the West sought after beauty as their highest ideal in life—not only the artists of the aestheticist camp, but also a great deal of the Romantic poets. John Keats asserted: "A thing of beauty is a joy forever."② One's life may be and ought to be dedicated to the pursuit of beauty in which dwells an eternal happiness or bliss. This kind of life ideal looks quite at variance with that of the Chinese, for whom the value of life consists exclusively in the perfection of virtue and nothing else. Everything else derives its right of existence only from its utility in the ethico-political structure it serves. Was it the Chinese character that inspired the doctrine of Confucius, or conversely did the doctrine of Confucius provide the Chinese with their characteristic features? The answer probably lies somewhere in the mutual magnification they exerted upon each other in the course of history.

Since the Confucian teachings stressed virtue in practical life to the neglect of the independent value of truth or beauty, politics as a matter of course came to take the lead: because what reigns in practical life is predominantly political force, which in ancient China was controlled by none other than the supreme imperial power. In general, one's attitude towards the ruling regime consti-

① Goethe, *Faust*, pt. 2, act 5, scene 4, trans. Albert Latham.

② J. Keats, "Endymion," bk.1.

tutes what is called virtue. In regard to governing, Confucius said: "The art of governing should be exercised by means of virtue. It may be compared to the North Star which keeps its place while all the other stars turn towards it."[①] And again: "If the people be led by orders and uniformity sought by giving them punishments, they will try to avoid the punishment, but have no sense of shame. If they be led by virtue, and uniformity sought by giving them the rules of rites, they will have the sense of shame, and moreover will become good."[②] In exercising political power it is not merely force that the ruler should rely upon. Only through governing by virtue can the best political outcome be attained, because it induces people to obey voluntarily instead of compulsively. Coercion is indispensable in politics, but sheer suppression is not enough. It has to allure or to appeal to the spirits of the people.

Besides coercion, the ruler has to persuade them to follow him willingly. And a virtuous (or benevolent) government will prove to be the best way for this. Herein lies the basic divergence between the Confucians and the Legalists. To persuade the people, the ruler has to bring forth a benevolent government, and this in turn will require the functioning of rites of propriety. Hence Confucius proclaimed: "To subdue one's self and return to rites (propriety) is benevolence (perfect virtue). Once a man can subdue himself and return to rites (propriety), all the world will ascribe benevolence (perfect virtue) to him."[③]

[VIII] The Rule of Rites

There is always something in the minds of men which does not conform to the rites (propriety), and therefore one has to "subdue one's self and return to rites (propriety)," that is to say, one has to restrain or control one's self in accordance with the Zhou institution as conceived by Confucius. Here is suggested an issue which is of cardinal importance in the history of philosophy. Confucius did not amplify his theory into a systematic philosophy; this task was eventually completed by the Song Confucians as late as in the 11th and 12th centuries. But still the question was already implied herein. Why is it that one has to "subdue one's self and return to rites"? Is there something in human nature which is born

① *Analects*, bk.2 "On Governing," trans. James Legge, with alterations by the author.

② Ibid., trans. James Legge, with alterations by the author.

③ Ibid., bk.12 "Yan Yuan," trans. James Legge with alterations by the author. As is well known, during the early seventies as Lin Biao cited these words, "Subdue one's self and return to rites (propriety)," and there was launched in China a campaign of "criticizing Lin and criticizing Confucius."

evil and not in conformity with good propriety, so that one must subdue it to lead one's self back again to the way of good propriety? If there is, how can man achieve genuine good? Mencius took it for granted that human nature is born good. In the popular reader of the bygone days *The Classic in Three Words* (*San Zi Jing*), the opening sentence runs, "In the beginning, human nature is good." If it is born good, why need it be subdued or restrained? After all, there must be something in it which is not entirely good and consequently has to be subdued. Here is involved a basic issue of philosophy in China, i.e. that of the origin of evil. From where do the evils in society and in our minds come, and where do they go? If human nature is born good, then where do the evils come from? To this question, the Song Confucians elaborated a theory of the struggle between the Heavenly Principles and the human desires (or lust). Heavenly Principles as the primordial principles stipulated by Heaven, are by nature good in themselves. But alongside them there are human desires (lust). Human desires should not be wholly equated with the normal desires. There are good desires as well as bad ones. Confucius said, "Whenever I desire benevolence (virtue), there is then benevolence (virtue) here."[①] Such a desire is a good one. We need not seek it outside of ourselves, for it is already there within our inner heart. It is a desire without any lust. Yet there are surely some desires which are no good at all, such as the pursuit of sensual enjoyments, which should be identified with lust. As to why there are such lusts, Confucius gave no answer. He took it for granted that humans were able "to subdue themselves and return to the rites (propriety)" through their proper cultivation and earnest efforts. Later generations worked out various explanations on this question, which formed one of the basic issues in the history of philosophy in China. Though Confucius himself gave no answer to this question, it is he who first formally put forth such a perennial question.

The overemphasis on benevolence and rites brought forth a byproduct in the Chinese way of thinking, i.e. it tended to obliterate the value of the pursuit of truth and beauty, as mentioned above. And such an outlook on life can hardly be taken as a wholesome and well-balanced one. On many aspects of the natural world and the spiritual world, the Confucians lacked a serious interest and a sound understanding. They never encouraged people to study natural phenomena or technical knowledge and contributed very little to theories of social and emotional life (or even of romantic love). At any rate, all the complexities of the world and of our life cannot simply be reduced to an ethico-political framework

① *Analects*, bk.7 "Transmitting", trans. James Legge.

as the sole account. In this sense, the Confucians are monists, not pluralists. For them, all started from an ethico-political norm and returned to it again. Thus was formed the age-long tradition of Chinese culture. When a scientist is in search of truth, he would take no care of what is benevolence or rites (propriety). Scientific truth has nothing to do with either of them, and nor do our emotional lives. We have to admit that, after all, these elements also form the integral parts of humanity, to the totality of which the Confucians never paid due attention. We cannot substitute the whole living facts of our lives and social activities by or configure these into a framework of ethical preachings. Yet it is this tradition which afforded the Chinese minds an unshakable credo. What is generally known as "the doctrine of names" (*zheng ming*) or "the teaching of rites" (*li jiao*) is at bottom supported by such a framework of mentality. Perhaps we should not demand a philosopher do so much as to comprehend all the various aspects of life. But we have the right to ask him to not stress only one aspect of it, to the oblivion of all others. With virtue being valued above all others as the sole criterion of our thoughts and activities, the Chinese mind was thenceforth constrained by a one-sidedness, as though once separated from virtue, all would lose their value. Such a prejudice certainly tends to lead to hypocrisy and not to a vigorous, colorful and well-balanced life.

[IX] The Ethico-Politico-Centric World-View

Virtue is first of all embodied in the superior men (gentlemen). Confucius said: "The virtue of the superiors is like the wind and that of the inferiors the grass. The grass must bend, when the wind blows across it."① Hence the virtue on the part of the rulers is of the utmost importance. Virtue and law are mutually complementary; law entails a coercion, but it has to be based on virtue. Coercion by itself would not work in the long run. But will virtue avail by itself? Aristotle in his treatment of various political institutions remarked that each of them would of necessity degenerate into a worse one. With this remark in view, we might as well say that when the teaching of rites (propriety) degenerates, it would become a hypocritical formality. The overemphasis of virtue would bring about a great deal of artificiality or affectedness. It would be against what is natural in human desires and consequently become very unnatural. In course of time it would be destined to become ever worse.

① Ibid., bk.12 "Yan Yuan," trans. James Legge, with alterations by the author.

We may indeed remember the two orientations in philosophy: one in search of mysteries of the world, the other in search of the wisdom of life. The former is for the sake of knowing, the other for the sake of good living. What the Confucian school stressed is the latter and we should evaluate them from this aspect, more than from the former. In their investigation of inner spiritual cultivation and moral self-perfection there is a great deal of incomparable value, for they have left us a profound revelation on the wisdom of life. The famous saying of Confucius: "If a man in the morning hears the (right) way, he may die in the evening without regret",① gave a good description of this inner perfection of a moral life, rather than the satisfaction brought about by mere curiosity one might entertain for the outside world. This state of mind resembles very much what Rousseau described in his *Emile*, that one should be educated to fulfill his moral life so that one could die at any time without regret or remorse. Such longings lie within one's life ideals. Confucius described himself with these words: "He [Confucius] is simply a man who in his eager pursuit forgets his food, who in the joy [of its attainment] forgets his sorrow and who does not perceive that old age is coming on."② Once the inner perfection he had eagerly pursued was attained, all other things would be of little importance. The joy Confucius and Yan Yuan were in eager pursuit of was but such a mental state of inner perfection. It is unconditionally self-sufficient.

The Confucian ethic is in its reality just an enlargement of the family ethic. The society or the nation is but an enlargement of the family. Benevolence (*ren*) is derived from the nature of one's status as a member in the family, e.g. the father should be kind and the son filial, etc. And the sovereign of a nation is simply the embodiment of the power of the father (*patria potestas*). All come from the inborn nature as was summed up in the notion of benevolence. In the Confucian conception, politics was simply the family relationship on a larger scale. The sovereign is the father, and hence is called the sovereign-father or father-sovereign; and the subject the son, and hence the subject-son or son-subject. The nation is a product of nature, not something artificial or man-made. Therefore the relation between the governing and the governed is not that of contract or coercion, but that of natural bondage. Down to the Song Confucians, this idea was even further enlarged; not only the nation but the whole world or the universe at large was but the embodiment of the family ethic. The ethical

① Ibid., bk.4 "In Neighborhood of Benevolence" (Li Ren), trans. James Legge, with alterations by the author.

② Ibid., bk.7 "Transmitting", trans. James Legge, with alterations by the author.

idea was then extended and transformed into the substance of the universe. If one follows the ethical maxims, then his actions would be in harmony with the principles of Heaven. Today we regard the natural world as an objective existence in itself and by itself, but in the eyes of the Song Confucians the entire objectively existent world was but substantiation or transubstantiation of the moral ideas which governed the whole world (natural and human) and which identified themselves with that world. We have to see that this is the way of thinking characteristic of the Chinese. It may be termed a moral or ethico-centric world-view which subordinates the whole world to the sovereignty of a supreme ethical principle. Moral ideas were thus transubstantiated into the vital principle of the entire universe. This way of thinking survives in contemporary China under the dictum: "Politics (i.e. virtue) is the commander; politics is the soul."

Ethical principles govern not only our inner world but also the external world. For convenience of interpretation, we might also differentiate what is generally called philosophy into two constituent parts: one is to answer the question what is the world and what is life, the other is to answer the question of how we philosophize or how we deduce our philosophical arguments. As to the latter question, the Chinese way has always been to employ the family ethical model in their philosophizing, sometimes leading to a too far-fetched analogy. If one fails to grasp this peculiarity, one would easily miss the key to comprehending their characteristic mode of argument (such as, the governors are to bestow favors and the governed are to repay them).

In sum, Confucius and his school established what has been the most fundamental element in the Chinese mentality, i.e. the primacy of ethical utility in the practical life. At its best, it has been of great social and political use; while at its worst, it discarded all earnest pursuit of truth. Philosophy is and ought to be the love (philo) of wisdom (sophia); but the Chinese way of thinking was led to allow ethical dogma to reign over theoretical argument. The content of the term "rites" (propriety) in ancient China far surpassed what it would mean today. It denotes the entire norm of the social order. Conformity to rites meant the obedience to the established political and social norm. To probe the optimum value in conformity with the rites (but not in conformity with truth) was what the Confucians aimed at. Confucius taught: "Don't look at what is contrary to rites (propriety); don't listen to what is contrary to rites (propriety); don't speak what is contrary to rites (propriety); and don't take any action which is contrary to rites (propriety)."[①] He tried to confine human desires within the bounds of ethics. But, ultimately, on what the human desires are, Confucius gave no definite answer. Nor did the Song Confucians who stressed so strongly the struggle between the Heavenly Principles and the human desires. In his last years, perhaps he himself had found a way out which allowed him to say, "At seventy, I could follow what my heart desired, without transgressing what was right."[②] How he could attain such a state of mind and whether it was of universal application—he made no indication.

Though Confucius was never complacent with any success in carrying out his way (Tao) during his career, even complaining "as to the failure of Tao (the right principles) to make progress, I am fully aware of that",[③] after his death he was venerated as the arch-pontiff "whose virtue matches the universe and whose principle (Tao) crowns eternity."[④] His place and role in history may be compared to that of Jesus Christ. Though Christianity influenced the history of the West tremendously, Jesus himself in his lifetime had never achieved any illustrious career. Rather, it may be said there have been two images of Jesus and two of Confucius. One was Jesus the man, or Confucius the man, in his own time; the other was the sanctified Jesus and Confucius molded by later ages. For the sake of an overall comprehension of such historical figures, we have to pay due attention to both of their aspects. Further, it is noteworthy that the Jesus or Confucius who played the most influential role in history was not the one in his own time, but the one which was molded by later ages. That is the reason why history has to be always rewritten, because each epoch has its own ideas with which to comprehend the past. Moreover, the history of the past itself will never die out; it varies but it never dies. It lives still in later ages and it still exercises its influence. The evaluation of Confucius depends not only on his role in times passed but also in times to come. It varies with the variation of his role at the present time and in future. Will Confucianism radiate its past luster again in future, or will it fade away with the course of modernization? For this we have to wait and see.

All theories or ideas have two aspects or rather possess a dual character. One is its historicity, since it is a product of history, conditioned by certain historical circumstances and reflecting certain historical environments; another is its eternity, or its non-historicity, which transcends all historical surroundings.

① Ibid., bk.12 "Yan Yuan," trans. James Legge, with alterations by the author.

② Ibid., bk.2 "On Governing," trans. James Legge.

③ Ibid., bk.18 "Wei Zi," trans. James Legge, with alterations by the author.

④ A couplet found at the front of all Confucian shrines.

It is not merely a historical product; once it is given birth, it becomes an eternal entity and can never be eliminated from history. So is the case with arts, so is the case with sciences; and so also is the case with all philosophies and ideas. Once a philosophy or a set of ideas is formed, it then passes from history into eternity. Some would say: all depends on the time, the place and the conditions. Yet this proposition itself seems not to depend on the time, the place and the conditions. In short, all thoughts and philosophies are endowed with this dual quality: historicity and eternity. It is left for us to see it steadfastly and to see it whole in both of these aspects. And so in treating Confucius we have to study this historic figure both as he was in his own time and as he has been in later ages.

Chapter Two: Mo Zi and the Mohist School

[I] Origin of the Mohist School and Their Characteristics

The life of Mo Zi (Mo Di, Zi meaning "master") is generally dated around the years 480 to 420 B.C.,① somewhat later than Confucius. Of all ancient philosophers, the dates of his life were nearest to Confucius. In comparison with some ancient schools which were not much in vogue in their own times, nor exerted much influence on later ages, the Mohist school together with the Confucians were generally held as the two foremost schools, or Prominent Learnings (*xian xue*) in ancient times. But the historical fates of these two schools contrasted sharply with each other. The Confucian school having undergone a long process of evolution was eventually to assume the sole orthodoxy in the world of learning and ideology, while the Mohist school, after a short period of renown in the intellectual field, had fallen rapidly into oblivion with no remarkable consequence at all.

All culture of all times might be roughly classified into two levels: the upper and the lower. The culture of the upper level belongs to the elite, i.e. to those who are more well-cultivated in academic learning and intellectual tastes. But side by side with the elite, there is at the same time always the popular culture of the masses which prevails among the less educated or less cultivated people of the lower strata in the society. The lower strata of the society also have their own cultural works which, however, as a rule often vanish with the passing of time. The works of the upper class are much better preserved and remain easily accessible for the people of later generations. The works of the great poets Li Bai and Du Fu are preserved in a rather complete

① Qian Mu, *A Chronology of the Pre-Qin Philosophers*, vol. 2, 31.

form from their own times down to the present day, while most of the folksongs and folklore of that time are mostly lost except for fragments. Due to this state of things, the study of popular culture would present special difficulties. So is also the case with our study of the Mohist school. The history of human ideas covers two such levels: that of the elite, such as what Confucius has left behind him in his *Analects*, or Mencius in his *Book of Mencius*, which fairly accurately records their sayings and actions; but in contrast the lower strata of the common people could hardly be afforded the chance of putting their ideas down to leave to posterity. The Mohist school which we are going to deal with belongs in a considerable degree to the popular culture of ancient China.

In comparison with the Confucians, most Mohists came from amongst the craftsmen. Hence their characteristic features are shown in the following ways. Firstly, a large amount of their works is devoted to the recording of applied science and technology. Confucius and Mencius never mentioned any practical or technical knowledge whatsoever.

Yet the Mohist school paid much attention to it, because it was required in their daily life. For the craftsmen, the practical knowledge in the productive process was necessarily of utmost importance to them, as much as the ritual knowledge was to the Confucians. We find in the works of Mo Zi and his followers a large amount of knowledge of physics, mechanics and optics which had long been neglected by nearly all scholars for more than two thousand years. It was not until the late 19th century that they were rediscovered. Surely it must be admitted that there were many scientific and technical contributions made in ancient China, but science never constituted an independent subject and discipline in the Chinese intellectual tradition. So it is no wonder that few scholars along the traditional academic lines had ever seriously taken up the task of studying the scientific knowledge of the Mohist school. A widely circulated story of Mo Zi himself runs thus: Mo Zi preached vehemently the doctrine of "universal love" and "non-aggression." Once the greatest craftsman of the time Gongshu Ban designed a scaling ladder for the state of Chu, for an attack on the state of Song. On hearing the news, Mo Zi hastened to Chu to meet Gongshu and urged him not to invade Song. He made clear that if it were invaded, he and his disciples would at once come to the rescue of Song. Then Gongshu and Mo Zi began to engage in a mock battle. Nine times Gongshu tried to break Mo Zi's defense, but nine times he failed.[①] The story shows that the knowledge of the Mohist school is mainly concerned with practical technique.

① *Book of Mo Zi*, "Gong Shu."

Indeed, record of practical technique is very rarely found in most ancient Chinese writings and only in fragmentary forms. We find a record in the Rites of Zhou that the ratio between the circumference of a circle and its diameter is 3:1 ("the circumference in 3 to the diameter in 1"). It may well be imagined that this knowledge came from the craftsmen's practical operation. But as to who had first discovered it and under what circumstances, there could be found no mention at all. In truth, it could only have been discovered by some of the earliest craftsmen when making wheels. Since most Mohists came from the lower strata of the laborers, it is no wonder that they had accordingly in their professional activities embraced more knowledge of this kind than had other schools. The Mohist classics afford abundant records of ancient scientific and technical knowledge which must be acknowledged as the greatest treasure for the study of the ancient science and technology of China.

The second characteristic of the Mohist school is that, since they were mostly from amongst the lower strata of society, they were more than other schools destined to entanglement with some popular and even very primitive beliefs and superstitions. This is inevitable not only in ancient times but also in later ages, especially during the peasants' uprisings. In the Mohists classics there are many paragraphs dealing with the superhuman and supernatural spirits which never appeared in the Confucian classics—a basic distinction to be noted with due attention. The worship of the spirits, gods and ghosts may be regarded as a particular relic of the primitive beliefs among the masses of the ancient people.

The third characteristic of the Mohist school is that, again due to their lower-class roots, they needed a strong organization for mutual aid and cooperation, something like the brotherhoods of the mediaeval West or secret societies in mediaeval China. Such organizations were maintained by rigorous rules and disciplines, their members often living together and helping one another. As an organization under the head of an absolute leader by the name of "the Great Master" (Ju Zi), the Mohist school even resorted to armed operations as the above story showed: if the state of Chu attempted to attack the state Song, they would come to the rescue of Song, defending against the Chu invasion. In the book *Huai Nan Zi* (composed about the 2nd century B.C.) it was recorded that the members of the Mohist organization numbered one hundred and eighty, always ready to confront a life and death struggle without the least hesitation.[①]

① *Book of Huai Nan Zi.*

One scholar① even went so far as to identify the Mohist school with the tradition of Chinese chivalry (*xia*). In ancient China there were two groups of persons who proved often repugnant to the ruling authority: the Confucian scholars and the men of chivalry. The foremost Legalist Han Fei (280-230 B.C.) remarked sharply: "the Confucian scholars are prone to spoil the laws with their learnings and the men of chivalry are prone to break the legal prohibitions with their arms."② The Confucian scholars criticized the current affairs by professing their own opinions which would often run counter to officialdom and lead to ideological and intellectual chaos. Meanwhile the Mohist school was not a purely academic group, because it often resorted to taking up arms. The famous historian Sima Qian in his *Records of the Historian* wrote a specific chapter dealing with the ancient Chinese knights-errant. In the early years of the Eastern Han Dynasty (1st century), the famous general Ma Ruan addressed a letter to his nephew Ma Yandun which became a model of belles-lettres in posterity. This Ma Yandun was very "fond of criticizing others for their merits and defects and of commenting on the current political affairs"③ and was thus in danger of offending officialdom. Many chivalrous figures in the Han period, such as the well-known Zhu Jia and Guo Jie, represented a considerable social and political force and exerted great influence on their time. As a matter of course, it was easy for them to come into conflict (sometimes open, sometimes hidden) with the officials. The Confucians were more flexible in maneuvering and more prone to compromise with those in power, and hence gradually attained their position of hegemony, whereas the Mohists were more rigid and scornful of compromise with the political authorities, and finally experienced their own short-lived glory.

Among the various schools of the pre-Qin period, the Confucians and the Taoists persisted down to later ages, the Legalists merged with the Confucians, the *Yin-Yang* school was in the main also absorbed into the Confucian school, and only the Logicians and the Mohists declined and extinguished after a short period of success. The cause of the Logicians' extinction might be attributed to the underdevelopment of science in China, for without rigorous scientific development there would be no inducement to the development of methodology in thinking. As to the cause of the extinction of the Mohists, it might be properly attributed to their origin in the lower social strata, which handicapped them from

① Feng Youlan, *History of Chinese Philosophy*, appendix.

② Sima Qian, *History*, "Lives of the Knights-Errant."

③ Ma Ruan, "Letter to His Nephew Ma Yandun," in *Anthology of Ancient Essays*, ed. Yan Kejun.

elucidating in full their theories and techniques. According to the record in the *Book of Mencius* "nowadays the words of Yang Zhu and Mo Di fill the world. People's discourses have adopted the views either of Yang or of Mo."[①] Yang was by then the arch-proponent of individualistic doctrine in ancient China, while Mo the foremost spokesman of altruism. From Mencius' declaration that all the world was clinging either to Yang or to Mo, it might be seen how influential these two schools had once been, during the classical age of ancient China. But unfortunately, the sayings of the Mohist school had never been properly understood by scholars until the late 19th century, when Sun Yirang produced his excellent study of Mo Zi entitled *Commentaries on Mo Zi* (*Mo Zi Xian Gu*). After more than two thousand years' oblivion, the Mohist school was again made known to the reading public.

[II] Morality and Utility in the Mohist Teachings

Mo Di known as Mo Zi, the founder of the Mohist school, was a native of the state of Song (now the eastern part of Henan Province). Song was a small but culturally very significant country, because many eminent historical figures came from Song. Mo Zi spent a long time in the state of Lu, and was possibly affected by the influence of Confucianism, positively as well as negatively. It was said that he had engaged in the Confucian education. But he developed in a way quite different from the Confucians. The Confucians stressed benevolence or the inner cultivation, and were always inclined to return to the rites of Zhou, while the Mohists advocated "working to one's utmost" for (or rather, mainly for) the benefit of the country and the people, and their idol was not the founder of rites, the Duke of Zhou, but the great ancient sage-king Yu, who according to legend had overcome the flood through his death-defying labors. The Mohists claimed themselves to have inherited the spirit and ideals of the great Yu. Prof. Gu Jiegang in his *Examinations on Ancient History* (*Gu Shi Bian*) suggested that the later ages were in the habit of fabricating fables attached to the ancients, the later the more so, thus each school customarily exalted an ancient sage for their specific veneration. The Confucians deified the Duke of Zhou, then Yao and Shun; and the Mohists held the great Yu as their idol of hard labor and self-sacrifice.

The images of Mo Zi and the Mohists might be more appropriately seen

① *Book of Mencius*, "Duke Wen of *Teng*," pt.2, trans. James Legge, with alterations by the author.

through the eyes of their opponents. Generally speaking, we find in ancient literature that what was asserted by their opponents was in the main more credible. The Mohists and Taoists were against the Confucians, and their criticisms of Confucianism to a large extent had some grounds. Conversely, most of the boasts and self-praise from each school were often unreliable. Zhuang Zi (some two centuries after Mo Zi) in his "The World" (*Tian Xia*) described the Mohists in these words: "the Mohists never take a rest day and night, driving themselves on to the bitterest exertions. 'If we could not do the same,' they say, 'then we are not following the way of Yu, and are unworthy of being called Mohists.'"① And again, "Mo Zi (of all ancient philosophers) alone declares there is to be no singing in life, no mourning in death." And Zhuang Zi went on to criticize him in these words: "If he teaches men in this fashion, then I fear he has no love for them; and if he adopts such practices himself, then he surely has no love for himself." And further: "I do not mean to discredit his teaching entirely; and yet men want to sing and he says 'No singing'; they want to wail and he says 'No wailing,' they want to play music and he says 'No music'—one wonders if he is in fact human at all. A life that is all toil, a death shoddily disposed of—it is a way that goes too much against us. To make life toilsome, to make death lamentable, to make the Way (Principle) a mere hardship; to make men anxious, to make them miserable—such practices are hard to carry out, and I fear they cannot be regarded as the Way (Principle) of the sage. They are contrary to the hearts of the world, and the world cannot endure them. Though Mo Zi himself may be capable of such endurance, how can the whole world do likewise? Departing so far from the ways of the world, they must be far removed indeed from those of the true [sage-]king."②

Now for some remarks about Zhuang Zi's criticism of the Mohist school. I'm of the opinion that Zhuang's criticism came for the most part very much to the point. An ethical criterion, in order to claim validity, has to be universally practicable. As we have said above, if an ethical teaching asks all people to sacrifice themselves entirely for others, then its logical result would come to null and nothing. For then who would be benefited by such a wholesale sacrifice? The meaning of sacrifice exists only in so far as it provides more happiness to more people; otherwise it will be entirely meaningless. The maxim of the Mohists was to sacrifice oneself unconditionally for others, but when carried to the extreme all men will be sacrificed for no one. The logical

① *Book of Zhuang Zi*, "The World," trans. B. Watson, with alterations by the author.

② Ibid., with supplements and alterations by the author.

presupposition of the dogma "for the people" is the existence of the people whom one is supposed to serve. The logical presupposition of happiness is the existence of the happiness for which one is striving. When the happiness of the people itself has no objective existence except in the very striving of the subject (as in the Mohists, who "never take a rest day and night, drive themselves on to the bitterest exertion"),[①] then you need not find happiness elsewhere except in the reform of your own state of mind. This is clearly not for the sake of the happiness of the people, but simply for the sake of transforming and reforming the very idea of the happiness of the people. Once your idea of happiness is transformed and reformed in the style of the Mohists, then happiness will be right here in your heart. Of course, the idea of happiness inevitably contains a certain spiritual element, but ultimately there must be some universal and eternal criteria (such as material welfare, personal freedom, etc.) which should be invariably available to all. At any rate, it seems that history is still too short to make such a topsy-turvy transformation successful. In other words, "to drive oneself on to the bitterest exertion" is only a means to some end (happiness), but it is not and cannot be an end in itself. The Mohists mistook the means for the end, and thus put the cart before the horse. Their professed end is to make people happy, but the means to it is to transform their idea of happiness by taking suffering or hardship as happiness. Such was the conclusion the Mohist way of philosophizing led to. The danger thereof lies in the fact that to ask people to sacrifice themselves as the highest morality always tends to satisfy only the ambitions of the few who, in the name of some high ideal, would use those people as their instruments. Had the Mohists ever come to power, we can hardly think their rule would bring forth more happiness or welfare than other ideologies might.

It reminds us of Bentham's famous dictum: "the greatest happiness of the greatest number." Morality consists in nothing else than in making people happy. But what is it that constitutes this happiness, whether of an individual or of the people? In the last analysis, there would always be something in it which springs purely from personal feeling. Then there would be a paradox. If one deemed a situation as happy while the other did not, unhappiness would be called happiness, and to make others happy would be totally meaningless.

Furthermore, too great a moral requirement would surpass the reach of the ordinary people and hence would prove impracticable. Hence Zhuang Zi judged the Mohists severely, as contradicting the nature of most people. "They

① Ibid.

are contrary to the hearts of the world, and the world cannot endure them. Though Mo Zi himself may be capable of such endurance, how can the rest of the world do likewise?" Even viewed from a modern standpoint, this criticism sounds quite reasonable and well-grounded. You cannot and should not ask all men to do what only an exceptional few (of whom Mo Zi was undoubtedly an outstanding example) are capable of. If a maxim of morality can only be achieved by an exceptional few, then it would not and should not be held as universally valid. And if it seems to diminish the happiness of the greatest number, or tries to enforce the so-called happiness dictated by one party instead of a universally acknowledged norm, then it nullifies itself. Thus Zhuang Zi criticized Mo Zi as "departing so far from the ways of the world, they must be far removed indeed from those of the true [sage-]king." Here "the true king" signifies an ideal philosopher-king. Translated into modern terminology, it means that the way of Mo Zi would not lead to a good ruling order, because it is so far removed from the people. After all is said and done, morality and utility are not separable from each other, but should converge in unity. True morality will never discard happiness, nor happiness morality. The banner the Mohists upheld is "the great happiness (great profit) of the country and the people." But, in the end, what constitutes this "great happiness of the country and the people"? It was on this issue that the Mohists stumbled and fell.

As a doctrine of morality or ethics, Mohism had to satisfy two conditions. First, it had to be of universal validity to everyone, i.e., the criterion should be the same and common to all. It would be a logical fallacy to assert that this or that means happiness to one but unhappiness to some other. Second, it had to be practicable in our daily life. If one takes self-torture ("the bitterest exertion") as happiness, then there would be no common practicability. To demand that all men suffer forever in the name of the happiness of "the people" would be simply nonsense. Suffering is for the sake of happiness, but suffering itself is no happiness. One should not confuse the means with the end. The Mohists (and those who are in tune with them) have inverted the right order, and took the means as the end.

The *Book of Mo Zi*, or the *Mo Scripture* (*Mo Jing*), like all other ancient classics, was not an individual work, but a collection of the Mohist school. As the learning of the Mohist school had long been lost, there appeared many challenges, both in the text and in its interpretation. The greatest academic contributions of the Qing (17th-19th centuries) scholars lay in their critical examination of nearly all the ancient classics. Without their works, much ancient literature would remain incomprehensible to us. By the late 19th century Sun Yirang's commentaries on Mo Zi provided us with a comprehensible reader for Mo Zi's works. Later in the 20th century, both the German scholar Forke and the British scholar Needham made some penetrating studies on Mo Zi. With their modern scientific training, they had made outstanding research into the scientific and technical contents of the Mohist school.

[III] The Mohist Items and Their System

In the Confucian scripture the *Great Learning*, the procedure of attaining a perfect personality had to undergo the following stages: "investigation of things" (*ge wu*), "extension of knowledge" (*zhi zhi*), "sincerity of thoughts" (*cheng yi*), "rectification of the heart" (*zheng xin*), "cultivation of the person" (*xiu shen*), "regulation of the family" (*qi jia*), "governing the state" (*zhi guo*), "pacification of the world" (*ping tian xia*), together traditionally called the eight items (*ba tiao mu*) by later generations. As might be easily seen, these eight items represent a clear logical order from inner cultivation to outward achievements. In contrast to these eight Confucian items, the Mohists had articulated theirs in a group of ten at a much earlier date, being: "universal love" (*jian ai*), "anti-militarism" (*fei gong*), "agreement with the talents" (*shang xian*), "agreement with the superior" (*xian tong*), "the will of Heaven" (*tian zhi*), "belief in spirits" (*ming gui*), "anti-music" (*fei yue*), "anti-fatalism" (*fei ming*), "frugality in expenditure" (*jie yong*) and "frugality in funeral" (*jie zang*), each of which constituted a main topic of the theses in their book. Those closely-related items form a systematic theory of the Mohists. From the universal love was derived "anti-militarism," from the belief in Heaven and spirits the subservience to the superior and the talents, while "driving oneself on to the bitterest exertions" would render people necessarily "anti-music," "frugal in expenditure," etc. The Mohists tried their utmost to save the world from chaos and misery by their doctrines and practices. But would their doctrines really lead to a well-ordered society? And are their prescriptions really practicable?

The doctrine of universal love supposes that it is possible for men to love, instead of to encroaching upon, one another. Once this doctrine were realized, the world would be in an ideal state of peace and prosperity. But in the history of mankind, never had such an ideal state come true, although it has remained the most enchanting dream in nearly all ages. The notion of love—it seems many an idealist lost sight of the inherent logical implication—carries as a prerequisite the notion of not loving someone or something. Where there is love, elsewhere there will be no love. Love and non-love each necessarily entail the existence of the other. If everyone is to take as much care of others as of himself (or even more than of himself, as some often like to say), then there would be no one who would take care of himself. The result would be that everyone will take care of all others—a result which is theoretically unjustifiable, and gets nowhere in practice. The Mohist altruism had fallaciously neglected the fact that the love of others presupposes the love of self. If the self is not worthy to be loved, then how can the love of others' selves be justified?

Hand in hand with this fallacy, the Mohists also crudely neglected (or consciously rejected) the cardinal impetus in the progress of civilized life, i.e. human creativity through the freedom of thought. As we have seen, the Mohists formed a strictly organized and disciplined group, something like a secret society, all members of which were required to give themselves up perfectly and completely at the will of their leader, and hence they maintained most forcibly "agreement with the superior." Carried to its extreme, this would naturally lead to the dictatorship of the leader, to the thorough obliteration of any individual initiative. A political and social organization must have a leader, and the leader after all is also a human being and is liable to err ("to err is human"). What then is it that may be used to prevent him from going astray? In modern times people devised various mechanisms of checks and balances, such as the separation of the three powers (legislation, judiciary and executive). But under the rule of a sole dictator, there is no force capable of keeping him within bounds. The progress of culture requires unity and variety, both being *sine qua non.* Unity without variety leads to uniformity and petrification. Variety without unity leads to disorder and tumult. Only a synthesis of unity in variety and variety in unity can afford the peace and order necessary for an exuberant blossom in the intellectual garden. Unity dwells not in uniformity but in variety. The more fully individuality is brought into play, the more exuberant and colorful the contents in the unity would be. In other words, unity is not achieved at the price of giving up individuality, but conversely it consists exactly in the full blossom of individuality. As early as in 1848, Marx in his *Manifesto of the Communist Party* had already remarked: "the free development of each is the condition of the free development of all."[①] Without the free development of the individual initiative, there can be no development of the society at large. The society

① K. Marx and F. Engels, *Manifesto of the Communist Party*, chap. 2 (Beijing: For. Lang. Pr., 1972), p. 59. The original German text reads, "die freie Entwicklung eines jeden die Bedingung für die freie Entwicklung aller ist." (Beijing: For. Lang. Pr., 1965), p. 61.

should keep definite unity simply because this requirement guarantees the free development of each individual. If individuality is entirely negated, there will be no culture. A society of bees or ants cannot create anything of humanistic value, because each member in it has neither individuality nor freedom of intellectual initiative. Human culture consists in there being unity in variety and variety in unity. Unity depends on variety and exists in variety, and vice versa. Otherwise, the society would be a uniform one, invariable to eternity. This is just what the Mohists failed to realize. Human culture exists nowhere except in the elevation of humanistic values which are by themselves non-utilitarian in nature. The Mohists considered this only from a utilitarian view-point, to the total neglect of the basic truth that all utilities presuppose some humanistic, non-utilitarian values as their premises and their ends. That is why Xun Zi criticized Mo Zi as "being eclipsed by the utility and knowing nothing of what is humanistic and human."① They imagined, either due to foolishness or to ignorance, that a society of uniformity was the best. According to them, everybody would speak in a uniform tone and think in a uniform way. If things really did go on in this uniform fashion, society would become unchanging and unchangeable forever, and human culture could achieve neither progress nor evolution, just like the society of the bees or ants. It is a simple fact of human history that, in the ages of pluralism and tolerance, cultures would flourish in their most colorful and richest fashion. It was in such a time of unprecedented variety that China's classical culture reached its zenith, including the contributions of the Mohists themselves. Zhuang Zi criticized the Mohists, "though with their good intentions, they are wrong in their practices."② They had stressed uniformity with no regard to diversity and variety. Throughout human history, when a culture has been such that everything and everyone in it submitted to a single authority, that culture did not thrive or last long. The vitality of culture dwells not in an absolute authoritative decree but in the myriad of opinions. This is the second point of our criticism of the Mohists. Our first point starts from a theoretical view, and our second from a historical one.

Did Mo Zi himself or the Mohists perceive the fallacy in his or their own theory? At least, it can fairly be affirmed that his emphasis on "the Will of Heaven" and "the Belief in Spirits" showed his worship of intellectual uniformity, outweighing his regard for intellectual variety. Believing that behind and beyond the world of our actual life, there are Heaven and Spirits whose will we

① *Book of Xun Zi*, "Enlightenment."

② *Book of Zhuang Zi*, op.cit.

must obey,—among all schools in ancient China, such a naked and unrestrained theism could be found only in the Mohists who were certainly the sole school to preach their teaching through the divine. It is most interesting to note that Mo Zi himself openly admitted that such a practice of preaching about the divine was in a certain sense just a political strategy, yet indispensable in bringing all things into uniformity—a frankness rarely seen in other philosophers. In the course of Chinese history, there have been many such practices of resorting to divinity, by claiming the support of the will of Heaven. The question is whether those who professed it really did believe in it? As late as the second half of the 19th century, Hong Xiuquan was professing himself the son of Jehovah and the younger brother of Jesus. Did he really believe what he professed? The answer probably may only be given by applying psychoanalysis. Perhaps at first he was in need of something to deceive others, but in the course of cheating others he also needed something to deceive or to delude himself; for without a psychic support he could hardly gather up enough courage to deceive others. In cheating others, he cheated himself at the same time. It provides a spiritual anesthetic for others as well as for himself.

Side by side with his theism, Mo Zi elaborated a theory of "anti-fatalism." It is interesting to inquire why he was against the idea of destiny. Destiny has been an idea prevalent since antiquity. Early in the 11th century B.C. King Zhou of Shang, faced with the rebellious princes, proclaimed arrogantly: "Is not my fate destined by Heaven?"[①] If it seemed that the course of one's life lay outside of the will of oneself, then one would be led to think it was arranged by Heaven. More than once Confucius acknowledged the existence of fate and of Heaven. His disciple Zi Xia once heard from him: "Death and life have their appointment by Fate, riches and honors depend upon Heaven."[②] When his beloved disciple Yan Yuan died ("unfortunate, cut so short by Fate"[③]), he lamented: "Alas, Heaven is destroying me! Heaven is destroying me!"[④] He described himself: "At fifty, I know the decrees of Heaven."[⑤] When Huan Tui was trying to hurt him, he said: "Heaven produced the virtue that is in me—what can Huan Tui do to me!"[⑥] Once. when he went to pay a visit to Nanzi (a famous beauty in the harem of the Duke Ling of Wei), Zi Lu (his disciple) was displeased, and the

① Sima Qian, *Records of the Historian*, "Chronicle of Yin."

② *Analects*, chap. 12 "Yan Yuan."

③ Ibid., chap. 11 "Xian Jin."

④ Ibid.

⑤ Ibid., chap. 2 "On Governing."

⑥ Ibid., chap. 7 "Shu Er."

Master (Confucius) swore, "wherein I have done improperly, may Heaven reject me! May Heaven reject me!"① All these showed Confucius' acknowledgement of Heaven and of Fate. In this regard, the Mohist doctrine of "anti-fatalism" was the antithesis of the Confucians' teaching. The Confucians believed in Fate and the decree of Heaven which destined events inviolably, while the Mohists emphasized human endeavors, as against fatalism.

We must admit that there are some greatly positive elements in the Mohist doctrine of anti-fatalism, i.e. relying on their own strenuous effort they would never submit to unfavorable circumstances. But the question is how to reconcile this anti-fatalism with belief in the order laid down by Heaven. Are not the two in contradiction of each other? Mo Zi seemed to have found a way out, very similar to that of the Calvinists in the 16th century. For the Mohists, Heaven had indeed prescribed human fate; it was the decree of Heaven which disposed everything in the human world. Yet the will of Heaven favored those who engaged in ceaseless effort. He who engaged in such efforts would be rewarded by Heaven. This argument comes very near to Calvin's. John Calvin (1509-1564) preached a doctrine of predestination in which he still left enough room for personal struggles. Here we are involved with a very delicate issue, i.e. the duality of the human being: a man is free on one hand, yet on the other hand unfree and determined. Just because men are free, their voluntary efforts are not nonsense; if all was but the outcome of predestination, then men would powerless in trying to do anything, and consequently all human efforts would be meaningless and come to nothing. Faced with this dilemma, most philosophical schools seemed to swing between the two extremes, i.e. between total fatalism and total voluntarism. Voluntarism is obviously not in conformity with the content of our experiences, for the outcome of anything is not in proportion with the input of our effort. But if all human endeavors and efforts are but vain and void, then human motives and volitions would lose the least bit of significance. In order to reconcile the two extremes and find an optimum position in between, we have to admit both the significance of human efforts as well as the uncertainty of our willed efforts simultaneously. In Calvin's opinion, all is predetermined by God, but God favors those who are earnest in their effort; the more earnest you are in your work, the more God would bestow his favor upon you, so that your earnest effort would not be in vain. (It seems Lao Zi right in saying, "The way of heaven plays no favors, but it is always in accord with good men.") According to some (Max Weber being one), the Calvinist doctrine paved

① Ibid., chap. 6 "Yong Ye."

the way for the accumulation of early capitalism, in the presupposition that the success of a businessman was a reflection of the divine grace bestowed upon him. At any rate, this sounds a rather justifiable compromise in the perennial conflict between the divine will and human effort. The affirmation of predestination need not nullify personal effort; on the contrary, the former exacts even more of the latter. And this is just the idea the Mohists intended to amplify. In their stressing of anti-fatalism, they demanded that every person should "strive to their utmost." But why is it that Calvinism helped stimulate the rise of capitalism, while the Mohists did not? This perhaps depended greatly on the historical conditions of their respective times. When the historical conditions were not yet ripe, even if there were such theories, they would not naturally lead to the road of capitalism. The intellectual component is not necessarily the sole, nor even the decisive factor in history. But conversely, we may well have grounds to assert that the theory of the Mohists had in a considerable degree refuted that of Max Weber. Since this kind of divine determination did not lead to the road of capitalism, as a consequence his theory cannot be considered as established. Ultimately, the verification and falsification of a historical proposition are not as evident as in the propositions of natural sciences.

[IV] The Mode of Thinking in the Mohist Teaching

Now, let us turn to the ways of thinking peculiar to the Mohist teachings. Every theory comprises two aspects: one is the contents and conclusions of its thinking; the other its mode of reasoning or the way of its thinking. The methodology of Mo Zi was named by himself "the method of the three tests" (*san biao fa*) which might give us some hints about a characteristic of the Chinese way of thinking, i.e. to start the process of reasoning from an ethical standard, or an ethico-politically centered ideology, as was stated in the foregoing chapters. None of the philosophies in ancient China (the most scientific and technically-inclined Mohism included) took their approach from natural philosophy; on the contrary, all based their conclusions on their ethico-political premises. The "test" (*biao*) by the Mohists literally means a criterion or standard (*yi*). Then, what are the three tests? In Mo Zi's system, this method of "the three tests" consisted of "its basis, its verifiability and its application."① As to the implications of the three tests, he expounded them as follows: "On what is it to be based? It should

① *Book of Mo Zi*, "Anti-fatalism (I)."

be based on the deeds of the ancient sage-kings. By what is it to be verified? It is to be verified by the senses of hearing and seeing of the common people. How is it to be applied? It is to be applied by adopting it in government and observing its benefits for the country and the people. This is what is meant by the three tests when judging any doctrine."① That is to say, in judging a truth, the norm of the ancient sage-kings should be held as the supreme touchstone above all else—a way of thinking again characteristically scholastic rather than scientific or philosophical. The second test sounds somewhat like a naive empiricism, or rather a shallow sensualism, since—as is generally acknowledged—the sensory perceptions of our daily experience are always deceptive and unreliable, and should never be taken as an invariable and infallible criterion for truth. The third test might be classified under the ethico-political pragmatism which, as we have repeatedly pointed out, has served as the backbone of the Chinese way of thinking since antiquity. Therefore we may identify Mohist philosophy as another significant phase in the philosophy of ancient China.

We may, for simplicity's sake, classify the modes of reasoning into two basic norms: one begins with a definite conclusion, and then articulates the argument for it by reasoning from an unproven premise (a hypothesis of convenience); the other first only grants a premise but with no pre-determined conclusion, and then proceeds to draw out its conclusion, no matter what conclusion may result. The ethico-political mode of reasoning follows the first norm, i.e. it has its conclusion given beforehand and then proceeds to find out the argument for it. Or to put it in a simple way, in the former "the end justifies the means," while the other is the reverse. Most religious and political ends are to be justified through the former norm of reasoning, while most scientific and academic ends by the latter. From the "method of the three tests," it may be easily seen that the Mohists started not from natural phenomena or facts but from a transcendental norm in the wake of the dogmas propounded by the ancient sage-kings, that is, all truth ought to be derived from the ancient sage-kings, who thus provided the sole criterion of truth. This implies that truth is at bottom revealed by some superhuman authority rather than by human intellect. Such an approach is diametrically opposed to any speculative reasoning in the true sense of the word philosophy. A truth, in so far as it is qualified to be deemed a truth, should be capable of being either verified or falsified. But a truth revealed by transcendental authority can be neither verified nor falsified, because it is given *a priori*, invariable and subject to no revision whatsoever. In the main, this mode of

① Ibid.

thinking took the upper hand and lasted in China for more than two thousand years, down to modern times. It may help to explain from the intellectual viewpoint why science—in the sense of modern science pursued consciously with a strict discipline—developed so slowly in the course of China's history.

The "second test" of the Mohists, i.e. "the senses of hearing and seeing of the common people" should be recognized as bringing some positive factors into their epistemological theory, because it afforded proper room for our experience, from which all our knowledge is derived. But when considered in synthesis with the first and the third tests, its validity may appear to some extent less assured. Without doubt, all our knowledge comes from experience. But experience alone does not lead to knowledge. Experience provides only raw materials which only after a process of our mental manipulation can result in a definite form of knowledge. Pure empiricism or knowledge through experience alone can never be tenable in any sense. Thus the second test of the Mohists had to resort to the first and the third tests for its availability and validity. The first test is wholly *a priori* by its very nature as shown above. The third test means that a truth should be tested by its political effects. Of course, the political effects are their "benefit to the country and the people," as the Mohists would claim. But what exactly constitutes the "benefit to the country and the people" would depend after all on how one would like to define or interpret it. Each person may have his own view and his own interpretation. The Mohists have their own views on happiness and on the value of human life, as stated in the foregoing paragraphs. Theirs is a peculiar kind of utilitarianism which can hardly be accepted by most people, for it would benefit only those who share the same idea of happiness that the Mohists did. If happiness be accepted as a common measure of the benefit of any policy, then this idea of happiness should have to be common to all. But if every one has an idea of happiness in his own way, then purporting to use happiness as a common measure would come to nothing. Furthermore, if one could be happy only with the provision that one must first have one's idea of happiness converted and recast so as to match others', then it would rather be a matter of ideological remolding and reforming than a pursuit of happiness in the ordinary sense.

We find in the Mohist doctrine a strange mixture of empiricism, asceticism, utilitarianism and transcendentalism in a fashion grotesque and impracticable, which went so far as to even approach the opposite of itself. These inherent shortcomings helped to explain why the Mohist school was so ephemeral and short-lived. Its utilitarianism was pushed to such extremes as to throw out all things that would not bring forth immediate and direct utility (e.g. music). A man under such circumstances, where utility is carried to such an extreme, would not be a human being but a mere instrument that could hardly enjoy happincss in any sense. An end may perhaps justify means, but means can never justify an end. A theory like the Mohists professed, when extended far enough, would turn to its own opposite. A truth overstated or overdone may turn into absurdity. The Mohist teaching and practice would tend toward negating precisely the ultimate end which they emphatically professed to serve. Bees and ants toiling and moiling their whole life are mere instruments, and they can hardly be said of having any intrinsic value in their lives. But human life ought to be otherwise; it has its inalienable value, intrinsic in and proper to itself. It is not and ought not to be a mere means whose value exists simply and entirely in its utility to serve some end. Otherwise, where does the difference between a human being and an ant or bee lie, in respect to their morality as well as to their nobility? For humans, we ought to assign a human use, and not treat them simply as tools. Consider the bees and the ants laboring year in and year out for the benefit of their community, far more dedicated, concentrated and earnest than human beings, never a moment for their individual enjoyment—is this the highest perfection of the Mohist ideal? The Mohists, it appears, lacked a sense of any humanistic value which alone could constitute the core of human life. A human being is more than a means to some utilitarian end. He is an end in himself and by himself. Man is an instrument only conditionally, by no means an instrument alone. He has to labor in order to earn his living, but he is not a machine existing simply to earn that living. If he were only such, then life would be worthless. In the last analysis, the highest state of life the Mohists preached would precisely reduce human beings to plain instruments. Such a utopia, once realized, would be a state in which all existed for one, while the one exists for none, or rather a fascist regime in ancient dress. This is just where a demand of unconditional dedication would lead. Some persuasive talkers may say that the value of life exists in wholehearted consecration. Perhaps so. But this can never be unconditional, that is, a man cannot and should not consecrate everything of his. He ought not dedicate his independence, his dignity, his thought and judgment and his natural rights to either the community or to anyone in it. He should not consecrate himself for the sake of consecration. Unconditional consecration would be meaningless and absurd. Any sacrifice or dedication is for some definite purpose. The Mohists were obsessed by their own fanaticism and tried to fanaticize others. In my opinion, this is the reason why the Mohists so prevailed over the world at that time, such that Mencius once lamented: "The words of Yang Zhu and Mo Di fill the world. People's discourses throughout the world have adopted the views either of Yang or Mo."[①] But equally, it is also the reason why the Mohists died out so soon and so prematurely. Their utopian aspiration incited people's passion, but their intrinsic theoretical defects led to their short life and rapid annihilation.

Now a few words about the intrinsic value of life. The Mohists who viewed life from a mere utilitarian light fell short of a true understanding of the humanistic value of the spiritual life, which stretches far beyond the narrow bounds of material utility. When we enjoy a piece of music, we appreciate it for music's sake, not for any material benefit,—conceded that sometimes music may bring some kinds of benefit, financial or other. Furthermore, the fact that the Mohists in the last resort appealed to a superhuman divine force reflected convincingly that they had no faith in the strength either of the people or of themselves. Herein is implied a very delicate problem. They urged people to strive to their utmost, yet human strife was not enough to solve all problems. To interpret it from a lower level in real life, it may be put thus: what attitude ought one to adopt in confronting the existing social order and its inequity? Should one accept it with docility or even complete resignation, or recast it with vehement and strenuous effort? The fatalist regards the existing social order as inevitable, so that one must give up any endeavor to change it. Yet there are always those who go over to the other extreme by completely rejecting the existing social order and trying their best to reform it in accordance with their own will. In reality, most people ponder, and swing between the two extremes, neither resigning voluntarily to all that is imposed upon them by the external world, nor able to reshape it in accordance with their will. It seems the solution lies somewhere in between. In regard to this, we may readily recall Hegel's contention that the world is wholly rational, and that it is the function of philosophy to discover that rationality in it. It implies that all things that exist have their reason for existence, that is, there has to be a reason why a thing is so and not otherwise. Such a theory when applied to actual life may readily provide an apology for the existing social order, entailing that the existing social order is rational and, therefore, one is obliged to submit to it. But later, as we can see, this well-known proposition was employed by the Young Hegelians for just the opposite interpretation. Marx in his early years was one of the Young Hegelian camp. Their political position was far more radical than Hegel himself. Hegel's intention was to uphold the then existing social order and political institution (the Prussian autocracy). But the Young Hegelians were strongly against the

① *Book of Mencius,* "Duke Wen of Teng," pt. 2, trans. James Legge, with alterations by the author.

monarchy, while upholding the cause of a democratic republic. Nevertheless, they used the same argument that Hegel had: our rebellion has real existence, so it must be rational. The same theoretical proposition may be employed by the positive as well as by the negative side—a phenomenon not unusual in the history of ideas. It is indeed worthy of note that altruism, once led to the extreme, would utterly preclude what it originally meant to realize.

[V] The Mohist Idea of Equality

Another significant peculiarity of the Mohist theory is their stress on the equality between man and man. This tendency reflects the wishes of the lower social classes. Roughly speaking, people of the higher social strata with possession of more power and wealth are inclined to justify the rationality of the social hierarchy, affirming that the superior should rule over the inferior, and the inferior should obey the superior. But people of the lower social strata are likely to uphold the cause of equality. Since the Mohists belonged to a social group made up small craftsmen, they were naturally more inclined to stress social equality than other schools, especially compared with the Confucians. The Confucians emphatically distinguished the superior men, or gentlemen (*jun zi*), and the small men (*xiao ren*), implicitly referring to the upper and the lower social classes. The distinction is a social one, while also being a moral one. A gentleman in the Confucian sense is taken for granted to be a man of higher moral integrity, but the Mohists conversely laid stress on the identical aspect in the upper and the lower classes. Mo Zi declared that all states, whether large or small, are "the cities of Heaven"; and all men, whether of noble or low birth, are "the subjects of Heaven." This contention sounds very similar to the mediaeval pagans in Christendom, who preached that all men and women are the children of God and hence ought to be equal to one another. It reflected the naive but natural wishes and hopes of the lower social strata, who longed for a better life with more equality between man and man.

But how could such a better society be reached? The Mohists were the upholders of "anti-fatalism." The fates of men, and consequently their respective social status, were not destined unalterably to be so. It could be changed through our own effort, or in Mo Zi's own words, by "striving to the utmost." Here the phrase "striving to the utmost" should be understood in a historically determined condition. The ancient laborers engaged in simple manual work where the increase of productivity depended entirely on the prolongation of labor time and the aggravation of labor intensity, and hence had very limited efficiency within a very small dimension, since human energy and physical strength are necessarily restricted by natural limits. In ancient times, the growth in production purely through the exercise of manual labor was, as a matter of course, extremely low. The way to the efficient growth of production can only be found in the enhancement of productive efficiency by the advancement of science and technology. But any idea of the continual progress in science and technique was beyond the reach of the knowledge of the ancients, and therefore they had no other choice than to appeal to aggravated exertion in simple manual labor. This explains why the Mohists persistently insisted on "striving to the utmost." Here we encounter a somewhat more complicated factor in the development of human society. The advancement of science and technology, regarded in present-day China as the primary productive force, depends more on mental than on manual labor. So far as manual labor is concerned, human labor is much inferior to that of an ox or horse; but when mental work is required, all other species are incomparable to mankind, because human beings are endowed with wisdom (*homo sapiens*) and with the successive accumulation of knowledge through which they are capable of perpetual progress and endless innovation. Meanwhile, all other species must begin anew from the same spot where their ancestors started. The whole epoch in which Mo Zi lived was not yet ripe for recognition of this, and we should not demand too much of the ancients. Nonetheless, the role of this "striving to the utmost" was very limited and could not improve the living conditions of the laboring masses in any substantial or sustained way.

Though the Mohists arose from the lower classes in society, many of their doctrines and theories did not exist in unison with the characteristics of the Chinese cultural tradition. Among all philosophical schools in ancient China, it was the Mohists and the Logicians who were the earliest to have extinguished in history. The basic reason for this lay precisely in the fact that their teachings did not accommodate themselves well with the essential Chinese characteristics. The Mohists preached a peculiar kind of religion, but the Chinese people (at least the Hans, which form the main bulk) have always been too practical to embrace any religion seriously, or what is the same, they may embrace any religious belief or dogma whatsoever. The Mohists demanded an unconditional consecration which by its very nature undermined its own value. To demand the total consecration of all men is equal to denying the ultimate value of life of all. Such a demand is valueless (for what end would it serve?) and meaningless (sacrifice as a means is turned to an end). The Mohist teaching's canonization as a "prominent learning" (*xian xue*) depended on historical circumstances which were by themselves not sustainable for long. First, it required a strictly disciplined organization, which is not capable of being sustained for long under normal conditions, and can only be maintained in wartime. Any doctrine, in order to survive for long as an inspiring spiritual force, cannot depend on compulsion by sheer force. It has to carry with it something appealing to the hearts of ordinary people in their day-to-day lives. Second, a strictly disciplined organization of such a militant character has to rely on a great leader who would rule not only with an iron fist but, more importantly, with sufficient goodwill and intelligence. The Mohist injunction to "agreement with the superior" demands uniformity with their leader (Ju Zi, or the "Great Master"). But then the outcome of this obedience would essentially depend on the personal quality of the leader himself. A leader is also a human being. "To err is human," as a well-known proverb says. So the vitality of the Mohists, or indeed of any school which shares a similar view, lies nowhere else other than in the personal ability and goodwill of their leader, instead of in the wisdom of their doctrine. This would be a fatal perversion, for the vitality of a philosophy must dwell in its profundity and soundness, and not in any personal quality or character. The Mohist doctrine, depending too much on the personal ability of the leader, is evidently unreliable. The situation would constantly vary, according to the quality of the leader. After the death of Mo Zi, the founder of the Mohist school, the school was split into three sects, or so the ancient literature recorded. With the splitting up of their school, the Mohists were drawing into their later stage. The later Mohist school, in differentiation from the earlier, was more and more inclined to engage in scientific and technical knowledge, while the strong political hue of the earlier Mohists was gradually fading out. But scientific and technical interests were not enough to sustain the later Mohists for long in a primarily ethico-political environment.

[VI] The Utopia of the Mohists

Xun Zi lived in the later stage of the Warring States Period (5th-3rd centuries B.C.) and in one chapter of his book entitled "*Against the Twelve Philosophical Schools*" (*Fei Shi Er Zi*) had severely criticized them individually, one after another, the Mohists included. Xun Zi judged the Mohists as "advocating utility, proclaiming frugality and overlooking the social differentiations"①—a keen criticism. The Mohists did not properly realize the

① *Book of Xun Zi*, "Against the Twelve Philosophical Schools."

immense variety of men and things in the real world and in real life. They tried their best to force all men into a utopian state of affairs created by their willful imagination, or wishful thinking. Mo Zi made a vital mistake by disregarding the infinite varieties of men and their social lives while mistaking uniformity for unity. They took the unity of social lives not as a unity in variety but as a unity in uniformity. In fact, the unity of society consists in the differences and divergences between man and man; unity never means uniformity. The gospel of uniformity could only result in the ossification of human intellectual culture; the more people are diversified in their ways of thinking and living, the more varied and colorful will be their intellectual culture. In the course of human history, intellectual tolerance has always proved far superior to intellectual intolerance. The more the variety, the more vigorous would a culture be. The uniformity of life and thought would be disastrous to any ideology, Mohist thought providing a salient example. In short, unity exists in variety, not in uniformity. Uniformity is not and can never be unity. The Mohists designed a utopia the essential principle of which was "agreement to the superior," that is, to follow a leader supposed to be the incarnation of the absolute truth. However, practical enactment of such a teaching would bring a lot of problems. As we have come to see, virtue itself is very hard to measure. Never yet have people devised a mechanism that could afford any practically operational standard for measuring virtue. In regard to this, Mo Zi elaborated his doctrine of "agreement with the superior." And the "agreement with the virtuous" meant nothing other than the "agreement with the superior." For, other than the superior, who would be qualified to be called virtuous? "One who has stolen a sword would deserve capital punishment, but one who has stolen the whole country would deserve to be crowned a prince",[①] asserted the prominent ancient historian Sima Qian. "Those who succeeded would become kings and princes, but those who failed would become thieves and bandits," proclaims an age-old Chinese proverb. Virtue cannot be measured efficiently, and what is called virtue is in the last analysis just the will of those in power. In this way, "agreement with the virtuous" was turned into "agreement with the superior." Since whoever is superior is virtuous, to agree with the virtuous can only mean to agree with the superior. The hierarchy of virtue becomes then, in its essence, the hierarchy of power. Here lies a process of ideological transmutation which reveals the secret of ancient Chinese ideology. With the advent of the "agreement with the superior," the Mohists accomplished the quintessential part of their ideological structure. Mo Zi went even so far as to

① Sima Qian, *History*, "Lives of the Knights-Errant."

maintain that the royal throne should be passed to the virtuous and the talented. Here the issue is this: among all people, who should be presumed virtuous? The idea that the virtuous (the superior) should rule, and the less virtuous or the unvirtuous (the masses) obey, had its origin in the ancient Chinese philosophies of Confucius, Mo Zi and others. And since that time on, it had become a rule of thumb in the history of China. This way of thinking, that the leader is forever the superior who should rule over the masses, while the inferior masses should always follow and obey, never to attempt to become the masters, helps explain why there had never been the idea of popular sovereignty and democracy in China since old times.

In political theory, Mo Zi founded a doctrine roughly with the effect that, before the emergence of the civil state, each person had his own criterion of right and wrong, and since there was no unity among peoples' opinions, the world was doomed to chaos. Hence there was an urgent need that "the persons of virtue and talent and of wisdom and intelligence should be elected the Son of Heaven [the sovereign] under whom the different standards in the world might be unified."① From among the virtuous and the talented, the Son of Heaven would choose the leaders of different echelons with whose help it would be possible for him to unify the thoughts and wills of the whole people. This meant agreement with "the Will of Heaven"—a term which was in fact synonymous with the will of the sovereign. Consequently the very end of the unification of thoughts was the uniformity of thoughts—a prerequisite which paved the way to absolute despotism. It is really a pity to see that the seeds of fascism might be found everywhere since antiquity. Hence Meinecke, Germany's leading liberal historian, was strongly against the prevailing idea that Nazism was a specific product of the German culture. Is it impossible, so he would ask, to engender fascist ideas at all in other countries? Certainly not. And it is more a pity to see how the most populist-inclined doctrine, such as the Mohists', turns to be its own opposite—to some kind of intellectual serfdom or fascism in its antique dress. This intellectual tradition permeated the long course of later history in China, sometimes hidden and sometimes open.

An ideal, when too much idealized, will always tend to turn against itself. What the Mohists preached offers a striking example. In the state of nature, so they argued, everyone followed his own will and there could then be only disorder everywhere. Later, as they came to realize that disorder was caused by the state of anarchy, they chose a virtuous and talented person as the Son of

① *Book of Mo Zi*, "The Agreement with the Virtuous."

Heaven. Thenceforth the community would step from the state of disorder into a state of order, that is, from the state of nature into the civil state. This theory of the origin of the state looks very much like early modern Europe's contract theory of the state, especially that of Hobbes. Such an interpretation, to be sure, was unhistorical; but it was still one of jurisprudence. In a certain sense, our different ways of thinking might be classified under two heads: one is historical, the other jurisprudential. The former answers the question of how something comes into being in history, the latter how it is established jurisprudentially; the former deals with what it is (sein), the latter what it ought to be (sollen). For instance, marriage in the early stage of human history generally took the form of capturing the fair sex by violence; later in a more civilized stage it became more and more a matter of contract, often a matter of bargain. This is a simple historical fact. But when viewed from a jurisprudential standpoint, nearly all marriage laws, whether in the East or in the West, prescribe love as the sole basis upon which marriage is to be founded, neither the winning by violence nor the bargain by money are allowed legally. Historically, few marriages are found to be based purely on love, most of them based instead upon the consideration of certain social conditions, and hence are not free. But jurisprudentially, marriage has to be prescribed as unconditional. Thus we are faced with two different ways of reasoning: the historical and the jurisprudential. The way of reasoning of the Mohists is jurisprudential, but it leads to a conclusion extremely non-jurisprudential or even anti-jurisprudential. Politically, they advocated "agreement with the superior," "not to make any analogy with the inferior," obliging the masses to follow their superiors in their judgments of what is right or wrong. This kind of duty-bound uniformity inevitably includes a great deal of hypocrisy, for people can never agree in all judgments homogeneously and unanimously. Moreover, there can never be a leader who is forever infallible in all things, with every word of his an irrefutable truth. If every man is required to agree with his superior and to identify himself with his superior, the end would be a despotic regime, no more, no less, though under the trappings of antiquity. In the case of the Mohists, we see how the most populist school becomes one of the most detrimental to the interests and wishes of the people. Such is the cunning of historical reason, which seems to be always teasing us.

The Mohists supposed that in order to realize an ideal political system as they had designed, all men had to share and observe a uniform idea and action. But to maintain such a uniformity would infallibly lead to the stereotype of the life of the community at large. All men speaking with the same voice would mean the ossification of human culture. As we have observed above, the ethico-politico-centric ideology constituted the axis of the Chinese way of thinking. The Mohists were no exception. But this trend also brought with it a misfortune, because it smothered any individual creativity. At bottom, the progress of any community has to depend upon the full display of the innovative talents of all men. Unity—let's repeat it again—is not uniformity, but the synthesis of variety. A community can hardly make any advancement if unity is suppressed by uniformity, as the Mohists once exhorted so devoutly. From this they drew out many naive ideas, taking all leaders as wise and well-intentioned. It seemed as though they never gave a hint that an authority might by chance neither be wise nor have good intentions, and they committed fatal errors thereby. Their greatest hope was summed up in their slogan: "the great benefit to the country and the people." But a petrified community would certainly benefit no one. We may agree with the superior—so far so good, provided the superior be forever intelligent and good willed. But what would the case be, when the leader proved not so intelligent or his intentions not so good? A man's thought is above all a product of his existence in real life and forever varies with it. The existing living conditions determine one's consciousness, and a superior can never be infallible—especially when he is unrestrained in his power over the inferior, such as we have too often observed in the wanton and capricious conducts of many emperors in the history of China ever since antiquity. After all, the best-governed state should be that which makes possible the greatest display of the people's liberty.

[VII] The Mohists and the Confucians

Still another point to be distinguished and discerned is that the idea of good and evil should never be equated with that of right and wrong. The former is an ethical judgment, while the latter a scientific one. The idea of good and evil should not be identified with right and wrong because they belong to different categories. The fault of the ethico-politico-centric tradition is to have mistaken the two as one and the same. If Confucianism has influenced the later ages openly and profoundly, then Mohism has undergone its course in a clandestine way, its influences sometimes open and sometimes hidden, but never completely extinguished. The former has consistently upheld the principle of hierarchy, professing the inequality of men, while the latter has brought us to a strange rendezvous of the two extremes, starting with the equality of men but finally arriving at an absolute despotism. If we ignore the essence of this ethico-political tradition, we would never be able to reach the core of the Chinese ideology.

There was an obvious divergence between China and the West from the very beginning; the road the West took was that of wisdom or of intellectualism, giving priority to knowledge. But the road the Chinese philosophy took is that of virtue, giving priority to morality. As an academic study, we are here concerned not with a value judgment, i.e. which is the better of the two different roads, but only with a basic historical fact. No matter how wide a gap there might seem between the Confucians and the Mohists, there might yet be found a keen consanguinity with each other. At first sight it looks as though there was a great difference between Confucianism and Mohism. The Mohists preached "universal love" without differentiation, while the Confucians a "love with differentiation (or, in different grades)." What dominated the Confucians was the principle of hierarchy dividing people into various levels and ranks. The idea of benevolence (ren) in the Confucian doctrine is a process of enlarging oneself to others, i.e. "to care for my elders and then for others, to care for my youngsters and then for others."① In it there was a series of gradations. The Confucians represented the interests of the upper social classes, who were naturally prone to view people through a perspective based on differentiation. The Mohists represented the lower classes and hence naturally demanded more equality instead of social differentiation. Both looked rational from their own standpoint, but not so coherent theoretically as they might appear at first sight. What we may call rules or principles in life arise, so to speak, either by nature or by convention. The natural ones are not man-made or artificial, while the ethical ones are. Nearly all schools in ancient China, the Confucians and the Mohists included, had tried voluntarily or involuntarily to integrate the two into one. Hence all the confusions in their arguments and speculations. It is the task of the reader to distinguish them, rendering the natural to nature and the man-made to man. There is and can be no problem of good and evil in the natural world; ethics concerns itself with what ought to be (sollen), but never with what really is (sein). Ancient Chinese philosophers were always obsessed by a desire to integrate them in one, taking the natural world as immediately identical with the ethical. It became even more so in later ages. We'll come to it in dealing with the disagreement over the inborn goodness or evil of human nature—obviously an inverted way of putting questions—in the long ages to come. And then during the late middle ages, the natural world in the Neo-Confucian conception was no more and no less than an aggrandizement of the inner moral world. The moral principle

① *Book of Mencius*, "King Hui of Liang," pt. 1.

was said to permeate and be embodied in the material world. This is where the ethico-political world-view leads and ends. Herein one may find the reason why the Chinese way of thinking always tended to lead to the utopia of virtuocracy.

After all, Nature by itself does not engender any moral principle in human society. It was in just their treatment of the natural evolution of the world that both the Confucians and the Mohists failed in their attempt in framing a coherent theory of philosophy. The Mohists' "universal love" was impractical in its operation, because it was not in conformity with the natural law. After all, ethical value and natural law are different in kind and cannot be identified as one and the same. Both the Confucian and the Mohist schools, two of the earliest in the history of China, confused the one and the other into a muddle, and henceforth it became an essential feature in nearly all the philosophical schools of China. In fact, there is no problem of what is good and evil or beautiful and ugly in the natural world itself. The ideas of good and evil or of beauty and ugliness are but creations of men, imposed by men on the natural world. The natural world and the ethical world are independent of each other. It is beyond the capacity of human intellect either to derive the one from the other or to impose the one on the other.

In their treatment of human nature, both the Confucians and the Mohists were entangled with this fallacy. What they treated was not the real human nature, but their own idealized human nature. The Confucians supposed that the idea of benevolence was common to all. The Mohists' "universal love" was also a fiction imposed by them on all men. Maybe this "universal love" did exist in Mo Zi himself and some of his followers, but has surely never been thoroughly realized by most people. Granted that human nature is what is natural, it must be admitted that there is something in it which encourages "mutual aggression" toward one another, just as there is something which promotes "mutual love and compassion" toward one another. In any given time and in any given community, the total amount of wealth and power is destined to be limited. Then there is the problem of how to distribute this given amount to each one rationally. Distribution of a limited amount would unavoidably cause competition. And in competition there will necessarily be fair-play as well as foul. Hence there are in human nature always the elements of "mutual love" as well as those of "mutual aggression." Both the Confucians and the Mohists viewed human nature from an irrational standpoint arising from their wishful thinking. Human nature is too many-sided and variegated to be reduced to a homogeneous and simplified channel. In our life, we have to admit that there are cases where one is able to sacrifice oneself for others and yet there are also cases where one is to benefit only oneself at the price of others. Both cases are undeniable and indisputable facts of our experience. In a certain sense, some of the attributes of human nature are given as our inborn natural instinct, while some are the outcomes of social circumstances. From a commonplace point of view, let's admit there are innate as well as conditioned elements in human nature. But the leading philosophical schools in ancient China mistook the two as one and the same, and, what was worse still, they tried to identify their own ideal as the sole reality. Thus they were led astray by their well-intended wishes and failed to arrive at a comprehensive and steadfast understanding of human nature. All this was due to the fault in their ethico-politico-centric doctrine.

Chapter Three: The Mohist School and the Traditional Mode of Thinking

[I] Why the Mohist School Vanished in History

As a matter of course, the original teachings of the founders of each school underwent a process of development in the hands of their followers, and they often became differentiated to a considerable degree. According to ancient literature, after Confucius the Confucian school was split into eight sects, and after Mo Zi the Mohist into three. But as to their contents and their differences, few clues can be found in the existing materials. As a rule, those materials provide only fragmentary records, which are more often than not the ill-intentioned attacks of their opponents. While each school ceaselessly attacked others, they were at the same time assimilating each other.

Considering the arguments in their mutual attacks, most of them appear rather plausible. Of those who attacked the Mohist school, the two foremost were Zhuang Zi and Xun Zi. Zhuang's criticism of the Mohist school was already mentioned in the foregoing chapter, most of which—so far as we might evaluate—was very much to the point. Now let us turn to Xun Zi's criticism of the Mohist school. Xun Zi himself was the last and the greatest Confucian master in the last stage of the Warring States. In his refutation of the twelve schools, he sharply criticized Mo Zi and his school, and the main substance may be summed thus: 1). the ethico-political theory of the Mohist school did not and could not provide a universal maxim, because it was attainable only for a very few. A universal ethical maxim, in order to be genuinely universal, has to be tenable and accessible for all people. If it is practicable only by a very few, to the exclusion of most people, then the theory itself is doomed to be defective or fallacious. 2). The

Mohist theory was in reality impractical, since everyone was required to think only of the happiness of others but never his own. Here is implied a logical paradox. If everyone is to think only of others in spite of himself, as if he can have no happiness whatever of his own, then there will be no happiness at all; because if everyone has no happiness of his own, there will be no happiness among all. If one is to interpret one's bitterness and suffering as happiness, then the pursuit of happiness would be totally meaningless. If the maxim that one should think only of others but never of oneself is to be universally binding, then to give up oneself for the sake of others would be in vain. When I give up my share to feed others, because others are hunger-stricken, it is a praiseworthy act. But when others are not hunger-stricken and in no need of being fed, then my act of giving up my own things to others would be morally no good at all. Here lies the logical paradox.

Hence, all moral preachings ought to satisfy the following two prerequisites. The first is that the theory can be universally adopted. If it is tenable only for a few, instead of for all or most people, it cannot have universal tenability. The second is that it should be workable in practice. If a man never thinks of his own feelings, we can hardly think it possible for him to think of what others would feel. If he has no knowledge of what he himself requires, then how could he know what others require? Confucius once said: "Do not do to others what you do not want done to yourself"① Surely this is a universal moral maxim, but it presupposes that you have to think of yourself before you think of others: what you want and what you do not. If you really never think of what you do or do not want done to yourself, then you would never know nor be able to do what others want, nor not do what they do not want. To know oneself is the prerequisite of knowing others. With this in view, we may fairly say that the Mohist teaching is rather strongly permeated with a religious impetus or a blind aspiration to self-sacrifice, never giving a thought to its theoretical justification nor its practicality in real life. And this, as strange as it may seem, would come into contradiction with the Mohists' own doctrine of utilitarianism. As a professed utilitarian, a Mohist should take into consideration what is beneficial, and an action would be valueless if it brings no benefit. But religious dedication is often non-beneficial, or at least one should never take into consideration what benefit it might bring. It exacts sacrifice for sacrifice's sake, dedication for dedication's sake. It is a central religious sentiment that one ought not to ask what benefits one's sacrifice or dedication would bring. We may as well say that in

① *Analects*, chap. 15 "The Duke Liang of Wei," trans. James Legge with alterations by the author.

all religious sentiments there is always an element of asceticism. For a devotee, self-sacrifice is not a means of utilitarianism, but is a moral end in itself. This is probably the most incomprehensible feeling in the depths of the human heart, as though it is only in their unconditional dedication or suffering that people may enjoy a profound self-satisfaction. According to the teachings of Christianity, men are born with original sin, and people can redeem their sins only through voluntary self-sacrifice. This perhaps reflects one of the profoundest instincts in human hearts. As regards this inexpressible secret of the soul, each school provided its own way of salvation, and in China it was only the Mohist way that was permeated with such a deep religious flavor.

Many of the ancient philosophical schools in China have spread down to later ages, with the exceptions of only the Mohists and the Logicians. And the Mohists and the Logicians had many features in common. One of the basic reasons why only these two schools vanished over time is that they did not conform to the national characteristics of the Chinese. The Chinese people, or at any rate the Han people, are extremely practical, yet the teachings of the Mohists and the Logicians were notably impractical. They had lost sight of the most practical demands of the Chinese people, i.e. subsistence in their day-to-day lives and pursuit of worldly benefits. This can be regarded the fundamental reason for their decline and fall. A doctrine may be followed for a certain period of time by a group, and even followed devoutly and thoroughly. But its real vitality lies not in the devotion of a small group of people at certain times, but in its appeal to the great multitude in the long run. Both the Mohists and the Logicians failed the test of satisfying the Chinese national character over the duration of history.

[II] Natural Philosophy vs. Ethico-Political Philosophy

Since the Mohist school sprang from the lower strata in society, they were specifically interested in science and technique from the craftsmen's point of view. Especially with the later Mohist school, their moral preachings lessened while the logical, scientific and technical content was greatly increased. The writings of the later Mohist school dealt mainly with epistemology, logic, optics and mechanics. But unfortunately their intellectual trend did not include natural philosophy. This is certainly an issue worthy of serious consideration. In the West, ancient Greek philosophers took the way of natural philosophy from the very start, their interests being concentrated on the topic: what is the essence that constitutes the world? Thales held water to be the thing from which all else was created. Heraclitus identified the essence with fire, ever changing its form in its manifestation of all things. Whether it be water, fire, or anything else, the principles and essence of the outside world had always been their main concern. In contrast, the philosophy of China from its very start followed an ethico-political line, its starting point invariably being moral ideas such as benevolence, duty, etc. Confucius predominantly stressed benevolence (*ren*), his view based not on the natural but on the moral world. Some ancient sources recorded that Mo Zi had learned Confucianism in his youth while staying in the princedom of Lu, the home of Confucius and his school. Even with its strong scientific and technological interest, the Mohist school still ultimately chose an ethico-political orientation, not one of natural philosophy. An approach inspired by natural philosophy first tries to understand what the natural would is made of, and from there to derive how our life and the human world ought to be. The ethico-political mode of thinking is just the contrary; it tries to ask what the ethical relationship between man and man ought to be, and from there to broaden, to develop and to extend it to the whole world, the mechanics of which are after all but a copy or imitation of the functioning of our moral world.

In later ages, the Neo-Confucians (of the Song period) viewed the whole universe as a mere extension of moral principles, which dominated not only the human world but also the whole universe at large, as though the fundamental principles of the universe were composed entirely from these moral obligations. The ethical (and hence political) orientation of philosophy in China from its very beginning, in differentiation with that in the West, has lasted down to modern times. Modern philosophy in the West started in the main from natural science (since Francis Bacon and Descartes), from which certain ideas and methods were drawn for application to the human world and human life. But philosophy in China took the reverse route. It has always been an extension from the ethical to the natural world, as though the latter was a by-product of the former.

There was a still further technical reason which might help explain why the Mohists, with their strong scientific interests, failed to take the path of natural philosophy. Since the Mohists were mostly practical craftsmen, what interested them was how to perform practical production. Most of their knowledge (and hence their way of thinking) came from practical interests. They were not concerned with the speculative problems of how to elevate their knowledge to a philosophic level. Ancient Greek philosophers were, as a rule, free citizens who did not engage in manual labor, and therefore were free to indulge in artistic and scientific activities. They were infected with a genuine pleasure in speculative thinking, which their slaves engaging in manual toil would have no interest in at all. This seems to be a material factor which led the Chinese of both the upper and lower classes to concentrate on practicality, the upper class from an ethico-politico-centric standpoint, the lower from a mostly utilitarian consideration. The Greek philosopher Aristotle took disinterested contemplation of the world to be the highest ideal of human life. In modern times, Pascal, the preeminent scientist and philosopher of the 17th century, expressed his ideal for life in this well-known aphorism: "Toute notre dignité consiste donc en la pensée… Travaillons donc à bien penser: voilà le principe de la morale."[①] For a Chinese philosopher, the word "pensée" here should be substituted by "ethical practice," and then the sentence would run thus: "*Travaillons à bien pratiquer éthiquement: voilà le principe de la pensée.*" And the German philosophical poet Goethe expressed his life ideal through the mouth of a watchtower man in these words: "*Zum sehen geboren, Zum schauen bestellt*" ("to see is my dower, to look my employ").[②] But for Mao Zedong, for example, practice is primary, and then follows knowledge.

Such a contemplative attitude toward life would never be found in the thoughts of the Chinese philosophers. The life ideal of the Chinese, no matter the school, has always aimed at the practical realization of its ethical postulates, and never pure contemplation or speculation on life as such. As a result, there arose many extremely minute and penetrating observations on optics, mechanics and logic, such as the Mohists had produced, yet they never tried to draw any conclusions of natural philosophy from this. Mo Zi was a contemporary of Democritus, the foremost representative of atomism in ancient Greece. The Greek atomist taught that all the world was at bottom composed by invisible and indivisible particles called atoms. Though the atomic theory of modern science is not exactly the same as that of the ancient Greeks, it is nevertheless derived and developed from the ancient Greeks, or rather the philosophical view in its root and by its very nature is still essentially that of the ancient Greek atomists. Yet the Mohist theory did not lead to any form of atomism. Some argued that there might be found some elements or traces of atomism in the Mohist classics. But in fact we can hardly discover any credible evidence to support such arguments. In "The World" of Zhuang Zi, there is a proposition which reads: "the infinite great has nothing outside of it, and so it is called the Great One; the

① "All our dignity consists therefore in thought… So let us work at thinking well; this is the principle of moral reflection." B. Pascal, *Pensées*, ed. L. Brunschvicg (Paris: Hachette, 1912), 347.

② Goethe, *Faust* pt. 2, act 5, sc. 4, trans. A. Latham.

infinite small has nothing within it, and so it is called the Small One."① Some identify this "Small One" as the atom. Reasoning logically, this seems plausible. Etymologically, "a" in Greek means "un-" and "tom" means "divisible"; so an atom is literally that which is indivisible. But so far, this notion of the infinitesimal in Zhuang Zi has never been amplified into a theory of atomism, or of any natural philosophy by which the universe and the human lives in it were to be explained by the idea of the atom. We should not cite a single sentence at random and impromptu and assume that it is the philosophy of atomism. We may also find in the same chapter of the *Book of Zhuang Zi* a proposition with great philosophical and scientific significance, i.e. this assertion: "a rod of a foot long, being taken daily by half, will never exhaust unto eternity."② In modern terms, this is an infinite series in algebra. It is really a most brilliant and wonderful proposition for ancient times. It is the basic idea in modern higher mathematics, i.e. the idea of the limit and the infinitesimal. Nevertheless, we are by no means qualified to assert that Zhuang Zi had already conceptualized modern higher mathematics. After all, he did not deduce from this point any further part of modern higher mathematics. Similarly, we have no reason to assert that the idea of "the Small One" might be identified with that of the atom. Contemporaneous though the Mohist school was with the Greek atomists, the Chinese philosophers never worked out any version of atomism. The reason for this lies in the particular Chinese way of thinking, which is ethico-politically centered and diametrically opposed to the analytic and mechanistic way of thinking.

There has never been a theory of atomism in China, nor could any have arisen in China. This fact is very much in close connection with the basic fact that an individual in China has never been an atom, and has forever been regarded as a "particle" governed by a much larger "field"—to borrow a term from physics. Human society is but a field that governs the particles in it at all points and all times. The individual particle is neither independent nor isolated by itself or in itself. There has never been atomism in China because there has never been individualism in any sense in China, for the essence of an individual has been identified as a mere function of the ethical relationship between man and man. Confucius stressed: "Let a prince be (what) a prince (ought) to be, a minister be a minister, a father be a father and a son be a son."③ Such is the ideal

① *Book of Zhuang Zi*, "The World."

② Ibid.

③ *Analects*, bk.12 "Yan Yuan."

human society as conceived by the Confucians. That is to say, an individual is much more than merely his natural existence. The essence of being human exists in the fact that he ought to do what his social status (and his ethical obligations thereby) requires him to do. To do one's ethical duty is what makes a man a human being. A human being is above all an instrument in the broad network of ethical relationships: be he a prince or a minister, a father or a son. A man is in the first place not a mere individual *per se,* but a *homo ethicus*, and it is only in his ethical relationship that he is endowed with the very nature of what makes a human being a human being. It is the network of ethical relationship which makes the human being, not the human being that makes the ethical relationship. Man is not the law-giver but the morality-bearer. Since individualism has never existed in China, there has consequently been no atomism, nor any form of the atomic philosophy. Here lies the secret of the way of thinking characteristic to the Chinese.

What traditionally interested the Chinese was not any kind of pure contemplation or speculation, but the realization of their ethical worth in the world of our daily lives. Nearly all philosophical schools in China, the Confucians and the Mohists included, turned to an ethico-political end as their final spiritual resort. It is worthwhile to note that as the later Mohists became more and more interested in science and technology, they simultaneously approached their final decline ever more rapidly. They were moving too far away from the traditional Chinese way of thinking, which might be readily summed up in the slogan, "science (or knowledge) in service of politics." What is ethics is politics, and politics ethics. All sciences were employed for the sake of ethico-political expediency. Science itself is something secondary, used to serve some ethical purpose of a higher level. Knowledge was considered to have no value of its own. The search for truth is only for its utility in serving an ethical end. This is even so in modern times. Marx himself emphasized that his theory was scientific socialism, in contradistinction from all the former socialisms, which were to him utopian in nature. He held that his theory of socialism was the product of science, and that for him science (rather than any ethical or political ideal) was primary and predominant, and hence politics should be put under the guidance or the command of science. Socialism is the conclusion of science, and science should govern politics. But in China, as is generally known, it is politics that is given the command (or "let politics take the command"). And hence the slogan "science in the service of the proletarian politics," instead of politics being derived from science, which would make it subject to science (i.e. let science take the command). Here emerges the question of how to situate truth and utility (or science and politics) in relation to each other, or which of the two should be given priority. Should truth be submitted to expediency, or expediency to truth? Does knowledge have its own worth, or should the ethico-political exactions reign over the dignity of truth? It has to be noted that in the traditional sense of value in China, truth has never been held as a good in itself and by itself (e.g. people never praised those who dedicated their lives to the pursuit of truth, such as Bruno or Galileo), and neither has beauty (such as might be seen in whole-hearted devotion to art or to romantic love). It is only virtue which deserves the name of goodness and is the sole measure of goodness. Thus it can be seen that what the Chinese believe and admire is nothing else but virtue, or "virtuism." Virtue is forever deemed cardinal, supreme and primary. All else is subordinated to it and serves it. Whoever fails to grasp this would lose sight of a proper perspective of the Chinese world-view (Weltanschauung).

As to those parts of the Mohist classics dealing with science and craft, the readers may consult J. Needham's monumental work *Science and Civilization in China*, especially the chapter in Volume 2 dealing with the Mohists and Logicians. In other parts of his book, he discusses separately the optics and mechanics of the Mohist school. It is science and logic in particular which are neglected by most scholars studying the history of philosophy in China, and which have hence never received further scrutiny down to this day. The exact meanings of many prominent paragraphs in the Mohist literature are still ambiguous. It was not until the early 20th century that people began to achieve a preliminary understanding of their scientific content, which had not been comprehended before. The Mohists were indeed greatly interested in science, yet their influence on the history of science was very limited. The reason for this paradoxical phenomenon may also be found in other similar cases. We may observe any theory from two aspects: one is its influence, i.e. its effect or role in history, while the other is its own theoretical merit independent of its historical context. The epigram we have cited above from Zhuang Zi, "a rod of a foot long, being taken daily by half, will never exhaust unto eternity," is certainly highly admirable in its theoretical reasoning, but it exercised little influence in the history of ideas. So it often happens that the historic significance of a theory or of an opinion is not necessarily in proportion with its scientific or philosophic merit. The same is valid with regard to all historical figures. We ought to evaluate them duly from both aspects, not solely from their merit nor from the effect of their historical role alone. An all-round evaluation requires the combination of both sides. There are times when what has value in science or theory may have little impact on history; and conversely there are times when what is of little value in science or theory may be of great significance in history. Without a sound and well-balanced comprehension of both sides at the same time, we can hardly behold the whole of the truth of history. The most prevalent doctrines at any time are often not the most valuable. It often takes a very long time to test the most valuable. To cite an example at hand in modern intellectual history: the works of Liang Qichao and Wang Guowei, both generally acknowledge as leading scholars and thinkers. Some of Wang's works, such as his *Dictum on Poesy* (*Ren Jian Ci Hua*) are full of aesthetic profundity but seem to have had little impact on his own time or on later ages. In contrast with Wang, Liang's works were very much in vogue all over the country, and their influence is unparalleled in modern times, even though Liang himself was greatly regretful of their superficiality. Guo Moruo confessed in his memoir that almost none of his generation in the early 20th century escaped Liang's influence, even if in disagreement with Liang's viewpoint. This is an indisputable historical fact. Liang's significance lies in the impetus he gave to the Chinese enlightenment, comparable roughly to Hu Shih's role in the New Cultural Movement of the "May Fourth" period. Hu's works, if reconsidered purely from an academic angle, would not seem to have much value. But one should not evaluate him from one aspect only, and one should pay due respect to his historic role as well. In evaluating our forerunners, we should take proper care on both sides.

It was not until modern times that the Mohist scientific and technical records were rediscovered and studied, but in a broader sense the Mohist tradition had never completely vanished; for wherever there have been craftsmen, the Mohist tradition has been passed on. One example is furnished by the book *The Exploitation of the Works of Nature* (*Tian Gong Kai Wu*) written by Song Yingxing, the foremost technical expert of the early 17th century. Needham evaluated it as the encyclopedia of technical science of that age, because in it are summed up nearly all branches of technical knowledge known at that time. But it was lost in China for centuries. Not until the end of the 19th century was this book reintroduced into China from Japan. The reason for its loss in its native land is very simple, just as its author had explained in his preface: "This book has nothing to do with what concerns official rank or worldly honors." Ultimately, most people are inclined to indulge in the pursuit of honor and wealth, and so the book was lost to the later generations. Everything bows to social requirements. Song's lot reflects the fate of all artisans and craftsmen in traditional China. It is appropriate to note that all cultures move along two different levels: one associated with the upper social strata, with more sophisticated intellectual resources, whose legacy is often more easily preserved for posterity; the other that of the lower social strata (mostly laborers) whose contributions are rarely kept for posterity, since they do not belong to the sphere of refined taste, and often lack written records, their legacy consequently lost for the most part. The long tradition stretching from the Mohist classics to Song's work has been almost entirely lost. Song's whole life has to an extent faded into oblivion, and we do not even know the activities of his last years or the exact date of his death.

Now what we are able to discuss is only the internal coherence of the Mohist philosophy with their logical and scientific knowledge. It should be noted that the Mohist philosophy so far as we are now able to observe was still ethico-politically centered, because its main concern was directed to an ethico-political end. Thus essentially it shares some basic features with the Confucians, though with great divergence in their respective inclinations. Needham held that the greatest misfortune in the history of science in China was the fact that the naturalism of the Taoist school failed to unite itself with the logical study of the Mohist school. If the two were combined, philosophy in China would have been more likely to have developed along the naturalistic line; and then science in China would probably have thrived more exuberantly. In my opinion, Dr. J. Needham here overlooked the other aspect, i.e. the Chinese mode of thinking or the Chinese character. As stated above, the Chinese were a people of extreme practicality. Both logic and science are, in a certain sense, divorced from practical utility and have nothing to do with worldly prestige and profit. The eight-legged essay ("ba gou" style of writing—an official style in the imperial examination) has no scientific value whatsoever, yet it ruled over the realm of the Chinese literati for centuries. Why is it that this absurd style of learning could maintain a widespread reign over Chinese intellectuals for so long, while by contrast the study of science never attained a dominant position? The answer may readily be found in the words of Ma Chunshang, a *dramatis personae* in the famous novel *An Informal History of the Confucian Scholars* (*Ru Lin Wai Shi* by Wu Jingzi) in the 18th century, who professed with these frank words: "If you do not [engage in the study of the eight-legged essay], how can you hope to get a position in officialdom!"① This confession comes to the point plainly and sharply. The effort to study a stereotyped and sterile norm of learning is made purely to get a high position in officialdom and the wealth it might bring. It serves as an instrument for the highest fulfillment of practical life in the vanity fair. From Ban Gu, the leading historian of the 1st century, down

① Wu Jingzi, *An Informal History of the Confucian Scholars*, chap. 13.

to Zhang Taiyan, the preeminent scholar in the early 20th century, a long series of thinkers have revealed this truth relentlessly. Yet Needham missed precisely this characteristic of the Chinese mentality: it was their practicality that impeded them from the pursuit of any object of pure spiritual value, truth and beauty included. They admire virtue just because the appearance of virtue can afford them an easy means to their practical ends. They are equally ready to accept any moral or political doctrine, provided it satisfies them practical interests, and they are just as willing to abandon it, once it fails to meet their needs. In the depths of their minds, scientific truth has no independent worth of its own. It only serves a practical purpose, under the name of "virtue," and otherwise has no value at all. Yet the worth of scientific truth does not lie mainly in its practical means toward some worldly end. Scientific truths may possess high theoretical value, but be of little practical use (such as was the mediaeval Ptolemaic theory, taken as supporting papal orthodoxy). Religion, in the last analysis, is also of no practical value, unless endowed with a theocratic connotation. And it is in just this respect that the Mohists made their unique contribution to the tradition of Chinese culture.

The Confucians never preached any religious doctrine, while the Mohists by contrast strongly professed their religious beliefs; but they transformed religion into something like a means to practical utility. Among all schools of the pre-Qin period, only the Mohists advocated religion, and the manner of their preaching was characteristically Chinese. Needham developed his inquiry simply from a technical point of view, to the neglect of the deeper social and cultural factors.

The reason that philosophy in China did not take the way of natural philosophy is precisely because of their deep-rooted pragmatism. It was presumed that science should serve certain political ends and hence has to be distorted to adapt to certain social and political purposes, in spite of itself. Above all, it is the political and social utility that has to be taken into consideration, not the dignity of scientific truth itself. This was where the Chinese way of thinking led. And it was only the Mohist school which kept a lively interest in science and technology and bequeathed a wealth of intellectual and scientific thinking, the intellectual value of which makes it worthy of exploration and absorption by modern people.

[III] The Ethico-Political Doctrine of the Mohists

Now some more words on the religious and political theory of the Mohist school. Nearly all political theories in China have been ethical injunctions, instead of pure political studies. In the Mohist doctrine they are summarized under ten items: universal love, anti-aggression, agreement with the talents (or the virtuous), agreement with the sovereign, the will of Heaven, existence of the spirits, anti-music, anti-fatalism, frugality of expenditure, and frugality in funeral. Those ten items formed a coherent system for their reasoning. Anti-aggression is the natural corollary of universal love. "The agreement with the talents (or the virtuous)" and "the agreement with the sovereign" signify the identification of the talented (the virtuous) with the sovereign—a typical mode of thinking in Chinese tradition. As is generally known, in China the sovereign is as a rule identified with the sage. Judgment of right and wrong is passed by the sovereign, and the people are required to conform. In this respect, the Mohists kept themselves within the parameters of the general Chinese tradition. What distinguishes the Mohists from other schools is their prominent emphasis on the will of Heaven, which made them the most religiously inclined school. Their demands are all supposedly derived from Heaven. Since there is a Heaven, there are spirits. This formed a vivid contrast with the Confucians. Confucius never affirmed the existence of gods and spirits: "The subjects on which the Master [Confucius] did not speak were extraordinary things, feats of strength, disorder and spiritual beings."① Not only did Mo Zi acknowledge the existence of spiritual beings, but he even went so far as to admit with naive frankness that he holds this doctrine purely for the purpose of teaching and guiding the people. Mo Zi was a thoroughgoing utilitarian, his theism also serving a utilitarian purpose. And likewise with his other doctrines. Confucians always gave priority to rites and music. But to the Mohists all rites and music were superfluous and useless, assessed by utilitarian purposes. This again constituted a sharp opposition to the Confucians. The Confucian culture was essentially one of rites and music which served to set up a norm or ideal of social life and social order. In opposition to this, the Mohists held these matters as useless extravagances. Both the Confucians' over-elaborate formalities expressed in rites and music and the Mohists' oversimplified abrogation of the same are characteristic of Chinese culture and Chinese thinking: the underlying motive is their thor-

① *Analects*, chap.7, "Shu Er," trans. James Legge.

oughgoing practicality. The Confucians valued them highly, because they took rites and music as indispensable to a well-governed society. Conversely, the Mohists would abolish them entirely, because they took these as totally useless in practical life. These two diametrically opposed theses came from the same starting point. Unless we have grasped the Chinese insistence on practicality, we can never fully understand the various differences as well as the uniformities of these philosophical schools. Confucians represented one extreme, while the Mohists the other. In their deepest hearts both were equally practical, down to the very marrow of their bones. Perhaps it might seem that the Mohists were less intelligent than the Confucians, for the latter came to realize that rites and music may be employed in guiding the people, and hence were not useless. The demand for frugality reflected the simple wishes of the Mohist artisans from the lower social strata, contraposed to the luxurious lives of the upper classes. Since kinship in traditional China is extremely strong, a large amount of wealth would often be squandered in the funeral ceremony. Frugality of expenditure implies, as a matter of course, the greatest prodigality, i.e. spending on the funeral.

When the approach of a thinker takes the road of natural philosophy, his idea of human nature is dominated by his idea of nature: such is nature, and so also is human nature. Down to modern times, the interpretation of human nature has always started from that of nature, and the interpretation of the birth of the civil state from that of the state of nature (as seen in Hobbes, Locke and Rousseau). As there had been no such naturalistic approach in ancient China, the Chinese philosophers (of nearly all schools) started not from nature but from ethical ideas, which as a rule were identified with human nature. The Mohists preached universal love because they presumed it mutually beneficial to everyone. Their standpoint is a utilitarian one. Yet as far as utilitarianism is concerned, there may be two different ways of argumentation. One expounds that everyone is selfish, but that selfishness when carried to such an extreme as to threaten annihilation of all others would be impracticable and harmful to oneself. Hobbes supposed that every person is a wolf to every other, risking the result of a war of all against all;[①] but a society of wolves against wolves surely could not survive long. To fulfill one's own selfish self-interest, one has to help keep the society in good order, and this requires a coercive authority to prevent men from devouring men. Indeed, starting from such a premise, the only natural conclusion would be that there has to be a coercive power or sovereignty, which could allow everyone to live in an orderly society. Hobbes' stance

① Hobbes, *Leviathan*, chap.13.

is derived from his theory of human nature, such that everyone is a selfish being and malign to others. But in the end he concludes that everyone has to submit to a coercive power in order to live for his better self-interest. This utilitarianism is drawn from a thoroughgoing individualistic, or egoistic, theory. But the Mohists thought otherwise, theirs instead being an altruistic or collectivistic reasoning. They took it for granted that men were born with a fine sentiment for loving others. The relation between men and men was by no means that between wolves and wolves. Most of the theories of human nature in the history of China followed this trend more or less. Mencius, in proclaiming his theory that men were born good, cited a well-known example: "If men suddenly see a child about to fall into a well, they will without exception experience a feeling of alarm and distress."[①] This feeling comes from the innate goodness of human nature. Both the Confucians and the Mohists were committed to the belief that human nature is created good and that the love of others follows naturally. However, when preaching love for others, the Confucians started from one's family, which is bound up by consanguinity. When the ethics of the family is enlarged, it will lead people to take care to "treat the elders in one's own family so that the elders in the families of others shall be similarly treated; treat the young in one's own family so that the young in the family of others shall be similarly treated—thus the whole land may be made to go round in one's palm."[②] In comparison with the Confucian ideal, there is a much stronger hue of egalitarianism in the Mohist preaching of universal love. The Confucians took the family (the unit in the context of consanguinity) as their axis. Since the Mohists were accustomed to the communal life of the craftsmen, they took a collectivist idea as their origin. The divergence in their respective starting points caused the divergence in their respective reasonings. The arguments of the Confucians proceeded from the premise of "endearing those who are dear to you in blood relationship" (*qin qin*), and thus Confucius said: "The father conceals the misconduct of the son, and the son conceals the misconduct of the father. Uprightness is to be found in this."[③] In other words, the relationship between family members reigns over others. But in the collectivist view, what reigns supreme is not the family bond but the community. Uprightness for

① *Book of Mencius*, pt. 1, "Gongsun Chou," trans James Legge.

② Ibid., pt. 1, "King Hui of Liang," trans James Legge, with alterations by the author.

③ *Analects*, chap.13 "Zi Lu," trans James Legge. Hence in the traditional historiography of the Confucians (or what is generally known as "the writing style of the *Spring and Autumn Annals*"), an orthodox historian should always make sure "to conceal the misconduct of the honorable, to conceal the misconduct of the endeared and to conceal the misconduct of persons of outstanding worth."

the Mohists exists in the reverse of the Confucian ideal, hence "there are those who may be styled upright: if their fathers have stolen a sheep, they will bear witness to the fact."[①] For the Confucians, the community or society is nothing more than the enlargement of the family, while for the Mohists the community is primary. Herein lie the different concepts of love of the two different schools. And that is also one of the reasons why the Mohists fell into oblivion in later ages. Meanwhile the Confucians demanded one should conceal the misconduct of honorable persons, dear ones, and the talented or virtuous.

Nevertheless, viewed from another aspect, there is yet a striking similarity in the theory of human nature of both the Confucians and the Mohists, i.e. both started by taking human nature as something inborn and given prior to experience. Whether there is an inborn element in human nature, we will leave outside of our consideration for the moment. What is to be considered here is this: what we call human nature dictates the social nature of human beings, which is and can be only shown in their social life. Without the experience of social life, there can be no human nature as such. To Robinson Crusoe on the deserted island, there is and there can be no elements of human nature such as "loving others as oneself" or "universal love." On this issue the ancient Chinese philosophers committed a fatal error by identifying what is conditioned (social nature) with what is innate (inborn nature).

The Confucian doctrine of love (or charity) consists in a process of gradation which stresses the differentiation between those dear to you and those who are not; while the Mohist "universal love" denies this differentiation. While the Mohists deny the gradation of human love, the Confucians deem "universal love" impractical. Perhaps on this point the Confucians come nearer to the truth than the Mohists, and are hence more reasonable. Suppose the Mohists came into power, what would happen then? Before they came to power, they might profess an array of fascinating theory. But as soon as they were really in control, their theory would be conditioned by the circumstances of social life, such as with their proposed redistribution of social wealth—which must be of a limited amount at any given time. Then their preachings would very probably be twisted into deceitful rhetoric leading to hypocrisy. In the "middle ages" of both East and West, theology often preached a philosophy of love (or charity), but these sermons were often accompanied by behavior to the contrary. When most people are in most cases unable to carry preaching into practice, these moral exhortations necessarily become turned into political fraud. When a set of

① Ibid.

sublime ideals does not work in practical life, and yet people are still required to preach it, it will result in nothing other than for the collaborative fomenting of a great fraud. This is just as Hans Christian Andersen described in his well-known fable "The Emperor's New Clothes," where everyone lies in their joint performance of a farce. "Power corrupts, absolute power corrupts absolutely," Lord Acton's dictum again proving pertinent.

When Mo Zi himself was proclaiming his doctrine, it was based on the experience of his own life. Because he and his disciples came from the lower social classes, it is natural that they bore a resentment of the upper classes in their wielding of power and enjoyment of a luxurious life. In the Book of Mo Zi we find many passages fiercely attacking "the wealthy and the honorable, who are worthless." Against the social and political disparities the Mohists preached a vehement egalitarianism. Mo Zi proclaimed: "The dignitaries are not forever the honorable, the common people are not destined to be forever miserable. It is the worthy who should be promoted and it is the unworthy who should be demoted."[①] These words vividly reflect the Mohists egalitarianism, directed against the hereditary hierarchy of feudalism. Yet here also is involved the problem of its practicability. What would their ideas in practice turn out to be? It sounds quite proper to say that talent dwells in one's virtue and ability. But one can hardly locate an objective standard for measuring people's virtue. In practice, the measurement is always turned to its reverse, i.e. one's virtue and ability are generally measured by one's social and political status. Whoever holds a higher position is presumed more virtuous than others. Thus there results a logical reversion. This is the theory's outcome in practice. In modern times, in order to prevent such abuses people invented practices like the division of powers, to erect checks and balances against the abuse of power. But in the history of China, it has always been the ethico-political theory which prevailed over all others. Those on high are assumed to be endowed with higher virtue, and are consequently assumed as more qualified to rule over those of the lower classes. It is not the virtuous who are assigned rule, but the rulers who are presumed more virtuous. Then what is taken for granted in theory is turned into its reverse in practice. If it is not superior virtue, then what qualifies the ruler (or rulers) to hold his position? In its very essence, this ethico-political theory is anti-democratic. The prerequisite of a democracy is the supposition that all men are created equal and independent. Though virtue and talent may vary in each person, all are nevertheless equal in their rights. It is not the case that those

① *Book of Mo Zi*, "Agreement with the talents."

with higher virtue and talent by nature should rule over others while the rest should simply be subservient. On the contrary, the governed who are considered of lower virtue and talent ought to have the right to be the sovereign of the governing. Sovereignty dwells in the governed instead of the governing. The action of the governing should be sanctioned by the consent of the governed. This is the theory of popular sovereignty, instead of that of elite sovereignty as propounded by the ethico-political doctrines. In his *Civil War in France*, Marx formulated the fundamental principle of the Paris Commune of the year 1871 thus: the people have the right to recall and to replace all officials and functionaries of all levels at all times.[①] Such is Marx's idea of democracy.

The above issue involves a basic issue: how should one look at human nature? Both the Confucians and the Mohists embraced a naive idealism, taking human nature as something innately good. And what should be done for human beings is simply to bring it into full play. But other philosophers, especially the later Confucian Xun Zi and the Legalists, took it otherwise. They did not take human nature as something entirely good, so that the question is not simply how to bring it into full play, but how to prevent its bad elements from developing. This act of prevention was indeed more crucial than giving it a free rein. Thus they criticized both the Confucians and the Mohists. According to the ethico-political doctrine of the Mohists, the virtuous and the talented should be the rulers, and hence it is taken for granted that the sovereign ought to be the most virtuous and talented. But in reality, the case turned out to be just the opposite: whoever gets hold of supreme power will become the embodiment of justice, the spokesman and the bearer of virtue and truth. The highest talent as a matter of course dwells only in the sovereign (the Son of Heaven), whom everyone is obliged to keep in agreement with. Unconditional obedience to him—this is where the Mohists' "agreement with the superior (or the sovereign)" would lead. Hence the conclusion is that one should obligingly subjugate oneself to one's superior. This eventually can mean nothing other than sheer despotism by constructing a theory supporting the abolition of the people's democratic rights. It is indeed tragic to think that a doctrine for the people would turn out to be against the people, such as the Mohists' was. Any doctrine for the people should throughout be kept within the bounds of supervision by the people. Once the power of the sovereign surpasses that bound and renders him the overlord of the people, whom it should be the duty of the sovereign to serve, the aforementioned tragic transition (or transformation) is doomed to occur. It

① K. Marx, *Civil War in France* (second draft).

is left to the wisdom of the philosophers to design a mechanism such that the people could not for a moment lose their sovereignty over the sovereign. But the Mohists failed in this.

Besides, there is still another failure in the Mohist theory. In order to remain vigorous and thriving, a society must rely on its social mobility. At bottom the vitality of any society depends on its mobility. If a society were designed, as the Mohists would like, to line up all people in proportion to their alleged virtue and talents—like the heroes in the novel *Outlaws of the Marsh* (*Shui Hu*) each allotted in order to his given seat—and everyone were fixed in his appropriate position in the socio-political network, then the whole society would become immobile, save for an outburst of violence. For who is qualified to evaluate the virtue and talents of others? Virtue is invisible and talent exists in flux. Unless a mechanism is set up which allows social mobility its greatest flexibility, the fixing of one's social position by authority (i.e. "the agreement with the superior" in the Mohist terminology) would certainly lead to social stagnation, or to the violent revolt against that stagnation that so frequently happened under despotism. Following the Mohist teaching, each one would be fixed in his given position (as his virtue and talent allowed) without any possibility of mobility. The Mohists never designed any practical mechanism for social mobility, as though such an issue were out of the question. Gong Zizhen, the famous poet of the early 19th century, once lamented over the then immobile and stagnant society in these words: "It is really a pity that thousands of horses are all dull and mute." But is it not much more lamentable when millions of people all shout with the same voice? It was said that under the despotism of the Roman Empire there were indeed such happenings. Surely this is what was frequently found under the reign of imperial power in the history of China. It must be confessed that the Mohists' theory grossly missed the vital significance of social mobility.

The *philosophes* of 18th century France very naively conceived that human reason afforded the surest guarantee for human progress. Human reason had not yet fully developed because people had not as yet been sufficiently enlightened. Once people had undergone sufficient enlightenment, their fully developed reason would be enough to ensure that they would march on toward a perfect society. Though such a reverie looks too naive to be true, there are still people today who stick to it. At present there are still many people who hold that once the quality of a nation (presumably their knowledge and education) is heightened, all troubles would come to an end. Such a view identifies the full development of human reason (human understanding or speculation) as the sufficient guarantee of the progress of human society. This is no more than an eighteenth century naiveté. The good or evil of one's virtue and the greatness or smallness of one's knowledge are two entirely different kinds of thing. A well-learned man can do more evil than a less learned. One's virtue can by no means be identified directly with his knowledge. Such an automatic equation would be an over-simplified way of thinking. It is with this in mind that philosophers are prompted to design a mechanism which will not allow the members of a society to do evils. And the simplest and most ready-made way for that would be the preaching of divinity, by creating a god who would compel all people to obey through his strict fairness in meting out rewards and punishments. And this is just where the Mohist theorization led to. Mo Zi proclaimed that the will of Heaven exacted people to love one another. And woe to those who would try to go against the will of Heaven. "Those who love and do good to others will be blessed by Heaven; and those who harm and do evil to others will be punished by Heaven",[①] thus taught Mo Zi. In fact, all religions eventually lead to a moral sanction. Religion induces an inner constraint which may guide people towards good and away from evil. Such is the intention of all religious teachings, to which the Mohist school is no exception. Logically as well as practically this is where the Mohists' teaching led.

[IV] The Historical Fate of the Mohist School

The Mohists, as seen above, elaborated a rather systematic ideology, with its subordinate items closely interrelated. Furthermore, they greatly advanced the study of science and logic with a methodology of detailed thinking developed by their use of "the three tests." It is really unfortunate that in the last resort they fell short of stepping onto the road of natural philosophy, and failed to engage in the objective study of the laws of nature and then of the human world. Their final standpoint was still that of the ethico-political doctrine, which was essentially shared with the Confucians. The Mohist theory was logically more or less incoherent and pragmatically only valid for the few. In the foregoing passages we have already remarked that if a theory or an ideal is only valid for the few instead of for the greatest number, then it is not only unworkable in practice but also deeply questionable in its theoretical justification.

The Mohists were allegedly "seeking to suffer day and night the greatest

① *Book of Mo Zi*, "The Will of Heaven."

hardship as their ideal."[①] Such a demeanor, as we can fairly believe, might occur in a few persons in certain historical periods under certain circumstances. But it would be hard for most people in most times and under most circumstances to carry out such ideals. Theoretically there exists this dilemma in it: to make others happy one has to know beforehand in what others' genuine happiness lies. We have already treated this topic in dealing with the prevailing phrase "to take suffering as happiness." When a theory sounds its keynote at too high a pitch and is capable of being realized only by a very few, the outcome is always mere fraud, because it will be out of the reach of most people. Its adherents, once in power, will certainly push their theory with all kinds of political artifices through their strict administration. And their forceful persuasion could only lead to a gospel of uniformity, or rather a fascist rule, compelling everyone to adjust his own way of thinking in order to meet the will of ruler. The result would be to put the cart before the horse. The legality of a sovereignty rests on the support of the people, but now the people would be required to recast their ideas to meet the will of the sovereign by relinquishing their own ideas. Perhaps we should rejoice that the Mohists did not come to power. As is well-known, after the First Emperor of Qin—a thoroughgoing follower of the Legalist school—unified the whole country (221 B.C.), an absolutist rule was implemented which incited an unprecedented peasants' upheaval through the whole country. Later, after Confucianism was honored as the state orthodoxy in the mid-2nd century B.C., the original Confucian spirit was subsequently transubstantiated and turned into a sanctimonious dogma, a perfect fraud. Lu Xun, the greatest writer of our age, sharply criticized it, lamenting that behind their teachings of "benevolence and morality" there could be found nothing else but cannibal lust. This is similar to the 18th century philosopher Dai Zheng's comment that the hypocritical Confucians wanted only "to murder others with their so-called Principles." Had the Mohists really come to power, we would have had no reason to hope for any better. In the last analysis, it is men's existence that determines their consciousness and not their consciousness that determines their existence—here I freely borrow Marx's terminology. Once in power, what governs people's behavior is not their original exhortations, no matter how impressive and high-sounding they might be, but the requirements of their interests and power.

In the opening words of his *The Social Contract*, Rousseau declared, "In this inquiry I shall endeavor always to unite what right sanctions [i.e. the legal justification] with what is prescribed by interest [i.e. the social reality], in order

① *Book of Zhuang Zi*, "The World."

that justice and utility may in no case be divided."① It seems he meant that any doctrine ought to satisfy the following conditions: first, it should be plausible in theory, and second, it should be workable in practice. If a doctrine requires everyone to comply with extraordinary high standard, then it would become unworkable in practice. When it is carried out by force, it leads to sheer tyranny and hypocrisy. But this phenomenon should be studied with due respect for the dissimilarities between China and the West. The various philosophical schools in China, the Confucians and the Mohists included, each espoused a fundamentally ethico-political doctrine which, starting from a moral hypothesis, explicated their theory of politics with the aim to "save the world." They tried their best to reform or to transform the order (or rather the tumult and turbulence) of the existing world. In this sense, their doctrines were professed like the Gospels. Yet a difference between China and the West should be noted. In comparison with the Confucians, who preached "the way leading inwardly to be a saint and outwardly to be a sovereign" (*nei sheng wai wang*), Christianity preached only a spiritual cultivation or an inward morality. The Christian Gospels neither discussed nor desired reform or transformation of social and political reality. Jesus himself taught, "Render unto Caesar the things which are Caesar's; and unto God the things that are God's."② Here a strict line of bifurcation is drawn between the ethical and the political. The Christians as Christians are concerned only with the ethical, but never the political. Jesus had openly said that his kingdom was not of this world, that "the kingdom of God cometh not with observation" for "the kingdom of God is within you."③ Hence Jesus recommended faith, love and hope, but never proposed any political scheme. The kingdom of God is in another world and of another world. In the minds of the Chinese, there has never been and could never be another world except this one. To them, life after death is nothing other than a prolongation of this life in the present world. All ancient Chinese philosophers had designed their own ideal states as what they pursued, and these ideal states were aimed to be realized just in this world and nowhere else. They were without exception paradises on earth, but not in another world. If their doctrine could not be carried out in the present world, then all their theories and ideals would come to nothing. In the Confucian ideal of "inwardly a saint and outwardly a sovereign," the saintliness of a sage is to be realized in a well-governed state. And the Taoist ideal of

① Rousseau, *Social Contract*, bk. 1, trans. G. D. H. Cole.

② Matthew 22:21.

③ Luke 17:20-21.

"return to naiveté" (*fan pu gui zheng*) aimed too at the realization of an earthly paradise, though different in many aspects from that of the Confucians. Christianity paid little attention to the perfection in reality of governance, while almost all Chinese philosophers engaged with the issue of the good running of an ideal government. Above all, their theories were variegated systematizations and compositions of various ethico-political doctrines. So the test of their doctrines is dependent not merely on their logical coherence, but much more on their practical effects.

The Confucians taught both inner cultivation and outward practice. The Mohists placed their emphasis much more on the latter, i.e. reform of the political and social conditions of the existing world. To plunge into the arduous and strenuous effort of reforming political society, one has to be inspired by the spirit of a wholehearted dedication ("taking suffering as the highest ideal"). Is this spiritual dedication really practical for most people? After all, it is quite uncertain how many could be inspired by their ideals and could put it into practice persistently. The Confucian tradition is to teach people "to search where lies the happiness of Confucius and (his foremost disciple) Yan Hui." This happiness is a sort of inner satisfaction and self-sufficiency, no matter how far their social and political ideals have been carried out in real life. For the Mohists, there is no such inner satisfaction or self-sufficiency without the accomplishment of certain outward achievements. But both Confucians and Mohists never for a moment lost their aspiration for worldly endeavor. On the contrary, what Jesus sought was purely an inner perfection. Jesus taught his disciples to find their happiness (or rather blessings) in not worrying about worldly affairs. He preached: "Therefore I say unto you, take no thought for your life, what ye shall eat or what ye shall drink; nor yet for your body, what ye shall put on. Is not the life more than meat, and the body more than raiment?" And further, "behold the fowls of the air: for they sow not, neither do they reap, nor gather into bares; yet your heavenly Father feedeth them. Are ye not much better than they?"[①] Though the Confucians were also looking for a happiness—a purely spiritual or inner happiness—they never forgot their moral obligation to reform the social order in accordance with their designs. The Chinese philosophers have always been too practical to lose sight of the world of daily living. Until the world is well-fed and clothed, they could never give up the hope of realizing their ideal state. They are too practical to entertain any religion or science outside of the sphere of our day-to-day life. The secret why the Chinese

① Matthew 6:25-26.

had neither religion nor science in their history perhaps might be found in their thoroughgoing practicality. Any genuine religion or science requires a disinterestedness in everything practical. It has long been a popular topic of academic interest why China has had neither religion nor science. If the answer is to be found anywhere, it has to be in their practicality. It is primarily this quality which has prevented them from pursuing any thing without practical usage, such as religious fervor or scientific speculation. Or in other words, they are too practical to dedicate themselves to the cause of religious beliefs or scientific truth. Under certain circumstances they could accept the doctrine preached by Hong Xiuquan, the Taiping rebellion leader, not because he was the brother of Jesus as he professed, but because he could provide for their basic subsistence. And later they gave up their support for him, not because they recanted their former pledge of loyalty, but because he could no longer maintain their subsistence. Unless one can grasp this state of mind, one can never hope to reach the core of the Chinese mentality.

The Mohists vowed that they would dedicate all their heart and soul to the cause of social reform without the least concern for their own welfare. Yet could their pledge really change the world into a much better one? In order to launch a real social reform, people should in the first instance follow natural philosophy, that is, try to understand the world objectively without intermingling any tint of personal bias or prejudice. And secondly, one has to ascend a step higher from this, to apply that objective attitude and method to dissect human society and culture in spite of oneself. Until people have got hold of those successive steps of knowledge, they are not qualified to endeavor for social reform. Both the Confucians and the Mohists failed these tests. For instance, both of their views of human nature were biased and insane. Whether we assume an idealistic view of human nature, taking it to be extremely good by nature (such as the Confucians did), or on the contrary assume an opposite view, taking it to be deeply evil by nature (such as the Legalists did)—both are groundless and very partial. Human nature seems to be a medley of various complicated elements. Pascal was of the opinion that "*L'homme n'est ni ange ni bête.*"① But it seems to be more proper to say that "*il est ange et bête.*" In humanity there are elements both of the angels and the beasts. What we ordinarily designate as good or evil in human nature relates only to the social nature of human beings. It should be borne in mind that besides their social nature, there is still their non-social nature. If each member of a society is competing for his own selfish gains at the

① "Man is neither angel nor beast." Pascal, *Pensées*, ed. Brunschvicg, 397.

price of others, then it can hardly be imagined how such a society could survive for long. But if one goes to the other extreme by assuming all men are saints without exception, it would be far from reality. A wholesome and all-round view of human nature is the cardinal prerequisite for any sound ethico-political doctrine. It is a pity that both the Confucians and the Mohists failed in this respect. Most of the ancient philosophical schools in China took it for granted that the so-called good or evil in human nature was something given innately. They never conceded that what was "good" or "evil" in human nature was merely a social product. Apart from one's social life, it would be sheer nonsense to talk about the issue of "good" or "evil" of human nature. What is called "good" or "evil" is defined by the social norm, and hence is an artificial consequence, not an attribute given at birth.

In the main, it may be affirmed that human beings and the whole society composed by them are endowed with a natural intention or pursuing happiness, not unhappiness. All sacrifices are aimed at obtaining some greater happiness. If not, sacrifice for the mere sake of sacrifice would be completely meaningless. We might well imagine the ants and bees by their natural instincts toil and moil year in and year out to give themselves up totally in service of the community, fulfilling the Mohist ideal to the extreme. They might manifest a courage for self-sacrifice greatly elevated beyond what human beings can ever imagine. But can such a community be taken as the model of happiness? Hardly. Can a society in which everyone gives himself up wholeheartedly and completely and thence becomes a mere instrument for the (supposed) happiness of others, be taken as happy? And can everyone in such a society (or at least most people) be regarded as happy? A human being is endowed with his own value and dignity in himself and by himself. If he serves only as a tool for others, then the value of his own life would be nullified. Thus the society's value would be rendered to nothing, for after all the sum total of the happiness of each one is the measure of that of the whole society. Outside of the flesh-and-blood human beings, there can be no happiness of the society in general.

Every theory is the product of a particular historical epoch, but once it comes into being, it becomes independent to the background of its historical context. From then on theories have their own independent existence, just like a new-born baby possesses its own independent life at the moment when it separates itself from its mother's body. Their independent worth rests in their searching for and in their uncovering of some truth, and thus they can move from transience into eternity as an indelible part of history. Archimedes in ancient Greece discovered the law of buoyancy, known in history by his name. That law was, as a matter of course, discovered under certain historical circumstances; but although its given historical circumstances have vanished, the worth of Archimedes' law did not vanish with them. It has persisted down to the present day and will persist to posterity. Any theory once having come into being will possess an eternal worth. Such is the case not only with speculative thinking, but with all cultural treasures, for instance works of art. There is certainly something of immortal worth in any valuable theory. The purpose of our study of the past philosophers is nothing other than the absorption of their valuable features to enrich and inspire our own speculative thinking, so as to raise ourselves from our current state to ever higher levels.

As to the historical destiny of the Confucian and Mohist schools, Han Fei, the past master of the Legalist school, described it in his chapter on "The Predominant Schools of Learnings" (*Xian Xue*).

> The predominant learnings in this world are those of Confucius and of Mo Zi. The supreme representative of the Confucians is Confucius. The supreme representative of the Mohists is Mo Di (Mo Zi). After the death of Confucius there have been the Confucians following Zi Zhang, the Confucians following Zi Si, the Confucians following Yan [Hui], the Confucians following Mencius, the Confucians following Qi Diao, the Confucians following Zhong Liang, the Confucians following Xun Zi and the Confucians following Yue Zheng. After the death of Mo Zi, there have been the Mohists following Xiang Li, the Mohists following Xiang Fu and the Mohists following Deng Ling. Therefore after Confucius and Mo Zi, the Confucians have split up into eight groups and the Mohists have separated into three; their choices were different or opposite, yet all of them professed themselves to be the true Confucians or Mohists. Confucius and Mo Zi will not come back to life again, and who will be qualified to guide the learning of the later generations?①

Here we have an argument full of depth and wisdom. Every theory (as well as every thinker) is always undergoing a process of constant change. History itself is forever in a process of changing and development, and so is every philosophy and theory with it. Never in the history of mankind has there been any philosopher or doctrine that is unchanging and unchangeable forever through eternity. Hence there is and there ought to be no such problem as who or which sect is truly Confucian or Mohist, and who or which is fake. Intellectual culture belongs to the common treasury of all mankind, and everyone, whoever he may be, has the indisputable right to study and to interpret it in his own way.

① *Book of Han Fei Zi*, "The Predominant Schools of Learnings."

And it is natural that one person's understanding is not necessarily the same as another's. Each school inevitably undergoes a process of continuing change, and to argue who or which is the true one and who or which not, would be entirely nonsensical. Is it not that everyone has the inalienable right to worship the truth of God in his own way? Unfortunately, up to the present day there are still those who are interested in arguing who and which is the true one and who and which not. No doubt, there is certainly something more to it than mere stupidity. It involves a dispute over who is the legitimate heir to the founder of an academic dynasty, say that of Confucius or any other. But what should be argued is who comes nearer to truth, not who is the legitimate heir or who not. In the succession of the royal crown, we have witnessed too many feuds in political history. In China's long history of imperial sovereignty, blood lineage reigned over all other factors. So people are accustomed in ideological feuds to uphold the legitimacy of the orthodoxy of learning (*dao tong*, literally, the orthodoxy of ideology). This characteristic mentality reflected itself also in the field of philosophical learning, and surely proved to be an impediment to the vigorous development of Chinese thinking in the pursuit of philosophical truth. We should take care in our study of ancient thought to avoid being restricted by the narrow sectarianism of the ancients.

Incidentally, it may be mentioned that in recent decades the Mohists and other ancient schools have not been studied and emphasized as much as the Confucians. The reason perhaps may be that it is—as Marx would likely say—existence that determines consciousness, and not consciousness that determines existence. It is not because the theories of other schools are of less value than those of the Confucians. It is due to the fact that the reality of social life necessitated it, because after all the Confucian doctrine is much more closely suited to our present life, and hence has much more to do with the reality of life. Indeed, each generation looks back to the past from the standpoint of its present needs. It is in this sense that all past history is our present history and is in service of our present history. The reason for the negligence of the Mohist and other schools is to be found in present history and our present life, rather than in past history and the lives of the ancients.

Chapter Four: The Hundred Schools (1)

The various schools of the pre-imperial period are generally known as the Hundred Schools of Thought, or literally, the Philosophers and Hundred Schools (*Zhu Zi Bai Jia*). In the early 2nd century B.C., Sima Tan, father of the famous historian Sima Qian, drafted a famous treatise, entitled *On the Essentials of the Six Schools*, the Six Schools being the Confucians, the Mohists, the Taoists, the Legalists, the *Yin-Yang* school and the Logicians. In Ban Gu's *History of the Han*, there were enumerated nine or ten schools in these words, "Since the death of Confucius, his disciples separately elaborated their own doctrines, being nine in all: the Confucians, the Taoists, the *Yin-Yang* school, the Legalists, the Logicians, the Mohists, the Diplomatists, the Miscellanists, the Agriculturists." All these schools plus the Novelists make up ten. In the same book, it was asserted, "Of the ten schools there were only nine that were worthy to be held considerable."[①] As a matter of fact, in classical times the academic schools were in no way confined within the scope of the above-mentioned six or nine or ten schools.

This classical time was indeed one of the most brilliant periods in the history of Chinese civilization as well as in the history of mankind at large. It was then that we saw the emergence of the hundred rival schools in China; the age of the Sophists, the great systematic philosophers, the great tragedians and comedians, and the great poets and artists (such as Praxiteles and Phidias) in Greece; and the age of the foundation of Buddhism and Jainism among the ninety-six pagan schools of India. Thus was witnessed the first blossoming of human intelligence.

This historic period lasted from the later Spring and Autumn down to the end of the Warring States, from the 8th century to the 3rd century B.C., roughly corresponding to the period from the

① Ban Gu, *History of Han Dynasty* (*Han Shu*), "The Books of Literary Writing" (*Yi Wen Zhi*).

Epic Age of Greece to the Punic Wars in the Roman World. It was an age of violent political and social turbulence, or what was generally known in Chinese classical literature as an age of "the collapse of the rites and the decadence of music."① Rites and music for the ancients symbolized the rule of the age-old social order. "The collapse of the rites and the decadence of music" meant no less than the end of the older social structure, giving its way to the new social order of a coming new age. In almost all the separate nations that made up China at that time, we may find sources relating to radical political and social changes and upheavals in a similar fashion. The rule of the hereditary nobles was step by step replaced by the newly risen aristocrats, who came to prominence through their wealth and power acquired under the changing circumstances. In consequence, every nation was striving for "reform" so as to become strong and powerful enough to take a position of hegemony among the family of nations. The foremost among them were the Five Overlords (*Ba*) of the Spring and Autumn Period (i.e. Duke Huan of Qi, Duke Wen of Jin, Duke Mu of Qin, Duke Xiang of Song and King Zhuang of Chu) and the Seven Powers (*Xiong*) of the Warring States (i.e. the states of Qin, Chu, Qi, Yan, Han, Zhao and Wei). It was an age of international feuds and rivalries. Due to the urgent pressure caused by this rivalry, there poured forth a stream of different talented figures, each with his innovative doctrine trying to meet the new needs of the age. Thus were laid down the historical conditions for the thriving of the Hundred Schools. Some historians even go so far as to assert that intellectually fertile periods in history are as a rule accompanied by competition between states. The golden age in ancient Greece was stimulated by the rivalry between many thriving city-states. The intellectual achievements and cultural prosperity of Western Europe since the Renaissance have as background the rivalry among the co-existing city-states in Italy, and then that of the different nations in north-western Europe. So also was the case with China during the Spring and Autumn and the Warring States. Once the great unification was accomplished politically, it was followed as a matter of course by the rule of a unique ideology as its indispensable outcome. And the rule of an officially sanctioned ideology presented a severe obstacle for the existence and development of all other non-orthodoxy doctrines and schools. Judging from this aspect, one may fairly assert that the great unification of all China under the Qin Dynasty (late 3rd century B.C.) was an event pernicious and unfortunate for the proper development of China's intellectual culture. The life and vitality of thoughts and thinking lie nowhere else than in

① Ibid., "Life of Liu Xin."

their freedom. And without freedom of thought the life of a culture is destined to fade away. Ever since the great unification of the Qin Dynasty, there no longer existed the brilliant "contention of the Hundred Schools" as seen in classical times.

It is a matter of extreme regret that the sources and documents relating to the ancient philosophers that remain today are far from complete. There was still no printing at that time, and all writings were recorded on bamboo sheets or clothes. This can be contrasted with the papyrus common among the Greeks, which they could conveniently use to put down the words they had spoken. Thus the recorded literature in ancient China as a rule tended to be simple and compact, and its propagation was extremely difficult. Now all we are able to do is guess the theories of the ancients from the fragmentary materials, often taken from the works of their adversaries, and thus not without malicious intentions. This of course creates a serious limitation to our knowledge. The case of the ancient individualist Yang Zhu, whom we are about to discuss, furnishes a good example. There is nothing whatsoever of his teachings handed down to us in any direct or systematic form. What we can use to learn about his doctrine are all indirect quotations from the works of others lambasting him as an undesirable fashion. Many other schools are similar cases, though to different degrees. And as for those whose teachings were lost, or who had never been recorded at all, we must leave them to eternal oblivion.

The philosophical schools we are about to deal with appear to differ from the Confucian and the Mohist in that those two schools were then predominant and equipped with a set of relatively systematic theories, while all other schools appeared to lack such systematic form. At least, we do not now possess enough sources as to affirm that any of them had such. They were mostly sects derived from professional guilds of some sort. For instance, the Agriculturists propounded their theory from the standpoint of agricultural production and the Logicians were mainly concerned with speculation on logical concepts. Among them, we shall select only a few for our review and criticism.

[I] The Agriculturists

We have no direct literature on the Agriculturists, but in the *Book of Mencius* we may find some records about them. Mencius tells us:

> There came from the state of Chu to the state of Teng one Xu Xing, who gave out that he acted according to the works of Shen Nong [an ancient sage-king who

> taught people how to farm]. His disciples, amounting to several tens, all wove clothes of haircloth, and sandals of hemp, and wove mats for a living... It was reported that Xu Xing said: "The prince of Teng is indeed a worthy prince. He has not yet heard, however, the real doctrine of antiquity [Tao, the essential principle]. Now wise and able princes should cultivate the ground, equally and along with his people, and eat the fruit of their labor. They should prepare their own meals, morning and evening, while at the same time they carry on their government. But now, the prince of Teng has his granaries, treasuries and assurances, which is an oppression of the people to nourish himself. How can he be deemed a really worthy prince?"①

It seems that the Agriculturists upheld a thoroughgoing ideal of "eat together, live together and labor together"—an ideal characteristic of the small peasants of that antiquated time. After the above-cited paragraph, Mencius himself made a severe criticism of Xu Xing, set out from the standpoint of the social division of labor. There is no doubt that the division of labor laid down a great principle of social progress; at the same time, however, the ideal of equality should also be held as one of the most fundamental and basic moral values of mankind. There have always been those who uphold the division of labor over the principle of equality, and there have also been those who look at it the either way. Perhaps it is fair to say that both views are one-sided, each sticking to one part of the truth. Social progress requires both division of labor—and hence a certain differentiation of social status—and simultaneously a certain degree of fair play, social justice, or equality within reasonable parameters.

It was the common practice of nearly all philosophical schools in ancient times to assume some legendary figure, usually an ancient sage-king, as their founder and master. And their utopias are to be run by philosopher-kings, just as Plato of ancient Greece preached in his *Republic*. The legendary Shen Nong (literally, "the Miraculous Farmer") was an ancient sage-king. It was he who invented the art of farming, and thus people were enabled to lead settled lives based on agriculture. Maybe he was an ancient leader who contributed much to agriculture and became greatly sanctified by later legends. Even down to only a hundred years ago, when launching the Reform Movement of 1898, Kang Youwei still upheld (as is well known) the holy image of Confucius to support his claim of "reform based on the ancient tradition." It was an age-old tradition that the ancient thinkers would themselves defer to a sage of remote antiquity as their protector. They did not have the least idea that their theories were their own inventions, and nor was there considered to be any wrong-doing in merely

① *Book of Mencius*, "The Duke Wen of Teng," pt. 1, trans. Giles, with alterations by the author.

copying the words of the ancient sages. There was as yet no trace of the modern idea of the right of creation or of private ownership. The great historian Sima Qian in his immortal *Records of the Historian* had directly or indirectly copied and quoted large amounts from other ancient works. No one would think such acts to be plagiarism. So it is often very hard for us to judge which ideas should be attributed to which person. It seems more appropriate to take them simply as we find them in certain books.

The Mohists were a group of artisans, while Xu Xing and his disciples (among whom Chen Xiang was the most well-known) came from farm laborers. Their idea of "the prince and his subjects plowing together" reflected the primitive longing for equality, an equality without social differentiation. This was destined to be unrealizably utopian, because it ran against an essential principle of social progress—the division of labor. Their ideal was nothing more than nostalgia for self-sufficient life in a unicellular society. It was suited only to a primitive social formation and would hinder the progress of society. In the history of China down to the present day, this mental complex has repeatedly troubled the sound development of Chinese society. On the other hand, we should rightly acknowledge that the social division of labor will necessarily lead to social differentiation, a process which by its very nature will tend to be unfair, or in little conformity with the goal of social justice. In the course of this social differentiation, there will certainly emerge those who would exploit all possible advantages to become the privileged, while the majority of the population is doomed to rather miserable conditions. When social injustice is deepened to a critical point, there burst out violent uprisings or revolutions. In any given society at any given time, the total amount of the social wealth is always limited. And how to distribute this limited amount of wealth fairly among its members, so as not to shirk the requirements of rational justice, is of course a very complicated issue. But it goes without saying that no distribution in real life could fully comply with any standard of rational justice. Thus throughout the history of mankind there have always been social contradictions, sometimes hidden and sometimes open, sometimes alleviated and sometimes sharp. The most natural demand of the exploited and the suppressed was an appeal for equality. And the most ready way to achieve a state of equality would be a return to the state of primitive equality, i.e. "to eat together, to live together and to labor together" at the price of giving up the social division of labor and social progress. Equality in this sense would in the last analysis collapse into a fancy or fantasy. This criticism of the ancient Agriculturists would also be valid for all proposed naive reversions to primitive equality, arising throughout the long history of civilization. As there never occurred a scientific revolution and industrial revolution in the history of China as there did in the West, the history of China has never been able to escape the shadow of such a childish reverie, even down to very recent times. Well enough though the slogan "let foods be eaten by all and let clothes be worn by all" may be, you cannot help society develop through the motive of mere egalitarianism alone.

It seems to hold this dilemma: on the one hand you get the disparity of wealth and the polarization of the rich and the poor, while on the other absolute egalitarianism with no initiatives or inventiveness at all. And it looks as though the history of China has forever been groping its way forward in the grip of such an antinomy. The division of labor and social differentiation incite people to compete and to crave for efficiency, but when it leads to a certain degree of inequality, an outburst of social crisis would soon bring back a return to egalitarianism. The longing of the Agriculturists, with Xu Xing and Chen Xiang as their foremost representatives, reflected on the one hand the unhistorical and unrealistic fancy of returning to the good old days of primitive egalitarianism, while on the other a rational protect against the prevailing phenomena of social irrationality.

This current of thought was naturally not confined to the Agriculturists alone, and was shared alike by many other schools. Egalitarianism is eternally the most convenient weapon with which to fight social inequality. Mencius himself criticized the shortcomings of the Agriculturists, but he also uttered a similar protest against the then prevailing social inequality and injustice.

> [Mencius asked:] "Is there any difference in killing a man with a stick and with a sword?" The King [Hui of Liang] said, "There is no difference." "Is there any difference between doing it with a sword and with the rule of a government?" The King said, "There is no difference." Mencius said, "In your kitchen there is fat meat; in your stables there are fat horses. But your people have the look of hunger, on the wilds there are those who have died of famine. This is leading on beasts to devour men. Beasts devour one another, and men hate them for doing so. When a prince, being the parent of his people, administers his government so as to be chargeable with leading on beasts to devour men, where is his parental relation to his people?"①

In the *Spring and Autumn Annals* and the *Huai Nan Zi*, we find also mentioned the ideal of realizing "The Teaching of Shen Nong" as preached and practiced by the Agriculturists. It is only natural, when the society is considerably developed, for it to become impossible to ask all people to live together under the same conditions, leading the same life and laboring in the same

① *Book of Mencius*, "King Hui of Liang," trans. Giles, with alterations by the author.

way. However, it forever leaves its irremovable traces upon later generations. Whenever and wherever there has occurred a social tumult, especially peasants' uprisings, we are sure to find the resurgence of egalitarianism under different guises. Even the emperors were required to undergo a ceremonial plowing at the beginning of every year. The remains of the Agricultural Altar (Xian Nong Tan) in Beijing today still signify the remnant of the past reverie. Yet, any "prince plowing with his subjects together" is doomed impractical. Any ideal rationale has to accommodate itself to the then existing conditions and possibilities. The development of any society necessarily requires labor, and labor of different kinds. If a society remains in a state of unicellular self-sufficiency, there could never emerge the pluralism required for social progress. The ideas of the small peasants always leant toward self-sufficiency, conservatism and nostalgia for the remote past. While being ill-treated beyond forbearance, they would instinctively long for those good old days described by an old song,

> Go to labor when the sun rises,
> Go to rest when the sun falls,
> What then would the imperial power have to do with me?

But the plain, cruel fact remained: with social progress the imperial power, or the political and social coercion, would inevitably interfere upon the natural liberty of one's life. Thus, fulfilling the naive desire for a life of primitive liberty and equality, while paying due attention to the complicated yet unavoidable demands of social progress (such as the social differentiation and inequality necessitated by competition and selection), becomes the key goal of all political wisdom since antiquity. We possess no material whatsoever to let us know how this problem was dealt with by the Agriculturists. But it is the Agriculturists who first presented this issue vividly. And their view, like the Taoist emphasis of "the return to nature," reflected the bitter protest against the social injustices brought about by ever-complicated social life. We may consider any and every doctrine in respect of either what problems it proposed or what solutions it devised. The ideological contribution of the Agriculturists lay in the problems they articulated, i.e. those of social injustice, but not in the solution they offered.

[II] The Strategists

The Strategists were brought to the fore by the human lives and problems of their time. In ceaseless wars many principalities bitterly struggled for their existence, always with the consequences of "slaughtering the whole city" and "slaughtering the whole field." Thus an author lamented: "There was never a just war in the age of Spring and Autumn." Incessant warfare led people to study the principles and arts of war. Then came forth the Strategists, the most well-known to later generations being Sun Wu, Wu Qi and Sun Bin. There was also Sima Rangju, who according to legend left his work *The Strategy of Sima* to the world, but the version we now have is a fabrication of a much later date. The genuine work, if any there was, has been long lost.

The earliest and also the most eminent among the Strategists is Sun Wu. Of his life and activities, there are records in Sima Qian's *Records of the Historian*. It was said that Sun came from his native country Qi (now Shandong Province) in the early 5th century B.C., and left thirteen treatises on strategy. A widely circulated story describes him as follows. When He Lu, king of the State of Wu, ordered him to give military training to the 180 servant girls in his harem, he nominated two of the king's favorites as the leaders of the battalions and then beheaded them, using the excuse that they had disobeyed his order. This act terrified all the female soldiers, so that they dared not obey him. And Sun was thus known as a famous general ever since.

The civilized region of ancient China extended roughly to the area of the middle and lower valley of the Yellow River. During the period of Spring and Autumn it gradually expanded further to the valley of the Yangtze River. The newly risen states in the middle part of the Yangtze River were Chu, with its capital at Ying (now Hubei), and Wu in the lower part, with its capital at Wu (now Jiangsu). It was then that the well-known statesman and general Wu Yuan (or Wu Zixu) was in charge of the administration of the state of Wu, and successfully made Wu a new power among the family of nations. It was also he who singled out Sun to lead an army in an expedition with him "far into the west, defeated the state of Chu, captured its capital Ying, menacing the states Qi and Lu to the north, and enjoyed a splendor illustriously among the principalities."[①]

The Art of War by Sun Wu has 13 chapters, dealing mainly with the topic of strategy in the first six chapters and with tactics in the later seven. The whole book numbers about 5,000 words (roughly equivalent to the total of the *Book of Lao Zi*), and the content is extremely abundant and revealing, making it deservedly comparable with the *Book of Lao Zi*. In the 18th century the famous scholar Sun Xingyan compiled an anthology of the annotations on Sun Wu. In modern

① Sima Qian, *Records of the Historian*, vol. 65 "Life of Wu Qi," and vol. 66 "Life of Wu Zixu."

times the famous Strategist Jiang Baili commentated on Sun's book from the viewpoint of modern military science. For two thousand and more years Sun's work was generally recognized as the foremost classic in military science, and its influence was world-wide. What stands out in Sun's book is the fact that it starts from the angle of war but goes on to formulate the philosophical principles of change, thus in the most compact form producing an exposition of great philosophical depth.

> Military action is of vital importance to the state. It is a matter of life and death, a road either to safety or to ruin. Hence it is a subject of inquiry which can on no account be neglected.①

Thus runs the opening sentences of Sun's *Art of War*. It is the age-old tradition in ancient China that "the only things of vital importance to the state are the offering of sacrifice and the launching of war." Sacrifice in ancient times had a far deeper meaning than in later ages. It was not just a ceremony, but a symbolic embodiment of the whole social order, political power-structure and ideology. Therefore what is "of vital importance to the state" is nothing other than domestic governance and foreign war. The fundamental principles of war were epitomized by Sun under the following five items: "(1) Tao, (2) Heaven, (3) Earth, (4) the Commander, (5) Method and Discipline."② Here the implication of "Tao" made by Sun is quite different from that of both the Confucians and the Taoists. It denotes neither the principle (substance) of nature in the Taoists' sense, nor an ethical ideal in the Confucian sense. It signifies statecraft with special emphasis on morale. This is explicitly seen in his definition of Tao as follows:

> The Tao③ causes the people to be in complete accord with their sovereign, so that they will follow him in life and death without the slightest disloyalty.

For Sun, Tao signifies the perfect unity between the will of the sovereign and that of his people. Or, in other terms, military action is the extension of politics, provided the politics is good. The basis of military action always dwells in politics. Without good politics as its foundation, military action can achieve nothing. "Heaven" and "earth" in his terminology meant various natural and material conditions which constitute crucial factors influencing the outcome of the war. To disregard all objective conditions and plunge headlong into battle merely because of personal desire could result in complete failure. Next to external conditions come the subjective factors, in the role of the "commander" and the

---

① Sun Wu, *The Art of War*, chap. 1, trans. Giles, with alterations by the author.

② Ibid.

③ Ibid., "The Moral Law."

"method and discipline." It is the commander who has the talent for waging the campaign and enacting strict order and regulation. Sun asserts five prerequisites for being a good commander: "the virtues of wisdom, sincerity, benevolence, courage and strictness."① And he elaborates the fifth component, "By method and discipline are to be understood the marshalling of the army in its proper subdivisions, the gradations of rank among the officers, the maintenance of roads by which supplies may reach the army, and the control of military expenditure," ② or in other words, the staff and its personnel, transportation and logistics. War embodies the relationship of man to the external world in its most concentrated and intimate form. The theory formulated through the military reflections of Sun's *Art of War* is—in a certain sense—a profound philosophical treatment of how man and world relate to one another.

Another well-known Strategist is Wu Qi, who flourished in the late 5th century B.C., somewhat later than Sun Wu. He had assumed a governorship in the state of Wei, and then came to the state of Chu where he was entrusted with carrying out the Reform. This "Reform" was a common phenomenon across nearly all principalities during the transition from the Spring and Autumn to the Warring States period (5th-3rd centuries B.C.) The aim of these reforms was to remold the age-old political and social structure to meet the new conditions, both internal and external to the state. The distribution of power and wealth at any given time can never be fair and rational, and hence never stable. Under any given circumstances, the total population and wealth of any society are of particular (and hence limited) amounts, but the desire for power and wealth is always boundless. Consequently, there are always those who are more privileged and possess more power and wealth than others; meanwhile the underprivileged majority are always endeavoring to change or reform the present mode of distribution of power and wealth, and first of all to strip the ruling class of their privileges. Therefore, when a reform is launched, it is usually destined to be opposed by those representing the old order and institutions. This is the reason why many of the reforms in the history of China ended in failure. Such was the fate of Wu Qi, whose reform was met with bitter opposition from the old nobles of Chu who finally succeeded in murdering him. It seems as though the greatest art in launching a reform depends on how to weaken the opposition of the old privileged class. And perhaps the most realistic and practical way would be to let the old nobility to get enough profits from the process of reform, and at such

① Ibid., chap. 1.

② Ibid.

a price bribe them over to the side supporting reform. Of course, there have also been occasions of revolutionary eruption. But the problem here is always how to prevent the new rulers being transubstantiated into the new privileged class, and prevent the masses from becoming the new oppressors. And there have been too many antecedents of such transformation. Maybe there is no short-cut, and hence history itself is full of contradictions and conflicts. What Sun Wu asserted in his *Art of War*—"A skillful commander subdues the enemy's troops without any fighting"①—should inform our observation of the revolutions in history.

The writing of Wu Qi was known as the *Book of Master Wu* (Wu Zi). In Sima Qian's *Records of the Historian* we may find some record of him. A widely circulated story told that he had slain his wife. It was also said that he followed the great Confucian scholar Zeng Zi, and we find in him such Confucian moralizing as "what pays is virtue, not a fortress," and "instruct the people with rites, encourage the people with righteousness." The *Book of Master Wu* we have today consists of six chapters, very probably the result of revision by later generations.

Still another prominent Strategist was Sun Bin, a little later than Wu Qi. Sun Bin became famous for his triumphs in two decisive battles (the Battle of Kuei Ling, 353 B.C., and the Battle of Ma Ling, 341 B.C.) against the state of Wei, and thereby led many principalities to pay tribute to King Wei of Qi. "By these feats this name Sun Bin circulated from mouth to mouth all the world over, and his strategy was widely studied,"② wrote Sima Qian in his *Records of the Historian*. Sun Bin's *Art of War* was listed in the catalogue in the *History of Han*, but was not mentioned in the *History of Sui*—which shows that the book was already lost by the early years of the Tang Dynasty (early 7th century). Due to the ambiguity of its authorship, there was some confusion over his writings, and people even came to suspect that Sun Wu and Sun Bin were but one person designated by different names. Not until the 1970s, when there were unearthed two books in Mt. Yinque in Linye (Shandong Province) under the respective names *Sun Zi's (*Sun Wu's*) Art of War* and *Sun Bin's Art of War*, did people come to realize their separate authorship. Following the changing historical conditions, cities had begun to show unprecedented importance in political and social life. So Sun Bin paid more attention to the significance of direct attacks upon city sites and of camp-formation than did Sun Wu. Sun Bin upheld the principle of active attack, taking attack as the last method of defense, or as he

① Ibid., chap. 3.

② Sima Qian, Op.cit, vol. 65 "Life of Sun Zi and Wu Qi."

put it, "One has always to take the offensive, not the defensive."

Among the Strategists, another name that should be mentioned here is Sima Rangju. According to the record of Sima Qian's *Records of the Historian*: "King Wei of Qi while making use of his armies to enforce his hegemony, followed the method of Sima Rangju on a grand scale, and thus brought his principalities to pay homage to him. The King ordered his officials to record the Sima strategy of antiquity and to include Rangju in it, and entitled it the *Art of War of Sima Rangju*."① This paragraph is indeed rather ambiguous; but we know nothing more of this historical figure Sima Rangju's writing.

[III] The Logicians: Hui Shi

All theories may be considered from two aspects. On the one hand, they are the products of certain historical conditions; while on the other, once they have come into being, they are endowed with an independence in themselves. From then on they cease to be conditioned by the concrete circumstances of particular times and places and become objects of the critique of pure reason. When we take any theory into consideration, it goes without saying that we should investigate the concrete historical background under which it is born. Yet at the same time we should equally place enough emphasis on its intrinsic value, independent of the social and material conditions under which it was made possible. That is to say, it should be judged by its own merits with no attention to its background whatsoever. In evaluating the theories of the philosophers of bygone days, it is appropriate for us to lay more emphasis on their theoretical value, rather than on the historical conditions under which they were worked out. Let us cite a famous story in history for example. According to legend, Archimedes was once ordered to investigate whether the royal crown was made of real gold, but on the condition that the crown should not be broken in any way. This led him into meditation. One day he was taking a bath, and discovered to his surprise that his body floated up to the surface of the water. Suddenly he was enlightened, crying "I found it!" What he found was the famous principle known by his name. This principle, like all others, was certainly brought to light under certain given historical circumstances (here, the royal order, his bathing, etc.). Yet as soon as it was given birth, it obtained its own right of existence, independent of any circumstance there then might be. We understand it and

① Ibid., vol. 64 "Life of Sima Rangju."

evaluate it merely by the theory itself (*per se*), there being no necessity whatsoever to consider its relationship with its surroundings, such as how and why the king ordered him to inspect the crown or whether he found the secret in his bathing, etc. Viewed from this angle, it seems that most scholars engaging in research of the Logicians have not yet come to a just evaluation of them.

Such is the way we should look at all past theories, whether in the field of natural science or of humanities. It may be fairly asserted that if there are valuable elements in a theory, then once they have come into being, they enter instantly into eternity. The historical background helped to give birth to the theory, but is never able to refute it or to change it. It is no longer limited to the concrete conditions of a certain time and place and circumstance. One might discover a certain principle (say the Archimedes' principle) under a given circumstance, but thenceforth this principle exists in itself and is known and valued by itself, being completely divorced from its historical environment. We ought to look at any theory historically, yet we ought not to look at it merely in the light of history. People often talk about combining theory and practice, yet the idea of such a union itself presupposes the very distinction of theory and practice as its indispensable premise, without which the combination would be meaningless. Just because the two are not one and the same thing, so a combination is required; otherwise there would be no combination to be done. The marriage of the two presupposes their separation, differentiation and opposition, or in other words the two are not one and the same. What makes a theory what it is, is the fact that it is no mere reality. If it is simply one with reality, it is no longer a theory. In the same way, we ought not to turn our eyesight only to the theory's dependence on certain historical conditions, while neglecting the intrinsic value of the theory itself. In studying the ideas of the philosophers in history, both their historical and their intellectual content are equally worthy of examination.

Traditionally a mode of thinking has been universally employed in China, that is, when people evaluate the theories of their predecessors, it is often their habit to start from a presupposed moral criterion, or to look at the issue from an ethical viewpoint rather than from a purely analytical one. It is this bias which in former days led people to brand the pre-Qin Logicians as practicing pure sophistry. This approach is a common way of thinking, but certainly not a correct one, because it presupposes its conclusion and then argues for its justification. Its conclusion is not drawn from its argument, but its argument is led by its predetermined conclusion. Roughly speaking, the difference here resembles that between the mode of thinking employed in hermeneutics and that in science. In the history of mankind, to discard any ethical premise and to go immediately into the logical reasoning of things and facts themselves always signifies a great step in the progress of intellectual culture. The scene of the Scientific Revolution in modern history offered a most salient example. The great intellectual contribution of the Logicians—also their fundamental difference from the traditional Confucians—lay just in the fact that they abruptly threw away all untested ethical suppositions or beliefs. In some ways there was great resemblance between them and the Sophists of ancient Greece, even in the very words of some of their respective statements. If when reading the writings of the Logicians we compare them with the Greek Sophists, we are paid with many revealing discoveries.

If the Logicians indulged in mere sophistry, as some were prone to think, we could hardly explain why the Logicians' doctrines and arguments became so prevalent as to assume an influential current of thought at that time. Owing to the scarcity of existent materials, we are unable to restore the truth of the Logicians in their original state. Yet we have grounds to assume that the doctrine of the Logicians was closely related with the extremely complex and sharp struggles in political life at that time. Behind the abstract speculations were the cruel political realities which concerned the life and death of either the one faction or the other. Unfortunately, modern researchers including Prof. Feng Youlan and Prof. Hou Wailu (both being foremost scholars in the field of Chinese intellectual history) made no penetrating studies from this angle. In the main, their studies were confined to the explanation of the logical implications of the Logicians, i.e. what are the logical meanings of their apparently highly sophisticated propositions. But they missed the exposition of the political and historical background which made possible the emergence of the Logicians' doctrine and rendered it a strong current of thought. Why was it that disagreements over such issues as "a white horse is not a horse" became a theme of great debate even in the royal court? Socrates, as we would well remember, was regarded by the Greeks as a Sophist, though indeed he was not. But that did not matter, because he had something in common with the Sophists. Both he and the Sophists burst out of the confines of the traditional mode of thinking and hence constituted a dangerous intellectual menace to the orthodoxy of the political and social order. The Athenian authority sentenced Socrates to the death penalty, accusing him of misleading the minds of the young people by claiming that what was on heaven was on earth and vice versa. Both Socrates and the Sophists formed in common an impetus to the ruling order of that time and thus became intolerable to the ruling classes. In a similar way, besides their pure intellectual aspect, we should also pay enough attention to the political and social role of the Logicians. Unclear about the concrete background though we are, it is still clear that this was an age of violent turbulence, and that the great social and political upheavals would of necessity induce a great ideological upheaval. It seems clear that the Logicians launched their attacks on the traditional system of ideology with their non-orthodox and non-ethical weapons of logical and linguistic analysis. In modern times when the Chinese "*philosophes*" of the late 19th century launched another vehement attack on traditional ideology, they were also trying to break it through the introduction of new scientific ideas, such as the theory of evolution borrowed from Darwin and Huxley. Just because an attack launched from this angle is as a rule the easiest and most convenient way, the new logic of thinking is always brought to the fore in the intellectual battlefield.

What the Logicians were concerned with was "the name" (ming), or concept. All our knowledge is to be expressed in the form of concepts, and all our thinking is to be carried on in the form of concepts. If we say "man is an animal," here what is expressed by the term "man" is only a concept, and so also with the term "animal." In the sensory world we come into contact with a great variety of concrete people, but none of them can ever be identical with the concept of "man." Such is true also for the concept of "animal." All our concepts, like "man" or "animal" and "2" or "*x*," have no existence in the empirical, external world in which we live. They exist merely in our thinking. Yet, without concepts, we are unable to think at all. For instance, except in conceptual form, we are unable to think that "man is an animal," or "$2 + 2 = 4$," or "If $a > b$ and $b > c$, then $a > c$." Concepts have no material existence, nor are they the attributes of material things. Things in the external world themselves can never figure in such reasoning; it is our thinking that is responsible. We may perceive two eggs or two stones in the material world, but there is never such a thing as "2" (or "*x*") in it. Knowledge implies a process of transition and transformation, i.e. from material existence and then transformed into our thinking. This discovery should be attributed to the Logicians, who among all philosophical schools in ancient China offered the only definite elaboration of such a distinction. It is the Logicians who dealt formally with the relationship between "ming" (the name, or concept) and "shi" (reality, or material existence). We can make the comparison: all other schools dealt with the objective world, and it was only the Logicians who began to think about thinking. This is the unique contribution of the Logicians, which ought to be regarded as a great advance in the philosophy of cognition.

It has been an almost universal opinion that the Chinese mind is not skilled at logical thought. This is really a misunderstanding. Owing to historical reasons, this or that academic discipline or mode of thinking may not have flourished in the cultural and intellectual tradition of this or that people. But this does not in any sense mean that a people is predestined to be poor at an academic discipline or mode of thinking. For most of history there was no geometry in China. Geometry was introduced into China from the West at the turn of the 16th and 17th centuries. But once the Chinese learned geometry, they studied it quite skillfully. There is no reason to say that geometry is the knowledge of the Westerners (and not of the Chinese), or even of the Greeks or still earlier the Egyptians, though geometry originated in Greece and Egypt. Geometry is not an exclusive inborn privilege of the Greeks or Egyptians, just as the method of logical thinking does not exclusively belong to the Westerners as a whole. Where and when it originated and developed is only an accidental historical fact, the people's intellectual qualities being entirely irrelevant. From this aspect of consideration, the contributions of the Logicians and their historical fate are especially worthy of notice.

It is natural that the Logicians flourished in the early years of the Warring States Period, because then the intellectual field required a new start, which manifested itself in an outburst on the logical front. The foremost representatives of the Logicians, so far as can be known to us, were Hui Shi and Gongsun Long. But their teachings are preserved down to us only through second-hand narration in the works of others.

Hui Shi (ca. 370-318 B.C.), a native of the State of Song (now the border of Henan and Jiangsu), was roughly contemporaneous with the Confucian sage Mencius. According to Zhuang Zi, "Hui Shi learned widely, his books having filled up his five carts",[①] and hence in later generations when someone is praised for his broad learning, he is said to be "as learned as the five carts." Of him, the *Book of Zhuang Zi* recorded a story as follows:

> There was a wonderful man named Huang Liao from the south, who asked the reasons why the sky and the earth do not fall and collapse and why there are winds, rain and thunder. To this Hui Shi replied without a moment of hesitation or consideration and explained everything in full. He explained unceasingly and multifariously.[②]

This profound interest in searching the mysteries of nature reflected another phase of ancient philosophy in China which had taken natural philosophy for its inspiration. This is especially noteworthy when we keep in mind that China's

① *Book of Zhuang Zi*, "The World" (*Tian Xia*).

② Ibid.

ancient philosophy had taken a road quite different to that of the ancient Greeks, and that the road it chose was traditionally an ethico-politico-centric one, instead of that of natural philosophy. Generally speaking, traditional philosophy in China showed little interest in pure natural philosophy and pure speculation.

The Logicians started their thinking by way of logical and linguistic analysis. Philosophical problems were for the first time baptized by logic, with the purpose of clarifying their linguistic meanings. In ancient Greece, Zeno of Elea (ca. 404-430 B.C.) uttered a famous proposition, "The flying arrow does not move." He also thought that if Achilles and the turtle competed in a race, Achilles could never outstrip the turtle. Hui Shi the Logician too had advanced the same proposition. Their intentions were the same, i.e. to argue for the impossibility of motion through the same use of logic. By such logical analysis, the Logician endeavored to show that the problems customarily supposed by the age-old tradition were indeed not true problems, or not what the true problems ought to be. Many traditional problems, such as those propounded by the Confucians and the Mohists, were in reality only the expositions and affirmations of their own beliefs, and not the conclusion of speculative analysis. Their beliefs were taken for granted without any discerning reflection. It is here that the Logicians had taken a decisive step forward in their speculations. Their works have had a positive bearing on the development of our theoretical thinking. Yet their works—at least in so far as we have access to them—were so entangled in the discernment of the "name" and "reality" that they were led far from any formal inquiry into what people were most concerned with, i.e. the value, meaning and purpose of human life. Yet the problem of the vocation of man was the very center of all other schools' concerns. At a time when all other schools were trying hard to give out definite and detailed answers about the meaning of life, the Logicians kept themselves away and aloof from it. On this cardinal issue, the Logicians neglected the main current of thought of the age. Perhaps this is one of the reasons which led the Logician school finally into oblivion. What helped a school become widely propagated and a "prominent learning" (*xian xue*) is its capacity to meet the urgent requirements of society. If it cannot meet the social requirements, it will be stripped of the most important material condition which would make its propagation possible. Admittedly, as we have already stated above, the wide propagation of the Logician school certainly must have had some grounding in social reality. But unfortunately what these social grounds were like, we are not now in a position to identify.

Today, all our knowledge about the Logicians is drawn from the records of Zhuang Zi, who was an intimate friend of Hui Shi and held a keen appreciation for his talent. Zhuang Zi deeply lamented that Hui Shi failed to employ his wisdom on problems of a much higher level. Zhuang Zi gave a description of Hui Shi.

> Viewed from the Way of Heaven and Earth, the ability of Hui Shi may be comparable merely to the toils of a fly or a mosquito. What can it do with the things in the world?
>
> Hui Shi did not content himself with this. He never tired of pursuing all things of the external world and at last became known for his sophistry *par excellence*. What a pity! The talent of Hui Shi wandered randomly here and there and got nowhere. It traced all external things without ever returning to himself. This is simply like following the sound by its echo, or to make a race between a figure and its shadow. How miserable![①]

This commentary is full of Zhuang's appreciation, mourning and regret in memory of Hui Shi. To discuss reason by pure reason, to discuss concepts by pure conception without any relevance to the essence of the world and of life, to indulge merely in the technical operation of logic and linguistics—this would be just what Zhuang Zi lamented as "a race between the figure and its shadow," indeed something most lamentable. All logical and syntactic analysis should serve simply as a bridge to philosophy or to the ultimate truth of the world and of human life. Hence a man in pursuit of philosophical truth should, to use the words of Zhuang Zi, "forget the hook once the fish have been caught," and "forget his words when the meaning is grasped"—but not "forget the fish once the hook has been taken," nor "forget the meaning while the words are grasped." All knowledge and concepts, all abstraction and reasoning are but means leading to the truth, and only the value of life is worthy of being assumed as an end. One should not be entangled in means while forgetting the end—thus Zhuang Zi criticized the Logicians. I wonder if this criticism would offer some guidance in our evaluation of the present-day analytic school of philosophy.

It may fairly be said that philosophy is practiced for two reasons: knowledge and wisdom. Knowledge is not mere wisdom, nor wisdom mere knowledge. Knowledge consists in what we know about the world, while wisdom in how we accommodate ourselves to the world. Etymologically speaking, philosophy is but the love (philo) of wisdom (sophia). In the 17th century, when the Western missionaries came to China, the term "philosophy" was then literally translated as "the love of wisdom" (*ai zhi xue*). There is no doubt that wisdom is closely related to knowledge, but knowledge can not simply be identified with nor lead automatically to wisdom. What knowledge seeks is the mystery of the world; what wisdom seeks is the perfection of life.

① Ibid.

For the philosophers in ancient China it seemed that only a virtuous life could lead to perfect living, while possession of mere knowledge could never lead to it. That is why most of them rejected intellectualism, i.e. the pursuit of pure knowledge, but chose decidedly the search for the wisdom of life. They never pursued knowledge for knowledge's sake, as Dr. Faust did when he sold his soul to the devil in exchange for the knowledge of the world. For Zhuang Zi, genuine wisdom lies in nothing else than the comprehension and grasping of the Tao (i.e. the wisdom of life). Yet Hui Shi was content in confining himself within the limit of logical analysis, and thus failed to attain the heights of wisdom, i.e. the highest state of life. Even so clever a man as Hui Shi could get lost regarding the right way of life, to the great lament of Zhuang Zi. The Chan Buddhists were fond of criticizing others as "suffering death under the burden of words," meaning that people were entangled with mere words and failed to catch the higher reality behind and above the words. Zhuang Zi's criticism of Hui Shi was closely akin to Rousseau's criticism of Voltaire. Rousseau spoke regretfully of the fact that Voltaire, endowed as he was with all his unparalleled gifts, was puzzled amidst social affairs and had no perception of a higher level of intellectual creativity. Zhuang Zi was so fascinated by Hui Shi's talent that he sighed mournfully, "Since his (Hui Shi's) death, can I find no other to ask, can I find no other to converse with?"[①]

At any rate, the Logicians produced a great contribution, unprecedented and unparalleled in the intellectual history of China. Zhuang Zi left us ten propositions of Hui Shi, though we are now incapable of finding out Hui Shi's own argumentations and expositions of them. All explanations given by the later generations are but conjectures. The ten propositions of Hui Shi are as follows:

> ① The greatest has nothing outside of it and is called the Great Unit. The smallest has nothing inside of it, and is called the Small Unit.

By "the greatest" is apparently meant that thing which there is nothing greater than, and hence also which there is nothing outside of. If there is something outside of it, there is something beyond it, and it would not be the greatest. In the same way, by "the smallest" is meant the thing which there is nothing smaller than, and hence which there is nothing inside of. Otherwise, it would not be qualified to be called the smallest. This is exactly the notion of the infinite and of the infinitesimal in modern mathematics. What is infinite (or infinitesimal) is that which is greater (or smaller) than anything we could suppose.

① *Book of Zhuang Zi*, "Xu Wu Gui."

② That which has no thickness cannot be increased in thickness, yet in extent it may cover a thousand miles.

This proposition may be explained thus: a plane (in the geometric sense) has no thickness, but its area may extend over a tremendous width. Mathematically, the notion of a plane is different from that of volume.

③ The sky is as low as the earth; mountains are on the same level as marshes.

This proposition seems to show that in the light of the infinite or infinitude, the differences of all things (such as those between the sky and the earth or the mountain and marsh) are equivalent or may be equated to nothing. Or in mathematical terms, $1/\infty$ and $1{,}000/\infty$ are equivalent.

④ The sun at its zenith is simultaneously in its decline; the creature being born is simultaneously dying.

This is to say: when the sun rises to its peak height, it begins to decline; the moment when a creature is born is the beginning of its dying. It implies that the process of things' emergence and development is simultaneously the march to their end. A baby from its very birth is every moment approaching its death. Here Hui Shi expresses his world-view that all things are transitory and momentary, that nothing in the world is eternal or stable.

⑤ A great similarity differs from a little similarity. This is called the little similarity and difference. All things are similar, yet different. This is called the great similarity and difference.

⑥ The south has no limit and yet has a limit.

⑦ I go to the state of Yue (now the northern part of Zhejiang) today and arrived there already sometime ago.

We cannot be very certain about the definite meaning of these three statements. However, based on the foregoing principles, it may be conjectured that by these three statements Hui Shi intended to show: all differences and differentiations viewed from the standpoint of infinity or infinitude are non-existent and hence meaningless.

⑧ Linked rings can be separated.

Two inter-linked rings are endless circles and hence seem inseparable. A famous story ran thus: "King Zhao of Qin sent his envoy to present linked jade rings to the Queen of Qi, saying, 'As there are many intelligent people in the State of Qi, can they manage to separate these connected rings?' The queen showed them to her court, and no one knew how to separate the rings. The Queen fetched a hammer and smashed then, then replying to the envoy of Qin: 'Thus they are separated.'"[①] Maybe the intention of this statement is to

① *Zhan Guo Ce* (Statecraft of the Warring States).

show that although a problem may seem insoluble, on a higher level of scrutiny it is perfectly soluble. Considered with the previous statements, it looks very likely that Hui Shi was trying to contemplate the world of our daily life from a higher level. In that other world of a higher level, the problems of this world may vanish or be turned into problems of another kind. It is noteworthy that most Chinese philosophers since antiquity have insisted that there was only one world, i.e. the world of our normal everyday living. Only the Logicians insisted there were two worlds, the world of appearance and the world of reality. The latter is behind the former and is more real than it. All the apparent contradictions in the world of appearance are solved or even rendered non-existent in the world of reality.

⑨ I know the center of the world; it is north of Yan and south of Yue.

The State of Yan was in the north of China and the State of Yue in the south. In accordance with common sense the center of the world should be somewhere between the north and south, i.e. to the south of Yan and to the north of Yue. But from a higher point of view, say from the astronomical, there is no center whatsoever, or the center may be placed everywhere or anywhere. Anywhere may be validated as the center of the world.

⑩ Love all things universally; and the universe will be one.

This concluding proposition finally captured the essence of his philosophy, though permeated with a strong mystic hue. From the ten propositions enumerated above, Hui Shi had aimed at transforming the world of daily life into a world more real and of a higher level by means of a process of logical manipulation. This purported world of reality would be, so he assumed, a world of infinity and eternity containing no contradiction whatsoever, where all things are embraced by infinity. In this way, he reached his conclusion: if you "love all things universally" by melting yourself into the infinite universe, then the whole universe would be one with you. All religious followers and all mystics long for the blessed state of "communion of Heaven and Man" (*Tian Ren He Yi*, literally, "Heaven and Man in one"), wherein the ego completely vanishes into eternity. This goal may perhaps be the same wisdom which Hui Shi pursued in his philosophy.

[IV] The Logicians: Gong-sun Long

Another prominent representative of the Logicians is Gongsun Long (ca. 370-318 B.C.), about half a century later than Hui Shi. During the hectic rivalry for hegemony in the Warring States Period, each needed the service of the talented intellectuals as experts in politics, or to form a sort of "brain trust." Most of them were not only good at drawing up plans for statecraft, but were often excellent diplomats and orators. They had to master a breadth of knowledge and incisive eloquence. Among them came an outstanding sophist from the State of Zhao, Gongsun Long by name. It was said he had persuaded King Zhao of Yan to cease his attack on the State of Zhao, and had been a long-time guest in the court of Prince Ping Yuan, one of the four famous court patrons in the Warring States Period. Being a guest meant he was a member of his group of advisors. Customarily, the Logician school was divided into two groups: the group for "the union of similarity and difference" and that for "the separation of hardness and whiteness," the former group represented by Hui Shi and the latter by Gongsun Long. The former held the view that "all things are similar and different," i.e. all things have their similarities and at the same time their differences. Yet ultimately their differences are relative and temporary, while their identity is absolute and eternal. Therefore we ought to transcend their differences in order to grasp their eternal identity. Conversely, the group for the "separation of hardness and whiteness" was known for their contention that "a white horse is not a horse," and hence that the differences of all things are absolute and eternal. We should take care to distinguish the various constituent aspects of everything. Only these particularities are real and eternal. Perhaps we can say that both went too far in making one single aspect absolute, for all things without exception incorporate "unity in variety" as well as "variety in unity," i.e. all things consist of different qualities, yet all differences are united in an entity. But one group upheld identity and disregarded variety, while the other upheld variety and disregarded unity. Thus both in their logical reasoning committed the error of one-sidedness. Yet within their one-sided reasoning both made great contributions to the history of thought in ancient China. What follows is a short introduction to Gongsun Long's theory.

For Gongsun Long, the key step in right thinking is the distinction of concept and existence, or in other terms, the separation of understanding and sensation and of theory and practice. Only by recognizing that our concepts have no material existence are we enabled to engage in philosophical thinking. Thinking is by itself a process of abstraction. And what it deals with is only our ideas or concepts of things, not any concrete material object in itself. At this step, Gongsun Long may be said to have made a great leap in his unprecedented discovery of the mystery of thinking. Before him, people had taken for granted that the things involved in people's thinking were the material objects themselves, without considering that their thinking deals only with the ideas in their minds. It was he who first proclaimed that what people thought were not the material objects in the outside world but the ideas or concepts of the material objects, which exist nowhere else than within our own minds. If we fail to recognize that our ideas are separate from objective reality, we cannot account for the problem of the integration of theory with practice. It is just because theory (which necessarily has a form made up of concepts) is not and cannot be identified with objective reality that there exists the problem of how to unite or integrate them. It is only when the history of human thought has reached this realization that human thinking may be said to have attained a self-consciousness, and to have reached the height of philosophical thinking. In the last analysis, thinking is carried on by means of and in the form of concepts alone. Gong-sun Long gave a penetrating exposition of this viewpoint in his well-known "theory of the white horse."

This theory of his may be summed up in a rather simple proposition: "a white horse is not a horse." Gongsun Long explained thus:

> The term "horse" denotes a shape [of horse] and the term "white" a color. What denotes the color does not denote the shape. Therefore, I say a white horse is not a horse.①

The term "horse" denotes a material object, but in our thinking it remains forever a concept or an idea. The term "white" denotes an attribute of that material object, but in our thinking it remains forever a concept or an idea. "Horse" and "white" are two distinct and different concepts or ideas in our thinking and can never be confused into one and the same. We can never employ the idea of a certain color (here "white") to comprise that of a certain shape (here "horse"). Therefore, we are justified to assert, "A white horse is not a horse," that is, the idea of a "white horse" can't be equated to that of a "horse." Following this way of thinking, we may deprive an object of all its attributes (such as shape, color, etc.), then what will be left, i.e. that which it can never be deprived of, is what it genuinely is. However, we may as well suppose what makes a thing what it is lies exactly in the integration of its various attributes. For instance, what make a horse what it is consists precisely in the combination of attributes such as having four legs, galloping, long hair and so on. Stripped off all these attributes, there would be nothing left, and no so-called essence or substance. Of course, this is an argument which would never come to an end. At any rate, by raising this question, the Logician school had elevated the philo-

① *Gongsun Long Zi*, "Theory of the White Horse." (*Bai Ma Lun*).

sophical nature of our reasoning to a new height and into a wholly new region. It is really a pity this approach ceased to develop, or we may perhaps have had the struggle between nominalism and realism like that in the mediaeval West, and later the distinction of "primary qualities" and "secondary qualities" expounded by Locke. Locke considered the color of an object to be a secondary quality of it, so that we are justified in identifying the white horse as a horse and the black horse too as a horse. As we have mentioned above, this line of the Logician failed to make further progress and remained in its state of infancy.

Another famous argument of Gongsun Long's is his theory of the "separation of hardness and whiteness." A stone is hard and white, yet

> When we see it, we do not perceive what is hard, but perceive what is white without the hardness. When we touch it, we do not perceive what is white, but perceive what is hard without the whiteness.①

Here hardness and whiteness are two different attributes of the stone, each incapable of being substituted for the other and having nothing to do with the other. That is to say they are separated from and independent of each other. Or, as Gongsun himself put it, "Neither of them pervades the other. Therefore they are separate."② This doctrine made a significant distinction, roughly equivalent to that between essence and attribute in Spinoza. Both hardness and whiteness are attributes of things (here a stone) but not the essence of things which makes them what they are.

Furthermore, hardness and whiteness are concepts drawn from our perceptions and hence have no objective existence in themselves. There is nothing in the outside world which may be identified with "white" or "whiteness" by itself. So it is it also with "hard" or "hardness." Since "white" or "hard" have no existence in things themselves, they are but the "names" given by the cognitive subject, through which and only through which we can engage in thinking. Any thinking has to be carried on in the form of such abstract concepts or ideas. This makes up what is most essential and indispensable in our thinking. It is by means of those concepts that men are able to transcend the sensible world of their immediate perception and to ascend to the height of conscious deliberate thought. All philosophers in ancient times were engaged in thinking, but none of them, with the exception of the Logicians, ever undertook the task of reflecting on thinking itself. Thus it seems that this reflection on thought *per se* ought to be judged as the most valuable element in their philosophy.

A stone is hard and white. But white (or whiteness) is not hard (or

① *Gongsun Long Zi*, "Discourse on Hard and White" (*Jian Bai Lun*).

② Ibid.

hardness), nor hard white. They are two separate and different items in our thinking. Not only are white and hard separate, but also white, hard and stone are all three separate and different. Neither hard nor white is stone. So the three are different and take independent existence in our cognition, each by itself alone. According to common sense, a stone has an objective existence in the outside world, while "hard" and "white" are the subjective perceptions of our inner feeling, not the inherent attribute of the material objects. Thus, we have two kinds of existence, different from each other: one in the physical world, the other in our mental world. To analyze the issue along this line is undoubtedly the greatest contribution of the Logicians. And it is along this line of thinking that Gongsun Long propounded his famous "theory of notation and things" (*zhi wu lun*). For him "notation" means concepts, in contrast to "things," which have physical existence in the outside world. "Things" are the objects of our "notation." His statement reads:

> [In the realm of our knowledge] there is nothing that is not our notation, but notation itself is not a notation. If the world had no notation, things could by no means be called things. Without notations, the world would have no things; then can [notation itself] be called a notation? Notations are what do not exist in the [physical] world; things are what do exist in the [physical] world.①

That is to say, things in the physical world are objectively existent, while our concepts of them exist merely in our thinking, and not in the outside world. Thus Gongsun asserted: "There is nothing that is not our notation, but notation itself is not a notation." All things present themselves in our thinking by assuming the form of concepts, but our concepts themselves do not. Notation and the notated operate on two different levels (or worlds) of existence. We understand objective things by means of concepts, but concepts themselves are not objective things. This may remind us of Pascal's maxim:

> Par l'espace, l'univers me comprend et m'engloutit comme un point; par la pensée, je le comprends.②

Here Pascal's "comprendre" has a double meaning; it means to understand and it means also to comprise. A transition from the former sense to the latter may imply Gongsun Long's entire world-view: we are to understand and to embrace the universe by our thinking. Hence his dictum: "The world is but a notation, and all things are but a horse." This theory of notation and of things is not only his logic of thinking, but at the same time his ontology. It may be comparable to the Logos (Tao) of Lao Zi, which is not only the primary

① *Gongsun Long Zi*, "Discourse on Notations and Things," (*zhi wu lan*).

② Pascal, *Pensées*, ed. L. Brunschvicg, 348.

principle of the universe but at the same time its noumenon or ultimate reality.

There are two worlds in ancient Greek philosophy: the world of physical objects which is changeable and forever changing, and the world of ideas which is unchangeable and eternally unchanging. Similarly there are two worlds for the ancient Logician school: one is the outside physical world, the other the transcendental world of concepts. It seems the final aim of all philosophies is nothing other than to explicate the relationship of the two worlds. The combination of similarity and difference preached by Hui Shi stressed the world of the unchangeable and the unchanging, and hence the ultimate identity of all things. Or rather, in light of identity, the world never changes. The separation of hardness and whiteness propounded by Gongsun Long stressed the world of the changing, and hence the variety of things. From their different starting points the two groups accomplished in common—though from opposite sides—a great discovery in the history of philosophical thought, i.e. that thinking was performed only through the use of our concepts. It was under the guidance of the Logicians that people came to realize the nature and role of concepts in our thinking. Their work roughly corresponded to that of the ancient Greek Sophists. Traditionally, people used to regard the doctrines of the Sophists merely as specious rhetoric—hence the derogatory term "sophistry." It was not until Hegel that the value and contributions of the Sophists were afforded their due respect for achieving an unprecedented reflection on thinking itself. The Logicians' place and role in China may be compared to the Sophists' in the West, but their appearance in the history of China was only momentary and did not last long. What caused this (in addition to the political factors mentioned above) may perhaps be attributed to some mode of thinking characteristic of the Chinese mind. In general, the Chinese mind has been accustomed to poetic moods of expression rather than strict logical inquiries—or thinking in terms of images rather than logical deduction. That is why the ancient Chinese philosophers were far fonder of employing metaphors in their argument. For instance, the philosopher Gao Zi used water as an analogy to illustrate human nature thus:

> Human nature is like whirling water. Open a passage for it to the east, and it will flow to the east; open a passage for it to the west, and it will flow to the west.①

Anyone accustomed to the logical mode of thinking would be puzzled at Gao Zi's way of argument: why should human nature be elucidated by analogy to water, and why should it not be compared to something else (like fire)? This habit of Chinese thinking may be easily found in too many cases. The Greek

① *Book of Mencius*, bk. 9 "Gao Zi," pt. 1.

philosopher Heraclitus (533-475 B.C.) tried to show the passing of time by such a proposition:

> All things flow, nothing abides. Into the same river, one cannot step twice.

While Confucius expressed the same feeling on the river's side with the poetic epigram:

> Thus all pass away, day and night without ceasing.①

With the coming of the Jesuit missionaries into China at the beginning of the 17th century, when Father Mateo Ricci and Xu Guangqi (the foremost among Chinese scientists) collaborated in translating Euclid's *Elements of Geometry*, Li Zhizao was engaged in translating the *Logical*, a textbook of the University of Coimbra. It was the first book introducing formal logic into China. Though China had never come into contact with Western logic before that time, this book nevertheless left almost no trace at all on philosophical thought in China of the next three centuries. Of course, we ought not to attribute this to any feebleness of the Chinese mind as regards logical thinking. It was primarily due to the fact that the traditional style of learning in China was dominated by an ethico-political tendency, which was not at all interested in pure logical deduction.

In the history of Western philosophy, there was in the Middle Ages the dispute between nominalism and realism. The substance of this conflict was the question of how to deal with the problem of the two worlds. The nominalists held that our concepts were not inherent in the objective things themselves, but were the products of our abstract thinking and existed nowhere else than in our thoughts. The realists held that only the world of our ideas was real because it was eternal and unchangeable, while the phenomenal world was entirely transitory and ever-changing. Realism may be traced to Plato who posited an eternal world of ideas which was real and more perfect than the everyday sensory world, and claimed that all things perceived in our daily life were but imperfect copies of those perfect ideas. Surely this assertion is valid in some branches of our learning, such as geometry. In geometry a point, a straight line, a circle etc. all have eternal existence in their perfect forms only in our ideas; while the points, straight lines and circles as we perceive them in our daily experiences are all imperfect copies of the perfect ideas. At any rate, we are fully justified in holding that in China the framework of the two worlds was first propounded by the Logicians, and this occurred only once in history. All other philosophical schools in China insisted that there was one world only, while the Logician school maintained the existence of two worlds.

① *Analects*, trans. Giles, with alterations by author.

Gongsun Long's theory of notation and of things was in reality dealing with the relation of ideas to reality. From earliest times there could be found such sayings in the ancient classics, "What is metaphysical is called the Way (Tao) and what is physical is called the things (*qi*)." The Way refers to the abstract principles of a higher level, possessing universal validity, while things (physical objects) are objects in the sensible world. An abstract contemplation of the ideas themselves signifies a higher level of thinking, i.e. a reflection on thinking itself, for all our knowledge and thoughts are made possible only in the form of ideas.

Zhuang Zi, in his "The World", recorded the following 21 propositions of Gongsun Long:

> The egg has hair.
> A fowl has three legs.
> Ying [the capital of the State of Chu] contains the world.
> The dog may be a sheep.
> The horse has eggs.
> The frog has a tail.
> Fire is not hot.
> The mountain has a mouth.
> A wheel never touches the ground.
> Eyes do not see.
> Notation never reaches anywhere, and the reaching never ends.
> The tortoise is longer than the snake.
> A T-square does not make a square; a compass never makes a circle.
> Chisels do not surround their handles.
> The shadow of a flying bird never moves.
> There are times when a flying arrow is neither in motion nor at rest.
> A puppy is not a dog.
> A brown horse and a dark ox make three.
> A white dog is black.
> An orphan colt has never had a mother.
> If a rod of one foot long is cut short every day by one half of its length, it will never end in nothing even after ten thousand generations.

As to the definite meanings of these seeming absurdities, and how the author interpreted them in his own time, we can find no relevant source in the surviving documents. Any attempt at a full explanation would be far-fetched. Suffice to say that, though they are apparently contradictory to our experience, nevertheless through a logical manipulation of our ideas they clarify the nature of our knowledge and thinking. For instance, take the proposition "Fire is not hot." Here fire and hot have two different and distinct denotations. Fire denotes fire, not hot; and hot denotes hot, not fire. There is no logically necessary connection between the two. And again, consider the proposition, "A wheel never touches the ground." A circle intersects a plane only at an infinitesimally small point; hence a wheel (circle) never touches (intersects) the ground (a plane). We may fairly reason that the author was aiming to demonstrate what our ideas are, by means of logical analysis. Among the above propositions, "The shadow of a flying bird never moves" and "There are times when a flying arrow is neither in motion nor at rest" are exactly the same as proposed by the Greek Sophists. They are concerned with a deeply fundamental problem in natural philosophy, the problem of motion. Anybody at any given instant (a certain time-point) must be at a single particular position (a certain space-point); therefore at this certain time-point the object stays at rest (motionless) in a certain space-point. And the most noteworthy among those propositions is the last: "If a rod of one foot long is cut short every day by one half of its length, it will never end in nothing even after ten thousand generations." This deserves to be ranked among the most profound and striking thinking of ancient times. Mathematically it may be expressed by the equation: Σ — + — + — … — = 1. It contains not only the germ of the concepts of the limit and the infinitesimal, which constituted the starting point of modern mathematics, but also a brilliant demonstration of the infinite divisibility of things.

The proposition "All things are similar and different" implies a profound world-view of the Logicians too, i.e. all things in the world have their similarities and yet their peculiarities. All things are constantly changing, yet there are always unchanging elements in their change; otherwise there would be no continuity and identity in the world, and a thing would cease to be what it is. Mr. A and Mr. B must have something in common which makes them what a Mr. is. Yet they must also have something different which distinguishes Mr. A from Mr. B. Further, Mr. A today must have something different from the Mr. A of yesterday, yet no matter what changes may happen to Mr. A, there must be something persisting which makes Mr. A what Mr. A is. If the change in Mr. A is so great that there is nothing left in common with what Mr. A was yesterday, then we will have no way to identify Mr. A, and Mr. A would cease to be Mr. A altogether. The continuity and identity of something together with its peculiarity and variability are forever co-existent in an entity. A thing is to be identified as such a thing precisely because of its persisting identity; and it is distinguished and differentiated from other things as well as from its own past or future precisely because of its variability. What the Logicians sought was just this universal identity and this universal variability. We have to consider all this in terms of ideas, and what we are then thinking are not objects themselves but ideas of the objects in our minds. Truly, we have no reason not to acknowledge the unique contribution of the Logicians, the sophists of ancient China, and their unparalleled place in history.

Life is short while the universe is eternal and infinite. People are always striving to pursue and grasp something eternal and infinite in the short stay of their present life. All philosophers since antiquity have been in eager pursuit of some eternity—a perpetual worth or a cosmic emotion. The issue of how to unify the changing (the momentary) with the unchanging (the eternal) has become a basic concern, even a mental complex, for all philosophers, East and West, ancient and modern. In their heart of hearts, the Logicians were never restricted solely to logical and linguistic reasoning, but always longed for a deeper wisdom of life and living, a kind of spiritual immortality. The state of *summum bonum* and of eternal blessing so earnestly sought after by all philosophers—whatever school they might belong to—would finally lead to a state of ecstasy of a mystical quality. The Confucian Yan Hui was striving for such a state, the Taoist Zhuang Zi also sought such a state, and so also did the Logicians. Hui Shi eventually reached the conclusion that "The universal love of all things will lead to the unity of the whole world," founded on his argument that "All things are similar and different." This longing is the same as the Confucian's "Wherever the superior man (*jun zi*) passes through, transformation follows; wherever he abides, there is a spiritualizing influence. This flows abroad above and below together with heaven and earth."[①] It is also like the Taoists' "union of the universe and the ego." Philosophy aspires not only to satisfy our pursuit of theory and knowledge, but also to deliver us to a state of heavenly beatification. In this cosmic rapture the small ego of the individual would be led to return to the great ego of the cosmos, as Tennyson eulogized in his last hymn:

> When that which drew from out the boundless deep,
> Turns again home.[②]

Zhuang Zi made a similar remark with these words:

> Viewed from their differences, the gap between the liver and the gall-bladder is as far away as that between the state of Chu and the state of Yue; but viewed from their

① *Book of Mencius*, "Jin Xin," pt. 1, 13.

② Tennyson, "Crossing the Bar."

> similarities, all things are one and the same.[①]

On this, Guo Xiang (252-312) about five centuries later commented,

> Differentiating things by their differences, everything in the world is different from all other things; but identifying them by their similarities, everything in the world is similar to everything else.

This thinking of the Taoist school is akin to that of the Logicians. Again, almost eight centuries later, the famous poet and scholar Su Shi (Su Dongpo, 1036-1101) in his famous "Former Rhapsody on Red Cliff" expressed the same thought:

> Viewed from their changes, Heaven and Earth are no longer than an instant; viewed from their constancies, the world and I are infinite.[②]

There are ceaseless changes as well as eternal constancies in the world. If all things only changed, then there would be no things as such and no world as such. Life is forever limited yet forever in pursuit of infinity, and this is what Chinese philosophers have long so eagerly looked for: the union (or communion) of Heaven and Man. Such a cosmic state might appear rather mystical, but is not as mystical as we are apt to imagine. It is essentially a poetic (or artistic) world-view rather than a logical (or intellectual) one. It seems we have to choose a poetic angle in order to more keenly comprehend (or rather to "erleben"—to use a German term) traditional philosophy in China. It compels us to exchange the standpoint of intellectualism with that of intuition, for the ancient philosophers in China had taken the road of the poets rather than that of pure speculation. The Logicians, though having performed magnificent conceptual analysis, still ultimately stepped beyond logical reasoning into the realm of poetic illumination, which alone could bring the fulfillment of human life. In contrast and in opposition to the Confucians and the Taoists, the Logicians in their arguments seemed possessed of a thoroughly logical spirit, and yet their final ends were all the same. Through the elimination of all limitations and boundaries they strove to achieve the union of all things, leaving no trace of the differences and opposition between man and the world which confront us.

As stated above, the Logician school ought to be examined along two dimensions. Politically they had to be the product of the sharp political contradictions and struggles prevalent at that time, or they could not possibly have come onto the stage with such splendor. Prof. Hou Wailu held that the Logicians wished to solve contradiction through the negation of its very existence, and hence probably represented the privileges of the old nobility. By contrast, the

① *Book of Zhuang Zi*, "De Chong Fu."

② Su Shi, *Works*, "Former Rhapsody on Chi Bi."

masses of the lower class were prone to resort to uprisings, endeavoring to confront the contradictions face to face. However, we are as yet unable to gather enough sources about their political activities, and hence are obliged to confine our study to their theoretical character, as shown in the foregoing pages. After all, they were the first in history to engage consciously in the self-reflection of speculative thinking. It was they who for the first time in the history of human thinking realized that thinking was conducted only in the form of concepts, and that our thoughts do not really deal with objects *per se* but with the concepts of the objects.

According to some records, "[Gongsun] Long learned the ways of the ancient kings in his youth and later became skilled in the manners of rites and proprieties. He unified the similarities and differences, separated the hard and the white, affirmed what others did not affirm and avowed what others did not agree with; he puzzled the intellect of all scholars and refuted the discourses of other people."① These words succinctly summarized Gongsun Long's outstanding style and the role he played in his time. All things in the world have their aspects of similarity (universality) and yet also those of peculiarity (particularity). The Logicians had from different aspects identified all similarities and peculiarities into a unique entity (i.e., "all things are similar and different"). Everything had its different attributes (a stone might be hard and white and so on). The Logicians succeeded in discerning their various attributes by segregating the substance from the attributes—there was no intrinsic correlation between the idea of a stone and that of whiteness or hardness. At first sight, this seems to contradict the common sense of our daily experience. The Logicians "affirmed what others did not affirm and avowed what others did not agree with," or in other words, they asserted what others would deny and denied what others would assert. Their main inclination was to refute ordinary views by dint of their logical manipulations. Quite probably they were closely linked with the political orators and diplomats of the time. At a time of "the contending of a hundred schools" during the Warring States Period, the art of debate was a skill of cardinal importance, and so every school tried their best to refute other schools and thus attain a dominant position. It is natural that such schools became the "prominent learnings", including the Logicians. But as for their political activities, we still know too little to ascertain their content. What we are sure of now is only that it was this school which led people for the first time to reflect seriously on human thinking and to touch upon the real nature of human

① *Book of Zhuang Zi*, "Autumnal Water" (*Qiu Shui*).

knowledge.

Unfortunately, after the great unification of all China under the sole and supreme imperial reign of the Qin Dynasty, the absolute imperial power enforced a single ideology to support and strengthen its absolute rule, to the complete exclusion of any debate by different schools. It was a situation in which everyone "holds right what he thinks right and nullifies what he thinks null." From then onwards, the independent spirit and the freedom of thought slipped all the way downward, and in their place arose the worship of the imperial power, as we might similarly observe in the replacement of Greek classical civilization by the Roman imperium. A great unification, contrary to what many historians might take for granted, is not necessarily a superior state of affairs. It is not the case that all political unifications (at least, in the case of the Chinese) are necessarily much better than the co-existence of many independent states. It must be considered by whom the unification is accomplished and under what conditions. Is it a good thing to be unified by Hitler under Nazi rule? Perhaps much better not.

However, even under absolute rule, the classical legacy of the Hundred Schools did not all of a sudden completely vanish. They persisted down to later generations in various forms or were absorbed by other schools under different guises. Among all these schools only the Mohists and Logicians were lost to oblivion in China's middle ages. The reason might be in part attributed to the backward state of science in the mediaeval ages. The political and social conditions did not yet make possible the emergence of a scientific revolution in the modern sense, thus inducing a dogmatic orthodoxy under the supremacy of imperial rule. And as a result the Mohists and the Logicians, the most scientifically inspired schools, fell into oblivion. In the final analysis, this fact should be counted as a great misfortune in the history of philosophical thought in China.

Chapter Five: The Hundred Schools (2)

[I] The *Yin-Yang* School

Since earliest antiquity, people have been naturally interested in the phenomenal changes of the physical world, as each such change occurred in close connection with the course of their everyday lives. Occupied with those phenomena, they were eager to understand them and, what is more, to manage to make use of them for their own benefit. Hence the origin of scientific knowledge as well as of the *Yin-Yang* school in ancient China.

Etymologically, the term "*Yin*" designates the negative part of things and "*Yang*" the positive. It was generally conceded by the ancients that everything consisted of those two sides combined in unison. Those who engaged in studying the phenomena of the changes of the natural world were thus enlisted among the ranks of the *Yin-Yang* school. Perhaps in all cultures there are always to be found two different levels, the higher and serious versus the lower and vulgar. The latter often originally contains much that might be branded as superstitious or ignorant. Among this rank were to be found the witches, wizards and believers in fairies. Those engaged in this kind of profession in China were mostly members of the *Yin-Yang* school. According to historical resources, this school prevailed over the north-eastern part of the lower Yellow River Valley, their practitioners being called "the wizards"—fang shi, i.e., the performers of magic arts of Yan (now Hebei) and Qi (now Shandong). The states Yan and Qi were located by the seashore at the north of the Yellow River and the spectacular natural scenery was held by the ancient inhabitants as an actual apparition of fairies and the fairy world, and the most earnest among them aspired to find the fairies of the sea. It was generally acknowledged that the three mountains Peng Lai, Fangzhang and Ying Zhou at the sea were the residence of these fairies. This geographical background offered fertile soil for the growth and propagation of the *Yin-Yang* school. All those whose profession related to mystical practices can be ranked among them, including astrologers, prophets, practitioners of magic powers and witchcraft. Down to the present day, fortune-tellers and their like are still very popular amongst the lower social classes in China just as in many parts of the world.

In the history of all ancient peoples, scientific knowledge was generally mingled together with superstitions and magic. Ancient chemistry can only be found for the most part in alchemy. The ancient alchemists pursued only two magic arts: the elixir of life which protected people from getting old, and the stone capable of turning base metals into gold. Of course, such magic things can never be found in the world. But through their prolonged efforts, these alchemists accumulated little by little some useful scientific knowledge—learning, for example, that some substance (like spruce or mercury) may under certain conditions lead to certain chemical actions and reactions. Thus in their long-continuing professional practices, the *Yin-Yang* school should rightly be taken as the earliest ancient experimental scientists. Their learning was a medley of science and superstition. Ever since their emergence in the Warring States Period, this school had currency both in the royal court as well as among the populace for a substantial time. In the long history of China there were many emperors, nobles and people in other walks of life who indulged in the school's magic arts and consequently adopted many of its theories. In the early years of the Han Dynasty (2nd century B.C.), the famous scholar Sima Tan (father of the well-known historian Sima Qian) complained that there were too many taboos in their learning; and somewhat later another famous scholar Liu Xin criticized them for paying homage not to human beings but to spirits and ghosts.

The founder and the most influential figure of the *Yin-Yang* school was Zou Yan, later honored as the greatest master of the school. Because of his prominent skill in his discourse about the heavens, he was widely known as "Yan the astronomer." Zou Yan was a native from the State of Qi (ca. 305-240 B.C., during the reigns of King Wei and King Xuan of Qi). Some records affirmed that he and Gongsun Long, the famous Logician, held a debate over the well-known proposition "a white horse is not a horse" in front of the king of Zhou—a phenomenon not so rare during the contentions of the hundred schools, and in accordance with the manners of the age. From amongst the legacies of the age-long *Yin-Yang* traditions, Zou Yan elaborated his own theory, which was destined to play a role important in history and noteworthy for scholars of intellectual history. First among them was his philosophy of history. The term "history" in its literal sense denoted what has happened in the past, i.e. human actions and their thoughts. But behind the kaleidoscope of history people are always tempted to discern some deep-hidden laws or principles to explain or interpret all historical changes. This is what the philosophy of history aims at. And Zou Yan, earlier than any other philosopher in ancient China, provided a systematic philosophy of history known as "the Circulation (or the end and beginning) of the Five Virtues," which, as might be expected, was a medley of naive scientific ideas and superstitious elements.

While both ancient Greeks and Indians conceived of the world and everything in it as composed of four elements—earth, water, fire and air, in different proportions and modes—the ancient Chinese were much more fond of the number "five" rather than "four." In the earliest classic of China, the *Book of History*, the "five elements" were frequently mentioned.

Water, first; fire, second; wood, third; metal, fourth; earth, fifth.

Ever since then, almost all prominent philosophies of nature in China took those five as the primordial elements of which all things on heaven and earth were constituted. Side by side with the five elements, there arose corresponding ideas such as the five odors (representing vital energies), five colors, and five orientations, all with a somewhat mystical and supernatural import. Why is it that the Chinese preferred "five" rather than "four" ever since antiquity? This might find its answer in their deep-rooted predilection for the idea of Great Unity. For example, over and above the four directions east, west, south and north, there had to be crowned a "center." The name "China" itself literally means the Middle (*Zhong*) Kingdom (*Guo*).

Each of the five elements was assigned a specific "virtue." Here the term "virtue" (*de*) should be understood as a somewhat mystical power, though it also stood for a specific quality or function of a particular material substance. Each of the elements had its own virtue specific to itself, their interrelations existing forever in mutual germination while at the same time in mutual destruction, thus: earth begets metal, metal begets water, wood begets fire, fire begets earth; and reversibly: earth subdues water, water subdues fire, fire subdues wood, and wood subdues earth. As each of the five elements possesses its own specific power, when it is the turn of one of the elements to assume supremacy its virtue will reign supreme in that specific age in the course of history. By that time the rule of that specific virtue would come forth to rule over the world. For instance, the Qin dynasty came "to reign by its virtue of water," and its color "black" reigned supreme over all the land. For every virtue, there was a set of corresponding colors, costumes, manners, etc. Each element undergoes a certain cycle of rise and fall, in a perpetual cycle of superseding and then being superseded. This was called the "end and beginning of the five virtues." In accordance with this theory, the ancient sage-king Shun came to reign by representing the virtue of earth. And since wood subdues earth, the Xia Dynasty succeeded the Yu Dynasty (founded by Shun) "to reign by its virtue of wood." Metal subdues wood, and hence the Shang Dynasty came after Xia Dynasty "to reign by its virtue of metal." Fire subdues metal, allowing the Zhou Dynasty to succeed the Shang Dynasty came "to reign by its virtue of fire." And later the Qin Dynasty succeeded the Zhou because it is destined "to reign by its virtue of water." Thus is derived a complete explanation of the sequence of the reigning dynasties from a perspective both semi-naturalistic and semi-mystical. The five elements represent the power of the natural world, the changes in which are manifested in the ceaseless successions of days and nights, the cycles of the four seasons, the flourishing and withering of plants etc. It seems only natural to view all the fluctuations of human affairs by the same pattern and to reduce human history to the same cyclic repetition. As the five elements constituted the primordial substances of the natural world, so also must their virtue be the supreme sovereign of the human world. Thus the cyclic process of their mutual subjugation as well as their mutual promotion was embodied not only in the natural world but also in human history. There are altogether, so to speak, five historical formations, and their regular process of succession signifies a systematic philosophy of history. Whenever and wherever there was a signal of the decline of the present regime, it meant that its ruling virtue or power was in its waning phase and in its stead the next succeeding virtue or power was in ascendancy. Then those who assume themselves the representatives of the new virtue and power are qualified to launch an attack on the old ruling dynasty. In this fashion, this semi-mystical philosophy of history itself is as an active ideological factor and plays an important role in the making of history.

This theory of the succession of the five virtues was of course in its essence a cyclical one. Under the ancient conditions when production was carried out on the scale of simple reproduction (rather than the ever-aggrandizing reproduction of modern times) all people could conceive of were the repetitions of natural phenomena and human affairs (the rise and decay of the ruling dynasties) in endless recurrence. The succession of an orderly reign followed invariably by a turbulent reign looked just like that of the four seasons following each after the other. The ancients were not yet in a position to embrace any idea of an everlasting progress of evolution—an idea impossible in pre-modern times.

In antiquity, and indeed in any traditional society basically agrarian, the mode of production was a simple repetition year after year, accompanied by a mode of living without the least notion of transition from a lower level to a higher. Viewing history in this way, history itself seemed nothing more than a simple cycle, as though history were forever repeating itself again and again, age after age. History was not advancing—contrary to what most modern historians would naturally assume—toward an ever higher level, but only moving in endless cycles with no definite aim at all. Thus, they purported no heavenly city whatsoever that might lead people hoping for a higher end. It was in fact but a reflection of the naive mentality of the peasants. Yet at the same time, it furnished them with an ideological weapon: whenever and wherever they were oppressed by the old ruling class beyond their forbearance, they might resort to arms under the presumption of "the turning of virtues." Such is reflected in the well-known slogan of the protagonists of the Yellow Turban Rebellion, "The blue sky is dead; it is now the reign of the yellow sky." As might be easily imagined, not only the peasants but also any political force striving for power could exploit it to argue for its own right in assuming sovereignty. Therefore by implication, it meant that no existing regime or social order could assume eternal survival without change. Furthermore, the fate of history was logically not the creation of great personalities but the result of a natural process of cyclical motion. What was favored by this natural process would for the moment ascend to the fore, while what was not would descend as a natural result.

The above-mentioned theory was later recast by and absorbed into the Confucian doctrine. It should be noted that the orthodox theology lasting more than two millennia in Chinese history had embraced not only Confucianism but also other schools, into a complex system in which the idea of the turning of the five virtues formed a major constituent. This might be seen in the observations of Mencius, who was a second-generation follower of Zi Si, the direct disciple of Confucius. A famous remark made by Mencius reads thus:

> From Yao and Shun down to Tang was 500 years and more… From Tang to King Wen [of the Zhou Dynasty] was 500 years and more... from King Wen to Confucius was 500 hundred years and more…[①]

Yao, Shun, Tang, King Wen [of the Zhou Dynasty] and Confucius were all the greatest kings and sages in antiquity, and this assertion of Mencius was widely known as the theory of "the assured emergence of a sage-king every 500 years in history." These words sounded as though an ancient Spengler was

① *Book of Mencius*, "Jin Xin," pt. 2.

prophesying the coming of the golden age of a sage-king. A sage-king was supposedly destined to appear every 500 years—surely, this was a cyclical paradigm suffused with a mystic flavor. Yet indeed, the long coursc of Chinese history did resemble a pendulum, swaying forever between peace and tumult, flourishing and decay, order and disorder, prosperity and decline, unlike the 19th century positivist historians' image of history as forever progressing headlong from worse to better. A genuinely progressive outlook of history never found a proper place in the Chinese philosophy of history. Nearly all the noteworthy schools of the philosophy of history in China agree with a cyclical theory, of which the *Yin-Yang* school provided a basic model as shown above.

In addition to his philosophy of history, Zou Yan also elaborated an important theory in the field of cosmogony with a somewhat original world-view. All civilized peoples in the early stages of their history contributed their specific pictures of the world which were generally composed on the basis of their legends and myths. Since their knowledge of the outside world was greatly limited, they often resorted to conjecture. The ancient Hindus hypothesized that the world was surrounded by great seas and that the continent on which people dwelt was placed on the back of an enormous tortoise to prevent it from drowning. Amidst various cosmogonies in ancient China that of Zou Yan was the most clear-cut and influential. From their origin, the profession of the *Yin-Yang* school dealt with astronomy and geography. Zou Yan propounded a neat and well-ordered picture of the world which embodied the longings characteristic of the ancient magicians. Those magicians keenly sought fairies and in their pursuits they tried to go as far as the fairy land over the ocean and at the end of the world. As is well-known, the First Emperor of Qin (by the end of the 3rd century B.C.) launched a great expedition for overseas exploration in search of fairies and fairy lands. And in later ages, the most renowned Chinese poet Li Bai (in the early 8th century) was also famous for his romantic pursuit of the fairies. This tradition lasted down to modern times. All these stories belong to a spectacular and age-old tradition of Chinese cultural life.

Zou Yan affirmed that what people called the Middle Kingdom (i.e. China or *Zhong Guo*) was only a very small part of the world, called *Chi Xian Shen Zhou* (literally Red Region of the Fairy Land), which later became an alternative name for China as a whole. There were, he claimed, nine such regions in total, known by their collective name of the "Nine Continents." But these "Nine Continents" only formed one ninth of a still larger "Nine Continents." Hence China or *Chi Xian Shen Zhou* formed only 1/81 of the whole world. Again, this greater "Nine Continents" was surrounded all around by great seas. And still further, this great group of "Nine Continents" was part of a set nine in number, surrounded by still much greater sea. In this Zou Yan showed his unparalleled imagination *par excellence*, only to be matched by the ancient Indian myths. Just like his philosophy of history, the world-view he depicted was a mix of scientific conjecture and legend. The scientific (and hence rational) elements in it sprang from his awareness of the immense vastness of the possible world far surpassing the capability of our imagination, while the fanciful elements were added through his groundless exaggeration. This kind of search into the mysteries of the natural world was the earliest origin of science and philosophical curiosity, of which the ancient *Yin-Yang* school ought to be counted as foremost representatives. In them, superstition, fancy, and myth were closely correlated with a longing for the ultimate secrets of the universe and the human beings living therein. As earlier discussed, in the intellectual history of China the ethico-politico-centric ideology had always reigned supreme over all other learning and knowledge, and all values were reduced and oriented to the service of an ethico-political aim, with the corollary that any knowledge in itself had no intrinsic value at all. With this in mind, we can better understand how significant the interests of the *Yin-Yang* school were, as well as those of the Logicians and the Taoists, in their pursuit of knowledge beyond the narrow Confucianism of the predominant ethico-political dogma. They represented a deviation from the main current of thought and a genuine interest for pure philosophical and scientific truth. As long as knowledge was restricted by an ethico-political pragmatism, there was no choice but to submit to the orthodoxy and play the part of its servant maid. All histories, in China as well as in Europe, showed philosophy to have had an inescapable fate as the servant maid of theology in the pursuit of knowledge. Hence the quest of the *Yin-Yang* school, together with the Logicians and Taoists, reflected an effort for intellectual emancipation, and a longing for the liberation of human nature. A human being born with his intrinsic and inherent value ought never to be a mere obedient tool for the purpose of some ethico-political utility. To use the terminology of Kant, man himself is an end in himself and by himself, but never a means for others, and so you ought never to make use of others as mere means. Such an act of servitude would harm the dignity of humanity. It is in this sense that we may well assert: the above-mentioned non-ethico-political current represented a high tide of ancient Chinese philosophy in an unorthodox direction, on which there had not yet been focused sufficient attention. It is really unfortunate that this line of pursuit after knowledge and truth always remained in a lesser position and thus could only end in fruitless tragedy.

[II] The Political Strategists

The Political Strategists—or alternatively, the Diplomats—of the Zong Heng school, literally the school of research into political operation, were those who worked for the sovereigns and princes as their advisers and special envoys, somewhat as the employees in the Rand Corporation might do in present-day America. Again they were somewhat like modern professionals who wandered from nation to nation in the hope that some sovereign would be persuaded by their proposal and entrust them with a high rank and important political responsibility. Hence, this profession often proved an efficient short-cut to honor and success for the ancient intellectuals. But such a profession could flourish only in an epoch when many nations were in violent rivalry with one another. During the time of the Warring States Period (5th-3rd centuries B.C.) the incessant and turbulent inter-state struggles created urgent need for those professionals skilled in the art of war, diplomacy or political planning. Those skilled in the art of war came under the category of the Strategists as we have mentioned above. Those skilled in the art of diplomacy or political communication belonged to the Zong Heng school, dealing primarily with the complicated relations between states. The school's foremost representatives were Sou Qin and Zhang Yi, both according to legend the disciples of a semi-mystical personality by the name of Gui Gu Zi ("the master of the Wonder Cave"). It should be kept in mind that the transmission of learning in antiquity was always esoteric in nature. Gui Gu Zi was a legendary figure, widely known for his unparalleled military planning. There were still further such figures including Huang Shi Gong (Master Yellow Stone, of the 2nd century B.C.) who was the tutor of Zhang Liang. According to legend, Zhang Liang received from his master an esoteric book on the art of war which enabled Zhang to become the chief of staff to Liu Bang (the first emperor of the Han Dynasty) and helped him unify the whole realm of China. The emperor praised Zhang highly, saying "in planning from behind the curtain and winning the battle a thousand miles away, I'm far inferior to Zhang."[①] Obviously, Zhang Liang inherited the tradition of this school. Strictly speaking, the ideas of the Political Strategists fell under the category of practical politics, yet it also involved a philosophical aspect, for all ancient schools mutually influenced one another. Behind their

① Sima Qian, *Records of the Historian*, vol. 8 "Life of the First Emperor" (referring to the first emperor of the Han dynasty).

theories, political, social or ethical, one might well discover their presupposed philosophical outlooks.

On the lives of Sou Qin and Zhang Yi, Sima Qian's *Records of the Historian* offers very detailed records. Their political planning in many ways remind the reader of the "geopolitics" of Germany during World War II; if one likes, one may fairly call them the *Geopolitik* school of ancient China. Sou Qin had planned a scheme known as the vertical union, i.e. the union of the smaller countries in the east against the encroaching hegemony of Qin. His diplomatic work won him a great success, "the result being that the six [eastern] states were allied with Sou as their chief executive who concurrently became the minister to all six states."[①] His strategy became so illustrious that "the force of Qin dared not attempt a drive to the east in the course of 15 years."[②] Sima Qian evaluated Sou Qin by saying: "He became widely known through canvassing the princes with his skill for political maneuverings."[③] Zhang Yi was Sou's learning mate, and his career and achievements were similar to Sou's, the difference being that he served the kingdom of Qin instead of the other six kingdoms Sou Qin served. The aim of Qin was to annex the other six kingdoms in the east, hence generally called "the strategy for a horizontal union" (i.e. assimilation into Qin). And so Sima Qian was led to assert, "The achievements of Zhang Yi far surpassed that of Sou Qin."[④] The most well-known story about Zhang Yi told of how, when sent to the state of Chu, he managed successfully to deceive King Huai of Chu, and was thus able to finally defeat Chu.[⑤]

These activities of the Political Strategists were the principal inspiration for the saying "the intellectuals' vehement discourses on the topic of politics" (*chu shi heng yi*). This was a prevalent phenomenon at the time. Their exploits show that they were intellectuals who earned their living and tried to promote their social and political status through their political devices. Ever since mankind stepped into a civilized state, there have emerged surplus laboring forces able to support a part of the population who were not required to engage in daily manual labor (as the Bible put it: "thorns and thistles—all the days of their lives... by the sweat on their faces"[⑥]); and thereby a minority were liberated from the constraint of enforced labor to turn to other fields of activities, among

① Ibid. vol. 69 "Life of Sou Qin."

② Ibid.

③ Ibid.

④ Ibid., "Life of Zhang Yi."

⑤ Ibid., vol. 80, "Lives of Qu Yuan and Jia Yi."

⑥ Genesis 3:18-19.

which the profession of the intellectuals was the most noteworthy. The intellectuals were part of a wider group who engage in a specific field and support themselves through their specific training and capacities (i.e. their intellectual caliber). But whereas other walks of profession which were morally and ethico-politically neutral and maintained themselves merely through their non-moral skills, the intellectuals were otherwise. In the long tradition of Chinese political culture, an intellectual was compelled by nature to serve some political authority (often the imperial power). Consequently it was impossible for him to remain independent morally or politically. More often than not, it was likely that he must serve the imperial power. And once his service no longer satisfied the intentions of the imperial power, he would be destined to become its sacrifice. Herein lay the tragic fate of the Chinese intellectuals in their traditional culture. It was almost impossible for them to keep their independence—their independent ideas, ideals and judgments—outside of the imperial power.

The ancient document *Strategies of the Warring States* (*Zhan Guo Ce*) was a large collection of records of the speeches, discourse and activities of the Political Strategists. Their concern was how to establish a balance of power out of the feuds of the Warring States, and further how to promote the hegemony of the royal power they served. Naturally this incorporated a particular political philosophy and theories of human nature, social order and sovereign power. In their study of ruling power their interests were the same as the Legalists. The Legalists focused on the topic of power and the art of ruling, and so too did the Political Strategists. However, the Legalists stressed the ruling power of the sovereign over his subjects and possible rivals, while for the Political Strategists the balance and variety in international relations were primary. As stated earlier, the Legalist ideas were closely affiliated with those of the Taoists and the Strategists: their knowledge pertaining to the laws of behavior of the ruling power presupposed their knowledge of the laws of nature, from which they derived their laws of human nature and its habits. And this was the aim of the Taoists and the Political Strategists, long before the emergence of the Legalists. They drew their knowledge of the laws of the human world from the laws of nature. Since the laws of the social world were a derivation of the natural laws, they had to comply with those natural laws. Hence the Taoists' affirmation of a return to nature. But the Political Strategists and the Legalists seemed to reason thus: once human beings emerged from the state of nature and entered into the civil state, there was then neither the necessity nor the possibility of a return to nature. For better or for worse, they had to undertake the struggle for life, as dictated by the iron law of society, i.e. the law of *homo politicus*. Yet at the same time the other side of the struggle for life had to be a process of cruel selection, the inescapable result of the mechanism of the struggle for living. As can be seen in history, this was precisely the lot that fell upon some of the most prominent Political Strategists and Legalists themselves. Such was the bitter fate of the famous Legalists Shang Yang and Wu Qi as well as of the famous Political Strategists Sou Qin and Zhang Yi. Few, if any, were able to avoid a tragic end.

Faced with such conditions, the Confucians and some of the Taoists resorted to an idealized utopia, which they believed had existed in antiquity. Such a nostalgia for the good old days was expressed in the Confucian doctrine of the reign of the Three Dynasties (supposedly ruled by sage-kings) or in the Taoists' avowed return to the naiveté of nature. Surely these were but impractical longings without any basis in real life. In contrast, the Political Strategists and later the Legalists turned to focus on the practical issues of real life while totally neglecting the idealistic side of life. To be idealistic in this sense is to regard a life not merely as a constituent part in a tremendous machine, but as a thinking being with indispensable spiritual and mental values. A human being is not a mere instrument, but is an end in himself and by himself. For him, social justice and individual dignity are essential wherever and whenever. It goes without saying that total neglect of the spiritual value of humanity would mean disaster to the sound development of any community. Without a certain degree of social justice, there would be no peace or order at all. Throughout the history of mankind, the outbreak of revolutions is not always accompanied by the bitterest material conditions. The widespread tumults in the later years of both the Qin Dynasty (the end of the 3rd century B.C.) and the Sui Dynasty (early 7th century) are notable examples. Or again in the instance of the French Revolution in modern times, there appears no ground to assert that the material lives of most French people were at that time any worse than their neighbors, say the Germans or the Spanish. The course of evolution of human society is forever an interweaving of two dimensions: spiritual and material life. When their material lives were impoverished to such a degree that most people were no longer able to subsist, there was certain to be a storm of revolution. But it seems that the important factors are more likely to be spiritual. Without the Enlightenment—which had so excited French minds—one can hardly imagine that the French Revolution would have happened as it did. The cause of social upheaval is just as likely to be found in the demand for social justice as in material poverty. Even when the total amount of social wealth does not decrease, or even increases—as it did for instance during the reigns of the Qin and Sui dynasties in Chinese history—the social discontent can still burst forth in a most violent fashion. Therefore, the secret of social progress perhaps is to be found in keeping a balanced and synchronous development of these two needs side by side. A society could not subsist long by spiritual coercion or ideological indoctrination alone. But growth in material wealth with no regard to social justice or spiritual cultivation is equally destined to be short-lived. The Confucians and the Taoists resorted one-sidedly to the role of the spiritual force, supposing that all political and social problems could be solved purely by ethical and mental cultivation of the human mind. It was surely too idealistic to be realistic. In contrast, the Political Strategists and the Legalists were concerned solely with the mechanical balance of political and social forces to the total disregard of the spiritual role of people's ideals and aspirations. They were—so to speak—more power mongers than human beings in the full sense of the term. They seemed to have gone too far toward another extreme in their vulgar realism to pay due consideration to spiritual and idealistic issues. Since a sound development of any society depends on the concert of these two elements, all the aforementioned philosophical schools in ancient China fell short of being able to "see life steadily and see it whole," each in its own way and with its own limitations.

The job of a Political Strategist was decidedly not an easy one. It was required of him to be an expert in international affairs, possessing abundant knowledge of all things relating to power struggles, whether in a domestic or foreign arena. He needed a sensitive mind always ready to react swiftly to the circumstances of *Realpolitik*, as well as an eloquent tongue to deal with any changing situation, and to make firm and intelligent decisions. He had to have the courage to confront all unexpected events, forever ready to risk his own life in dealing with all possible complications in different political conflicts. He had to be an excellent diplomat and a sagacious power-broker. And just because of this, his theory often changed to match the requirements of the ever-changing political situation. Since the world of *Realpolitik* never unfolded in accordance to a logical structure, those Political Strategists were much more interested in the real gains and losses than in logic, philosophy or metaphysics. However, as their activities were inevitably guided by their world-views, which were at bottom a product of their epoch, we may discern something in their general outlook that came very near to the ideas of the Legalist school, whom we shall discuss in another chapter.

[III] Individualism in Ancient China—Yang Zhu

So tumultuous were the rapid changes in society during the Spring and Autumn and Warring States Periods (770-221 B.C.) that many determined thinkers came forth to commit themselves to the cause of "saving the world" by engaging in practical political and social activities, wishing to reform or reshape the real world with their own elevated ideas and ideals. Among them the most renowned were the "prominent learnings" of the Confucians and the Mohists. They (and together with them many other schools) engaged in the cause of "serving the world" wholeheartedly. In an elegy, Emperor Xuan of the Tang Dynasty (early 8th century) lamented over Confucius, "What was the Master striving for? So laboriously he had toiled all his life." This was a portrait not only of Confucius himself but of all the philosophers of that time: they toiled day and night in the hope that the "Way" (Tao) of their ideals might be realized, and thereby the people made happy and the world brought to peace and prosperity. But it was noteworthy that at the same time and in contrast with them, there were also those who sought not "to serve the world" but "to withdraw from the world" (Bi Shi[①] vs. Yong Shi), that is, to withdraw out of the political and social troubles of real life in order to develop self-preservation in the peaceful sanctity of one's own mind. Confucius once remarked, "Some men of worth retire from the world."[②] In the *Analects* were mentioned the names of "Jieyu" (a madman of Chu), Chang Zu, Jieni, "and an old man carrying across his shoulder a hoe,"[③] all of whom can be considered hermits as described above. They were those who tried earnestly to escape the world in which they lived. And they were simultaneously the reluctant protesters against the present world. Among them we will single out the striking figure of Yang Zhu as a representative, whose doctrine famously professed "the preservation of life" purely "for one's own self," reflecting clearly both the positive and the negative elements of his individualist theory.

Mencius characterized the age of his own generation,

> The sage-kings cease to arise, and the princes of all states give free rein to various lusts. Unemployed scholars indulge in unbridled discussions. The words of Yang Zhu and Mo Di [Mo Zi] fill the whole realm. All the peoples' discourses throughout adopt

① *Analects*, chap. 18, pt. 6.

② Ibid., chap. 14, 37.

③ Ibid., chap. 18, 5-7.

the views either of Yang or of Mo.[①]

And further:

Yang's principle is "for one's own self," which does not acknowledge the reign of the sovereign.

From the words of Mencius it may be seen how prevalent and influential were the two schools Yang and Mo. Mencius emphatically pointed out that Yang Zhu was "for one's own self" and Mo Zi was "for love of all equally."[②] That made Mo a radical universalist, and Yang a radical individualist. It is a matter of extreme regret that we know but too little about Yang the man and his doctrine—we are even not clear about his main achievements, when precisely he lived, or his central arguments. All we know of him comes from the fragmentary records of others, contemporaneous or later, and even those are mostly from his adversaries. Hence we are now obliged to try to reconstruct his arguments and conclusions out of these fragmentary pieces.

In our estimation, it seems that Yang Zhu stood somewhere between those who "serve the world" (*yong shi*) and those who "escape from the world" (*bi shi*), though he came nearer to the latter. Or, to employ a modern terminology, Yang Zhu was an individualist who paid attention to himself above others and held that, if everyone sought to do likewise, the world would proceed in the best way for all. Yang preached that one should not do anything for the benefit of society. This came very near to the teaching of Lao Zi: "So long as I do nothing, the people will by themselves be cultivated."[③] It seems that Yang Zhu never urged people to try to change the world in any way. All he advised was that one take care of one's own well-being. The logical implication was this: if each person is to take care only of himself without interfering with others, then there would be a much better world for everyone to live in. Though the existing sources offer no such analysis, this ought to be taken for granted as a reasonable inference. A person's greatest responsibility is to look after himself; and if he was allowed only to look after himself, then all would be well.

Yang Zhu might have flourished in the early years of the Warring States, somewhat earlier than Mencius, for Mencius had emphatically described and severely criticized him. Our knowledge comes in the main from Mencius' record. In addition, Lu's *Spring and Autumn Annals* (of the late Warring States Period, about 3rd century B.C.) and the *Book of Huai Nan Zi* (early Han Dynasty, about 2nd century B.C.), both belonging to the Miscellaneous school,

① *Book of Mencius*, "Duke Wen of Teng," pt. 2, 6. 9.

② Ibid.

③ *Book of Lao Zi*, chap. 57.

mentioned him. It appears that we can be certain of Yang Zhu's existence and his basic doctrine. His individualism must be taken as unique in the intellectual history of China, because almost all other prominent schools preached a collectivism, placing the community over and above the individual, who should unconditionally dedicate himself to the cause of the community. This collectivist orientation formed the cardinal tradition of the Chinese mentality. The value of the individual existed only in being an instrument for the sake of the community. Outside of this, an individual had no independent value in himself. In contradiction with this main current, Yang Zhu sharply upheld the individual over and above the community. If the community had any value, then its value lies nowhere else than in its service to the individual. According to the *Book of Mencius*:

> The principle of the philosopher Yang was "Each one for himself." Even if he could have benefited the whole world by plucking out a simple hair, he would not have done it.①

Adding to this statement, the Legalist Han Fei (280-230 B.C.) offered the description "never exchanging a hair from his body even for the great benefit of the world."② In the debate between altruism and egoism, most ancient Chinese philosophers were for altruism. It was particularly noteworthy that only Yang Zhu stood distinctly for egoism. The disagreement stemmed from the question of who or what ought to claim the right of priority. If it failed to recognize individual interest or happiness as its premise, the argument for altruism would nullify itself. What makes altruism valid is just that it presupposes the existence of each and every individual, and presupposes the potential happiness of the individual. And this implies that everyone could and should take the best care of himself, and that if everyone were given the full liberty to take care of himself, then the world would all be well.

Thus we may fairly suppose that Yang's basic statements "everyone for himself" and "accord priority to life" were in their essence striving only for the equal rights of life for everyone against oppression from others. Hence his famous dictum:

> If no one loses a hair and no one takes interest in the world, then there will ensue the reign of peace in the world.③

It was said that Yang Zhu once discussed the issue of how to rule a country with the king of Liang. And Han Fei even said of Yang Zhu that he was just like

① *Book of Mencius*, "Jin Xin," pt. 1, 26.

② *Book of Han Fei Zi*, vol. 19, "The Prominent Learning" (*Xian Xue*).

③ Liu Xiang, *Garden of Talks* (*Shuo Yuan*), notes.

Mo Zi in being endowed with the talent to rule a country. Yang Zhu's above argument naturally led to the ideal of anarchism, i.e. the best reign would be one with no sovereign at all, and therefore Mencius rightly said of him, "The principle of Yang Zhu is 'Everyone for himself,' which simply means to exist without a sovereign."① For Yang Zhu, one's life and living were much more precious than being a sovereign in possession of the whole country: for all amounts to nothing when one's life is lost. Obviously he held the life of the individual to be supreme, over and above the state—an argument in sharp contradiction with China's collective-oriented tradition. Mencius rebuked him bitterly: "Having no sovereign would be the same as beasts."② Han Fei, the foremost Legalist, also criticized him. Once Yang Zhu's doctrine was carried out, Han Fei surmised, "It would be impossible to persuade the people to dedicate their lives to their betters or their rulers."③ It seems that both the Confucians and the Legalists neglected the essence of Yang Zhu's reasoning that "everyone for himself" would logically imply "never interfering with others." In such conditions, an ideal society could be easily imagined thus: "those who governed would be virtuous and talented, with the greatest humility in doing what is virtuous without assuming themselves virtuous."

Not only did Yang Zhu advise people to refrain from harming others, but also "not to conquer things." His individualism seems to have been an inference from an all-encompassing naturalism. But for people to fulfill both requirements at one and the same stroke was no easy task. It exacts serious deliberations at every step in the course of our lives. Hence the widely circulated story about Yang Zhu's hesitation in confronting such a great issue as life itself. The story tells us that once as Yang Zhu happened to come to a crossroad on his journey, he sighed mournfully: "At this very spot, if one wrong step is taken, it will lead to a mistake a thousand miles afar."④ Not knowing which was the right direction to take, he wept bitterly. Once the wrong way was taken in life, it would result in disasters. It appears that the choice of individualism was after all not as easy as people might imagine. Thus Han Fei admonished that, as plausible as Yang Zhu's doctrine might sound, it could not adjust itself to social reality and hence proved impracticable.⑤

Does the dictum "everyone for himself" mean the mere prolongation of

① *Book of Mencius*, "Duke Wen of Teng," pt. 2, 6. 9.

② Ibid.

③ *Book of Han Fei Zi,* op. cit

④ Ibid.

⑤ Ibid.

one's physiological existence, or the satisfaction of some spiritual or mental aspiration? If the latter, it comes very near to Stoicism with a tint of Taoist naturalism, notwithstanding the fact the Taoists advocated inactivity in life while Yang Zhu activity in life. But in its defense of the individual's rights and interests, Yang Zhu's doctrine also ran counter with the demands of the ruling classes of his time, both the newly-arisen dignitaries and the old-fashioned nobility, because individualism could only mean a resistance to the rule of despotism, no matter whence it came. This was most explicitly expressed by Han Fei's denouncement of Yang Zhu as "a man who values his life so much ... that he is obliged never to remain in a besieged city nor even to pluck out a hair from his skin even for the great benefit of the whole world."[①] and who would thus never be able to do anything useful for his country. Both Yang Zhu and Mo Zi were forceful representatives of the laboring classes, Yang Zhu speaking for the small individual proprietors while Mo Zi for the organized artisans. Yang Zhu's foundation was "for the self" and Mo Zi's "universal love." In their religious attitudes, Yang Zhu was atheistic, while Mo Zi theistic. In comparing the two schools these differences deserve our careful study.

As stated above, most Chinese philosophers prioritized the group—a fact which makes Yang Zhu exceedingly significant. The essence of the issue again hinges on the dilemma between egoism and altruism. Or, whether the community exists for the sake of the individual, or the individual for the sake of the community? Which should take priority? From the perspective of logical order, it seems the individual should come first and then the community, the latter being but a collective term for the individuals who compose it. Or, to put it in another way: the means ought to serve the end, yet which of the two is the end and which the means? Are we to take human beings as mere means to serve some end which transcends its constituent members, or take each individual as endowed with his own worth as a human being independent of the community to which he happens to belong? It may be urged that community exists in nothing other than its constituent members, outside of whom it can have no existence whatsoever in any time or place. Community is not an empty concept, and dwells exclusively in the lives of its member. Thus what is called the welfare of the community can be nothing other than the sum of the welfare of its members. To demand that all men sacrifice themselves for the sake of the community, and to regard this as a universally valid maxim, would be a line of reasoning which precludes any universal validity. If moral commands are justified by their fulfill-

① Ibid.

ment of the greatest happiness of the greatest number to the greatest degree, then as a matter of course the greatest number means the greatest number of living individuals, and not an empty abstraction of mankind in general. Further, one may assert that any elimination of the "right to the pursuit of happiness" in the name of community, that is, a usurpation of human rights under the pretext of the benefit of the community, in fact proves advocates nothing more than the profit of the ruling minority. After all, the rights, dignity and values of the concrete individuals ought to be placed above the empty fiction of any supposed "community" whatever its name might be. If all (or the majority) are required to sacrifice themselves for the sake of the community, then for whose sake does the community exist? If one is to live or die for the sake of other people, then those other people ought not themselves to live and die for still others. If all were to sacrifice themselves unconditionally for others, then who in the last analysis would benefit from these sacrifices? The individualists assumed the individual as the starting point in their logically constructing a value system contradistinguished with the collectivist tradition. Herein lies the contribution of Yang Zhu's individualism to the perennial ethical debate—whether the individual exists for the sake of the community or the community for the sake of the individuals who compose it. Unless we suppose that the community is something of a supra-human nature, there can be no community that does not dwell in its individuals. Outside of the happiness of the individuals, there is no such thing as the happiness of the community. In the dictum "the greatest happiness of the greatest number," the greatest number can only designate the individuals and not a community in any abstract sense; whenever and wherever the individuals are subordinated to some idea of community, surely there is a rejection of human rights as seen in ancient and mediaeval despotism or modern fascism.

While Yang Zhu professed individualism and Mo Zi collectivism, Mencius took it as his moral obligation to refute both Yang Zhu and Mo Zi. So Mencius asserted,

> If the principles of Yang and Mo are not stopped and the principles of Confucius not set forth, then this perverse discourse will delude the people and hinder the way of benevolence and righteousness... Whoever is able to oppose Yang and Mo is the disciple of the sage [Confucius].①

And again:

> Those who are fleeing away from Mo naturally turn to Yang, and those who are fleeing away from Yang naturally turn to the Confucians.②

① *Book of Mencius*, "Duke Wen of Teng," pt. 2, 6. 9.

② *Book of Mencius*, "Jin Xin," pt. 2.

As is well known, the theories of both the school of Yang and of the school of Mo, by going too far to be realistic or practicable, were eventually replaced by the ideology of a synthesis of the Confucians and the Legalists, which is the theme of the last part of our book. What ought to be stressed is simply this: the emergence of such thoroughgoing collectivism as in Mo Zi and such thoroughgoing individualism as in Yang Zhu should be regarded as the pride of ancient China, both philosophies leaving a fruitful legacy for later generations to inherit, absorb and ponder. They reached a height never again seen in the long course of Chinese intellectual history for more than two millennia.

Some scholars took Yang Zhu's doctrine as reflecting the interests of the small proprietors who were then threatened with losing territory to larger rivals. They demanded minimal intervention from the political and social authorities in order to maintain their personal right and liberty, or in other words, the best government for them was that which exercised the least coercion. This indeed may be regarded as the *laissez-faire* theory in its ancient Chinese version, politically as well as economically and socially. On the ethical level, it meant at the same time a bitter protest against the hypocrisy of the moral sermons of the ruling classes. Since all ruling classes customarily resorted to high-sounding slogans as a handy means to exact dedication and sacrifice from the people, Yang Zhu spoke out confrontationally to uphold the right to life and liberty of the individual against the infractions of the ruling classes.

However, it was a time when the main trend of Chinese history was approaching headlong the establishment of a great unified empire under feudal despotism. This trend towards a great unification was as irreversible as the waning of Yang Zhu's doctrine. At any rate, as regards the value of his theory proper, it had greatly enriched the treasury of the ancient thought of China, worthy of study by later generations, though we can hardly restore it in its entirety. Among the documents of the various philosophical schools there was a book entitled the *Book of Lie Zi*, attributed to a legendary figure in antiquity known as Lie Yukou, in which a specific chapter was allotted to Yang Zhu. The *Book of Lie Zi* has long been identified as a forgery portraying Yang Zhu as a hedonist professing the satisfaction of gluttony and concupiscence, a theory far from conformity with the true spirit of his individualism. Indeed, no elements of hedonism are necessarily linked with individualism, though there is a long tradition in nearly all cultures of all nations of confusing the two. Since life is short and time past can not be regained, the best approach seems to be to enjoy life and living while one can. Thus were spoken the famous lines of the poet Li Bai (early 8th century): "Enjoy a simple cup of wine in the moment while we live; never care for continuing fame after our death." Or we can consider the lines of a popular Renaissance poem:

Youth is wondrous, but how fleeting,
Sing and laugh, and banish sorrow,
Give to happiness good greetings,
Place the hope not on the morrow.

or other works in the same mien in other countries, such as Omar Khayyam's *Rubaiyat*. But it was groundless for Lie Zi to count Yang Zhu among the hedonists. Rather, Yang Zhu was an individualist instead of a hedonist, and individualism by no means necessarily leads to hedonism. What Yang Zhu insisted was (as far as we can now ascertain) simply no more than this: there is no (nor can there be) collective welfare outside and independent of the individuals in whom the community consists. It may indeed look like a paradox that people have to admit the priority of the community's interests over those of the individual, and yet at the same time guarantee the personal rights of the individual which are always in danger of being encroached upon by the authority in the name of the community. And the course of human history seems to oscillate forever between the two extremes. With collectivism being carried to the extreme, the value of the individual is denied, and this leads unavoidably to the self-denial of collectivism itself. When its members are forgotten, what would the community bind itself to? Conversely, when individualism is carried to the extreme, the community is negated. After all, an individual can not exist by itself, for an individual can never be a self-sufficient entity; his existence depends on and is often determined by the community of which he is a member. To a considerable extent, his existence consists in being an integral part of the whole. An individual in a certain sense is an atom (or a monad in the Leibnizian sense), and yet not a mere atom. For the existence of the individual incorporates elements which do not belong to the individual, but to the community. Yang Zhu failed to place a proper valuation on the function of society. Here, the reader may find an Achilles' heel in his doctrine. If a community can not be measured in the lives of its individuals then it can not justify its own existence; and so also with the individual in his relation to the community. Individuality can not itself subsist without the community. A community has to realize itself through the individuals just as the individuals have to realize themselves through the community. Kant took a human being to be an end in himself, not a mere means. But without society, the end of a human being can never be realized. In the union of the two there ought be an optimum point, and any overemphasis on either the individual or the community would lead to an impasse. From a logical point of view, such an optimal condition can only be that under which the individual is able to realize his end and his value to their greatest extent. This state of affairs then would be what Marx described as "an association in which the free development of each is the condition for the free development of all."[1] It would not require everyone to sacrifice himself unconditionally for an abstract and transcendent community. To take human beings as an expedient means would disqualify the community of any legitimacy, because to do so offers no rule carrying universal validity. If everyone is to give all of himself, then the "free development of each" and consequently the "free development of all" would be rendered at naught.

That is enough on individualism and collectivism. Now we turn again to Yang Zhu and his time. More than a mere individualist, Yang Zhu might be further identified as a solipsist in ancient dress: Man (the individual) is the sole reality and the primary fact in the world. It follows that it is only the existence of one's self which is worthy of one's concern, so that all other thoughts and deeds should be submitted to this sole concern. And this mode of thinking leads his individualism astray to extremity. A theory once made absolute to an extreme will generally lead to its own negation. Yang Zhu's was no exception. It seems that to keep a modicum of modesty, a certain degree of eclecticism and intellectual compromise, is often the best way to remedy this.

The intellectual tradition of China having the group-oriented nature that it has had from its beginning, an individualist doctrine such as Yang Zhu's was bound to be severely criticized and pilloried by its adversaries, with all possible distortions and insults, and without the least tolerance or sympathy. As a matter of fact, the lack of individualism was precisely the strongest characteristic as well as the greatest shortcoming in China's traditional ideology. Just because of the lack of individualism in their political and social views, their views on the natural world were correspondingly incapable of embracing any atomism or accompanying mechanistic world-view—both being the starting points of modern science. Again due to the lack of individualism, there was an inevitable absence of democracy in either its ancient or modern dress, a further precondition for the development of science. There have been numerous instances in history which showed how the establishment of an absolute intellectual authority impeded the advancement of learning. Despite the fact that despotism was never a necessary attribute of Oriental civilization (contrary to the claims of some researchers about "Oriental despotism," as if all despotism is Oriental and

① K. Marx and F. Engels, *Manifesto of the Communist Party*, chap. 2 (Beijing: For. Lang. Pr., 1972), p. 59.

all that is Oriental is despotic), the plain fact remains that the rule of despotism long impeded the progress of science and democracy in China. It is in this sense that we ought to evaluate Yang Zhu's individualism more highly than people have usually done. We ought to regret that people have been prone to forget such a unique figure who initiated an individualist line of thought in China.

In the intrinsic logic of thought, individualism is not only in close connection with science and democracy, but also with morals and morality. Man is a thinking animal, and also an animal endowed with a moral sense. The behavior of all animals is dominated by their instincts, but men (and men alone) are further guided by their moral sentiments, rising high above the level of instinct. But at the same time, moral teachings can serve and indeed often have served as a means for cheating others.

Ultimately the hypocritical moral homilies enjoined giving up oneself for the sake of greatness and glory. Behind the all these high-sounding ideals, one may often discern the incursion of some underhanded, violent selfishness, just as Lu Xun wrote in his "Diary of a Madman"—behind all the sermons of benevolence and righteousness there lurked the simple bloody reality of "men devouring men." And Yang Zhu's bold support of individual rights against any supra-human moral dogma might justly be seen as a defense of human rights in an ancient form, and an affirmation and proclamation of the value of the rights of men. Man is an end in himself with his own intrinsic values, and never a subservient tool for others. One should never dedicate oneself unconditionally to a supra-human community (under what guise it may be), and one never has the right to ask others to dedicate themselves to be a mere tool in serving one's own end. In the doctrines of the Confucians and Mohists we find hidden the danger that they could be easily utilized to serve a hypocritical moralizing purely for the benefit of the ruling classes. The ancient Taoists rejected these hypocrisies simply through their attitude of indifference. But Yang Zhu dared confront it face to face by holding up the right of life against encroachment done in the name of the community. Why was it that Yang Zhu's doctrine once achieved such popularity in antiquity? Though few definite records were left to us, its strength doubtless lay in its insistence on the right to life and liberty and in its resistance to outside coercion. And in its turn, just because the individuals deprived of their right to life and liberty were obliged to prostrate themselves in front of the imperial despotism of the great unified empire, Yang's individualism after a short period of flourishing was doomed to swiftly fade away.

It may be observed that each time there occurred an anti-despotic upsurge, people would naturally turn to the cause of individual rights for their intellectual reinforcement against authoritarian control from above. In a certain sense, this was to resist the divine right of the sovereigns with the natural rights of men. Throughout the long course of China's history, so to speak, there can be witnessed five great movements for intellectual emancipation. The first was embodied in the ancient Taoists and the Yang Zhu school, who earnestly resisted external authority by resorting to the value and rights of the individual. The second was the emancipation of individuality in the Wei and Jin period (3rd-5th centuries), demanding freedom from the restraint of traditional mores through venerating the way of nature. The impulse of the return to nature was namely a return to human nature, which was simply an integral part of nature generally. Representative of the third movement was the idealistic current of thought of the late Ming Dynasty (16th-17th centuries) which rejected conventional authoritative bondage by the invocation of one's own inner authority (some kind of transcendental consciousness). The fourth drive for intellectual emancipation followed the Reform Movement at the end of the 19th century, which was characterized by a polemic between "the doctrine of human rights and equality" and the traditional dogmas of the feudal ideology. The fifth movement was the "May Fourth Movement", giving priority to "science" and "democracy" against all the traditional "ghostly nonsense" in the words of Lu Xun. Thus there has been a long series of conflicts in the intellectual arena between the rationalist appeal to reason and the fetishistic belief in authority. One could never overvalue Yang Zhu's place as a leading forerunner of intellectual emancipation in this sense.

Now let us turn to the ethical side for a rational implication of Yang Zhu's doctrine. Is there any meaning or aim in human life? Of course, one can not expect any final answer satisfactory to such a perennial question. Even in the sphere of natural science, there is and can be no eternally unvarying answer to a question; and such is even more the case with any value judgment beyond the reach of scientific research. To reduce the question to its most basic, let us deal with it from our daily experience. Perhaps everyone may agree with the simple point of view that life is the pursuit of happiness, or what is the same, men are born for happiness. But then, what is happiness? This is again a question hard to give a unanimous answer. A plain and handy solution is to define happiness as pleasure. And pleasure in a most simplistic way means nothing other than the physical enjoyment which in turn is but sensual satisfaction. But as everyone knows well, sensual satisfaction is but momentary and fleeting and can never endure long. Hence hedonism is destined to bring about its own self-negation. That is why mere sensual satisfaction can not provide a measure of happiness. Some are prone to take the possession of wealth to be the greatest or the sole happiness. But more wealth does not necessarily bring about more happiness—nor does it mean more sensual enjoyment. Sensual enjoyment has its limits and does not entail any psychic or mental satisfaction, which after all is the most important component in what may be termed happiness. As soon as the momentary sensual satisfaction is over, one has to seek new stimulus, and this leads to various lusts. But all kinds of lust will eventually result in disappointment. Instead of getting greater satisfaction, those indulging in sensual enjoyment invariably fall into deeper frustration and hollowness. For the moderns, their material enjoyment and sensual excitement surely far surpass that of the ancients, but whether they are much happier than the ancients living in the Tao Hua Yuan (Fountain of the Peach Blooms—a legendary Shangri-La in ancient China) or in Arcadia is very doubtful. There is implied here a twofold judgment, both on the ethical side and on the material side. The point involved here is just this: any satisfaction of a material or physical kind does not necessarily mean satisfaction in a mental or spiritual sense. These two kinds of fulfillment are neither parallel nor synchronic. The satisfaction of the one does not necessarily bring about the satisfaction of the other. Yet the condition of true happiness exists predominantly in a mental or spiritual state without which mere physical and sensual enjoyment comes to nothing. True happiness requires that any physical satisfaction be transmuted into a spiritual level.

In a certain sense both the Taoists and Yang Zhu, like many other ancient philosophers, took the pursuit of a state of true happiness as the cardinal aim in life. Or, in more general terms, each philosopher hoped to give rise to an ideal state of being in his utopia. But such a condition is found not in physical but in mental satisfaction. The same also held true for Confucius, who advised, "With coarse food to eat, with water to drink and my bended arm for a pillow—I have still joy in the midst of these things. Riches and honors acquired by unrighteousness are to me as a floating cloud";[①] and again: "With a single bamboo dish of rice, a single gourd of drink, and living in his mean narrow lane, while others could not have endured the distress, he [Yan Yuan, Confucius' disciple] did not allow his joy to be diminished."[②] We have to admit that this is really a state of happiness in its truest sense. And the Mohist maxim "for the benefit of the world" represents too a state of happiness, for happiness exists nowhere else but in one's earnest pursuit of happiness, just as truth exists nowhere else but in the earnest pursuit of truth. In the last analysis, all utopias refer more to a spiritual

① *Analects*, chap. 7, 76.

② *Analects*, chap. 6, 11.

state than to mere material conditions. So it may be asserted that the essence of happiness is something with a strong spiritual element.

As earlier articulated, the Chinese culture is one of a people above all most practical. Circumspection about practical gains and losses made them as ready to receive any teaching as to renounce it; therefore in their heart of hearts they never truly cared for it. They might easily accept a belief, and just as easily give it up. The reason is simply that they have no deep-rooted belief at all, just as they did not in the case of Hong Xiuquan. This pragmatic spirit or practicality constituted the basic characteristic of the Chinese mentality. Of course, it does not mean that the Chinese people were destined to be a people of practicality. The character of a nation is as a rule only a product of its specific historical conditions and background, and hence varies with them. Yet once it is formed, it becomes an integral part of their lives that will guide them in their reaction to the outside world. The Chinese people with their deep-rooted practicality have been a non-religious people, and have never embraced in their innermost hearts any faith, religious or other. They accepted any belief just as easily as they might renounce it. The reason perhaps should be sought in the lack of individualism in their cultural tradition. An isolated individual, a forlorn particle in the infinite universe confronting the insoluble mystery of reality and life, would naturally be led to probe into an ultimate answer, and this gave birth to scientific inquiry. And in the sphere of faith he will long for some spiritual sustenance, leading to the birth of religion. But in the Chinese tradition the individual was completely merged into the community, and their sole concern was nothing other than the overwhelming obligation of the individual to the community in practical life, beyond which they never took any interest. Both science and religion are motivated by a longing (a kind of *selige Sehnsucht*) for something or somewhere in the beyond. The precondition of such a spiritual longing is the opposition between, on the one hand, the infiniteness of the individual and the universe and, on the other, our daily life. As mentioned above, the Chinese mind never worried itself with anything beyond the practicality of our daily life or what was outside of realistic utility. The Confucian teaching says, "The subjects on which the Master [Confucius] did not speak were extraordinary things, feats of strength, disorder and spiritual beings."[①] And similarly, "What is beyond the realistic world, whatever it may be, a sage never speaks of"—these were all embodiments of this spirit. But the Taoist teaching of the return to nature also exemplified the search for an enjoyable natural life, and they never tried

① *Analects*, chap. 7, 21.

to probe the mystery beyond or behind the realistic world in which they led their lives. Thus they urged: "Banish wisdom, discard knowledge."[①] As for the *Yin-Yang* school and the Legalists, all their ideas were completely permeated with a spirit of worldliness, what they pursued belonging exclusively to this world and nothing beyond. Since family and political ethics provided the final ends for the individual, they accounted for everything that was demanded of him. We may well remember that when one of the first astronauts in space established contact with the surface of the earth, he was asked: "Do you feel lonely in the space?" To this he replied, "Not at all, I know there are millions on earth who are supporting me." This way, he dispelled the loneliness of an individualist. In the intellectual tradition of China, the family and the authority of the state with its political ethics took priority in the life of the individual and reigned unconditionally over the individual. The requirements of these were given categorically and were not derived from the logical reasoning of the individual. And they carried closely related views on the world and on life. And further, it was intrinsically linked with the often-controversial question of why China never developed science (no modern science, to be exact). Since there had been little individualism in China, there was no mechanistic or atomistic thinking in their natural outlook, and hence no science in an orderly form. So rare was individualism in the Chinese tradition, more space should be allotted to Yang Zhu's ideas.

Yang Zhu's maxim of "for the self" did not lead to the conclusion that one was allowed to do whatever one would like to the neglect of others, as at first sight it might seem. This was just because keeping harmony with the outside world (both natural and social) was of the utmost importance for one's happiness. For oneself, indulgence in concupiscence was surely not a way leading to real happiness; hence in the pursuit of the greatest happiness, one had to be moderate. As we may see, this was the key point which led to the birth of Stoicism in the West. In a certain sense, the Taoists and the Yang Zhu school also had much in common with the Epicureans. All of them knew well that the sole way "for oneself" consisted in the best preservation of oneself, which logically included the best preservation of the world one lived in. To take no care of the outside world and others would result in disasters for oneself. If one were to take care only of oneself to the complete neglect of others, the whole world would fall into chaos and one would not be able to get what one wanted. This seems to be the natural conclusion an individualist ought to reach.

---

① *Book of Lao Zi*, chap. 19.

Striving to "see life steadily and to see it whole" in order to serve the purpose "for oneself" to the best would teach a person how to keep an optimal balance in the relationship between the individual and the community. The course of human history—so it seems—marches forward amidst the antinomy between individualism and collectivism, either of which would lead to its own denial if carried to an extreme. Such an extreme case with its inevitable disasters is shown manifestly by the realities of our own age. By implication, it seems that any theory when pursued to its fullest would end only in its own abnegation. Thus a certain degree of intellectual and theoretical moderation, even humility, would seem conducive to the progress of humanity. The intellectual culture of a society is by its very nature a pluralistic synthesis and can only find sound development through a process of unity in variety and variety in unity. Neither regarding some authority as the sole truth nor acting as one pleases irrespective of any regulation would do any good to the development of intellectual culture. Man is a rational animal and rationality itself comprises moral rules, including respect for others. All animals act by the impulse of their instincts; it is men and men only who act with a moral sense. But morality when over-puffed becomes a hypocritical preaching with immoral consequences never found in any other species of the animal world. The most unholy catastrophes of human history have as a rule been conducted under the pretense of the most holy and sacrosanct slogans.

Yang Zhu's principle, "Each one for himself"—so that he would not pluck out a single hair even if it benefited the whole world—in fact implies: I do *not* benefit the whole world by plucking out a simple hair, nor does any one else by plucking out his. Yang Zhu apparently recognized the role of human desires as objectively existent and ineradicable. Consequently, how to satisfy our desires most favorably and optimally became the nucleus of the theory whereby "Yang Zhu valued the self."① Yang Zhu's solution was to "never go so far as to harm one's body" and "to keep moderation in order to give a rein to our desires," i.e. to find a rational limit. This solution would be more reasonable and practical than any hypocritical moral preaching. Unfortunately, throughout the history of China, there has been more moralistic hypocrisy than realistic humility in confronting the weaknesses of human nature, and this inevitably hindered the spiritual enrichment of the people. Hypocrisy could only result in various kinds of fraud, and the elevation of spiritual life is brought not through bluffing but in, so to speak, "the happiness through sorrows" (durch Leiden Freude). Any

① *Spring and Autumn Annals*, "Bu Er."

communitarian preaching which totally obliterated the rights and natural desires of the individual was both illogical in theory and unrealistic in practice. The value of a theory exists in its capacity for achieving an optimal satisfaction of various and even conflicting human desires.

All philosophical schools in the classical age tried hard to "save the world" by earnestly propounding their own ways (Tao). What was of cardinal significance in saving the world was certainly the role of the political power. Following Yang Zhu's teaching, if all were not to pluck out a hair for the benefit of the whole world, then not a hair would be plucked out in the whole world; and if not a hair is touched in the world, then the world will be in good order. Such a theory in its essence might be identified as the forerunner of modern liberalism: everyone is the best judge and guardian of his own welfare, and if each is permitted to take care of himself and to act by himself (*laissez-faire*) without any outside interference, the community would naturally proceed in the best possible way. In other words, a government which interferes the least would be the best. It seems as though what Adam Smith professed in his *Wealth of Nations* has the same validity in the political realm. And it is really a wonder that we find one of its precursors in ancient China. But for all ancient and modern liberals, the same basic issue confronting them was this: would human nature with no outside interference whatever proceed automatically towards an increasing improvement by itself? And could we thus expect increasing political and social betterment? Further, is human nature predestined to be so good as to lead us necessarily to an earthly paradise, as long as it is not affected or coerced by any external force? Herein is implied a logical presupposition about human nature.

In Yang Zhu's reasoning, if no one was to pluck out a hair for the benefit of others, then everyone would be permitted to keep his life in the best way. The premise of "the preservation of life" was that one should not be interfered with by external force, hence in the political realm entailing anarchy. Because of this, Yang Zhu was lambasted by Mencius as "not acknowledging the sovereign," just as in the same way Mo Zi was criticized for "not acknowledging the father."① In traditional Chinese manners, the greatest evidence of one's evil was "not to acknowledge the sovereign, nor the father." Hence Mencius' conclusion that it was "the same as beasts."②

We can recall the legend of Yang Zhu weeping in bitter frustration when

① *Book of Mencius*, "Duke Wen of Teng," pt. 2.

② Ibid.

faced with the choice of paths at a crossroad. This fable may serve as symbolic illustration of Yang Zhu's intellectual puzzlement. The fabric of social life was variegated and the roads in our lives manifold. It was indeed very hard to choose the one which would prove best for the preservation of life. Yang Zhu's doctrine reflected the mentality of the small proprietors who, while wholeheartedly concerned with their own preservation, did not understand well that an individual was at the same time but a particle interwoven within a certain social context, and could by no means be separated and segregated from its social role, even in a life of self-preservation. At this juncture, ancient philosophers might be classified into two camps: one actively engaging in the reform of the world at large, while the other passively escaping from it. Among the former were the prominent schools of the Confucians and the Mohists who tried to improve their lives by remodeling political society. In the latter camp were the Taoists, the hermits and the Yang Zhu school, who tried to escape from political society in order to preserve themselves in the state of nature. The former group often fell short of their ideals and ended in hollow rhetoric, for real society was after all independent of their wills and wishes. As for the second camp, not only did their practice get nowhere, but even their theory was deficient. The preservation of individual life after all could not be maintained as an ultimate value, for the value of life ought be sought beyond the sphere of one's mere existence—in his pursuit of truth, goodness and beauty beyond the bounds of his personal preservation. Inner satisfaction does not have its own existence independent of the outside world. At any rate, ever since mankind entered into the civil state out of the state of nature, no individual could have independent existence outside of the community. Hence there is no possibility for the existence of an independent, self-subsistent and self-sufficient state of happiness without the social conditions in which the individual lives, even though logically we must admit the sum of the happiness of all the individuals to be the measure of the community's worth. The whole secret of an ideal state lies in finding the optimum union of the two contraries: personal freedom and communal coercion. Throughout the long course of Chinese history, her predominant ideology has always been collectivism, i.e. anti-individualism. Yet alongside it has always been a current demanding the autonomy of the individual, the Taoists and the Yang Zhu school its foremost representatives. A famous maxim of Confucius runs, "I'll find the ardent and the cautiously-minded [as my companions]. The ardent will advance and lay hold of something [truth]; the cautiously-minded will keep themselves from something [wrong]."[①] Those of the ardent camp were the determined social reformers while the cautiously-minded the passive non-conformists. And any passive non-conformist was at bottom a protester against the existing social order. (As Confucius said, "Some men of worth retire from the world."[②]) To the former camp belonged those who "know the impracticable and yet will do it,"[③] while to the latter belonged those who knew the impracticable and would not do it. Here lies the distinction between the two different currents in the realm of ancient thought.

The late Prof. Hou Wailu, the foremost Marxist historian in the field of the intellectual history of China, in his monumental work *A General Intellectual History of China* remarked that it was Yang Zhu who in ancient China was the first to discover that besides the interpersonal context there was still the existence of the individual *per se* who had his own value. Here Prof. Hou's remark came very much to the point. The orthodox thinking of China has been accustomed to view the individual as a mere vehicle amidst the complex of interpersonal relationships, and so much so that it never considered the plain fact of the existence of the atomic man. Man is not merely a component of an ethical context. He was first of all a living being independent of and in confrontation with the world around him. He was a being of blood and flesh with his own dignity, not simply a vehicle for some lofty ideals. Human life is endowed with intrinsic and inalienable value, and is hence not just an instrument, even though its fulfillment is inseparable from the conditions of the outside world. Viewed in this light, Yang Zhu ought to occupy a much higher place than he is usually allotted.

---

① *Analects*, chap. 13, 21.

② Ibid., chap. 14, 37.

③ Ibid., chap. 14, 38.

Chapter Six: Xun Zi

[I] Xun Zi and Coufucianism

Confucius, Mencius and Xun Zi have been generally acknowledged as the three greatest masters of the pre-Qin Confucian school. Both Mencius and Xun Zi venerated Confucius highly, but in very different ways. Like almost all ancient philosophers, the exact dates of Xun Zi's life cannot be ascertained. He came roughly a little over a century after Mencius (ca. 4th-3rd centuries B.C.), that is, he flourished in the century just before the great unification of all of China under the First Emperor of Qin.

Geographically, various schools were distributed and propagated mainly in different areas; the Confucians in Zou and Lu (now Shandong), hence being called "the gentlemen from Zou and Lu," the Taoists in the south (now the Huai River Valley), and the Legalists in the three Jins (i.e. Han, Zhao and Wei, now Shanxi and around). Xun Zi was a native of Zhao and became the foremost predecessor of the Legalist school. He traveled for a time in Jixia (of the Qi State, now Lingzi in Shandong) where the Academy was the center of the teachings of various schools. Each school was trying hard to win over the patronage of their sovereigns, promoting their specific plans and ideas for reforming society and thereby fostering their own advancement. Later, Xun Zi left Qi and went to Chu, where Lord Chunsheng appointed him as the mayor of Lanling, and afterwards he discussed warfare with the king of Zhao. When Lord Chunsheng died, Xun Zi came back to Chu and settled down at Lanling.

Xun Zi's family name was Sun with the given name Qing. Among all the then existing states, Qi ranked as the most wealthy and populous, and all schools were permitted academic freedom. The learning at Jixia reached its culmination during the reign of King Xuan and King Wei. According to Sima Qian's *Records of the Historian*, "King Xuan was fond of the literati, of whom Zou Yan, Chunyu Kun, Tian Bing, Jie Yu, Shen Dao, Huan Yuan and others, totaling seventy-six in number, were all bestowed houses and high ranks as senior counselors (*dai fu*), participating in political consultations without holding specific office; and it was then that the Jixia Academy of Qi flourished once more with hundreds of scholars therein."[①] According to the record of Ying Shao's *General Treatise on Customs and Manners*, Xun Zi "had three times assumed the position of dean [of the Jixia Academy]." And Sima Qian in his *Records of the Historian* had called Xun Zi "the foremost master" of his age. But his posthumous fate underwent a rather different course to that of Mencius. Mencius during his lifetime was not so illustrious, but after the reign of the Song Dynasty he was honored as the vice-sage, second only to Confucius. In contrast, Xun Zi's place came much lower and lagged far behind Mencius' in China's long history. Yet it is noteworthy that in recent decades Xun Zi has been evaluated ever higher. Firstly, because both Confucius and Mencius are labeled as idealists and so considered deserving of scorn, while Xun Zi was a materialist; and secondly because Xun Zi had a close relation with the Legalists, who were highly praised especially in the years of the Cultural Revolution (1966-1976) when in the course of the campaign of "the struggle between of the Confucians and Legalists" Xun Zi's place was heightened together with that of the Legalists. In reality, there is no such thing as a philosophy that is one hundred percent purely its own, and each philosopher is of necessity influenced by others as well as influencing others. Strictly speaking, everyone is a product of varied origins, and Xun Zi was no exception. It is impossible for him to have been otherwise. Of him, Tan Sitong (1865-1898), the outstanding philosopher of the late 19th century, launched the criticism, "All the politics of the last two thousand years have been those of the Qin Dynasty, for they were all bandits and robbers; all the learning of the last two thousand years has been that of Xun Zi, for they were all hypocrites and good-for-nothing." Tan's remarks are worthy of consideration—though from the reverse side. Traditionally, people took the teachings of Confucius and Mencius as the predominant learning of the last two thousand years. So Tan Sitong endowed Xun Zi with a historic significance quite contrary to the generally accepted tradition. One may find intriguing and penetrating insights in these remarks of his.

The conditions in which Xun Zi lived had already greatly changed from

① Sima Qian, *Records of the Historian.*

that of the time of both Confucius and Mencius. In the time of Confucius, the traditional socio-political order, though unstable, had not as yet collapsed, and Confucius longed to sustain it through some measures of reform. In this sense, Confucius was a conservative. By the time of Mencius the traditional order had already given away, and every state was undergoing a series of reforms, the ancient civilization of rites and music thus impossible to maintain as before. Mencius' whole life was spent disputing with his opponents. "Indeed, I am not fond of disputing, but I am compelled to do it,"[①] he sighed. In the *Book of Mencius*, we discover few of the political ideals as embraced by Confucius. "In the last month of spring, with the dress of the season all complete, along with five or six young men who have assumed their caps [representing adulthood], and six or seven boys, I would wash in the Yi River, enjoy the breeze among the rain-altars, and return home singing."[②] These sentimental and pastoral longings of Confucius could not be found in Mencius. The age of Xun Zi was drawing ever nearer to the great unification under the sole imperial sovereign of Qin. It was already apparent that a forthcoming great war of unification was inevitable. Hence Xun Zi focused much more on the outside world than on the moral cultivation of the innate mind. Besides, Confucius and Mencius were not at all interested in the natural world, while Xun Zi discussed natural knowledge at length, intending to more closely link the natural world with social life through his philosophy.

Mencius professed the inborn goodness of human nature, but Xun Zi professed the inborn evil of human nature. "The nature of man is evil; his goodness is only acquired training",[③] thus runs the opening sentence of the chapter on "The Evil of Man's Nature" in the *Book of Xun Zi*. In the Chinese lexicon, the term "*wei*" means either falseness (contrasted with truthfulness) or artificiality (man-made, contrasted with what is natural). This term "*wei*" in Xun Zi means what is acquired by human effort instead of what is endowed by nature. Mencius claimed goodness is inborn in nature, but Xun Zi held that it was acquired by human effort. Confucius and Mencius both emphatically professed the need to develop the goodness in human nature, recommending that, if everyone tried hard to develop it, the world itself would improve. But Xun Zi stressed the "persuasion of learning," i.e. the inner self being remodeled by external education. It is exactly because of this point that Xun Zi was praised

① *Book of Mencius,* "Duke Wen of Teng," pt. 2.

② *Analects,* "Xiang Dang."

③ *Book of Xun Zi,* "Xing E."

so effusively by researchers in recent decades.

There are still other aspects wherein Mencius and Xun Zi differ from each other. People often take Mencius as "a follower of the ancient kings" and Xun Zi "a follower of the later Kings." The "ancient kings" are the idealized sage-kings of antiquity such as Yao, Shun, Yu and Tan, whereas the "later Kings" are King Wen and King Wu of the Zhou Dynasty. This shows that Xun Zi's sights fell on the more modern times rather than on the idealized bygone days. Mencius preached "the way of benevolent governance (wang dao)," while Xun Zi "the way of high-handed governance (*ba dao*)"—the former ruling by virtue, the latter by force. But we shall see later that there is essentially little difference between Mencius' "ancient kings" and "benevolent governance" and Xun Zi's "later kings" and "high-handed governance." In addition, Mencius emphasized "obligation," which formed the nucleus of his thought, while Xun Zi placed much more emphasis on "utility"—a divergence leading to the polemic between obligation and utility in later ages. It might be seen from this that Mencius and Xun Zi represented respectively two main trends of pre-Qin Confucianism. Prof. Feng Youlan in his *History of Chinese Philosophy* said that Confucius' place in China resembles that of Socrates, Mencius' that of Plato and Xun Zi's that of Aristotle. Yet in a very significant respect, Xun Zi fell distinctly short of being on a par with Aristotle; for through the long mediaeval times it was Aristotle (not Plato) who was hallowed as the sole authority, but in China that glory belonged not to Xun Zi but to Mencius. In mediaeval China Xun Zi had long been neglected, and not until the Qing Dynasty with the flourishing of textual criticism was his thought studied scrupulously.

There are thirty-two chapters in the *Book of Xun Zi*, circulated down to the present day, but it is likely that some were not his own writings. And the chapter "Refutations of the Twelve Philosophers" resembles very much the chapter entitled "The World" in the *Book of Zhuang Zi*, both sharing the aim of criticizing the philosophical schools then in existence. From his criticism of other schools, his own views were clearly shown. The chapter on "Refutations of the Twelve Philosophers" affords us certain information not to be found elsewhere in ancient literature. For instance, it mentions the relation between Mencius and the doctrine of the "five elements"—something not discussed in other sources, not even in the *Book of Mencius* itself. Xun Zi's time was not long after that of Mencius, so this assertion ought to have its grounds, thus giving us a very valuable source in the study of ancient intellectual history.

The thought of Xun Zi did not evolve into the form of an independent school, except in that some elements were transmitted into the Legalist literature. Confucianism in the later ages primarily adhered to the legacy of the Confucius-Mencius teachings, and what flourished was the idealistic component of their ethics. In contrast, Xun Zi's teachings were significant because he, in his role as the last master of classical Confucianism, expounded its materialistic parts and along this direction promoted the theoretical foundations of the forthcoming Legalist school.

[II] Human Nature and Social Order

Like so many ancient Chinese philosophers, Xun Zi also took his basic evaluation of human nature as the foundation for his theory. For Mencius, human nature is what makes man a man, while for Xun Zi human nature is merely the animal instinct; therefore his evaluation of human nature is just the opposite of Mencius'. Mencius' theory of the goodness of human nature assumed that the seeds of benevolence, obligation, rites (propriety) and intelligence were already intrinsically given in human nature, but Xun Zi declared with certainty, "The nature of man is evil; his goodness is only acquired training."① For Xun Zi, the distinction between good and evil was no more than this: "Nature is the unwrought material of the original; what are acquired are the accomplishments and refinements brought about by cultivation and observation of the rules of proper conduct. Without nature, there would be nothing upon which to cultivate the acquired. Without the acquired, nature could not better itself."② What is implied by "the acquired" (wei) in the terminology of Xun Zi is this: human nature can be and ought to be perfected only through a strenuous process of acquired training. Hence he gives an exposition of human nature in argument.

Now man, by his nature, loves profit at his birth; and if he follows this tendency, strife and rapacity come about, whereas courtesy and yielding disappear. Man at birth is envious and hateful, and if he follows these tendencies, injury and destruction result, whereas loyalty and faithfulness disappear. At birth he possesses the desires of the ear and eye and likes sounds and beauties, and if he follows these tendencies, impurity and disorder result, whereas the rules of rites and obligations and finish and orderliness disappear. Therefore to give rein to man's original nature and to follow man's feelings means inevitable

① Ibid.

② *Book of Xun Zi,* "On the Rites."

strife and rapacity, together with violation of etiquette and confusion in the proper way of doing things and a reversion to a state of violence. Therefore the civilizing influence of teachers and laws, and the guidance of the rules of proper conduct and standards of justice are absolutely necessary. Thereupon courtesy results, culture is developed, and good government is the consequence. By this line of reasoning it is evident that the nature of man is evil and his goodness is acquired.[①]

From these lines it seems as though Xun Zi was in direct opposition to Mencius, but on further inspection the main tendency and goal of both were substantially the same, i.e. both strove for the rule of a sage-king. Here lies the basic watershed between Chinese classical philosophy and that of ancient Greece. Hence Tan Sitong accused Xun Zi of "endowing the sovereign with the supreme power to rule over the country by his sole monopoly of the learning of the rites."[②]

For Xun Zi, human nature is made up of the inborn natural desires of human beings, or their natural instincts, hence his well-known premise: "What makes one's life as it is, is called human nature."[③] Evils come out of human nature, goodness is the result of the remodeling of this nature, and hence is the result of human effort. On this premise Xun Zi went along with the theory of Thomas Hobbes which assumed that all humans are selfish and in pursuit of their own profit, thus the relation between people in the state of nature being like that of wolf to wolf in a situation of constant brutality, a war of each against everyone.[④] Such a state of nature surely cannot subsist long, and consequently people are obliged to reach an agreement of obedience to a generally acknowledged rule. For Xun Zi, people are born evil by nature. There is no innate goodness whatsoever in it—if there were, such inborn goodness once given an outlet would spontaneously result in the good of all. For Xun Zi, goodness could only be attained through a process of strenuous effort. Hence the chapter "Persuasion on Learning" in the *Book of Xun Zi* urged people to learn and to reform themselves unceasingly. In contrast to Xun Zi's emphasis on the reformative function of artificial education, Mencius claimed that the goodness of human nature is not "what is formed outwardly." The seeds of goodness dwell already within us, and the point is only to develop them to the greatest degree. In short, Mencius held a theory of moral spontaneity, while

① *Book of Xun Zi,* "The Evilness of Nature."

② Tan Sitong, *The Learning of Benevolence.*

③ *Book of Xun Zi,* "Rectification of Names."

④ Hobbes, *Leviathan,* chap. 13.

Xun Zi demanded conscious endeavor. Mencius took what ought to be as what is, and Xun Zi conversely advised reforming what is into what ought to be. In later ages, we may find there were always two different approaches to self-perfection: one is the elevation of our intrinsic virtue, the other the pursuit of learning and conscious cultivation. "Elevating our intrinsic virtue" implies that there are virtues already innate in us, and all that is left for us to do is to elevate and develop these virtues. This approach urges the self-cultivation and self-perfection of our mind, whereas the other professes reliance on learning alone, through which one can hope to grasp exact knowledge and do good. It might be seen that Mencius and Xun Zi initiated these two different approaches respectively. The divergence arises both from their personal philosophical temperaments and their specific ways of thinking. Ever since the 17th century, the main tendency of thinking in the West has proceeded along two different lines. One extols logical speculation, starting with Descartes and culminating in Enlightenment worship of reason and the scientific positivism of the 19th century, while the other upheld the priority of the heart over the brain, beginning with Pascal who preached "le coeur a ses raison que la raison ne connait point,"① that is, man thinks not only with his brain but also with his heart. This latter approach lasts down to the present day and results in the theories of Continental philosophy such as existentialism. This phenomenon of a synchronous divergence in the modern West allows a fascinating comparison with that in ancient and mediaeval China.

Mencius proclaimed, "Everyone can become a sage like Yao and Shun." Xun Zi also declared, "Every man in the street can become a sage like Yu."② Yao, Shun and Yu were the legendary sage-kings. Mencius' assertion and Xun Zi's are similar, but the paths leading there are quite different. For Mencius, everyone may become a sage by developing his innate goodness, while Xun Zi on the contrary held that only by means of learning is one able to attain sagehood. Thus he said, "What cannot be learned and cannot be engaged is called nature. What can be learned and mastered and can be engaged and accomplished is called the acquired training." And again: "What gave Yu the qualities of Yu was that he put into practice human-heartedness and righteousness and was obedient to law and uprightness. So there is the possibility of knowing and practicing human-heartedness, righteousness, and obedience to law and uprightness. This being so, an ordinary man in the street has the capacity for knowing

① Pascal, *Pensées*, ed. Brunschvicg, 277.

② *Book of Xun Zi,* "The Evilness of Nature."

human-heartedness, righteousness and obedience to law and uprightness, as well as the means to carry out these principles. Thus it is evident that he can become a Yu."[①]

Both Mencius and Xun Zi took sagehood to be "the culmination of humanity," but as to how one can attain such a state of perfection, they proposed different ways. For Xun Zi, human nature inherently included desires and sensuality which once let loose would degrade a man into a beast. In this aspect the human being is the same as the beast. Yet after all human beings are not on a par with beasts, so Mencius asserted, "That whereby man differs from the beasts is but a trifle. The mass of people often cast it away, while the superior men preserve it."[②] Mencius identified this trifle with the goodness inborn in human nature. But for Xun Zi human nature is composed entirely of natural desires and concupiscence, which once given a free rein can never be satiated. Yet it came forth out of nature, and so could neither be easily suppressed nor freely let loose. Therefore the issue lies in how to find an optimal point which could arrange human desires and lust so as to mitigate harmful effects. All those who subscribe to the theory of the evilness of human nature attempt to solve this problem by such an approach. If one gives up oneself completely to instincts, there would be no virtue at all. In a certain sense, virtue consists just in our subjugation of our instincts. The Hobbesian state of perpetual war of everyone against all of course cannot subsist long and the only way out is to agree upon coercion common to all, and thereupon a political and social authority is established.

Human nature *per se* carries no social implications whatsoever, and the idea of good and evil is a social product. For a Robinson Crusoe living on a desert island, the idea of good or evil is non-existent and meaningless. It is only when people leave the state of nature and enter into a civil state that there emerges what we call goodness and evilness. But the ancient Confucians, both Mencius and Xun Zi, had confused these two different states of affairs. Confucius and Mencius thought—decidedly too naively—that once the goodness inherent in human nature was set free, all would be well under the sun. The social background at the time of Xun Zi had greatly changed from that of the preceding centuries. During the late Warring States Period (3rd century B.C.) international wars and civil strife became so frequent and violent that "Slaughters caused the corpses of the dead to lie abundant in the fields." Under such circumstances the old-fashioned preaching of benevolence and obligations

① Ibid.

② *Book of Mencius,* "Li Lou," pt. 2.

(originating in Confucius and Mencius) was out of date and useless. At this historical juncture, Xun Zi emerged to maintain the social order by fortifying the rule of the rites (i.e. social and political regulations). Just before his time, nearly all states had undergone a process of "reform of laws and institutions" to meet the urgent needs of the time. Among these the most well-known were Shang Yang's reform in Qin and Wu Qi's in Chu. As the conventional institutions and orders could no longer support themselves, new ones were worked out to replace them—this was the substance of the "reform" of that time. As discussed previously, the conventional institutions were based on blood lineage and governed by the *patria potestas*. As the seven warring states each ruled over millions of people, the social and political conventions needed drastic adaptation to accommodate the new autocratic rule of a centralized government in place of the former hereditary nobility. Later under the rule of the First Emperor of Qin, "[hereditary] feudalism was abolished and [imperial] prefectures were established",[①] the aim of which was still the ongoing reforms, i.e. to centralize political powers in the hands of the royal regime. To meet such a transition of power, a new ideology was an urgent requirement. Xun Zi's theory of the rule of rites fit. A drastic reform was destined to conflict with the privileges of the old nobility, so the reforms were carried on through a series of bloody clashes. Such was the historical background to Xun Zi's theory, as well as the Legalists who succeeded him.

The course from Confucius' "benevolence" to Mencius' "obligation" and then to Xun Zi's "rule of rites" delineates the whole ideological course of Confucianism, forming an axis of Chinese civilization. The rule of rites was used to pacify social and psychological unrest, or in other words, to strike the best equilibrium for the people's minds as well as for the relations between people. This function of the rule of rites signifies Xun Zi's conception of civilization. It is a sort of modification of our inborn natural desires, after which an ideal state of civilization can be attained. In his "Theory of Rites" Xun Zi summarized his view of the origin of civilization in these words:

> Wherefrom does the rule of rites arise? The answer is that man at birth has desires. Where these desires are not satisfied, he cannot remain without seeking their satisfaction. Where this seeking for satisfaction is without measure or limit, there can only be contention. Where there is contention, there will be disorder; where there is disorder, everything will be destroyed. The ancient kings hated this disorder, and so they established the rule of the rites and obligation so as to set limits to this confusion and to satisfy men's desires and give opportunity for this satisfaction, in order that desires

① Sima Qian, *Records of the Historian*, "Life of the First Emperor of Qin."

should not be stretched to the breaking point by things, nor things be used up by desires, that they both should support each other and continue to survive. This is how the rites originated.①

The problem of the origin of civilization is a perennial question. It is only natural that when human desires are let loose, disorders and disputes will surely ensue. The rites are therefore instituted to regulate human behavior and set up a balance in the harmonious relationship among men. In another passage, he dealt further with this issue from the standpoint of his natural philosophy:

> Water and fire possess forces but are without life; shrubs and trees have life but no knowledge; birds and beasts have knowledge but no rite. Man has force, life, knowledge and also rites. Hence he is the highest being on earth. His strength is not equal to that of the ox; his running is not equal to that of the horses; and yet the ox and horse are used by him. This is because men are capable of social organization, whereas these others are incapable. How is it that men are able to form social relationships? Because of their social distinctions. How can these distinctions be carried out? Through their obligation.②

From this comes the conclusion: since man is bound to obligation, he is able to proceed "from distinction to unity, unity leads to uniformity, uniformity brings about force and force brings about strength, and strength overcomes all things." This is accomplished by means of the power that man has acquired over all others; hence man cannot live without social organization. Here is a semi-biological and semi-utilitarian theory of the origin of civilization. On the one hand Xun Zi explained from a biological perspective why men were civilized, while he also treated this topic from a utilitarian viewpoint. Civilization is nothing other than a social order, which originated through the quality which distinguishes man from other animals, i.e. his sociability. This is what enables man to master all things.

Xun Zi contended that, because the ancient sage-kings established the rule of rites, they made possible the transition from the state of nature to a civil state, from disorder to order. In this theory of the origin of civilization or his philosophy of history, it is noteworthy that the rites (indeed, civilization itself) were instituted by the ancient sage-kings. Herein lies the remarkable difference between the Chinese view of civilization and the Western (or, between the ancient and the modern). The Chinese view held civilization to be entirely an invention of the sage-kings, or what would be the same, the welfare of the people depended on the mercy of the sage-kings. In contrast, the modern view,

① *Book of Xun Zi,* "On the Rites."

② *Book of Xun Zi,* "On the Kingly Reign."

though granting the necessity of the social order and coercion, took it not as an invention of any governing sage or superman but as the consent of the governed and the establishment of social institutions as its consequence. The critical step by which man entered from the state of nature into civil state was realized—as the Chinese philosophers conceived it—by the sages, but to the moderns it was through contract, or the consent of the governed. This transition may be roughly summarized in H. Maine's famous dictum "from status to contract."①

Like all the pre-Qin philosophers, Xun Zi too nurtured his own utopia, or his "Tao" (Way), with the aim of saving the world. What distinguished him from others is his specific emphasis on the rule of rites, which was endowed with special significance in later ages. In a certain sense, Chinese culture is a culture traditionally based on rites. The notion "rites" embraces two meanings: one is the innate virtue and its outward expression, the other the social regulation and constraint on personal actions. In his idea, as in those of all other Confucians, the creation of the rites was attributed to the sages. They were in essence but the moral incarnations of the *patria potestas*. The subjection of the people to the rule of the sovereign was just the same as the children to their parents. Hence the ascriptions "sovereign-father" (*jun-fu*) and "subject-son" (*zi-min*). The state is just an enlarged family. The Chinese saw their utopia as a sweet home, and even the revolutionaries regard their community as "a great family of revolution." The Chinese followed the way of the sages, while the ancient Greeks that of the wise. In the city-states of ancient Greece, there was the custom out of finding a wise man to set legislations for them rather than a sage to rule over them. The wise men serve the country with their wisdom, whereas the sages rule over the country by their virtue. Xun Zi's utopia is a country under the "kingly institution" in which utility is united with morality. It was the sole example of this in classical China, and it was there where Xun Zi deviated remarkably from Confucius and Mencius. Hence Xun Zi made the famous statement, "The rites are the culmination of humanity."②

In another passage, Xun Zi amplified his ideal of the rule of the sages further, "The sovereignty should be assumed by the right man [i.e. the sage]. The empire is the weightiest thing there is. Only the strongest is able to bear its weight. It is the largest of all things. Only the most discriminating is able to work out its proper distinctions. It is the most populous. Only the wisest is

① H. Maine, *Ancient Law,* chap. 6.

② *Book of Xun Zi,* "On the Rites."

able to harmonize it."[1] Only the sage is the strongest, the most discriminating and the wisest. Only the sage possesses such excellent qualities as to be able to bear the burden of ruling the nation. The ideal of the ancient Greeks was a philosopher-king, while that of the Chinese was a sage-king both morally and intellectually. And just because the Chinese have been so prone to sage-worship and personality cult, they generally neglected the issue of how to design an institution to guarantee the normal operation of the political order. The tradition of their political ideals has always been to place their hopes unconditionally in a certain sage-king, never on the rule of law run by the multitude. That is why the Chinese in ancient times dreamt of a sage-king and in modern times a prophet-leader who would come forth to enlighten the people. Admittedly, it indeed ought to be a minority who assumes the ruling power instead of the majority of the common people supervising over the power of the rulers.

Confucius and Mencius preached benevolence and obligation, while Xun Zi stressed the rule of rites; this shows the difference between the earlier and later Confucians. But Xun Zi's doctrine—"heaven begets the people not for the sake of the king while heaven sets the king for the sake of the people"[2]—is still in line with Mencius' idea that the people are the root of the country. This is populism in its ancient sense, but not the modern idea of democracy that the sovereignty dwells in the people. In the last analysis, the thinking of the ancients relied on the benevolent rule of an enlightened prince but never of the people themselves. Hence Xun Zi made the conclusion: "The son of Heaven [i.e. the king or prince] is supreme in his power and position and is invincible under the sun."[3]

In the classics of ancient China, the term "sage" refers exclusively to the king or prince who is "the son of Heaven" and bears the mandate of Heaven. This theory has reigned over the Chinese mind for thousands of years. The hope for a wise sage-king to rule over the population has become an integral part of the Chinese way of thinking. It never occurred to them to design a mechanism by which the common people might take over the reins in ruling the country or supervising the ruler. It seemed as though a nation can only be run by the genius of a sage-king. Adam Smith's *Wealth of Nations* was published in 1776 and Kant's *Perpetual Peace* in 1795; both in their basic presumptions came very near to Xun Zi's that man is born selfish or even evil. Smith's theory was

① *Book of Xun Zi,* "On Politics."

② *Book of Xun Zi,* "On the Main."

③ *Book of Xun Zi,* "On Politics."

a deduction from his idea of human nature, i.e. man as a *homo economicus* is forever in pursuit of his greatest profit. In an imagined society where everyone is a saint and never concerned with his own profit but wholly dedicated to the cause of others, the Smithian economic theory would have no application. For Smith, the self-interest of everyone will successfully (though invisibly) lead to the harmony of the whole society. Herein lies the secret of the free market, which possesses the facility to regulate itself. Kant elevated Smith's theory of human nature to a philosophical level. Kant admitted the search of self-interest to be the instinct of everyone, but in so doing an optimum point might be found such that the self-interest of everyone might be satisfied while the harmony of man and man might be fairly maintained at the same time. Such a state of things depends on the establishment of a civil state based on the rule of law. In his thesis *The Idea of a Universal History from the Viewpoint of a World-Citizen*, Kant expounded his idea of man's "unsocial sociability." Man, though endowed with sociability naturally, is nevertheless gripped by an inclination to do everything in accordance with his own self-interest which is entirely unsocial in character. Thus there is the need of an optimal arrangement to both maintain social life and satisfy the self-interest of everyone as well. For Kant, the way out is no less than the formation of a universal civil state in which the unsocial character of everyone might be put to a reverse end and help the progress and development of the whole society. To raise interpersonal society to a still higher condition, the same must be done with international society. If each nation intends to conquer others for its self-interest, the world will fall into chaos. Therefore a program has to be established to ensure eternal peace in the world. The end of a civil state is just this eternal peace. This is the main thesis of Kant's *Perpetual Peace*. It is surely the best conclusion that human reason could ever reach. Yet Chinese philosophers have oriented their thinking in a different direction to this.

[III] The Political Ideal of Xun Zi

Since Confucius and Mencius stressed the goodness inborn in human nature while Xun Zi stressed its evilness, Xun Zi seems more modern in his quality as a competent thinker. Confucius and Mencius both appear to have failed in finding an equilibrium between utility and morality, but Xun Zi did identify such. Xun Zi found it by his design of a mechanism run by the rule of rites—a mechanism which turned out more practicable than phony moral sermonizing. It seems

Xun Zi succeeded where Confucius and Mencius had failed. A well-developed society should be designed and maintained, so to speak, not only by science and technology in the material sphere but also by the social and political and other superstructures (ideas, arts, etc.) that conform with it. In endeavoring to draw wisdom from the legacy of traditional thought, we will very probably find much more from Xun Zi than from Confucius and Mencius.

Confucius and Xun Zi both stressed the importance of the rites, but each had his own specific connotation. Confucius laid down the rites on the basis of the natural spontaneity of one's innermost heart, it being impossible for our virtue not to comply with what the rites required. Confucius said of himself, "At the age of seventy, I could follow what my heart desired, without transgressing what was right."① Etymologically, "what was right" was the "rule" (*ju*) which conveyed a sense of external regulation. Confucius' compliance with external regulation was but the natural outflow of his innermost heart. In contradistinction with Confucius, the rites conveyed for Xun Zi an idea of much greater external regulation, on the grounds that "human nature is evil, his goodness is only acquired training."② What is good in human conduct is not the inner heart's natural tendency but a strenuous effort of conscientious regulation of his nature, and hence Xun Zi paid more attention to external modification than did Confucius. In the time of Confucius, the conventional social mores—though already shaken—had not yet fallen apart and still retained its former structure. Down to the age of Xun Zi, the society had undergone a series of changes and transformations during a span of more than two centuries. The greatly complicated social relations could be maintained only by means of a set of stricter external regulations. New problems of the new age had to be dealt with by new means, Xun Zi surpassing his predecessors precisely in his claim of the necessity of an external norm, i.e. the rites. Considered from this viewpoint, Tan Sitong's assertion that all the learning in China for the past twenty centuries has mainly been that of Xun Zi might be taken as justified. For Xun Zi accepted in part the Confucian doctrine of rites, while also initiating the Legalist doctrine of coercion.

The greatest representatives of the Legalist school were Han Fei and Li Si—the latter being the key designer of the political mechanism of the Qin Dynasty—and both were the direct disciples of Xun Zi. "Outwardly Confucian but Legalist within," or in other words, "the mixture of both a kingly reign and

① *Analects,* "Wei Zheng."

② *Book of Xun Zi,* "The Evilness of Nature."

a despotic rule," has ever since formed the essential ingredient of Chinese politics—a kingly reign being the Confucian ideal and despotic rule the statecraft of the Legalists. Since then, the basic political model has stabilized and lasted for more than two thousand years. Both the school of Xun Zi and the political manipulations of the Qin Dynasty were the products of the age. Each age has its corresponding superstructure and the theory of Xun Zi was simply the superstructure corresponding with the requirements of his age.

The rites of Xun Zi were different from those of Confucius in conceding the evil in human nature. Yet in another aspect Xun Zi was akin to Confucius and Mencius in contrast to the Taoists. The Taoist school opposed any civilization and called for a return to nature in direct contradiction with any human artificiality. In sharp opposition to the Taoists, Xun Zi denounced such a return to nature and proclaimed the utmost importance of human efforts through the rule of rites. Instead of an attitude resigned to longing for a primitive naiveté, he upheld the ideal of positive proactivity, and in this he showed himself a genuine successor to the Confucian spirit of positive engagement and boldness, i.e., "The ardent will advance and lay hold of truth."① Prof. Li Zehou held that it is precisely Xun Zi's emphasis on experience and practice in our actual life that reoriented the evolving trend of Confucianism. If the Confucian school had followed the line of Confucius and Mencius entirely, it is probable that it would gradually turn into a religious mysticism pursuing only inner cultivation and inner perfection. It was Xun Zi who through his reorientation of Confucianism replaced the purely inward scrutinizing and stressed the external influence of human activities and the rule of law and rites, thus opening a new path of development.② For human thought has often stopped before an impasse, before which Zhuang Zi resorted to the renunciation of any positive pursuit after knowledge, since the only knowledge we are able to acquire will be significantly limited.③ The more science advances, the greater becomes the sphere of what is unknown to us. The more you ponder over it, the more the universe seems inconceivable. To confront such a dilemma, the Taoists adopted an attitude of humility by preaching what is unknown or unknowable and resigning themselves to what is inscrutable. But the Confucians resorted much more to a positive attitude of ceaseless effort and pursuit. And Xun Zi further advanced this attitude against the Taoists. Prof. Li Zehou argues that Xun Zi constituted a mid-way

① *Analects*, "Zi Lu."

② Li Zehou, *Essay on Ancient Chinese Thoughts, A Resumé on Xun Zi, the Book of Change and the Doctrine of the Mean.*

③ *Book of Zhuang Zi*, "Yang Sheng Zhu."

link between Confucius and the *Doctrine of the Mean*, thus exerting a major influence on later ages, for the *Doctrine of the Mean* constituted an integral part of the Four Books, becoming one of the sacred texts in the cultural life of China.

Following Confucius and Mencius, Xun Zi also highly revered the sages, since the rites were instituted by the sages and without this contribution there could be no civilization at all. This pragmatic spirit of his was nowhere more clearly shown than in his assertions that the sages were only the consequence of a long process of self-reformation, and that morality came solely from the constant accumulation of our spiritual cultivation. Most Chinese philosophers from Confucius down to the Neo-Confucians of the Song period regarded morality as something given *a priori*, but for Xun Zi it was something *a posteriori* or wholly man-made. Though the Song philosophers lauded the role of human effort, it was nothing more than an outward manifestation of what was already innate within ourselves—a traditional teaching inherited from Mencius. On this, we may aptly compare some analogous literary theories. One school holds that art is but the natural outflow of our emotions. Another school opposes such a theory of spontaneity by insisting that art is an artificial recasting of what is in nature and is natural. In Mencius' theory, benevolence and moral obligation are innate in human nature, not something "acquired from the outside," and hence he proclaimed, "All things are already complete in us. There is no greater delight than to be conscious of sincerity on self-examination."① So long as you examine your inner heart, morality will become manifest by itself. But for Xun Zi, the case is otherwise: morality has to be acquired through a process of outward cultivation, and hence it is the outcome of human efforts. These two viewpoints might also be found in contemporary events, such as in the Cultural Revolution when one side held that the proletarians are born revolutionaries while the other held that Marxism has to be instilled into the proletarians from outside.

Men are born with their natural endowments, such as appetite and sexual longing, but evidently the civilization of mankind is not a natural thing. Civilization is entirely something that is consciously and conscientiously man-made. People's material lives as well as their social and spiritual lives are for the most part the product of their own will and their own creation. In regard to this topic, the Confucian spirit seems to come nearer to the truth than does the Taoist. The question is not how to escape from civilization by returning to nature, but how to remold our nature so as to adapt ourselves to society.

① *Book of Mencius,* "On Mind," pt. I.

Rousseau in his first dissertation (in answer to a question set by the Academy of Dijon in 1746, "Has the restoration of the sciences and arts contributed to purify our morals?") propounded that the advanced sciences and arts are artificial products tending to lead people to be more hypocritical rather than honest. Both sciences and arts lead people more and more astray from the plain truth of nature. Therefore people ought to strive for a return to nature. This is precisely what the Taoists professed so earnestly. The Taoists repudiated all civilizations and man-made institutions, and blamed all corruption and degeneration on the influence of civilized live. Both the ancient Taoists and Rousseau took civilized life to be something unnatural, and hence called earnestly for a return to nature. Xun Zi held just the opposite standpoint. At the time of Confucius, the Taoists were not as yet a prevalent school, and few of the Confucian arguments were directed against the Taoist school. Later, by the time of Xun Zi, the Taoist ideas had already become popular, and hence a part of Xun Zi's doctrine was directed against the Taoists—a point which has not yet been fully treated. Xun Zi upheld the positive effects of civilization as an antithesis to the call for the return to nature. There thus appears to be an antinomy which was neglected by the ancients. Civilization cannot emerge spontaneously by itself, and is always the outcome of human ingenuity and speculation. Human beings cannot survive without civilization, nor can they remain eternally in the state of nature or the state of animals. But meanwhile, civilization is by its own nature an artifact, not something given readily by nature itself. Thus it is by its own nature a recast of what is in nature, and hence cannot remain the same as the original state of nature. The result can only be that all civilizations are inherently different to the state of nature. Yet, mankind is a part of nature and cannot be separated and made independent of nature. Man has to comply with what nature dictates and cannot become alienated from the rule of nature. So there is both divergence between civilization and nature, and at the same time a harmony between them. People cannot one-sidedly emphasize the conquering and remolding of nature while wholly neglecting submission to and harmony with nature. Even in the modern world, at the beginning of the process of modernization, this had not been given enough attention. Yet human history (or rather humanistic history) is advancing through the labyrinth of just such an antinomy. Nature and man are synchronously advancing both in conflict and in unison. There always remains the question of how to keep the two on an optimal balance, i.e. to manage a golden mean between man and nature. In a certain sense, all philosophers seek nothing more than that optimum point so as to profit both the human world and the natural world to the greatest extent, just as I. A. Richards thought the function of art to lie in its satisfaction of our whole-bodily consciousness to the greatest extent.[①]

There was a tendency in modern civilization that with the unprecedented success in reforming nature, people readily embraced a scientistic inclination and took science as the sole criterion of everything or reduced all values into the channel of science. This tends to be a narrow intellectualism instead of a broad humanism. After all, human life is far more complicated than the conclusions of logical speculation alone. There is indeed much in our lives that belongs to the sphere of pure reason, but meanwhile there is also a great deal in our lives that cannot be simply brought under the rule of pure reason. As to how the approach of scientism was applied to social and moral life, we may find a handy example in the case of Xun Zi and the Legalists. The Legalist doctrine might be taken as an ancient breed of social science endeavoring for a scientific and objective understanding of social reality, e.g. how to deal with others by threats and enticement so as to make them submit. But we will see in the chapter on the Legalists that they greatly limited their interest to political intrigue and maneuvering, such that all humanistic values and ideals disappeared entirely. In the study of economics, one may fairly treat a human being as a mere *homo economicus* without considering other incentives save the economic one. Thus, under the condition of a free market everyone tries his best to obtain his own greatest profit—this is the starting point of modern economics based on its presupposition about human nature. Such a theory does not, nor needs to see human nature in its whole. It needs only to take a human being as a *homo economicus*, not to take him simultaneously as having other qualities. Yet any sound philosophy in the sense of the love of wisdom is obliged to see human beings in their entirety. Xun Zi and his Legalist followers took into consideration only the *homo socialis* or *homo politicus* at the price of ignoring other humanistic values and ideals. It is there that the turning point showed itself much more strikingly in Xun Zi than elsewhere. And we should also pay enough regard to the abuses of the doctrine of rites once it had become stereotyped. Once stereotyped, it could turn into an evil instrument used to humiliate human nature, just as was severely lamented by Lu Xun. It was in his "A Madman's Diary" that Lu Xun so relentlessly unveiled the cruel "cannibalism of the doctrine of rites" that had so brutally trampled on the vitality of the Chinese nation.

Qin and Chu were at that time the two greatest countries, both having been visited by Xun Zi. Both countries had their own cultural peculiarities, being

① I. A. Richards, *Principles of Literary Criticism* (London: Kegan Paul, 1924).

distinct from each other. The culture of Chu possessed a romantic and fanciful atmosphere, while Qin was plain and simple with a wholehearted engagement in the practicality of farming and warfare. The main likelihood then seemed that sooner or later the great unification of the whole of China would be accomplished either by Qin or by Chu, thus inspiring a proverb: "Even if only three households remain in Chu, it must be Chu who will smash Qin." At any rate, it shows that in the eyes of the peoples at that time, Chu was a qualified match for Qin. Though the great unification under Qin was short-lived, the Han Dynasty succeeding Qin further consolidated the institutions initiated by Qin and formed the general norm for rule in China. Supposing it had not been Qin but Chu that achieved the historic feat of the great unification of China, the ensuing history would be greatly different. But the fact remains that it was Qin and not Chu that completed the great unification; and so it remained for Xun Zi and his Legalist descendants to come forth to predominate over ideology for millennia to come. The question whether it was to China's good fortune or not, will be left with the reader to consider.

In Xun Zi's "Strengthening the Nation," he praised highly the political mechanism of Qin, and the seeds of the Legalist ideas were evident when he gave his impression of Qin, "It was not luck but a matter of course that Qin was so successful within the span of four succeeding reigns. It is what I personally witnessed there. Hence I conclude: easy-going yet well-governed, simple yet scrupulously ordered, it achieved so much without much trouble. This is the culmination of a good politics. And Qin is nearest to that state."[①] This political ideal of Xun Zi's strongly conveyed a sense which was later associated with the Legalists. Mencius had minutely described his utopia, holding high the ideal of a "kingly reign." Xun Zi had developed his utopia too, which also brandished the ideal of a "kingly reign." But Xun Zi's ideal of a "kingly reign" is quite different from that of Mencius. In reality, Xun Zi's "kingly reign" came very near to Mencius' "reign of hegemony" which Mencius had so strongly opposed. In later generations, the difference between these two sorts of reign had been a perennial topic in the intellectual history of China. For Mencius, to lead the people by virtue is kingly reign, while to rule the people by force is hegemony. But down to Xun Zi they began to bear a very different connotation. Although Xun Zi made a proposal to Li Si, his pupil and the prime minister of Qin, that the regime of Qin should "stop its practice of force and carry out a benevolent rule" since it was still somewhat far from the ideal of "the best government,"

① *Book of Xun Zi,* "Strengthening the Nation."

he nevertheless affirmed: "To reign with virtue and to enforce with coercion—without either of them, a regime would be doomed to collapse."[1] For Mencius, a kingly reign and hegemony by force were essentially two diamctrically opposed political systems; but for Xun Zi the difference between the two was not one in essence but one of degree. Carried out in purity and entirety, it was kingly reign; otherwise it was hegemony. Here arose the question of whether the two were indeed different in kind or in degree. And this was a question not only of politics, but also relating to their world-views and scientific outlooks. We shall deal it in detail in later chapters.

The discernment and contention between the kingly reign and the hegemonic one lasted from the classical era down to modern times. For instance, Zhu Xi (1130-1200), the leader of Neo-Confucianism in the Song Period, launched a famous debate with his friend Chen Liang (1143-1194) over the distinction between the two types of rule. Zhu Xi inherited the conventional view that the ideal state of politics existed only in archaic times and all reigns of later ages were hegemonic, a degeneration from the older time. Against this thesis, Chen Liang contended that there was no essential distinction between the politics of antiquity and that of the later ages (say of the Han and Tang dynasties, which were generally known as the most prosperous epochs). The distinction dwells merely in the fact that the ancient sage-kings had carried out this ideal to its fullest extent while the later rulers did not.

As is well known, Mencius proposed to follow the line of the "ancient kings" while Xun Zi that of the "later kings." But the difference between them is not as great as people are apt to suppose. For in Mencius, the ancient sage-kings included King Wen and King Wu of the Zhou Dynasty. For Xun Zi, the later kings were none other than King Wen and King Wu of the Zhou Dynasty; but meanwhile he proposed to follow the ancient kings too. So their difference is but one of degree rather than one of substance. What led Xun Zi emphatically to follow the later kings was simply that the later kings came nearer to the social reality of his time and were hence more practical. Therefore Xun Zi asserted:

> Hence it is said: If you wish to see the footprints of the sage-kings, then look at where they are most clear, that is to say, at the later kings. To give up the later kings and follow those of archaic antiquity is like giving up one's own prince and serving another's prince. Hence it is said: If you wish to know a thousand years, then consider today. If you wish to understand hundreds of thousands, then examine one or two. If you wish to know the course of the Zhou Dynasty, you must learn from the proper man, i.e. the

① *Book of Xun Zi,* "Kingly Reign and Hegemony."

superior man.①

The "superior man" here was Confucius. The real distinction between Mencius and Xun Zi consists essentially in this: Mencius exhorted developing human nature's innate goodness to its fullest extent, while Xun Zi preached the subjugation of human nature's innate evilness by the function of the rule of rites. Mencius took the later sage-kings as the direct heirs apparent of the ancient ones, while Xun Zi took the later sage-kings as a higher stage of their ancient predecessors, who as a matter of course provided the model for us to imitate. Thus we may perceive another distinction between the two philosophers, i.e. Xun Zi had embraced a progressive conception of history much more than Mencius. The idea of progress is nowadays common sense, yet it was not so before modern times. In ancient China, as in most pre-modern cultures, both the Confucians and Taoists viewed history as a course of retrogression. The finest days in human history were the days long past under the reign of the archaic sage-kings. The emergence of the idea of progress in the West was something of later ages too. It was not until the days of the Enlightenment and especially of Darwin's theory of evolution in the 19th century that the idea of progress became fortified in its predominant position, the idea of progress then becoming something generally taken for granted. In the long history of China, very seldom can we find the idea of the progress of history, and conversely what we find more frequently is the idea of retrogression. People were well acquainted with these sayings: "public morals are declining day by day," "the world is getting ever worse and worse," or "the public morals are degenerating and not the same as before." Thus the famous poet Du Fu longed so sentimentally "to help the sovereign to become the equal of Yao and Shun so that the manners of the world can once more be purified." It reflected the poet's reverence for the good old days. We should recognize that Xun Zi's conception of historical progression is one of the rarest and most precious legacies in the treasure of China's classical thought.

A wide-spread primer in China, the *Classic in Three Words*, had as its opening sentence, "In the beginning, human nature is good." This shows how far Mencius' theory of the goodness of human nature surpassed Xun Zi's theory of the evilness of human nature. However, it can be seen that both theories committed the same error, i.e. both took good or evil as something endowed inherently. In fact, the conception of good or evil is a social product and hence not innate or inborn. Robinson Crusoe on his desert island can do whatever he

① *Book of Xun Zi,* "Against Physiognomy."

likes or think whatever he likes. It involves no goodness or evilness whatsoever. Only when placed in the community can his ideas and behavior (i.e. the expression of his human nature) be identified as good or evil. Human nature in itself has nothing to do with goodness or evilness, and there is neither innate goodness nor innate evilness in human nature. What is called good or evil refers to its social effect. It is only when it brings about certain social effects that it involves what we call goodness or evilness. In the last analysis, goodness and evilness are not things that can be innate in human nature, but determined by its social effects. So the concept of goodness or evilness can only be a socially defined idea. But nearly all Chinese classical philosophers stumbled on this point. For two thousand years they were entangled in a pseudo-problem, i.e. the innate goodness or evilness in human nature—a problem which assumed a cardinal place in the intellectual history of China.

[IV] Man and Heaven

Philosophy aims at the inquiry of three basic relations: first, the relation of man to nature; second, that of man to man; and lastly, that of man to himself. Traditional philosophy in China seemed predominantly interested in the second aspect rather than in the other two, and hence its ethico-political orientation. On the relation of man to nature, Xun Zi dealt much more with it than did either Confucius or Mencius, who said little about the way of heaven, while Xun Zi talked emphatically about the way of heaven (or rather, the way of nature). This interest in nature showed Xun Zi's realistic spirit. Any philosophy which paid too much attention to one aspect to the neglect of the others would be self-defeatingly one-sided and limited. For Xun Zi, nature was something given, while value consists totally in human initiative. "Heaven begets everything but it does not control them, the earth loads all people but it does not control them; all things in the universe, human beings included, have to wait for the sage-king to make distinctions among them."① That is why Xun Zi promoted "adapting Heaven's Fate and making use of it," that is to say, since the civilization's development is not necessarily the product of nature, it depends upon the voluntary actions of man.

His book contains a chapter "On Heaven" from which many paragraphs have been frequently cited. He proclaimed, "Heaven has a constant regularity of

---

① *Book of Xun Zi,* "On the Rites."

activity. It did not exist for the sake of Yao [the legendary sage-king] nor cease to exist for the sake of Jie [the well-known capricious tyrant]; the four seasons succeed one another; the *Yin* and *Yang* go through their great mutations."[①] The ways and movements of the natural world have their own constant regularity, independent of human factors or human volition. Truly, this deserves to be ranked as a brilliant proposition, possessing a hue more or less of the modern scientific outlook. Nature itself possesses no ethical value whatsoever. It moves by itself independent of any human volition. Yet most Confucians had been so used to expanding their ethical principles that it seemed to them the whole natural world was but an enlarged embodiment of their ethics. To them, the heart of heaven consisted of benevolence, because the human heart is made up of only benevolence. The universe is but the incarnation of human morality. Nevertheless, Xun Zi drew a distinct demarcation between the objective existence of the natural world and the ethical norm of the human world. They are two entirely different and mutually independent worlds. Thereupon he undertook a decisive step in defining a basic starting point for scientific knowledge, without which no scientific knowledge is possible. There was long an ideological factor which seriously impeded the development of science throughout the long history of China; i.e. their way of thinking projected the hierarchy of social and ethical inequality onto the natural world. This prevented them from knowing nature as it is. The natural world was not seen as a matter of fact, but an embodiment of an ethical principle. But one cannot understand the natural world by sanctifying it into an ethical structure. To foster scientific knowledge, one must discard all fictitious ethical attributes imposed upon the natural world. Xun Zi claimed, "Heaven has a constant regularity of activity. It did not exist for the sake of Yao nor cease to exist for the sake of Jie." And this affirmation represented an unprecedented scientific approach. Science has its own independent dignity, and is no servant-maid to any theology or ideology whatsoever.

Again Xun Zi proclaimed, "To make complete without acting, and to obtain without seeking: this is what is meant by the activities of Heaven... The fixed stars make their round, the sun and the moon alternately shine; the four seasons succeed one another; the *Yin* and *Yang* go through their great mutations; wind and rain are widely distributed; all things acquire their harmony and have their lives; each gets its nourishment and develops to its appointed state. We do not see the cause of these occurrences, but we do see their effect: this is what is meant by being spirit-like. The results of all these changes are known, but we

① *Book of Xun Zi,* "On Heaven."

do not know the invisible source: this is what is called Heaven." The natural world follows its own rule, unlike human affairs, which are from beginning to end permeated by our conscious deliberations. That the theological conception of nature had formed a serious obstacle to the development of modern science is well known to everyone, and on the whole China was no exception. Viewed in the light of a theological outlook, all things in the natural world are inter-associated into an organic hierarchy in accordance with ethical gradations. But the premise of science exists exactly in the supposition of a quantitative world-view instead of a qualitative, that is, a scientific outlook demands that all things are taken equally, regardless of their rank, status and value. Once there was a time when the celestial bodies were considered sacred and hence perfectly luminous without any spots on them. They were hallowed, and since the circle was supposed the most perfect figure, so the loci they described had to be perfectly circular. This was what the Ptolemaic astronomy of the Middle Ages taught. It constituted an example of teleological reasoning. Not until the time of Copernicus and Kepler was this superstitious fable brought down. Its outlook had insisted on the unequal gradation of nature, i.e. things in the natural world were unequal, some were created nobler, some humbler, with respect to their innate differences. So in the human world, people were seen as having been created unequal, some nobler and some humbler, their inborn qualities being different. This world-view of inequality so impeded the progress of science that science had to break it down in order to make room for the advancement of true learning. Thus modern science began by discarding the traditional qualitative world-view by up-holding in its stead a quantitative one that regarded all things being equal in themselves, their differences existing only in their quantity instead of in any supposed quality. The sun and the atom are different from each other only in their quantity and not in which of them is nobler than the other, just as in human society all humans are created equal and no one is born nobler than others. In the West, it was only after the revolution of modern science that the quantitative world-view substituted the qualitative one and held its dominant place by taking all things equally with no regard to any difference in their substance. In light of this, we may find some thoughts in Xun Zi which comprise elementary ideas essentially scientific in nature. Further, as an inference, the difference between a kingly reign and an autocratic hegemony is not (nor should be) one of quality but one of quantity. It implied the deduction (as later expounded by Chen Liang of the Song period in his polemic with Zhu Xi) that their principles were of one and the same, the difference only that the ancient sage-kings carried it to its fullest extent while the later kings did not. Maybe this way of reasoning might have opened a broad prospect for the emergence of science in China. Nevertheless it was a pity that the traditional way of thinking was too much confined to the ethico-political mode to allow itself to be aligned in any fashion with the process of scientific reasoning.

The scientific mode of thinking contains a premise which treats all objects equally without discrimination of their moral features. However, an ethical world-view had to differentiate people into different categories of the higher and the lower, such as the gentleman and the small-minded, etc. Projected onto the natural world, such a world-view would of necessity arrange it into a hierarchy of different ranks and grades. Xun Zi challenged this ethico-politico-centric view, declaring: "When a man is hungry he desires to eat; when he is cold, he desires to be warm; when he is tired he desires to rest; he likes what is beneficial and dislikes what is injurious. Man has these ways of acting from birth; he does not depend upon something to get them. In these things, Yu and Jie were alike." Then, "Wherein is it that man is truly man? Because he makes social distinctions."[①] And again: "What makes a sage the same with the multitude and no different from them is nature; and what makes him different from and surpassing the multitude is his acquired training."[②] For Xun Zi, the nature of a sage and that of an evil tyrant had no substantial difference, nor was there any difference between the nature of the sage and that of the multitude. The sage transcended the common people merely in that he was able to remold himself better that others. The distinction lies only in the degree of their remolding. Men are born with the same nature, equal to all. And from the equality of human nature one might easily infer the equality of man and man. Such an inference is of course very dangerous to the stability of the traditional hierarchical social formation. It amounts to denying the very foundation of the legitimacy of the hierarchical institution—the fundamental principle upon which the traditional political and social order was founded. At this point we encounter the intrinsic link between science and democracy, i.e. science presupposes the equality of things, and democracy that of human beings. Consequently, the idea of equality may lead both to science and to democracy.

Xun Zi had outdone other philosophers in his world-view in that he had prepared for others a door leading to the hall of science. No one else had ever achieved such a contribution. He assumed first of all a world in which all things and persons are created equal and hence are substantially homogenous, not

① *Book of Xun Zi,* "Against Physiognomy."

② *Book of Xun Zi,* "The Evilness of Nature."

heterogeneous. This premise being founded, it is made possible for science to grow. The natural world has its habits independent of human factors. It is not a world based on the hierarchy of different ranks but on equality, difference existing only in quantity, never quality. Then why is it that Xun Zi's ideas failed to lead to the birth of systematic scientific research in China? The reason is perhaps twofold. First, the material conditions were not as yet mature. China remained in an age-old agrarian mode of production, in a form of simple reproduction which had little connection with the progress of science (unlike modern industry). Second, Xun Zi did not reach the idea of quantification, without which our knowledge of natural phenomena could never have been raised to the height of science in the strict sense. In China, it was not until the early 17th century that one of her foremost scientists, Xu Guangqi (1562-1633), formulated a definite theory of how and why all scientific knowledge ought to be summed up in mathematical form.

There is an often-quoted line in Xun Zi's "Treatise on Heaven" which reads, "Instead of exalting Heaven and pondering it, why not gather wealth and use it to our advantage? Instead of obeying Heaven and praising it, why not adapt Heaven's ordinance and make use of it?"① Prof. Feng Youlan held this line as "the most definite and the most sonorous slogan calling for the reform of the natural world."② Here is man standing against Heaven and Nature. The relation between Man and Heaven (Nature) might be seen as the absolute subservience and unconditional obedience of Man to Nature, Man's efforts doomed in the face of the power of Nature. This is the attitude of the Taoists. But Xun Zi thought the other way—he claimed that men should endeavor to control and master Nature in order to serve himself. Again in this we find another factor in his thought with a somewhat modern intent. The famous dictum of Francis Bacon, the founder of modern science, pronounced loudly that "knowledge is power," that is, once we possess the knowledge of the natural world, we will be capable of using it to better serve our own ends. This is exactly what Xun Zi meant when he urged people to "adapt Heaven's ordinance and make use of it." This idea of his was pregnant with a modern sense in its positive aspect, but if it became lopsided it would bring forth its own disaster. For the sake of development, mankind had to utilize, to reform and to conquer Nature, and this contention is surely one of Xun Zi's outstanding contributions to the history of classical philosophy. But one cannot stop short at the conquering, utilizing

① *Book of Xun Zi*, "On Heaven."

② Feng Youlan, *New Versions of the History of Chinese Philosophy*, vol. 2, p373.

and explaining of the natural world, one has to further see to it that a mutual harmony and balance between Man and Nature is also of the utmost importance. The counsel "to adapt Heaven's ordinance and to make use of it" has long been generally overvalued. In fact, it touches on only half the matter, failing to recognize that after we have mastered Nature to serve our ends, we must further administer this service so as to obey Nature's law to the advantage of Nature. Xun Zi did touch upon the issue of how we should eventually bring ourselves in conformity with all-merciful Nature. But this had been even more markedly pointed out by Mencius already: "If the seasons of husbandry be not interfered with, the grain will be more than can be eaten. If nets are not allowed to enter the pools and ponds, the fishes and turtles will be more than can be consumed. If axes and saws enter the hills and forests only at the proper time, the wood will be more than can be used."[①] The relation of man to Nature is not simply one of the exploiter and the exploited; they mutually nourish and supplement one another. If we are planning to make Nature serve our purpose with no regard for our eventual return to nature, it would result in what Russell described as "the rape of the earth" and finally in the disaster of humanity itself. The balance of the natural world and the human world once broken, it would not only be the natural world but also the civilization of mankind that would suffer irretrievable disaster. Today all of us have learned to know what disasters the rape of the earth has brought us in the last two centuries. Xun Zi persuaded people to conquer and to exploit the natural world, but neglected the necessity of nourishing it so as to attain an ideal state of equilibrium and co-existence between men and Nature.

It is a truth generally neglected that the later generations are always prone to interpret the preceding generations according to their own understanding, disregarding the original intentions of their ancestors. Thus Xun Zi had been left to oblivion for thousands of years, but in recent decades there appeared a tendency to overvalue him to a new height. There are two reasons for this. First, it is said that he embraced a clear scientific outlook, based on the above-quoted lines, "Instead of exalting Heaven and pondering it, why not gather wealth and use it to our advantage? Instead of obeying Heaven and praising it, why not adapt Heaven's ordinance and make use of it?" And second, he was venerated as the founder of the Legalist school, who were considered to be the reformers representing progressive social forces. Indeed, these two points are dressed up in too much wishful exaggeration and greatly deviate from Xun Zi's own intention.

① *Book of Mencius*, "King Hui of Liang," pt. 1.

Undoubtedly, we may readily discover in ancient documents many propositions that carry certain scientific implications. Nevertheless, whether there is any scientific connotation is one thing, but whether in fact it led to the progress of science is another. These are two different issues. The advancement of science requires two indispensable conditions: first, a favorable social mechanism; second, the scientific spirit or scientific mode of thinking. Yet these conditions were what the Chinese cultural tradition lacked. Xun Zi, though he made some remarks with a rather scientific overtone, did not step from there onto the main road of scientific knowledge. On the contrary, the route he chose was still the ethico-politico-centric one passed down in the tradition from antiquity, which paved the way for the emergence of autocracy rather than science. In comparison with Confucius and Mencius, Xun Zi stressed much more the realistic and negative (or naturalistic) side of human life and human nature, while discarding the idealistic elements of his predecessors. Yet, it was just along this road that the Legalist school developed further and further, so as to set free some of the darkest and most corrupt ingredients in life and human nature to be aggravated ever more. Thus was formed another age-long tradition in Chinese culture. Whether it was fortunate or not for Chinese intellectual history, we shall discuss in detail in the chapter dealing with the Legalists. On the whole and in the long run, Xun Zi might be evaluated as equally balanced in his merits and demerits. In him we may find a keen insight into the innermost qualities of human nature, as well as an anti-humanist tendency leading to the degenerated influence of the Legalists.

In his book, there is a chapter with the title "The Elimination of Our Ignorance" specifically discussing how our knowledge is constrained by many factors, so that man can only hope to attain true knowledge after he escapes these confines. This chapter was a concentrated exposition of his epistemology. On reading it the reader may be readily reminded of what Bacon once bemoaned: human knowledge is always under the constraint of various sorts of idol-worship. People often identify our knowledge as the reflection of the objective world, but the history of science shows it has never been that simple. The objective fact is one thing, but our knowledge of it is quite another. Our knowledge of it incorporates subjective elements. Of course, it is common to hold such a very naive account, believing that what our knowledge reflects or represents is indeed the objective reality, or at least it is forever approaching this reality. But on thinking it over, we find that such a view can hardly be defended. There have been revolutions in the history of science too. Each such revolution is a complete overthrow of the long established ideas. If human knowledge was more or less a truthful reflection of the objective reality, then it could not be subverted so thoroughly, because the reality of the natural world can not be similarly turned upside-down. But what constituted our scientific knowledge or theory can be and indeed has been more than once completely overthrown (e.g. the Five Elements theory, the Ptolemaic theory, or the phlogiston theory). Our knowledge of the outside world cannot be correlated straightforwardly with the objective reality of the outside world. Natural phenomena as the objects of our knowledge are objectively given, but our knowledge of them includes much that belongs to the realm of our subjectivity. For instance, the whiteness of the snow is entirely caused by our perception of its light wave. It is we ourselves that perceive its whiteness, whereas the natural object (snow) itself has nothing of whiteness (or blackness). What snow itself has is just a certain light wavelength. Our perception of white or black is something purely subjective, not objective. Still, there is another prevailing view that although we do not completely and exactly know the objective truth, we are at any rate constantly approaching it. This argument cannot support itself logically or empirically. After all, truth is not something like the North Pole. When we are going straight northward we may eventually stop somewhere and proclaim with full conviction: "This is the North Pole, we can go northward no further." However, no one can claim his knowledge to be the exact ultimate truth. If it were so, the later generation would not be able to make any further advancement at all. There is a logical dilemma for those who insist that though we have not as yet reached the ultimate truth, we are nevertheless ceaselessly approaching it. If we do not know exactly where that truth is, then how can we be qualified to say that we are approaching ever nearer to it? First you must affirm with certainty that the truth is somewhere, then you are qualified to ascertain you are approaching ever nearer to it. As we have no right to ascertain where this ultimate truth is, how can we ascertain that we are approaching it unceasingly? We can know we are approaching the North Pole, because we know beforehand that there is a North Pole and we know where it is. But we have no right to ascertain this ultimate truth as existing somewhere. Truth, as we get hold of it, is not an object given before us (Gegenstand) but a mental framework based on our perception (Zustand). Hence those parts of our discourse which we might call true actually consist of two aspects: the perception of a given object and our comprehension of it. The latter of the two is always made up of a subjective framework, although it has to be well-grounded and in accordance with the known data and with logical reasoning. Our comprehension is in no way objectively given. In our knowledge there is always involved an element of subjective construction which is never objectively given ready-made. There is no such thing as purely objective knowledge.

The Confucians seldom paid attention to epistemology. Both Confucius and Mencius seldom dealt with it, but Xun Zi showed more interest in it. Xun Zi asserted that our knowledge is often lop-sided and hence incapable of reflecting the whole reality of things: "The defect of man is that he is closed on one side to the neglect of the whole matter. And the reasons that caused such lop-sidedness were manifold," "convention caused it, desire caused it, disgust caused it, the start caused it, the end caused it, the far caused it, the near caused it, the broad caused it, the shallow caused it, the bygone caused it, the present caused it, all things are different and are mutually closed to one another."[①] It is only when these factors which impede our proper knowledge are expelled that we can reach a true knowledge of the object. And further: "All that enables us to know is within human nature; and all that can be known is within the rules of things."[②] In other words, everything that can be employed to gain knowledge of external objects falls within the realm of human nature. Men are born with the faculty to know the outside things which can be known by men. Hence our knowledge is a union of the subject (the knowing) and the object (the knowable). The object that is known is objective, whereas our knowledge of it is subjective. In the exposition of their epistemology, the Buddhists distinguished what they called the relating (Neng Yuan), the related (Suo Yuan) and the relation of the relating and the related (Suo Yuan Yuan). The relating denotes the act of knowing, the related the object of our knowledge, and our knowledge is a relation between the relating and the related. Our knowledge is forever something that involves our subjective mechanism; and it is just this that makes scientific revolutions possible. If science were merely a plain reflection of the objective fact, no more no less, then no scientific revolution would ever be possible.

Our thinking is never a simple and passive reflection of external things, for it is our subjective understanding of the outside object but not the outside object itself. In other words, it is ultimately an intellectual composition or structure. In his epistemology, Xun Zi touched on the issue without giving a definite answer. Compared with the West, the study of epistemology seemed a weak point in the traditional philosophy of China. They failed to scrutinize in depth what constituted the intellectual factors in our knowledge. Even when they had established some criteria for testing truth, these criteria themselves had not yet been tested. If a practice is the test of truth, then the practice itself ought to be tested for its

① *Book of Xun Zi*, "Elimination of our Ignorance."

② Ibid.

own validity beforehand.

In another chapter, Xun Zi dealt with the issue of the test for truth, proclaiming, "To hear about is by far less than to witness, to witness is by far less than to know, to know is by far less than to practice. The end of learning is to practice."① Here he engaged the problem of the relation between knowledge and practice, though he was far from getting a satisfactory answer to this age-old problem. This problem has forever been a fundamental controversy in the history of philosophy in China. Almost all great philosophers dealt with it in some detail. The Confucians upheld a set of ethical ideals, and moral cultivation was regarded as the final end of knowledge. But in a deeper sense, one can hardly accept that "practice" should be limited to the sphere of moral perfection unless we adopt a thoroughly ethical world-view like the Confucians, for the world is after all wide enough to embrace many practices that are beyond the sphere of morality. We can consider a story told by George Santayana. The Spanish seafarers piously believed in the miracles of St. Theresa, and whenever they were in danger on the sea, they would pray to her, and they would get ashore safely. Can it be said that in this sense their practice (praying to St. Theresa) is the test of truth (her miraculous power)? In reality, Xun Zi like all Confucians took moral cultivation as the sole "practice" (*xing*). But one can hardly agree that the concept of "practice" can be defined in this way.

In his book, Xun Zi frequently mentions the two terms: "Heaven" and "Way" (or "Logos"). On the one hand, they denote the natural world, Heaven being nature and Way the principles of nature. On the other hand, the two terms denote something else—not the natural world, but moral ideals and norms. The notions of knowing (*zhi*) and practicing were mostly seen as confined to the sphere of morality. These two meanings were so often mixed together that we have to discern them carefully. We thus come to the issue of the relation between language and philosophy. Up until today, most philosophy has been expressed with the vehicle of language. But language often fails to convey an exact meaning. Many philosophical problems are ultimately problems of language. This led the contemporary analytic school to engage specifically in the linguistic analysis of philosophical propositions. Classical philosophy in China had talked a lot about "Heaven" and "Way." But after all, what did these terms mean? To answer this would require analysis and clarification of language.

There is another interesting passage *in the Book of Xun Zi* which reads, "How can a person know the Way [Logos or Tao]? Through the mind. How

① *Book of Xun Zi*, "The Effect of Practice."

does the mind know? By emptiness, unity and quiescence."[①] Indeed, how can we know the Way? According to Xun Zi, as mentioned above, the Way is made known to us by our practice or action. But here the answer given is "emptiness, unity and quiescence." Here arise two problems. The one is, as we mentioned above, that our mind is not just a passive reflection of the outside world, not simply a mirror. If it were only a mirror passively reflecting the outside world, then it could show only the falling of an apple, but nothing at all of the "law of universal gravitation." This law of universal gravitation is our mental construction. Our knowledge is in the last instance a systematic structure created by our reasoning, while the outside world can by no means present us a ready-made theory. Mere "emptiness, unity and quiescence" cannot provide us any knowledge. The other point in his assertion is this: "emptiness, unity and quiescence" signify a negation of practice or action—a postulate with a strong Taoist bent. The Taoists are known for preaching emptiness in opposition to any human activity, while Xun Zi strongly promoted human exertion. Then why did he propagate the Taoist-inclined "emptiness, unity and quiescence"? It is very likely that Xun Zi accepted some of the Taoist ideas, as we can find later in the case of the Legalists. No doctrine in the world is totally pure. Each doctrine is unavoidably under the influence of some other. Even the refutation of a doctrine may be studied in the light of the influence of other doctrines from its opposite side. Mencius fiercely criticized Yang Zhu and Mo Zi, but this very fact showed also how significant a place Yang and Mo occupied in his thoughts. Common sense shows us that there are always subjective parts to our thoughts, and it is impossible for anyone to simply reflect the outside world like a mirror or a pond of still water. Just because of this, people often hold different ideas about the outside world. If our minds are just reflective mirrors, then all men would share the same knowledge and as a consequence there would be no further advancement of learning. It is just because there are subjective elements in our knowledge that our knowledge is capable of being perpetually remodeled and made bettered. We ought not to be overcritical of the ancients in this respect. Yet it should be justly admitted that it is a failure in Xun Zi's doctrine for not acknowledging this issue properly.

In other chapters of his book, Xun Zi also discussed some philosophical issues where his world-view and moral view were clearly shown. In the chapter on the "Rectification of Names" he succeeded and developed Confucius' ideas. Confucius had already propounded the theory of the rectification of names, that

① *Book of Xun Zi,* "Elimination of our Ignorance."

to ensure order in society and peace for the state it is indispensable to rectify the names, "Let the prince be prince, the minister be minister, the father be father and the son be son,"[①] that is, to make everyone be what he ought to be so that all will be well. Xun Zi went still further as to assert: "Names have no corresponding actualities that necessarily relate to themselves. There was an agreement and things were named; when the agreement had been made and become customary, these were called related to actualities, when different with the agreement, these were called unrelated to actualities."[②] Names were not invariable, being only an expedient agreement or convention. They were only symbols and hence meaningless by themselves. Names were but a general agreement or convention. By and by they become customary. Herein Xun Zi differed greatly from Confucius. For Confucius, names were destined innately to be so. But for Xun Zi, it was but an expediency, not something *sine qua non*. Yet once this agreement or convention is established, it would be "inappropriate" to violate it. Again Xun Zi asserted, "A name has no definite substance. It is an agreement which is established to designate the substance. When the agreement had been made and became customary, people took it as a substantial name."[③] Or, a name was originally not destined for a certain object, and there was only a general agreement in using it to designate a certain object. But once it became settled as a custom, it would not be changed any more. On this issue of the relation between a name and the reality it refers to, we may find a striking resemblance to the debate between the nominalists and the realists in mediaeval scholasticism. The nominalists claimed that our concept of an object was no more than a name (term) used to designate it, while the realists insisted that the idea had an existence more real and lasting than the transitory existence of any object it referred to. The realists took the idea itself as something real and everlasting. The nominalists held that the idea was but a name imposed by men which became customary by usage. Incidentally it was this view of Xun Zi's which did not prevail in later generations, while Confucius' affirmation of the supremacy of the transcendent ethical categories reigned for too long a time to come. Later, the Song Confucians preached their moral codes as something given *a priori* and *sine qua non*. In accordance with Xun Zi's reasoning, we ought to admit that ethical ideas are not given *a priori* but are only general agreements for our utility, or a "convention apparatus." What is given *a priori* is

① *Analects*, "Yan Yuan."

② *Book of Xun Zi*, "Zheng Ming."

③ Ibid.

not any ethical code (those heavenly ideals of benevolence, obligation, etc.) but human nature (desires and lust included). Moral codes are expedient agreements which became customary and—contrary to orthodox Confucianism—not something exacted by supernatural decree. Conventions as they were, they were yet indispensable in maintaining a society. Under unbridled nominalism all would be purely ephemeral, and even ideas themselves would become impossible. Thus, some Buddhist sects regarded even all names (nomen, "idea") as wholly fictitious and meaningless. Such an extreme view would not be profitable to the advancement of our learning, for the progress of our knowledge as well as of our society surely needs certain generally accepted conventions. When driving, one will stop at the red light and move past the green one—this is also a convention which is absolutely indispensable. Therefore Xun Zi's viewpoint, when properly measured, comes nearer to the point than does Confucius'.

[V] Xun Zi's Criticism of All Schools

In the chapter "Refutation of the Twelve Philosophers," Xun Zi specifically criticized various schools of his time. He was of the opinion that all schools of the age had their faults. From his criticism of them, his own position and viewpoint can be clearly seen. He paid specific attention to the role of rites and music (*li* and *yue*) which served as the most important means in regulating the order of a society and which represented the concrete embodiment of social order. Therefore he criticized Mo Zi's preaching of "frugality in funerals," "frugality in expenditure" and "anti-music" as "being confined merely to expenditure and knowing no culture." The Mohists were ultra-utilitarian, holding utility as their sole criterion of all things and totally neglecting any humanistic value or ideal. But Xun Zi affirmed not only the practical value of music, but also its intrinsic value. A civilized life possesses not only its practical value but also its own intrinsic value, that is, it will bring happiness to mankind merely by its existence, in e.g. a fascinating piece of poetry or music. Civilization should be measured not only by its practical values, but even still much more by its spiritual values, which are an immeasurable contribution to humanity. In this respect, Xun Zi's criticism of the Mohists was very reasonable and ought to be regarded highly.

Xun Zi criticized Hui Shi, claiming he was "entangled with phraseology and did not know the reality." Hui Shi was a great master of language and logic. Xun Zi judged him as merely indulging in terminological play, and claimed that he knew nothing of the real state of things. Such a criticism was very much to the point too. Even nowadays the analytic school could hardly avoid the similar accusation that they are too much involved in mere logical analysis of language and thus lose sight of the real fundamental issues. Philosophy after all has to deal with questions of cardinal significance such as the ultimate end of our life and so on. But the analytic school discarded them all at one fell swoop. And Xun Zi's criticism—"entangled with phraseology and did not know the reality"—seems also valid for today's analytic philosophy.

In his criticism of Zhuang Zi, Xun Zi stated that Zhuang Zi was "entangled with Heaven and did not know humanity." Here the term "Heaven" refers to Nature. Zhuang Zi was a thorough naturalist who proclaimed the best way for everything and every man was just to let it (or him) follow the way of nature perfectly without the least coercion or exertion. This was just the opposite of Xun Zi, who professed "*wei*" (exertion) and human efforts, aiming to create humanistic value through a process of remolding inner nature (human nature) and outer nature (the natural world). Xun Zi criticized Zhuang Zi as "knowing nothing of what humanity is," that is, he knows nothing of humanistic values and ideals and nothing of the fact that civilization could only be the fruit of human efforts and exertions.

From Xun Zi's criticism of various schools, it is evident that Xun Zi among all thinkers offered the most well-balanced account. Compared with all others, he was less biased and better grounded, and hence deserves to hold a prominent place in the intellectual history of China. Matthew Arnold's description of Shakespeare, as one "who saw life steadily and saw it whole," in a certain sense may justly be applied to Xun Zi. Turning our sights to the long run of history, we may perhaps get a more appropriate evaluation of Xun Zi's historic place. In the Middle Ages of the Western world, people's thoughts were under the dictatorship of God. It was an age of religion and theology. After the Renaissance, Man awakened and God withdrew step by step behind the curtain. The role of the dictator was then replaced and replayed by Reason. About 400 years from the 16th to the 19th century it was Reason that came forth to take the place of God. Now this "Reason" was the reason of the narrower sense, namely the human understanding (instrumental reason, or logical reason). But Man is a complex entity and does not act consistently in conformity with his logical reasoning, which—however—has for a long time been hallowed as supreme. In the 18th century Kant made a distinction between understanding and reason by dividing our spiritual faculties into the three levels of sensibility, understanding and reason. Human knowledge begins with the perception of external objects. But mere sensibility does not form our knowledge. It depends on our logical faculty to process it by developing systematic knowledge. This is a result of the function of understanding. Reason possesses a much broader implication on a higher level. For instance, our morality comes from the command of our practical reason, not from a conclusion of logical reasoning. Our aesthetic feeling does not come from our intellectual reasoning but from our faculty of judgment. After long years of the autocratic reign of pure instrumental reason (understanding), it eventually fell from its throne in the last years of the 19th century. In the realm of natural sciences there emerged experiments and theories that shook the classical scientific mansion at its very foundations. In the realm of intellectual speculation there emerged various schools opposing the classical mode of thinking, similar to the approach initiated by Blaise Pascal in the 17th century in contention with the traditional rationalists. This line was represented successively by Kierkegaard, Stirner, Schopenhauer, Nietzsche, contemporary existentialists and others. It no longer scrutinized instrumental reason, but penetrated straightforward into the depths of the value and meaning of life itself.

In contrast to this line of intellectual development, it can be seen that in the history of ideas in China there had never existed the autocracy of an anthropomorphic God nor that of an irrevocable instrumental reason. It was not until the last years of the 19th century when China came into direct contact with the Occident that the Chinese began to accept the rule of science as the highest criterion. And since then science assumed—at least nominally—its supremacy as the measure of all things and ideas. This quickly led to the road of scientism, with science afforded the role of final judge and the dictatorship of instrumental reason. Instrumental reason had governed the Occidental mind for nearly four hundred years, and though it has not so impacted upon the Chinese mind, it has effected an influence. Before this time, neither God nor science had ever ruled over the Chinese mind. This mentality could be considered a strength, in that the Chinese possessed a peculiar soundness and practicality, and would never submit to any authority to its extreme, whether God or science. Yet considering the negative aspects of this mindset, it was in essence a spiritual numbness, as though insensible of the world, and hence inspiring no passion for the pursuit of any truth. They were ready to accept the authority of any person or faith according to their indoctrination, and just as ready to renounce it whenever they were taught otherwise. There have been too many examples of this in their history to enumerate one by one. This peculiar practicality of the Chinese mind furnishes us with a key to understand the seeming enigma both of their history and of their ideas: why was it that they were so quick to accept any authority, and just as quick to abandon it without yearning for it any longer?

Xun Zi venerated Confucius greatly and professed himself a successor to Confucius. But most scholars of the later generations proclaimed only Confucius-Mencius, never Confucius-Xun Zi. At any rate, what we take to be the Confucian school should never be confined only to Confucius and Mencius. The main trend of Confucius and Mencius was an idealistic one which, by sticking to a presupposed moral ideal, firmly believed in the possibility of the betterment of human life and the human world so far as this ideal was realized and enlarged. Hence they engaged all their life in the perfection and realization of this inner morality within human hearts. Alongside this line, there was another line held by Xun Zi—the line of realism which proposed the earnest reformation of human nature, without which human beings could never be perfected. It seems the greatest weakness of the idealists was that their ideals were as a rule too far detached from reality to be realized. Therefore, the effort of the idealists would as a rule fall into the posture of a hypocritical preaching, just as when in later ages the Neo-Confucians were often censured as mere "phony-Confucians." Reality is not the same as they described. In fact, the sages were always only a small number, and we cannot expect most people to attain that state of sagehood. Ban Gu in his *History of the Han* had remarked that in the Han dynasty the Confucian learning had already become a means for personal gain. Zhang Taiyan in modern times also criticized the Confucians and pointed out that their greatest defect was to lead people in the pursuit of personal profit. Once morality becomes an expedient means for selfish aims, it is doomed to turn into a fraud. In fact, it is impossible to ask all people to become sages. The radical Confucians in the late Ming period were ridiculed as holding that "swarms in the streets are all sages." Their ideal is after all not fact. To understand the world in this light is surely to present it in a distorted and absurd fashion. And a world-view formed upon such fictions could be neither true nor real. Thereby realism came to its rescue. Xun Zi's basic proposition, "The nature of man is evil; his goodness is only acquired training," had a more realistic ring. This Hobbesian attitude came forth just in time to compensate the shortcoming of the Confucian idealism by presenting a world-picture more real and more reliable. The advancement of knowledge and learning needs a realistic spirit, not a utopian one. In search of truth, one has to get rid of any idealistic fancy and stick to tough facts. It is this spirit which paves the way leading to true knowledge. To be sure, science may have its ideals. But it is furthered not by idealism but by the realistic mode of thinking. Without this realistic spirit, no ideal can sustain its own vitality. In this respect, Xun Zi's contribution surpassed that of Mencius. The way of Mencius led to the inner perfection of mind, the end of which was a perfect sagehood, but never a realistic understanding and remolding of society at large.

Generally speaking, the Confucians never attached any importance to the study of science, while more often than not they were intentionally hostile to it. Yet the case was not the same as in the mediaeval West under the spiritual dictatorship of God. Some scholars are of the opinion that Confucianism proved to be a hindrance to the development of science, for what the Confucians sought was moral perfection but not knowledge. The Confucian overemphasis on moral perfection in practice led people away from seeking scientific knowledge of the outside world. Furthermore, the Confucian ideological preaching became more and more an expedient instrument for personal gain in officialdom, and thus deviated further from an earnest seeking of scientific knowledge. The royal examination system based on the format of eight-legged treatises (*ba gu wen*) was merely a stereotyped exposition of the Confucian dogma in a degraded form, with no new ideas at all. It seems that there has reigned a perennial contradiction of virtue vs. knowledge (or virtue vs. talent). When virtue gained supremacy, talent and knowledge were pushed naturally to the background. People were led to adjust themselves according to the ethico-political privileges rather than intellectual merits. And certainly, no science would be possible, if there is no genuine interest in knowledge itself. The idealism of Confucius and Mencius needed realism to make itself balanced, and Xun Zi came forth to meet this need. That is the reason why in the history of China the Confucians as a rule did not treasure science or nourish any scientific attitude, though some among them, Zhu Xi for example, were scholars possessing a good amount of scientific knowledge. To this, the realism of Xun Zi presented an effective remedy, without which Confucianism may very likely have developed along the idealistic line and become entirely a mediaeval theology under the dictatorship of a supernatural God. It was Xun Zi who opened a door leading to possible scientific studies. He exceeded Confucius and Mencius in that he stressed the objective existence of the natural world and its inevitable and inexorable laws. "Heaven has a constant regularity of activity. It did not exist for the sake of Yao [the sage] nor cease to exist for the sake of Jie [the tyrant]." For him, objective laws and rules existed beyond and above the ethical values which had always been the basic axiom of the Chinese way of thinking. Surely, to arrive at such an understanding is no easy thing, if we consider the fact that even in contemporary China it is a prevailing idea that science does not have its own independence and its vocation is but to serve certain ethico-political ends as a faithful servant maid. That truth, beauty and goodness each has its own independent realm and is not subservient to any of the others, or that truth exists for truth's sake, or that "A thing of beauty is a joy forever"[①] has never secured a legitimate place in the Chinese ideology. Hereby we may reach a better apprehension of Xun Zi's unique role in the intellectual history of China.

Any thought once carried to the extreme will lead to partiality. Xun Zi's contribution lay in the fact that his realism helped to counter-balance the one-sided idealism preached by Confucius and Mencius. But Xun Zi's realism when carried too far would also be tripped by its own shortcomings. On this point we may readily cite Tan Sitong's criticism of Xun Zi that the learning in China for more than two thousand years has been nothing but Xun Zi's teaching, which resulted in good-for-nothing or good-for-everything, and Confucius himself had made a severe attack on this point: "The good-for-nothing is the thief of virtue."[②] What Confucius taught was to be ardent or cautious in decision: "The ardent [Kuang] will advance and lay hold of truth; the cautiously-decided will keep themselves from what is wrong."[③] Such was Confucius' ideal of life. If one was neither so ardent as to "advance and lay hold of truth" nor so "cautiously-decided to keep away from what is wrong," then he would surely be a good-for-nothing blindly following the vulgarity of fashion. Yet in our real life, what we see has always been the simple fact that most people have taken the road of the good-for-nothing, a road which is the natural fruit of too much realism. Realism needs Idealism to come to its rescue no less than idealism needs realism to correct its defects.

In his criticism of all schools, Xun Zi pointed out that each of them had only got hold of "one corner of the whole." For him, the Way (Tao) is constant but the modes of its manifestation are varied and manifold; so we cannot get hold of the totality of the Way (Tao) when considering from any single angle. Thus each school had grasped only one aspect of the Way (Tao). True knowledge ought to contain the truth in its totality. It seems Xun Zi's view came nearer to reality than the teachings of Confucius and Mencius, who paid attention only to inner cultivation, while Xun Zi came to acknowledge the effects of coercion and acquired training. The rule of virtue preached by Confucius taught that coercion alone would lead people to "try to avoid the punishment but have no sense of shame."[④] Yet the rule of virtue without the supplement of coercion would also

① Keats, "Endymion."

② *Analects,* "Yang Huo."

③ *Analects,* "Zi Lu."

④ *Analects,* "On Governance."

be of no avail. In searching for an optimum point between moral preaching and legal coercion, Xun Zi found his way out in the rule of rites, which consisted of both the inner morality and the outer coercion. In this, Xun Zi went a step further than Confucius and Mencius in the direction of realism. But to keep the two sides well-balanced is like the performance of a tightrope walker. A slight slip toward any one side may result in tremendous disaster. And we shall see in the coming chapter how Xun Zi's doctrine was transformed into the Machiavellian statecraft of the Legalists.

In temperament, Xun Zi differed very much from Confucius and Mencius. What Confucius and Mencius pursued was an inner spiritual state of life, while Xun Zi sought a pattern of social life which was practicable for and common to all people. Hence Xun Zi never preached sagehood for the common people. When a philosophy tries to probe into the ultimate meaning of life, it certainly comes into contact with what is ineffable or indescribable, a certain kind of mystic experience in life. For instance, the Confucians were often inclined to study the mystic happiness (an ecstatic state) of Yan Hui, Confucius' favorite pupil. In the history of mediaeval Christianity, we see the mystics seeking a state of ecstasy in which one achieved communion with divinity. Mencius ultimately hoped to merge as one with God and Nature, because "all things are already complete in me. There is no greater delight than to be conscious of sincerity in self-examination," "whenever the superior man passes through, transformation follows; wherever he abides, his influence is of a spiritual nature. It flows abroad above and beneath, like that of Heaven and Earth."[1] Heaven and Earth represent God and Nature. Such a communion is an ineffable and supernatural state of mind which has forever been the final end of most philosophical endeavor. Buddha himself arrived at his final mental state as "the Enlightened." But Xun Zi mentioned nothing of this sort, and he advised only a process of self-cultivation which was a step by step course in our daily life, its end never a transcendental mystic state. Yet the Confucians of the later ages mostly followed Confucius and Mencius' inner way of cultivation rather than Xun Zi's outer way, a habit particularly evident in the Song Confucians (the Neo-Confucians of the Song period). Thus Xun Zi's thought did not occupy the place that it deserved. By accident it was the side of him influencing the Legalist school which persistently infiltrated the main current of Chinese ideology. In a certain sense, the Legalists only employed Xun Zi's way of thinking to meet the needs of statecraft. By the later years of the Warring States Period (3rd century B.C.),

---

① *Book of Mencius,* "Culmination of the Mind," pt. 1.

the current of classical populism and humanism was fading out while the spirit of legalism was ascending to the fore. In contrast to the ethical implications of Confucius and Mencius' moral preaching, Xun Zi and his followers the Legalists resorted much more to the outer coercion of legal enforcement.

Prof. Li Zehou thought that the doctrine of Xun Zi, with its critical reason, had counterbalanced the various prevailing superstitions, teleology, voluntarism and mysticism, and thereby helped the Chinese mind to stay cool and clear. It kept the Chinese mind away from the rule of theocracy and theology, which are clearly observable in the mediaeval history of other peoples. Surely it was so, but unfortunately the Legalist preference for the trickery of power politics became ever since an integral part of the Chinese intellectual tradition down to the later days, whereas the more significant contributions in his thought, i.e. the realistic spirit leaning toward science, was grossly obliterated. Such a scene is indeed a pity in the history of philosophy in China.

Chapter Seven: The Taoist School

[I] Taoism and Lao Zi

The Taoist school is not only one of the most significant schools among the philosophies of the pre-Qin period, but also one of the most significant integral parts of intellectual culture throughout the long history of China. What deserves specific attention in the Taoist doctrine may be roughly summed up in the following lines:

Firstly, this Taoist school proposed a philosophy indigenous to the mainland of China, which as an extremely vigorous and tenacious current has persisted unbroken down to later ages, unlike other schools such as the Mohists and Logicians which utterly vanished in China's middle ages.

Secondly, among all schools in ancient times, the Taoists are the most philosophically-minded and the most philosophically-oriented in the proper sense of the word "philosophy." All other schools dealt with ethico-political preaching, while the Taoists—in addition to their ethico-political discourse—worked out a systematic theory of philosophy.

Thirdly, in contrast with all other schools, the Taoists were permeated with a keen interest in the observation of the natural world, and consequently are most closely related with the study of natural sciences in China. The Confucians had little interest in science. If one is interested in the history of the sciences and scientific thought, he can find it nowhere better than in the legacy of the Taoist documents. Any philosophical theory, provided it can be properly so called, must deal with the relationship between man and nature; yet most other schools, especially the Confucians, showed little interest in it. It was the Taoist school which exhibited a keen concern for natural philosophy and a naturalistic world-view.

Fourthly, as a philosophy of the upper classes at first, Taoist theory gradually intermingled with the popular beliefs of the common folk and eventually developed into a religious sect known as Taoism, which became the sole indigenous religion of China. It has survived two thousand years with its Chinese features in its entirety, exhibiting an enduring vitality. It exercised a profound influence on both the intellectual mentality and the daily life of the Chinese people, so much so that even the Confucian ideas of the later ages were strongly imbued with a Taoist intonation. The Taoists figured in both the "Six Schools" of ancient times and the "Three Doctrines" of the Middle Ages.

The teachings of Taoism penetrated the depths of the Chinese mind from the upper to the lower classes, so much so that its permeation among the masses equaled that of Confucianism. Some researchers even went so far so to propose that Taoism be seen as the major trend in Chinese culture. As a matter of fact, we should not ask who deserves to be credited as the proper representative of Chinese intellectual culture. The issue of "who is the legitimate representative" is valid only in the field of political legitimacy, and can by no means be applied to the realm of ideas and knowledge, for example inquiring who is the genuine Confucian and who is the pretender, or nominating Confucius as the undisputed representative of Chinese culture. For we may fairly retort: why is it not the grotesque figure of Ah Q? Is not Ah Q as well qualified in representing one of the most essential aspects of the Chinese mind? To attempt to argue legitimacy in the field of ideas is mere nonsense.

In respect to Taoism as the sole popular religion in China, it seems proper first of all to consider what constitutes the salient intellectual feature of the Chinese national mentality. Perhaps the most ready answer is simply their practicality in their behavior. Throughout their long history the Chinese people have laid particular emphasis on practical utility. Perhaps this furnishes us with a key to unlock the secret of their way of thinking and their general intellectual habits. For example, considering how clever they have proven, and the many inventions they have created, why did they still never develop modern science in their history? Again, why in their history did they never embrace genuine religious belief and worship, nor enter into any religious war? The reasons may all be traced to that practicality which became the innermost ingredient of their national character. They are too practical to engage in the pursuit of anything which is impractical or of no use to them. Their minds are dedicated wholly to what is of practical value, while both science and religion in the last analysis pursue something of the infinity beyond the practical world. A man of practicality would never have any interest in pursuing such things. The Chinese sages taught people not to talk about what is supernatural[①] (i.e. what is impractical). The Chinese were taught that a sage admits but never discusses what is beyond or behind the world. They never engage in studying what is outside the sphere of their practical life and practical interest. Therefore the Chinese people showed no intention to search for the secrets of the universe and the human mind. They are content with what concerns the practical satisfactions of their daily life. They are never willing to scrutinize what is beyond. They may readily accept any belief or indoctrination and just as readily give it up, depending on whether it might provide them some immediate practical utility or not. It is in this sense that Taoism survived as a religion with a peculiar Chinese form. And the teachings of Lao Zi and Zhuang Zi have—amazingly—been intermingled with the common longing for worldly reward.

In essence, religion pursues what is beyond of the present world of our immediate day-to-day life. And only this other-worldly ineffability can fulfill the deepest needs of the human heart. But, on the contrary, the ideal of the Taoists is merely prolongation of the enjoyment of the present life in this present world. This longing expressed by the Taoists vividly reflected the national ethos of the Chinese people. It has been absorbed into the marrow of their bones and embodied in their practices. That is why in modern times so many representative figures of the anti-traditional current have in one blow condemned both the Confucians and the Taoists as the greatest obstacles to China's progress. The iconic cultural critic Lu Xun (1880-1936) sharply attacked this traditional Chinese ethos. Similarly, the poet-scholar Wen Yiduo (1899-1941) criticized traditional intellectuals for aiming at nothing but wealth and a high position in officialdom. This is how a person earned respect as a proper Confucian, before later retiring to his hometown to enjoy a life of luxury—and thereby becoming a Taoist. Confucianism and Taoism were thus supplementary to each other and laid down the basic tone of intellectuals' life-view. This criticism from Wen seems to be an overly harsh judgment of Chinese intellectuals. Yet the fact is: the history of mankind has seen so many religious wars throughout the world, but none happened in China. This may show how far the Chinese people have been from any religious faith in its proper sense. We need neither to beautify nor to vilify what has happened in history. To keep a value-free standpoint would help us attain a deeper understanding of the past.

For all that happens in history, there always exist features which are

① *Analects*, chap. 7, 21.

cherished as well as those which are despised, both favored and unfavored going hand in hand. Modern China, strongly bound up by her long tradition as she was, was painfully obstructed in her progress toward modernization; hence the radicals tend to hold an extreme disgust for the unfavorable elements in the traditional culture, taking a thoroughly critical attitude. In their view, many of the Taoist ideas should be abruptly cast off. Of course, the question of which elements are the dross and which are the essence in traditional culture is complicated, and it is hard to draw a clear-cut demarcation. The relevant criterion is generally not unvarying, but always dependent on different times, places and circumstances. And furthermore, the alleged dross and essence may each turn out to be its opposite under different conditions; what is miraculous may turn out to be dross and vice versa. There is no ground for supposing the existence of an absolute criterion forever indisputable. What we can judge or measure is only its role under the present circumstances.

The origin of the Taoists was at least as early as that of the Confucians, if not earlier. And just like Confucianism, Taoism has survived down to modern times, and permeated throughout every aspect of Chinese cultural life. We are not justified in specifying any one philosopher or school as the sole representative of the Chinese spirit, because a nation's ethos is a complex synthesis of various ingredients. There is no such problem as who or which school ought to represent the spirit of a nation. We can merely say that the Taoists are as influential in China as the Confucians.

Similar to the other schools of antiquity, the Taoists venerated an ancient sage-king, Huang Di (literally "the Yellow Emperor"), as their original founder. Hence they were in later days known as the School of Huang Di and Lao Zi, or simply the Huang-Lao School; and their theories and practices were known as the learning of Huang Lao or the arts of Huang Lao. As the greatest masters of this school were Lao Zi and Zhuang Zi, it is also known as the learning of Lao Zhuang. Both Lao Zi and Zhuang Zi were surely outstanding philosophers, but neither was a founder of a religious sect, nor did they ever intend to be such. Much later, by the time of the Han dynasty, Taoism gradually emerged as a religion. In the early years of the Han Dynasty (2nd century B.C.), after long years of war, the whole society was deeply miserable, and the royal court resorted to a policy of "quietness and inactivity," the main aim "to nourish a peaceful life" and "let the people have a rest." Thus the rulers tried not to interfere with the people, nor to make demands of them, hoping that the social and economic life might soon improve. Then in the last years of the later Han Dynasty (early 3rd century) political corruption induced great social turmoil.

A certain Zhang Daoling founded a Taoist sect with a strong political appeal. Since then various sects sprang up and proliferated from time to time, here and there. One of his descendants founded a site at Mount Longhu (literally "Mount Dragons and Tigers") in Jiangxi and assumed the title of Heavenly Master. His heirs succeeded generation after generation with acknowledgment from the royal court. A great deal of Chinese popular customs, mores, witchcraft, medicines, alchemy and ideas originated in them. But all this occurred in the later ages, and what we are concerned with now are the ideas of the two leading philosophers of Taoism in classical times, Lao Zi and Zhuang Zi, who had little to do with the theories and practices of the Taoist religion of later ages.

[II] Lao Zi

There is still no definite conclusion on the dates of Lao Zi's life. But it is generally accepted that Lao Zi lived some time before Zhuang Zi. It is likely that Lao Zi flourished in the early years of the Warring States (5th century B.C.), an age of extreme disorder and constant war. There is a famous saying in the *Book of Lao Zi*, "Weapons at best are tools of bad omen."[①] Some took this as meaning that winning a war is of no good at all, while others interpreted the word "good" (*jia*) as "only" (*wei*), signifying that launching a war is of no good at all. It seems more likely the latter interpretation comes nearer the original meaning, since it was the time of the Warring States.

The earliest record of Lao Zi's life is found in Sima Qian's *Records of the Historian*, which, however, did not give any definite information about him. This shows Sima Qian's prudence as a classical historian. He faithfully recorded what was commonly believed but never inserted his own opinion. The details of Lao Zi's life in his *Records of the Historian* are all preceded by phrases such as: "It was said," Sima Qian never adding his own affirmation or negation.

It was said that Lao Zi's name was Li Er or Lao Dan, and that he had served as the royal librarian at the Royal House of Zhou. Again it was claimed that he traveled far westward and then disappeared forever. When he was passing the Han Gou Pass, the guard of the pass urged him to write out his work into a book. Thus we were left the *Book of Lao Zi*, sometimes known as the *Canon of Tao and Virtue* (*Dao De Jing*). There was also a prevailing legend that Lao Zi influenced Confucius on the issue of rites. So according to this legend,

① Trans. R. B. Blakney. Another translation reads, " the best war machines are the instruments of disaster."

Lao Zi was a predecessor of Confucius.

There are three points of contention here: first, the time of Lao Zi himself; second, the time of the compilation of the *Book of Lao Zi*; third, the time of the formation of Lao Zi's doctrine. Logically, the formation of the ideas expressed in the *Book of Lao Zi* ought to have occurred sometime between his own life and that of the book's completion. It seems likely that the book was completed sometime between the middle and late Warring States Period (3rd century B.C.). The ancients had no idea of private authorship or copyright in the modern sense, so after a long process of copying by hand and revising, the final version would certainly have undergone considerable modification from the original. Zhuang Zi closely associated himself with Lao Zi, and in the *Book of Zhuang Zi*, Lao Zi was revered as "the great wise man of antiquity."① This shows Lao Zi to have preceded Zhuang Zi. The *Book of Lao Zi* was written in beautiful rhymed verse, a style suggesting an origin later than that of the *Analects*, the *Analects* being recorded in plain and compact prose-dialogue.

What is the main intention of the *Book of Lao Zi*? Ban Gu's *History of the Han* had it that the *Book of Lao Zi* explained statecraft, "the art of ruling for the sovereigns." As we have said above, all ancient philosophers aspired to rescue the world from chaos and misery through their political theories and programs. Lao Zi said, "To rule a large country is like cooking a small fish."② The term "sage," appearing so frequently in his book, denotes the sovereign. Both the starting point and the end of his book are the issue of how to rule a country, and how to realize an ideal utopia. This reflects the general aim of China's classical philosophers. All of them began from political appeals, and ended in urging the realization of their ideals. This line of thinking, aligned with moral recommendations, constituted the basic thread of traditional Chinese ideology. In classical terminology, "sage" represents an ideal sovereign much more than it does a mere man of virtue, as we might readily observe in the *Book of Lao Zi*.

The *Book of Lao Zi* has its alternative name, *Canon of Tao and Virtue*, because it consists of two parts: the former part dealing with Tao, the latter with virtue. Some years ago a silk copy of *Book of Lao Zi* was unearthed in Ma wang dui (in Hunan Province) in which the part on virtue was put before that on Tao, while their contents were much the same. Lao Zi's introduction of the ideas of Tao and virtue must be regarded as the paramount contribution to the history of China's theoretical thought. By giving them a completely new connotation,

① *Book of Zhuang Zi*, "The World."

② *Book of Lao Zi*, chap. 60.

Lao Zi amplified their essence to a philosophical height never rivaled for ages to come. The Tao is literally the "Way." Confucius had dealt with Tao, saying, "My doctrines (Way) make no way. I will get upon a raft and float on the sea."① Here the Tao (Way) stands for his ideal or principle. And in another passage he says, "Since I cannot get men to pursue the due way..."② For Confucius, Tao (Way) means the ideal mode of proper behavior, carrying a purely socio-ethical implication. But for Lao Zi, the term Tao denotes immeasurably much more than this. Since it is the essential notion in Lao Zi's philosophy, it is hard to identify an English equivalent. Some translate it simply as the "Way," while others prefer the original term Tao (and hence Taoism and Taoists). What the readers should understand is that Lao Zi was the first in China to work out a systematic ontology, with the idea of Tao as the First Principle of the universe and human life. Personally I prefer to translate it by the Greek term "Logos." The opening sentence of the Gospel according to John runs, "In the beginning there is the Word, the Word is with God and God is the Word." Here the "Word" in English had its equivalents "Parole" in French, "Wort" in German or "Slovo" in Russian. "Word" in Greek is "Logos." In the Hellenistic period, Greek philosophy was influenced by Oriental mysticism, and Neo-Platonism was much in vogue. Its founder Plotinus (205-270) had elaborated in particular the idea of "Logos." Etymologically this "Logos" denotes a word, but, more so, it implies the noumenal totality of the material and the spiritual world. Some translate "Tao" as "Nature," which in capitalized form has a supernatural implication, as we might find in F. H. Balfour's English translation of more than a century ago. So after all, what does Tao mean? Let us suppose that all things are in a process of eternal change, whether rapid or slow. But no matter how a thing changes or transforms, there is ultimately something in it which remains unchanged and lasting. A thing can never become nothing at all. This remaining element (either physical or metaphysical) we can call substance (or essence), and is that which makes a thing what it is. The substance is unchanging amidst changes. The physical article changes, but its substance and the rules (say, the law of universal gravitation, or the atoms composing it) do not change. And still more, what governs these rules remains unchanged, or changes in accordance with an invisible unchanging hand. And this *Primum Mobile*, though invisible and imperceptible, ultimately governs the whole universe and the human world. This is the Tao, which governs the world and what is behind it and beyond it.

① *Analects*, chap. 5, 7.

② Ibid., chap. 13, 21.

In general, the more fundamental a philosophical idea is, the more difficult it is to define. The Newtonian system presupposes three fundamental dimensions: space, time and mass, but each of these is hard to define. We just take them as a generally acknowledged starting-point needing no further elucidation. It is difficult to make clear what time or space or mass is. The notion of law or rule similarly defies clear distinction. Contemporary physics holds very different views on the idea of "law" from the physics of the 19th century. And our modern idea of natural law cannot be straightforwardly identified with the Tao of Lao Zi. One ought not too quickly conclude that the Tao of Lao Zi is simply the same as our natural law.

At any rate, there is a twofold implication in Lao Zi's Tao requiring scrutiny: it refers to the immediately perceptible world, but at the same time its existence is not merely passive, for it is in constant motion and change, and the reason or principle governing these processes is Tao. The former aspect makes up the physical, the latter the metaphysical (i.e. that which is beyond the physical). The relationship between Tao and the objective world has been an age-long subject of debate. Some argued that Lao Zi is a materialist, insisting that Tao is just the law of motion and change immanent in the natural world. Others took Lao Zi as an idealist and his Tao as transcending the objective world. Or, another possible solution is this: his Tao is both transcendent of and immanent in the world. No matter the conclusion, his Tao is that which governs the whole world and human life, and is one with them. Hence:

> Tao (the Way) begot one,
> And the one, two;
> Then the two begot three,
> And three, all else.[①]

That is, all is derived from and directed by the primeval omnipresent and omnipotent Tao. Thus Lao Zi's philosophy reached an abstraction unequaled by all other classical schools.

The term "Logos" carries a certain ineffable tone, that leads us to identify Tao with a "hidden God." The idea of a hidden God had its origin in the *Bible*, and in early modern times Pascal expounded that God is a hidden God, not apparent in any definite form. In ancient Greece, a Sophist once contended: just as we imagine God in the form of a man, a cock would imagine God in the form of a cock. In the Middle Ages, Christian theologians were apt to say that God created Man after his own image. This is of course a primitive way of reasoning.

---

① *Book of Lao Zi*, chap. 42.

According to orthodox theology, God is omnipresent; and if he be omnipresent, then God would assume no definite form. As is well known, the Taoist master Zhuang Zi asserted that Tao exists even in excrement and urinc. Tao in the *Book of Lao Zi* is indeed somewhat like a hidden God, who dominates all things though hidden. He can be said to manifest himself and exercise his power in the existence of all things both in their changing and in their unchanging. Yet this interpretation seems more or less to dress up the thought of the ancients in a modernized garb—a tendency we should try to avoid. Philosophy is at bottom the elaboration of a comprehensive theory of the world—a world-view—and, among the ancient Chinese, only the Taoist school attained such an understanding, with Lao Zi as its earliest and foremost spokesman.

Our thoughts are formed and expressed through language and text. And so is it also with our understanding of others' thoughts. But for different persons, the same words do not necessarily convey the same content. We understand the ancients solely through their own words, but they did not intend their words to convey the exact implication that we perceive. The texts do not change, yet their implications are always changing in the course of time. It is indeed difficult to discern the different implications of the same words. This is especially the case with the "five thousand words" of the *Book of Lao Zi*. To be sure, we are to understand it through a process of translating it into our own understanding. Nevertheless, once it is translated into our modern terminology, what we understand is simply how we have translated it in our present thoughts. In other words, our understanding is doomed to never coincide exactly with the original text. The weight and content of the translated version can never be the same as the author's text. Maybe someday people can discover a device, like the mathematical formula in the study of physics, that allows people to reach common agreement on the classics of the ancients. But as long as we are obliged to employ the ordinary language of our daily life as the sole vehicle for expressing our ideas, we cannot entertain such a hope. The opening sentence of *Book of Lao Zi* reads, "There are ways, but the way is uncharted." In a different translation, it reads, "The Tao (Way) that can be told of, is not the eternal Tao." Yet another is, "If Tao could be defined, it would not be an everlasting truth." The different translated versions reflected different understandings and interpretations. And it seems very hard to single out which one comes closest to the author's original intention. Some prefer to identify "Tao" with "the law of nature." And the very term "law of nature" sounds rather ambiguous. In the 19th century this term carried a connotation very different from today. The scientist of the 19th century believed in the iron law of nature, which was unchangeable and necessarily true. Most people nowadays would no longer stick to such an inflexible and stereotyped notion of the "law of nature." The law of nature is no longer taken as something inflexible and immutable, because what we identify as the law of nature inevitably consists of some subjective elements on the part of the knowing subject in the process of our understanding. Can we assert that the idea of "natural law" we are accustomed to in modern science is the same as the Tao of Lao Zi? We may well suppose that Lao Zi envisioned nothing of the idea as formulated in modern science. Hence his Tao can in no way be identified with either law or rule or noumenon in their modern senses. Yet, although there can be no perfect coincidence between the ideas of the ancients and the terms of the moderns, we have no choice other than to understand the ancients in terms of our present-day language. Herein lies the insurmountable difficulty of understanding other people. In a certain sense, our understanding of others is just a process of translating their ideas.

After World War II, at the end of 1945, Einstein was attending a performance of Beethoven's Fifth Symphony conducted by Toscanini. After the performance Einstein went up to and congratulated him with the words, "Once more you proved to me the existence of God." As is well known, Einstein's God is a Spinozist God, i.e. Nature itself. God need not assume the figure of a human being. The term "Nature" denotes simply the objective world and the principles and rules governing it. We can remember John: "In the beginning there is the Word, the Word is with God and God is the Word." Maybe this was what led Pascal to assert that God is a hidden God. It serves as a proper footnote to Lao Zi's Way (Logos). God is invisible and imperceptible, but this does not necessarily mean that God is non-existent. The Tao for Lao Zi embraces a twofold implication, both nature and what is behind nature—something very akin to the Spinozist God. It comprises both law and what is more than law. It is in its very essence "Nature."

In one sense, Tao means the ever-flowing natural world, but the natural world in the last analysis must hold something within it which persists permanently and immutably. And Tao is just this substance. The entirety of the natural world is not only what appears to us, but also that which is invisible and imperceptible to us. It possesses its physical as well as its metaphysical aspects. And Lao Zi was the founder and foremost exponent of metaphysics and ontology in ancient China. What falls within the scope of metaphysics may be classified as noumenon, and it is in this sense that, logically, Tao is taken as the noumenon. If there is any reason or principle in this world, then this reason or principle can be nothing other than Tao. Thus the term Tao means both what belongs to the physical world as well as to the metaphysical world. This is readily understandable, for the ancients did not make the distinction between the two worlds that we do now. For the ancients, the natural world is not merely a heap of matters, but is endowed with a conscious reason or a sort of self-consciousness. Just because we share this very Tao, we are able to know what Tao is. This is the self-consciousness of the Tao, which is composed of both what is material and what is super-material. Tao is "Nature," encompassing both the material world and the spiritual world behind it.

Philosophically, the classical Taoist school went much further than the Orthodox Confucians. They produced more ideas of philosophical profundity than did any other school. Confucius and Mencius preached profusely on benevolence and obligation and other morals, but they never dealt with the fundamental principle (i.e. Tao or Logos) regulating life, history and the universe at large. It was only the Taoist school that worked out a systematic and comprehensive cosmology. As mentioned earlier, the *Yin-Yang* school worked out a detailed cosmography, but it only described the universe in which we live—akin to the ancient Chinese fable of how the sky was mended by the legendary Creator-goddess Nuwa, or the Christian mythology of the Creation and the Fall from the Eden. Whereas the central issue of cosmology is to deal with what constitutes the essence of "Being" in its broadest sense.

From where does "Being" arise? To this, the Taoist school devised a theory which would bewitch the Chinese mind for ages to come. Lao Zi asserted, "All things comes from Being, Being comes from Non-being."① The Taoist school held the Non-being (Nothingness) to be supreme. Being is the offspring of Non-being. This entails a logical antinomy. Similarly, Kant cited his first antimony.②

Thesis	Antithesis
The world has a beginning in time, and is also limited in regard to space.	The world has no beginning, and no limits in space, and is—in relation both to time and space—infinite.

① *Book of Lao Zi*, chap. 40.

② Kant, *Critique of Pure Reason*, trans. Meikljohn (New York: Colonial Press, 1900).

If the world had a beginning in time, then what was before that time? Either (1) there was something before that time, or (2) there was nothing at all before that time. If the latter, then we must admit that "Being comes from Non-being." If the former, then where did that something come from? As a matter of fact, these two answers are logically equivalent; neither is more reasonable or more well-grounded than the other, and neither argument is superior. Anyhow, the notion of "nothingness" became ever since then a key notion in the history of ideas of China. In the Song Dynasty there emerged a Diagram of the Ultimate Extremity (*Taiji*) showing how the universe was forever coming into being. In fact, this diagram illustrated the evolution of the world, or a cosmogony in symbolic forms, very akin to what we find in the mystic symbolism of various cultures outside of China. The Great Ultimate (*Taiji*) is "Nature", or "Being." The ancient Taoist dictum, "Being comes out of Non-being," became in the Song Confucians, "From the Non-Ultimate emerged the Great Ultimate." As the Great Ultimate differentiated, there successively came into being the two primary modes (*Yin* and *Yang*, or the positive principle and the negative), then the four phases (of the world), and then the Eight Trigrams, and more. The complexity of the world was originally derived from the Great Ultimate, which originally came out of the Non-Ultimate. The reason why the Taoist school upheld the notion of Non-being is closely linked to their world-view and their ideal of a life of humility and flexibility. Roughly speaking, the attitude towards life may be classified into two categories: one is positive aggressiveness, which includes the Confucians and Mohists; the other is passive flexibility, with the Taoists as its foremost exponents. Since the Taoists were most fond of flexibility and humility, Lao Zi customarily cited "water" as his favorite analogy in expounding the ever-flowing process of the world. He stressed "The highest goodness, water-like, does good to everything and goes unmurmuring to places men despise; But so is close in nature to the Way (Tao)."[①] And again: "Nothing is weaker than water. But when it attacks something hard, or resistant, then nothing withstands it, and nothing will alter its way."[②] Thus, his conclusion: "Alive, a man is supple, soft; In death, unbending, rigorous."[③] It is just by its softness and humility that water succeeds and overcomes all things. So it is with the human world too. In the age-old tradition of Chinese culture, this mentality promoted soft flexibility in

① *Book of Lao Zi*, chap. 8.
② Ibid., chap. 78.
③ Ibid., chap. 7, 6.

contrast to active initiative. And one has to admit that Chinese culture owed its long-enduring vitality to this flexibility no less than to its earnest vigor. When the famous Buddhist monk Xuanzang of the Tang period (mid-7th century) traveled in India, he translated the *Book of Lao Zi* into Sanskrit, instead of the classics of Confucianism. The Indians were a highly philosophically-minded people, and Xuanzang was well aware that the Taoists' philosophical depth surpassed all other schools.

The idea "Being" in its broadest sense exists in opposition to "Non-being." According to Lao Zi, "These two come paired but distinct by their names. Of all things profound, say their pairing is deepest, the gate to the root of the world."[①] So prevalent was this idea in the Wei and Jin dynasties (3rd-4th centuries) that the philosophy of that time was generally called "The learning of the profundity" (*xuan xue*), its purpose to discuss whether the essence of the world was "Being" or "Non-being." *Book of Lao Zi* together with the *Book of Changes* and *Book of Zhuang Zi* were regarded as the "Three Books on Profundity." And this approach was held as the only way leading to ultimate truth.

In modern times, as generally known, there emerged the idea of "alienation." Man is primarily a part of nature, but he is that part of nature which is made opposed to nature through a process of alienation. He is always intentionally acting against nature, with a motivation to act upon nature instead of passively following nature's course. In the *Book of Lao Zi*, the author strives to show that what is man-made is an alienation from what is natural and is hence unnatural, or directly against nature. The proper way of a human being lies just in casting away all that is against nature so that he may thus enjoy the good life in accordance with nature. Lao Zi proclaimed, "When wisdom and intelligence appeared, They brought with them a great hypocrisy."[②] Hypocrisy is the outcome of artificiality, and what is man-made is inherently opposed to what is natural. Wisdom is the outcome of human creation. Nature in itself carries no wisdom or intelligence, and hence no intellectual creation at all. In his view, all that is created by man is no good at all, because it is against nature. Hence Lao Zi was forever calling for a "return to nature." This reminds us of the famous opening sentence of Rousseau's *Emile*: "*Tout est bien sortant des mains de l'auteur des choses, tout dégénère entre les mains de l'homme.*"[③]

---

① Ibid., chap.1.

② Ibid., chap.18.

③ Rousseau, *Emile*, bk. 1.

How should we evaluate this life-view (Lebensanschauung) of Lao Zi's? In the late Qing Dynasty (early 20th century) one of the first moderns in China, Yan Fu (1853-1921), wrote a pamphlet, often neglected by the general reading public, with the title "Yan's annotations on *Book of Lao Zi*." He associated this doctrine of Lao Zi's with some of the fundamental ideas of modern naturalism and liberalism. It was Yan Fu who first introduced Adam Smith to China by translating Smith's *The Wealth of Nations*. As we earlier touched upon, Smith, a professor of ethics, taught that everyone is a thoroughly rational being, and that in an ideal free market everyone is motivated to seek his own greatest profit. According to such a theory of human nature, if everyone is set free in search of his own interests, then the whole society automatically steps into an optimal social order. An ideal state of free competition would logically result in the most effective arrangement meeting the self-interest of everyone to the greatest possible extent. And this is the idea Yan Fu used to expound the thought of Lao Zi. Set free what is natural, both in human nature and in nature as a whole, without the least coercion, and all will be well by itself. Yan identifies the "return to nature" as the very essence of Lao Zi's teaching. The best state of life and society is simply that which is never polluted by any artificial (i.e. unnatural) creation.

In the 18th century, as the foremost representative of the Enlightenment movement, Rousseau boldly raised his own cry for a "return to nature." Man should discard all that is unnatural (artificial or man-made) and return to nature. Indeed, on the one hand, we ought to admit that all civilization is an alienation from nature. But on the other hand, we have to admit as well that civilization in a broader sense is also a part of nature, i.e. that part of nature which is derived from nature but becomes alienated from it. It is the unnatural part of nature, so to speak. Those who entirely deny that this unnatural part of nature in fact derives from nature may be regarded as lacking a deeper understanding of nature. If there were no artifacts, we would not have the ingenuity of Lao Zi nor of Rousseau. Their thoughts were basically a profound reflection on nature, and on life and the world, but by no means the natural product of nature itself. We may fairly name it a sort of unnatural naturalness. Though unnatural, it is yet of naturalness. And above all, the naturalistic philosophers from Lao Zi to Rousseau failed to acknowledge the fact that humanity at bottom was still natural, and only nature alienated from itself. Without such an alienation, there would be no humanity, but only the animal world. If all were left to the mechanism of mere nature, there would never be speculations such as produced by Lao Zi or Rousseau. A return to nature exacts an earnest voluntary effort which can hardly be identified as natural. It is a strenuous, cultivated human effort, instead of a natural spontaneity. It is actually an ideal state of civilized life and of human culture. Lao Zi delineated it emphatically, "the straightest, yet it seems/ to deviate, to bend; the highest skill and yet/ it looks like clumsiness. The utmost eloquence/ it sounds like stammering."① Centuries later, the famous poet Su Shi (of the late 11th century, in the Song Dynasty) complemented this idea further by asserting, "The greatest wisdom looks like ignorance." The greatest wisdom of life—and this is what Lao Zi sought—looks like ignorance, but in fact is not. It is the result of our intentional intellectual pursuit, and not the product of the spontaneous course of nature. In a deeper sense the dialectics of Lao Zi seem to imply: Man is a part of nature, is alienated from nature, and finally returns to it again. Whoever fails to follow this line will be punished by nature. If you know the law of nature and follow it, you will exist in harmony with it and be happy. Civilization corrupted man and nature. If man is wise enough to know nature better, he sees that all that belongs to civilization is man-made. To discard civilization and to return to nature demands "non-activity" on the part of man. Hence "the mighty Way (Tao) declined among the folk/ And then came kindness and morality."② Once morality (a product of human invention) appeared, the natural Way was broken up.

Yet to return to the primeval state of nature is obviously impossible. Man is both a part of nature and at the same time a part of what opposes nature as soon as civilization starts its march. The march of civilization is entirely of humanity, forever a man-made process, and not something conferred spontaneously by nature. We may suppose that the evolution of mankind undergoes three stages. In the first, natural stage, man was nothing more than a part of nature. Second, man became alienated from nature, separating from it and remodeling it, such as when he cuts down trees into lumber and builds houses, there being nothing of "house" in the state of nature. Then there will be the third stage in which man, after his alienation from nature, returns to nature with his civilization in harmony with nature, i.e. not a simple return to the primeval state of nature but a return to nature on a higher level of consciousness through the ingenuity of man's wisdom.

Lao Zi espoused an extremely strong belief in the return to nature. Repeatedly he stressed the doctrine, "Doing spoils it, grabbing misses it."③

---

① Ibid., chap. 45.

② Ibid., chap. 14.

③ Ibid., chap. 64.

All human doings are rebellion against nature and eventually lead to disaster. In the last instance, man will return to nature. This is what Lao Zi meant in his preaching of Tao. He pointed out emphatically, "Tao is always still, at rest, / And yet does everything that's done."① Man should not try to interfere with the course of nature but should always be conscious that he himself is an integral part of nature, ever in obedience to its rules. Tao is always non-active, and any voluntary action spoils it. Hence, "The student learns by daily increment, the Way is gained by daily loss."② (Another translation reads, "As one is increasing one's knowledge, his apprehension of Tao is proportionately decreasing.") In summary, one should not try to meddle with the course of nature, but should submit to it obediently. The more one tries to control the course of nature, the further one runs contrary to it. Applied to the political and social realm, this might seem like a *laissez-faire* theory of ancient China. The less the sovereign tries to take measures, so much the better would things proceed by themselves. In other words, the civilization of mankind simultaneously means the fall of mankind. The *Bible* tells us how man fell from the Garden of Eden by eating the forbidden fruit of knowledge. Kant had it also: "The history of nature begins with good, for it is the work of God, while the history of human freedom begins with wickedness, for it is the work of man."③ Marx wrote that civilization began with the appearance of classes, and without the exploitation of man by man there could be no civilization. Thus human civilization since its very beginning seems to be simply the degeneration of mankind. How to keep humanity unspoiled with its merits while discarding its demerits is the problem so many philosophers have attempted to solve. Goethe taught that sorrows and disasters are unavoidable in life, and that one should entertain the hope of "durch Leiden Freude." It promises a higher level of happiness than normally conceived. If someday mankind's civilization is able to reach a more ideal state, it too could only be the kind of happiness that follows many sorrows and disasters.

Lastly, let us give some evaluation of Lao Zi's theory. He indeed produced a penetrating insight into the defects and disasters of civilized society, but he did not see it as a whole. We ought to confront face to face the wickedness in civilized (in contrast to natural) life, but we should at the same time take a broad view towards this wickedness. All civilization is but a reformation of nature. Man cannot remain forever in the state of nature. Yet if civilization goes against

① Ibid., chap. 37.

② Ibid., chap. 48.

③ Kant, *On History*, trans. L. W. Beck (Indianapolis: Bobbs-Merrill, 1963), p60.

nature, disaster inevitably follows. So the problem is how to arrange human activity in concordance with the requirements of nature, such that both may adjust to each other in the best possible way. Imitating Zhuang Zi's criticism of the ancient philosophers, perhaps we are justified to assert that Lao Zi "knows nature but knows no humanity." Humanity means a coercion of nature, but that does not mean a reconciliation cannot be found between the two. There should be a best possible way for this. However, what Lao Zi preached was only a simple return to the primitive state of nature—though the way leading to it still engendered great wisdom, such as one can only find in the leading Taoist philosophers Lao Zi and Zhuang Zi. Civilization is indispensable to humanity. Without human ingenuity, the advancement of humanity is simply impossible. There is an endless strife before this goal of a higher level of harmony with nature and a more conscious state of returning to nature. Humanity has to pay that indispensable price for its own betterment, Lao Zi himself being no exception. Without having experienced a great many hardships and pains himself, how is it possible for Lao Zi to arrive at such profound wisdom as is taught in his book?

Many researchers hold the view that Lao Zi desired a restoration of the ancients, or a return to primitive communism. Maybe it is so. Nevertheless, we have to see that, though any thought is inescapably the product of its age, once it comes into being, it survives by its own independent value. A thought possesses its own life independent of the author who gave birth to it. It has its own independent right to life and is to be judged by its own value independent of the circumstances behind its origin. The same social and historical background may engender different ideas, each of which has the right to clamor for its own survival. In the research on Lao Zi, some are inclined to raise him to such a height as if he had grasped the final wisdom—a judgment surely out of all proportion. Human knowledge and thought is a process of continual deepening and heightening, and the later ages as a rule come higher than their predecessors. But we ought to allot heartfelt praise to those whose theoretical insights by far surpassed their times. Admittedly everyone has his limitation, but at the same time we must scrutinize those ideas that are not confined by the limitation of their time. Keen and valuable theoretical insights are destined to be universally valuable, despite their specific backgrounds. To simplify intellectual achievements as mere products of their times and to arrogantly dismiss their independent value, or (on the other extreme) to elevate them to a height unsurpassable by later generations—both modes of evaluating our predecessors would be far from doing justice to them. Suffice to say that Lao Zi was one of the most profound philosophers in ancient China. It is he who first formulated a complete philosophical system with Tao (Way or Logos) as its essence, which expounded the first principle of the objective world as well as the law of humanity. It is he who founded a deeply important indigenous school of thought whose influence has been far-reaching and long-enduring. And Taoism as a popular religious sect bred the early germs of scientific research in China's history.

The influence of Lao Zi's teaching in the history of China has been tremendous. The early Han dynasty took his teaching as the guiding principle in ruling their kingdom, known as"the statecraft of the Yellow King [an ancient sage-king and the legendary founder of Taoism] and Lao Zi." And later the sovereigns of the Tang Dynasty venerated it as their state religion. Both Han and Tang Dynasties are generally acknowledged as the most flourishing periods in the long history of China. And thenceforth the three sects, Confucianism, Taoism and Buddhism, were universally accepted as the three prevailing modes of belief in China.

Considering Lao Zi and the Taoist school at large, both their positive qualities as well as their negative deserve minute examination. Among their positive contributions, it was due to their observations that people came to recognize the need to maintain the harmony between nature and man. After all, man is an integral part of nature and has to venerate the rule of nature above all. Man can neither separate from nature nor act against nature. Ultimately, man has to obey the rule of nature. Hence all that does not conform with nature should be resolutely denied, including all luxuries and hypocrisies in life, which are the inevitable products of civilized society. Lao Zi criticized them severely and justifiably. The negative elements in Lao Zi's teaching sprang from his overemphasizing the need to return to nature, causing him to neglect or even deny the value of the voluntary motives in human activity. We must acknowledge that every aspect of civilization is the product of human effort. Without such activity, mankind would remain forever in the state of mere animals. It is only through the progress of civilization that mankind is differentiated from the animals. Humanity dwells in just this. In the style of Zhuang Zi, we may well say that the Taoists were too overshadowed by Heaven (nature) to understand humanity. The good in humanity may promote further good, while the bad otherwise. All highly developed cultures in history are nothing other than the fruits of human intellectual creation. Lao Zi knew well that no matter how highly developed the culture of mankind may be, it must always conform with the sovereign Nature. But this by no means entails that people should annihilate all civilization as Lao Zi taught. Lao Zi did penetratingly and mercilessly expose the evils and hypocrisies of civilization, but he failed to recognize its positive values.

Every philosopher longs for his own utopia, Lao Zi being no exception. Guided by the line of his naturalistic nostalgia, he sketched his utopia.

> The ideal land is small,
> Its people very few,
> Where tools abound,
> Ten times or yet
> A hundredfold
> Beyond their use;
> Where people die
> And die again
> But never emigrate:
> Have boats and carts
> Which no one rides
> Weapons have they
> And armor too,
> But none displayed,
> The folk returns
> To use again,
> The knotted cords.
> Their meat is sweet,
> Their clothes adorned,
> Their homes at peace,
> Their customs charm.
>
> And neighbor lands
> Are juxtaposed,
> So each may hear,
> The barking dogs,
> The crowing cocks,
> Across the way;
> Where folks grow old,
> And folks will die,
> And never once,
> Exchange a call.[①]

As fascinatingly idyllic and pastoral as it sounds, it is yet contrary to the reality of the main current of the history of civilization. It is a utopia outside of this world, a land of the Blossom Fountain in ancient China or an Arcadian

① Ibid., chap. 80, trans. R. B. Blakney.

state somewhere in ancient Greece. People there enjoy themselves in their "sans souci" without troubling themselves in the least about the outside world. It is a single-cell self-sufficient community—an ideal which reflected the naive longings of the primitive peasants. Such a vision was popularly entertained in the very bosom of the ancient Chinese mentality, for traditional China predominantly consisted of small peasants whose life goal was no more than to enjoy the fruit of their own labors, and not to interfere with others nor to be interfered with by others. They had no idea of the complicated social division of labor and its manifold consequences, so indispensable in a modernized society. They never dreamt that any person, group, society or a whole nation at large can never be omnipotent and totally self-sufficient. They longed for an earthly paradise, which was isolated from the rest of the world while furnishing them with all their daily requirements, all walks of profession sufficiently provided for in a unicellular self-subsisting community. Surely this reflects the primitive mentality of the peasants and does not match the requirements of historical development. In such a state of things, civilization could never hope to reach an ever-growing height. Yet in the historical background of this Arcadian ideal, people's dreams could not be otherwise. Such a tradition lasted so long throughout the history of China that we may distinctly perceive its image in Kang Youwei's utopia in his *Book of Cosmopolitanism* (*Da Tong Shu*) in the late 19th century, as well as in the utopian experiment of the "people's commune" of mid-20th century China. All daily necessities were to be provided within a single self-sufficient community. On this point, we ought not to be over-critical of Lao Zi. It was the concrete conditions in history which caused him to embrace a nostalgic utopia styled after antiquity.

Another well-known passage in Lao Zi reads:

> Thirty spokes will converge
> In the hub of a wheel;
> But the use of the cart
> Will depend on the part
> Of the hub that is void.
>
> With a wall all around
> A clay bowl is molded;
> But the use of the bowl
> Will depend on the part
> Of the bowl that is void.

Cut out windows and doors
In the house as you build;
But the use of the house
Will depend on the space
In the walls that is void.

So advantage is had
From whatever is there;
But usefulness rises
From whatever is not.①

When making a wheel, you have to keep proper spaces between the spokes. The empty spaces are indispensable for the wheels. So it is with all things. Therefore "advantage is had / From whatever is there; / But usefulness rises/ From whatever is not." Because Lao Zi is good at observing whatever is not, he is capable to see clearly the usefulness of whatever is not. The late Prof. Hou Wailu held a somewhat peculiar view on Lao Zi's "whatever is" and "whatever is not." He suggested that they did not denote any material attributes, but represented exclusively the notion of commodity. Just as Aristotle had discovered the notion of commodity in ancient Greece, it is Lao Zi who found the notion of commodity in ancient China. "Whatever is" and "whatever is not" refer to the value of usefulness and the value of exchange. A marvelous innovation, indeed. Though many scholars did not agree with him, the late Joseph Needham (1900-1995) agreed unconditionally in his monumental work *Science and Civilization in China*. No matter the viewpoint one adopts, one cannot help but admire the depth of Lao Zi's thought. Such insights may be encountered in almost every word in his book.

There have been two main tendencies in philosophy ever since antiquity. One is to find a logical explanation of the world, the other is to search for the wisdom of living and life. Most philosophers in the West tried to explain the world in a logical way, and even the pious mediaeval scholastics were no exception. As for most philosophers in China, they have always engaged much more in the search for the wisdom in life—Confucians, Mohists and Taoists all being examples. And in this respect the Taoists seemed more flexible and penetrating than the Confucians. The Confucians urged human effort, while the Taoists emphatically preached humility, being concerned much more with the negative side of life and the viewpoint of "whatever is not." This tendency came

① Ibid., chap. 11, trans. R. B. Blakney.

very near to the pronounced individualism of Yang Zhu. It may be said that both pursued happiness by seeking the great wisdom of life. Lao Zi provided an answer, and indeed one of great profundity. Prof. Li Zehou said well that the Tao of Lao Zi was but his refinement or abstraction of this wisdom of life. And this line of wisdom differs very much from that of most Occidental thinkers. Many Western philosophers were fond of preaching the wisdom of life by elucidating the essence of Being and its First Principle. In contrast, Lao Zi started his argument by an elucidation of the immediate wisdom in life, and then employed this wisdom in abstracting from our immediate life to the natural world at large. Centuries later, we see the philosophers of the Song Dynasty also took this route by enlarging the knowledge abstracted from our daily life into a comprehensive cosmopolitan wisdom. One can hardly help experiencing a sense of shame when reading Lao Zi's vehement attack on the arrogance and corruption of the ruling sovereigns. It is there that Lao Zi showed vividly his sympathy for the unfortunate fate of the common people.

Now let us turn from Lao Zi to Zhuang Zi, the second greatest spokesman of the ancient Taoist school.

[III] Zhuang Zi

The thoughts of Zhuang Zi inherited Yang Zhu's doctrine of self-preservation and the idea of Tao from Lao Zi. And the logical analysis of the Logician school had undoubtedly influenced him in one way or another. From them Zhuang Zi worked out his own system—a system of philosophy worthy of note not only in ancient China but in the ancient world as a whole.

The life and activities of Zhuang Zi (369-286 B.C.), like that of most ancient philosophers, are not quite clear to us. Very probably he was a member of the waning nobility, otherwise his book would not be filled with so much irony, as well as so much cynical satire. It was said that once, when his friend Hui Shi (Hui Zi) was the minister of the kingdom of Liang, Zhuang Zi went to Liang and was expected to replace Hui Shi.[①] Zhuang Zi also paid visits to the king of Wei[②] and Duke Ai of Lu.[③] These legends might suggest that he was one of the nobles already displaced from power. Our copy of *Book of Zhuang Zi* includes three parts: seven chapters of "Inner Essays," fifteen chapters of

① *Book of Zhuang Zi*, "Autumn Floods."

② Ibid., "The Mountain Tree."

③ Ibid., "Tian Zifang."

"Outer Essays" and eleven chapters of "Miscellaneous Essays." It is generally agreed that the "Inner Essays" were his own writings, while the Outer and Miscellaneous were by his disciples and followers. The authenticity of their authorship can not be conclusively proven. Nearly all ancient classics may be properly regarded as the works of a school rather than of any individual author. The ancients did not have the modern idea of authorship or copyright. For instance, the chapter "The Turning of Heaven" dealt with the origin of the universe, and its topics as well as its exposition are almost the same as Qu Yuan's (the preeminent poet of the kingdom of Chu) "Inquiry into Heaven." And we find in *Book of Zhuang Zi* many propositions were the same word by word with Lao Zi's. This is why we take their books rather than their persons as the object of our study. In the present chapter we shall deal much more with *Book of Zhuang Zi* the book rather than Zhuang Zi the man. Every man's ideas may be here and there self-contradictory, and a collective work of a group of authors surely could not avoid inconsistencies. It is no wonder that we find inconsistencies in *Book of Zhuang Zi*, for it was prepared not by one hand nor at one time.

Above all, the great philosopher Zhuang Zi was the great poet and the great writer of belles-lettres, and the great poet and the great writer of belles-lettres Zhuang Zi was the great philosopher Zhuang Zi. This career may very well have been inspired by the culture of his native country Chu. The renowned poet Qu Yuan came from Chu and his poetry was filled with a romantic and fantastic profundity. Comparing his poems with those in the *Book of Songs* (one of the Five Classic works of China), one is strongly impressed by the differences between the style of the southern culture and that of the northern. The style of the *Book of Songs* was simple and plain even in its love poems, while the Chu poems were full of myths and legends of an extremely extravagant character. An analogous distinction may be found between the Confucians and the Taoists. The style of Confucius and Mencius was simple and plain, while Zhuang Zi's was one of extravagant linguistic embellishment. In the very beginning of the first chapter, "Free and Easy Wandering," the imagination of the poet-philosopher presents to the readers this scene:

In the northern darkness there is a fish and his name is Kun. The Kun is so huge I don't know how many thousand miles he measures. He changes and becomes a bird whose name is Peng. The back of the Peng measures I don't know how many thousand miles across and, when he rises up and flies, his wings are like clouds all over the sky.[1]

The reader may well imagine how far the author's imagination carried him away in such romantic exaggerations. Here the author was resorting to poetic imagination rather than to logical reasoning. Throughout the whole book we find such colorful metaphors and elegant euphuisms. What makes it so fascinating is its attractive and exquisite language, in addition to its philosophical depth. It reminds us of the works of Plato which are also full of poetic fantasy, fluently elegant in his narration of so many fables and myths. There is a popular idea that philosophy is an exercise of conceptual thinking, while literature is one of imagination. Yet there is no insurmountable obstacle between the two. It is surely not the case that the one cannot be well expressed by the other. We may have concepts-poesy (Begriffs-dichtung) as well as conceptual reasoning in poetic terms.

Zhuang Zi made several significant achievements. First, he was an unparalleled literary writer. The splendor of his composition should be acknowledged as among the highest in the history of literature. Second, in the different stories and fables of his book we find a wealth of historical resources of antiquity, not historical in the sense of historical facts, but as intellectual history. It does not record the factual deeds of history, but the intellectual sphere of that bygone time. Many times it narrates what Confucius or Lao Zi said or did. The portraits of these ancient philosophers are given in artistic silhouette. Zhuang Zi left us much on the arguments of the Logicians. Down to the present day, what we know of the Logicians derives mostly from the records left by Zhuang Zi. Third, and most precious, is the legacy of his philosophical thinking. Personally, I esteem Lao Zi and Zhuang Zi as the most profound philosophers among the ancients. Confucius, on the other hand, though the most influential figure in history, had little interest in philosophy proper. "The Master's [Confucius'] discourses about man's nature and the way of Heaven can not be heard"[2]—so his disciple informed us. Human nature and the way of Heaven have been forever the cardinal issues in philosophy, but Confucius showed little interest in the ultimate question of philosophy, because "as to what is beyond the Six Realms [i.e. the universe], the sage admits its existence but does not theorize."[3] And fourth, among all ancient schools of philosophy, it is only the Taoists who possessed a keen interest in nature and the way of Heaven, and hence made a

① *Book of Zhuang Zi*, chap. 1 "Free and Easy Wandering," trans. B. Watson, with alterations by author.

② *Analects*, chap. 5 "Gongye Chang."

③ *Book of Zhuang Zi*, "On Making All Things Equal."

genuine contribution in various fields of science, especially in what came to be chemistry and medicine in later ages. The Mohists, though with certain interests in handcrafts and artifacts, had little interest in scientific speculation other than optics; they adopted a view from the angle of craftsmanship. In this sense, it seems that the previous studies on the Taoists have more or less neglected their scientific research—a field which deserves our more positive evaluation.

Now we are trying to deal with these two aspects of their cardinal contributions, i.e. their philosophical thinking and their scientific thinking. The difficulty in this lies in the fact that most of Zhuang Zi's ideas were expressed in fables of an elegant, literary genre. How to understand them as they were really meant is a matter of extreme hardship. It would involve a great deal of hermeneutic procedures. And of course, every man may have his own interpretation.

Let us first cite some well-known fables from his book, the first from the chapter "Knowledge Wandered North."

> Master Dong Guo asked Zhuang Zi, "This thing called Tao—where does it exist?" Zhuang Zi said, "There is no place it doesn't exist." "Come," said Master Dong Guo, "you must be specific!" "It is in the ant." "As low a thing as that?" "It is in the switchgrass." "But that is lower still!" "It is in the tiles and shards." "How can it be so low?" "It is in the piss and shit." Master Dong Guo made no reply.[①]

This story demonstrates the omnipresence of the Way. It permeates throughout all things and exists everywhere. All submits to its operation and manipulation. Another story is found in the chapter "Autumn Floods."

> Zhuang Zi and Hui Zi were strolling along the dam of the Hao River when Zhuang Zi said, "See, how the minnows come out and dart around where they please! That is what fish really enjoy!" Hui Zi said, "You are not a fish —how do you know what fish enjoy?" Zhuang Zi said "You are not I, so how do you know I don't know what fish enjoy?"

This seems to illuminate the most delicate issue of knowledge, i.e. what we know and how we know. A well-known section of *Book of Zhuang Zi* occurs in the chapter "On the Equality of All Things."

> Once Zhuang Zhou dreamt he was a butterfly, a butterfly flitting and fluttering around, happy with himself and doing as he pleased. He didn't know he was Zhuang Zhou. Suddenly he woke up and there he was, solid and unmistakable Zhuang Zhou. But he didn't know if he was Zhuang Zhou who had dreamed he was a butterfly, or a butterfly dreaming he was Zhuang Zhou.

In another place, Zhuang Zi said, "One who dreamed of drinking wine would weep at day-break, and one who dreamed of weeping would go hunting

① Trans. B. Watson, with alterations by author.

at day-break." But when was one dreaming and when was one awakening? In the end, between Zhuang Zi and the butterfly, who was dreaming whom?

In the chapter "The Mountain Tree," it is recorded,

> Zhuang Zi was walking on the mountain when he saw a huge tree, its branches and leaves thick and lush. A woodcutter paused by its side but made no move to cut it down. When Zhuang Zi asked the reason, he replied, "There is nothing it could be used for." Zhuang Zi said, "Because of its worthlessness, this tree is able to live out the years Heaven gave it." ... Down from the mountain, the Master [Zhuang Zi] stopped for a night at the house of an old friend. The friend was delighted, and ordered his son to kill a goose and prepare it. "One of the geese can cackle and the other can't," said the son, "May I ask, please, which I should kill?" "Kill the one that can't cackle," said the host. The next day Zhuang Zi's disciple questioned him, "Yesterday there was a tree on the mountain that gets to live out the years Heaven gave it because of its worthlessness. Now our host's goose gets killed because of its worthlessness. What position would you take in this sort of case, master?" Zhuang Zi laughed and said, "I'd probably take a position halfway between worth and worthlessness."

A further story tells us that once Zi Gong, one of Confucius' disciples, met a gardener on his way who was preparing his fields for planting by watering them with an awkward pitcher. Zi Gong advised him to use a well-sweep machine instead. Thereupon "the gardener flushed with anger and then said with a laugh, 'I've heard my teacher say, where there are machines, there are bound to be machine-worries; where there are machine-worries, there are bound to be machine-cunnings in their hearts. With a machine-cunning heart in your breast, you've spoiled what was pure and simple. And without the pure and simple, the life of the spirit knows no rest. Where the life of the spirit knows no rest, the Tao will cease to buoy you up. It's not that I don't know about your machine—I would be ashamed to use it.'"① Hence the gardener preferred the primitive method and tool rather than the machine. Still another story tells us, "The emperor of the South Sea was called Shu ["Brief"], the emperor of the North Sea was called Hu ["Sudden"], and the emperor of the central region was called Hun-tun ["Chaos"]. Shu and Hu from time to time came together for a meeting in the territory of Hun-tun, and Hun-tun treated them very generously. Shu and Hu discussed how they could repay his kindness. 'All men,' they said, 'have seven openings so they can see, hear, eat, and breathe. But Hun-tun alone doesn't have any. Let's try cutting him some!' Each day they bored another hole, and on the seventh day Hun-tun died."②

---

① *Book of Zhuang Zi*, chap. 12 "Heaven and Earth." Trans. B. Watson, with alterations by author.

② Ibid., chap. 7 "Fit for Emperors and Kings."

All the stories cited above are concerned with the most fundamental issues in philosophy, many of which had never been touched upon by anyone. Plainly speaking, these fundamental philosophical issues involved questions like: What is reality? What is existence or Being? What is "I" (the thinking ego)? What is the relation between the ego and the objective world? How can I know the world? What place do I hold in the world? What are the meaning, the value and the end of life? Such are the perennial questions which are contemplated forever and yet never allow a final solution. The Confucians were as a rule uninterested in such issues. Confucius himself was interested merely in "benevolence" and "rites," and Mencius solely in ruling the state and pacifying the international family. It was only the Taoist school that speculated on these questions, to which they gave their answers.

What is reality? The answer might be: reality is objective existence. But such an answer looks like a tautology, because objective existence is reality, so conversely reality is objective existence. After all, what is meant by "objective existence"? An often quoted answer (and also a materialistic one, it is said) defines objective existence as that which is or may be perceived by our perceptions. Be it so, then what is not perceived would have no existence. Any objectively existing thing, strictly speaking, ought not to be dependent upon our perception; if it did, it would not objectively exist. But if objective existence does not depend on our perception, then one may still inquire what it means. If only what is visible or perceptible is existent, then it would not be objectively existent, but is dependent on our subjective perception. There are many things which are invisible or imperceptible, yet they can not be identified as non-existent. In the Newtonian system there are three basic dimensions, time, space and mass. Each of the three can hardly be perceived, yet the whole mansion of classical physics is founded on these indefinable ideas. They are imperceptible, yet they are comprehensible. In a certain mode, so it seems also with the basic issues in philosophy. Throughout the history of human ideas, posing a problem is as valuable as presenting answers. Sometimes the worth of a failure may be no less than that of a success. Herein lies the contribution of the *Book of Zhuang Zi*, who did not offer a final answer but led people to probe a more scrutinizing speculation. The problems he raised showed the depth of his philosophy.

Linked to the question of the nature of reality, there is the question: What am I (the ego)? Some extended this idea to say that everything that may be called "mine" is a part of "me." One may readily strip away all one's belongings, and have left only a physiological entity. Is that then entitled to be called "I" or "me"? For instance, deprived of my arms and legs, I am still "I." In the last analysis, my whole body may not be "I." And then what is left as the notion of "I" is merely a thinking ego, something like Wang Yangming's (1472-1508) "pure consciousness" (ling ming). Or what I am is but my consciousness, no more and no less. If the issue be reduced to such a state, then the fables in *Book of Zhuang Zi* would be outstandingly remarkable. Am I Zhuang Zhou or am I a butterfly? Is it Zhuang Zi who dreamt he was a butterfly, or was it a butterfly that dreamt of being Zhuang Zi? Logically, both cases are equivalent. We are not qualified to argue that it is more likely that it is Zhuang Zi who dreamt he was a butterfly than vice versa. Many people think life is but a dream and that when they enter into another world, they would awake from their dreams. How can we assert that it is Zhuang Zi who dreamed of being a butterfly? An easy argument for this is that the consciousness of being Zhuang Zi is continuous, while that of being a butterfly is not. But if the consciousness of being a butterfly is also continuous, it may be equally reasonable that it is the butterfly which dreamt of being Zhuang Zi. The question of what "I" (the thinking ego) am seems too hard to answer. If "I" am to be identified with the physiological "I", that would not be the issue our philosophizing aims to probe. Yet if reality or I the thinking ego can not be located anywhere in any way, then all other problems would come to naught.

We may find an answer to this in Zhuang Zi's chapter "On the Equality of All Things" in which he argues that all things in the world are equal and equivalent. In a certain sense, the essence of his ideas can be summed up in his basic notion of "making all things equal." The characteristic feature of Zhuang Zi's thought lies exactly in this endeavor to make all things equal or equivalent. To an ordinary person, the world seems multiply variegated. How could Zhuang Zi make all things equal and equivalent? Let us try to explain it in an easy and simple way. In mathematics, there is the notion of infinitesimal and infinity. For infinity, all numbers, no matter how large or how small, equal to naught. The totality of the whole universe, or the entirety of Tao (Way), may be regarded as an infinity in relation to which all things are but infinitesimal or equal to naught, and hence equivalent to one another. In this sense, all things are the same and equal. Of course, Zhuang Zi himself did not make such an explicit exposition, but this is his approach in comprehending the world. Things in the world are multifarious and variegated, but they all come under the rule of Tao and hence are the same from the viewpoint of Tao. Zhuang Zi cited many examples in illustrating this. "The morning mushroom knows nothing of twilight and dawn; the summer cicada knows nothing of spring and autumn"① because they are both so short-lived, while "long, long ago there was a great rose of Sharon [a large tree] that counted eight thousand years as one spring and eight thousand years as an autumn." And again he said, "Men claim that Lady Mao and Lady Li were beautiful, but if fish saw them they would dive to the bottom of the stream, if birds saw them they would fly quickly away. Of these four, who knows how to fix the standard of beauty for the world?" All standards in the world are purely relative, and would become null and void in the face of infinity. No measure whatsoever has the right to claim itself sole and invariable. Hence all different standards of measurement are logically equivalent, and there is no ground to assume any human standard as the only one to the exclusion of that of the bird or the fish. Viewed from the measure of the absolute, all measures are equivalent. This is what is meant by "making all things equal" or "the identity of contraries." That either Zhuang Zi had dreamt of becoming the butterfly or the butterfly had dreamt of becoming Zhuang Zi were all the same. There is no ground to expel the possibility of the butterfly having dreamt of being Zhuang Zi. We can have no right to judge one measure exclusive of all others. And no experience in the cognizant subject can claim itself the sole judge of the objective world. Some contended that the common saying, "Life is but a dream," only reflects the mentality of the declining social class, the argument being that a fighter finally victorious after a life-and-death struggle with his enemies could never hold that life is but a dream. But this is simply to judge reality by the criterion of our subjective impression. Logically we have no ground to assume one as the sole criterion of reality to the exclusion of the others. This formed the basis of Zhuang Zi's theory of the equality of all things. Zhuang Zi's whole book is the repeated defense of this point—what is today commonly called "relativism."

Since all differences are only relative, there is no truth nor falsehood, no right nor wrong in the strict sense, Hence Zhuang Zi affirmed, "Where there is recognition of wrong, there must be recognition of right; where there is recognition of right, there must be recognition of wrong." And "then we have the rights and the wrongs of the Confucians and the Mohists. What one calls right the others calls wrong; what one calls wrong the other calls right."② Each acknowledges what he thinks right as right and each takes what he thinks wrong as wrong. Each has his own measurement to judge what is right and

① *Book of Zhuang Zi*, chap. 1 "Free and Easy Wandering."

② Ibid., chap. 2 "On The Equality of All Things."

what is wrong. For Zhuang Zi, there is no measure common to all, nor can there be any. This naturally leads to the question: should no measure at all be taken as the sole measure? And since each has his own measure, then why should the equality of all measures or of all things be taken as having absolute justification? On this, Zhuang Zi gave no justification. Any philosophy, in addition to its interpretation of all things, ought to give a justification of itself. It would seem that a philosophy ought to prove the legitimacy of its own argument, yet all philosophies in the last analysis appear to fail in establishing a sufficient argument for why it starts from a particular foundation. Euclidean geometry starts from the idea of a "point," which is indefinable and unprovable. The particle in the Newtonian system follows the fashion of the Euclidean point, yet there is no particle at all in the physical world. All things occupy a certain space, no matter how trifling it may be, and a particle which occupies no space is simply non-existent. Yet it is exactly this idea which provides the starting point of a magnificent theoretical framework. Any theory when pushed to its finality reveals a starting point which in itself is unprovable and inexplicable. Yet if you do not accept such an initial assumption, you can by no means accept any of its consequent reasoning. Reasoning mathematically, Zhuang Zi seems to assert that from the viewpoint of infinity all things are but nothing. And hence "the right is an endlessness and the wrong too is an endlessness";[①] the right and the wrong, the good and the bad, the fair and the ugly are all equivalent before infinity.

Following this line of thinking, Zhuang Zi located the position of human life in the universe: one should expel all rights and wrongs as well as the good and the bad, the fair and the ugly, because all differences and differentiations presuppose an absolute standard of measurement. Since there can never be such an absolute standard, all differences and differentiations vanish before the infinite relativity. One can find no way to stick to a certain position in the immense universe. After all, the aim and meaning of one's life lies merely in the fact that he is an infinitesimal in the infinity of Nature, so he ought to let go of everything in obedience to the order of Nature. And just because Nature entails that all is but relative, so one ought not to seek the absolute whatsoever. For the Confucians, benevolence and obligation are absolute demands stemming from their innate values. But for Zhuang Zi there is no such thing as absolute value. The secret of Nature lies therein, and the meaning of our life lies exactly in knowing this and only this. The best life is simply that which follows only the way of Nature. Both Lao Zi and Zhuang Zi called earnestly for a return to

① Ibid., chap. 2.

nature, i.e. exalting the best life as that which follows the way of Nature. But it should be observed that there are two different ways of returning to nature. A modern man may rightly admit that man is by himself a part of nature, but he is that part of nature which through his own earnest effort is alienated from nature. Alienation was an idea first propounded by Hegel and later developed by Marx. Mankind underwent a process of alienation from nature, and after that there emerged human culture and civilization. Yet with their culture and civilization there also came into being a great deal of evils and disasters, and thus the call for a "return to nature" appeared, one of its foremost spokesmen being Rousseau in the 19th century. "Return to nature" means the return to the naiveté of nature without the evils and disasters brought by human (i.e. artificial) civilization. The natural way of life is supposed the finest. The life described by Lao Zi in his utopia of a small country with a handful of inhabitants is such a state of plain and simple life in full conformity with nature. There would not be the least amount of the hypocrisy and evil of civilized society. This ideal of Lao Zi's was substantially that of Zhuang Zi too. Wherever there exist civilized facilities, there must be an intention contrary to what is natural.① And this is doomed to lead people astray into a state of what Hobbes would describe as everyone against everyone.② To be sure, all human achievement is artificiality and hence is not natural. Here the question arises in challenge to the Taoists. Is not the wisdom venerated by the Taoists also a product of human ingenuity? Spinoza taught that all the world comes and goes according to the necessity of nature, yet at the same time he stressed the importance of self-cultivation (which is a volitional action arising through earnest human pursuit, and not a consequence necessitated in nature). The ancient Taoists in China seem to have been caught in the same dilemma. In a certain sense, the Cynics of ancient Greece were also trying to restore the natural state of life. They taught that human civilization engendered so many evils just because of segregation from nature. So the way out they recommended was a return to nature. The most noted among them, Diogenes of Sinope (408-355 B.C.), preached that men were happiest when they wanted nothing, and Lao Zi taught, "If things much desired are limited to our core needs, Disturbances will cease in the minds of the people"③ and "hence the Wise Man (Sage) wants the unwanted."④ When people return to the life of nature, then all will be well.

① Ibid., chap.12 "Heaven and Earth."

② Hobbes, *Leviathan*, chap. 13.

③ *Book of Lao Zi*, chap. 3.

④ Ibid., chap. 64.

Now let us try to propose some criticism of this line of thought. It should be noted that such thinking focused only on the original thesis in man's development, to the total neglect of its antithesis as well as of any higher synthesis. The state of nature was the thesis. Then mankind stepped into its civil state, which constituted an alienation (a separation or a segregation) from the original state of nature, and hence an antithesis to nature. Yet mankind still needs again to merge into and to mix as one with nature; mankind is a special, integral part of nature. This is the synthesis, which offers a theoretical understanding of, e.g., contemporary ecological issues. First, there is an alienation of mankind from nature, and then follows not a return to nature in a pure and simple fashion but an elevation of mankind through re-entry into nature. It is then not the state of nature in the original sense (i.e. not a simple reversal) but a synthesis on a higher level. The ancient naturalists (Lao Zi and Zhuang Zi included) aspired in vain for a return to the primitive life. They longed hopelessly for that archaic life *sans souci*. Along with the advancement of social productivity, social life is destined to become more and more differentiated and complicated. The longing for naive simplicity was just a dead end. Finally, Lao Zi and Zhuang Zi the philosophers were Lao Zi and Zhuang Zi the poets, and the poets Lao Zi and Zhuang Zi were Lao Zi and Zhuang Zi the philosophers. Their philosophical dreams were just their poetic nostalgia rather than logical study of society and history. Human history has advanced waywardly, but never retrogressively. Their utopia is ultimately unrealistic and impractical.

Still more, there is a mystic element in Zhuang Zi, as shown clearly in his description of the legendary magical beings the Yellow Emperor, Guang Cheng Zi[①] and others. It is no wonder that the Taoists of later ages venerated Lao Zi and Zhuang Zi as their archpriests. The ideal personality for the Taoists is a magical spirit like a fairy. Zhuang Zi professed that when one arrived at the ideal natural state that he described, one would live as wonderfully and joyfully as the fairies. This ideal became a tradition for the later Taoists so much so that the Taoist school developed into the Taoist sect, their ideal simply the life of a fairy. Each of the three traditional beliefs in China professes its own image of the perfect life: the Confucians aspired to be a sage, the Buddhists a Buddha (at least in some future life), and the Taoists a fairy. Sagehood is to be accomplished through social and ethical relationships, a sage representing the apogee of ethical virtue. Without social norms, there could be no sage. A sage exists in the world of daily living; sagehood is (and can only be) realized in this world. A

① *Book of Zhuang Zi*, chap. 11.

Buddha, being a different paragon of virtue, is neither a sage of this world nor a fairy in some fairyland. And a fairy does not care about any human relationship, but is concerned with living in perfect harmony with the natural as well as the supernatural world. The Taoist ideal personality is at one with the universe, or in the words of Zhuang Zi, "Heaven and earth were born at the same time I was, and the ten thousand things are one with me."[①] Evidently there is a strong mystic element in this. Such a longing is as old as China's traditional culture. At the turn of the 19th and 20th centuries, Kang Youwei in his *Book of Cosmopolitanism* sketched such a utopia, in which everyone is a perfectly liberated spirit enjoying all kinds of worldly pleasures at will in a heavenly garden. Kang's utopia symbolized how deeply the Chinese have been penetrated by a medley of Confucianism and Taoism, the two indigenous schools of teaching in China. Confucius never preached belief in fairies, his ideal being to strive for sagehood in this worldly life rather than to live a fairy-like life in an idealized world of eternal pleasure. Yet most people of later generations longed for a Taoist paradise, a prolongation of the pleasure in this life.

In the chapter "Autumn Floods" Zhuang Zi declared, "From the point of view of Tao (the Way, Logos), things have no nobility or meanness." As a rule, from the point of view of a human being, things do have their nobility or meanness. But viewed from Tao, there is no distinction between the noble and the mean. Nature itself makes no difference between the high and the low or the noble and the mean. All distinctions are man-made, and are hence not natural. Then, we can ask again, what is Tao after all? Yet still, Tao can not be given a name. What can be named is not Tao.[②] In a certain sense, Tao may be identified as the entity of Being, and therefore it can not be defined or limited by a name. A name means an affirmation, and an affirmation means at the same time a negation; that is it denies what it is not while it defines what it is. The early Confucians had already employed the term Tao (the Way), but to denote only an ethical or moral ideal with no cosmological or metaphysical connotation at all. It was the ancient Taoists who adopted the idea of Tao as the basic idea of their metaphysics. However, when the Confucians of later ages elaborated their own metaphysics, they adopted the term Tao as their First Principle. The Confucians of the Song Dynasty (from the late 12th century) named their teachings "The Learning of Tao." Since then the moral ideal of the ancient Confucians was completely mingled at one with the metaphysics of the ancient Taoists.

① *Book of Zhuang Zi*, chap. 2 "On the Equality of Things."

② *Book of Lao Zi*, chap. 1.

From then onward, the name "Tao" has implied a series of connotations on different levels. It denotes Nature, in the sense of both the natural world and what is behind and beyond it (i.e. the principles that govern both the natural world and the human world, or both the physical world and the metaphysical world). The whole world is driven by the invisible hand of Tao. In other words, Tao is a hidden God who moves in concealment, holding in his hand the reins of the world. This idea of a hidden God has even been supported by some of the greatest scientists in modern times, such as in Pascal's *Dieu caché* and Newton's First Mover. Sir James Jeans was fond of saying that God is a mathematician, just as the ancient Greeks were fond of asserting that "God does geometry everywhere." It seems that people are wont to suppose that there must be an invisible mover or driver behind the universe. This is roughly equivalent to the idea of Tao, i.e. the First Principle and its embodiment, both the metaphysical and the physical. Tao is omnipresent and reigns and rules over all things. In this sense, all things are equal under the reign of Tao, in spite of their apparent differences in magnitude, rank, etc.

The Confucians approved of social differentiation, holding that people ought to be classified into various ranks, each according to his appropriate value. Thus people are classified into the gentlemen and the inferior men, and things into the higher and the lower—e.g. the heaven is superior and the earth inferior. But for the Taoists, all are equal. It should be noted that this idea of the Taoists is not only democratic in spirit (because it implies all men are created equal), but also creates the foundation for science (because science takes all objects equivalently with no distinction between higher and lower). Ostensibly all things differ from one another, but really they are all the same. From the point of view of Tao, no distinction should be made among things. What is taken as the right or the wrong, the high and the low, etc, all lead to one and the same endless infinity, so that true wisdom is that which unites them all into a "Heavenly Balance," i.e. the harmony of Nature admitting the authenticity of all things but not forcing them into the channel of one and the same standard. Zhuang Zi talked a great deal about the relativity of our valuations: "There is nothing in the world bigger than the tip of an autumn hair, and Mount Tai is tiny. No one has lived longer than a dead child, and Peng Zu [the 'Methuselah' of China] died young. Heaven and earth were born at the same time I was, and all things are one with me."① All differences vanish before eternal infinity. "So the sage harmonizes with both right and wrong and rests in Heaven the Equalizer. This

① *Book of Zhuang Zi*, chap. 2, "On the Equality of All Things."

is called walking two roads."[①] When the greatest is identified with the smallest and vice versa, then the whole world is in a state of perfect unison and there is a communion of Heaven and man—a state of ecstasy so sincerely longed for by many philosophers and ascetics. Such a state of life is indeed what Zhuang Zi so eagerly exalted: "Heaven and earth were born at the same time I was, and all things are one with me." Along this line, it is but natural that from Taoism there emerged the Taoist sect that so prevailed in later ages, with its practices relating to longevity, alchemy and various kinds of witchcraft—an example of the confluence of elite philosophy with popular beliefs. The Confucians did search hard for a final mental resting-place, but they did not give rise to a religious sect. Spinoza took emotion and desire to be human bondage, just as indicated by Lao Zi: "I suffer most because of myself and selfishness. If I were selfless, then what suffering would I bear?"[②] If one is dissolved in and mixed up with Nature, then what sorrow would remain? It is only in this state of things that one may find absolute freedom without the least strain of human bondage.

Owning to the far-reaching and profound influence of the Taoists on the intellectual history of China, it would be appropriate for us to make some criticism of them as a concluding remark of the present chapter. Taoism, in its theory and practice, leads in the last analysis to nothingness as its logical conclusion. Yet at the same time the Taoists of later ages were inclined to preach indulgence in physiological lust as a supplement to their naturalistic (even ultra-naturalistic) teachings. Thus hedonism formed a necessary complement to their escapism. But any indulgence in lust is merely an anesthetic, which allows you to forget your sorrow by distracting you; yet you will be lost in even greater pain and sadness as soon as you awake. The way taught by the Taoists is not one of active initiative but negative inactivity. And an escapist attitude is apt to lead people just to muddle along, or just to get on so long as they live, no matter what cares and concerns there may be. Though this may lead people to see through all worldly worries and feel contented whatever the circumstances might be, it is ultimately directed toward nihilism. Our whole life and the world in which we live are very probably just a perfect emptiness. So all our efforts and pursuits are but vainglorious and meaningless. This intellectual habit of passivity and non-activity embodies another fundamental current in Chinese tradition—as long and as profound as the opposite tendency. The predominant intellectual tradition in China has always been identified in the sentiment, "Heaven, in

① Ibid.

② *Book of Lao Zi*, chap. 13.

its motion, [gives the idea of] strength. The superior man, in accordance with this, nerves himself to ceaseless activity",[1] i.e. the vocation of man lies in his ceaseless activity and pursuit. But in relation to this basic standpoint, the Taoists were countercultural. Their contrasting foundational assumption is the insistence on the "return to nature," which means for them passivity and non-activity, and thoroughly giving oneself up to primeval nature.

It should be taken into consideration that the advancement of humanity also constitutes a part of nature, though a specific part of nature. It seems as though—as Kant said[2]—man once created is endowed with the task of liberty. He has no choice but to engage in this task of liberty, although he may be not interested in bearing the concomitant burden. Once created, he has to become an integral part of Nature on a higher level through the pursuit of liberty, whereby a nature that only possesses self-existence evolves into a Nature that is also self-aware. After this, human beings cease to have a passive and unconscious nature. All human actions come about purely for the sake of reaching a nature on a higher level. Herein humanity is simply the way of Heaven, and Nature returns to the way of Heaven through the channel of humanity. Their philosophy ought to have led the Taoists to seek a return to nature at a higher level, but sometimes they fell into nihilism and could not find a way out. They were not good at realizing the function of liberty, and this failure was destined to be their lot. Even worse, they induced people to tolerate enslavement. This would keep people everywhere in chains.

The above remark is of course a humanist criticism of the Taoists' doctrine. Yet the fact remains that there are positive elements in the Taoist theory as well as the negative ones. The paradox is precisely that these negative features fortified the Chinese people with their unique capacity for survival in the most unfavorable and cruelest circumstances in history. This is also probably why we witnessed so many disasters and humiliations rarely seen elsewhere in the history of mankind. Such is the duplicity of history and such is the duplicity of all the history of ideas—and also such is the role of Taoism in the history of China.

Again, the Taoists taught, "Unbending rigor is the mate of death, and yielding softness, company of life."[3] That is, what makes a man able to survive is just his ability to yield, isn't it? Lao Zi compared human flexibility to the

---

① *Book of Changes*, pt. 1 "Qian," trans. James Legge.

② Kant, *Idee zu einer allgemeinen Geschichte in weltbürgerlicher Absicht*, fifth thesis.

③ *Book of Lao Zi*, chap. 76.

nature of water, asserting, "Nothing is weaker than water, But when it attacks something hard, Or resistant, then nothing withstands it."[①] All things possess a dual character, so we have to see its positive side as well as its negative. The two exist in an inseparable mutual dependence. It was precisely the non-activity advocated by the Taoists that engendered the strongest vitality. The Chinese people in the long years of their history have suffered immense hardship, almost unparalleled in its scale and depth. Yet they survived and even became the greatest nation in the world. It must be acknowledged as the greatest miracle in world history. Wherein lies the secret of this miracle, if not in the Taoist philosophy of flexibility and humility? If not in their almost unimaginable endurance for resignation and submission to all oppression, where can we turn to find the cause of this miracle? But for this mentality, the Chinese may have already perished like so many other ancient peoples did, despite all the glories of their brilliant civilizations. Should not the secret of China's survival be attributed to the Taoist tradition of indifference to all disasters in the spirit of an Ah Q? If we are to seek the Chinese spirit, we should seek it in the Taoist passive non-activity no less than in the Confucian activity. It is the pragmatic spirit expressed in their real life which constitutes the forbearing core of their persistent vitality. It is really a pity that this most characteristic feature of the Chinese mentality has been so often neglected by researchers. The late Prof. Wen Yiduo lamented: Many Chinese would take up official positions when blessed with worldly success (the Confucians) and yet equally readily become hermits when not successful (the Taoists). This aptly describes the duplicity of the Chinese philosophy of life. At any rate, when seeking the character of the Chinese people's philosophy we should search within Taoism no less than Confucianism. And the Taoist influence on Chinese people's negativity is by no means less than the Confucian influence on their proactivity.

Lastly, this world-view and life-view, so characteristic of Zhuang Zi, led naturally to his prophesy of such a tragic hue: Life is the unwilled performance of a role dictated by Nature. Lao Zi had asked, "Is then the world unkind? And does it treat all things like straw dogs used in magic rites?"[②] And Zhuang Zi went even further by lamenting, "Once a man has received this fixed bodily form, he holds onto it, waiting for the end. Sometimes clashing with things, sometimes bending before them, he runs his course like a galloping steed, and nothing can stop him. Is he not pathetic? Sweating and laboring to the end of his

① Ibid., chap. 78.

② *Book of Lao Zi*, chap. 5.

days and never seeing his accomplishment, utterly exhausting himself and never knowing where to look for rest—can you help pitying him?"[①] The pleasure and happiness in our life is only equivalent to the ennui and meaninglessness of our life—such is the end of life as taught in his "On the Equality of Things." It seems as though he perceived the eternal tragedy of life, just as Sophocles mournfully bemoaned in ancient Greece at about the same time, "Never to have been born is best."[②]

① *Book of Zhuang Zi*, chap. 2 "On the Equality of Things."

② Sophocles, *Oedipus at Colonus*.

Chapter Eight: The Legalists

[I] The Forerunners of the Legalists

It was on the eve of the great unification of China (3th century B.C.) that the Legalists came forth as a prominent school intellectually as well as politically. They may well remind us of the practitioners of *Realpolitik* in Germany before and during the Second World War, who were concerned wholeheartedly with the craft of ruling and conquering. Political formation and social formation are always mutually dependent, each being conditioned by the other. At first, the social formation of ancient China was based on blood lineage, but it later gradually transformed into independent feudal states (as was the general rule in world history). Along with the development of productive forces and the accompanying social changes, the former system of *patria potestas* became less and less capable of coping with the new social conditions. Thus a new form of the state came forth with the royal power at its head. A similar process can be seen in the transition of the political frameworks in the West from the Middle Ages to modern times.

The term "feudalism" is somewhat confusingly ambiguous. In late antiquity and the early Middle Ages, the barbarian German tribes conquered the Roman Empire and established their new nations. The process of the German conquest was at the same time one of feudalization, and similarly the conquest of the Early Zhou Dynasty over the eastern territory was accompanied by its own process of feudalization. The conquered lands were distributed to the conquering chieftains and each of them framed a new state—this is the origin of feudalism. China in the Spring and Autumn Period was a family of many such feudal nations, like in the mediaeval West. As a rule, the feudal principle was based on the blood-relationship, the sovereigns being hereditary. In the case of a larger state, the existence of various independent principalities might prove a disadvantage. For instance, too many tariffs and tax posts would be a great hindrance for commerce, the development of which required a unified system of measurement, currency and regulations and hence a unified royal rule. The way traversed by Chinese civilization was more or less similar to that of the mediaeval West. After unifying the whole land, the First Emperor of Qin abrogated the feudal institution of the former times and established the prefectural system of administration under the direct rule of the imperial power, and thus the old-fashioned feudal principalities came to an end. What was known as "the institution of prefectures" meant the rule of the hereditary nobilities was to be replaced by the imperial officials appointed by the emperor with the purpose of strengthening the royal power. Centuries later, the Chinese reading public's first contact with Marxism was via Japanese publications which rendered the term of feudalism as "*feng jian*." With this translated term in wide circulation, the traditional society of China before the year 1949 (the year of founding of the New China) was hence identified as feudalism. Thus there appeared two different notions of the term "feudalism": one denoting the ancient political system which was abolished by the First Emperor of Qin, the other the mediaeval social formation which existed down to modern times. The Legalists were those who consciously and vehemently upheld the new-born royal autocracy.

The history of human civilization is distinguished from the history of the natural world in this: human civilization is a process of perpetual change and accumulation, because human behaviors are actuated by their ideas, which are in perpetual development and accumulation. No idea is eternally unchanging and unchangeable. All ideas are at the some time both a continuation and yet a development of the past. This is valid both for an individual and for a community. A great turning point in the change of Confucianism occurred in the thought of Xun Zi. Confucius and Mencius were the representatives of the early Confucianism. But later with Xun Zi, there was a transition in its focus, shown in the fact that Xun Zi was much more realistic than his predecessors. And such a realism suited the age, for inner spiritual cultivation alone was radically insufficient for meeting the urgent demands of the time. A deluge of practical issues needed to be solved. It was the age of the contention of the "seven powers" (the seven states then existing), and the main historical trend was leading toward a great unification of the whole land. Already Mencius had said, "Wherein will the world be settled? Only in its unification."① But Xun Zi's realistic spirit contrasted strikingly with the pedantic idealism of both Confucius and Mencius. He stressed "taking the latcr kings as the model," the later kings being the sovereigns of his contemporaries. In contrast with his Confucian predecessors, Xun Zi turned his eyes toward the current age rather than focusing only on legendary antiquity. And what is more, in one of his most striking propositions he proclaimed "adopting ourselves to the appointments of heaven and making use of them,"② that is to say, by making use of the natural laws for their own benefit, people would be capable of reforming and transforming the natural world. This is an unprecedented world-view and life-view which far surpassed both Confucius and Mencius or Lao Zi and Zhuang Zi in its appeal to overcome nature. Such a spirit was incarnated in the Legalists in the form of their political appeals. The Legalists were a direct offspring of Xun Zi and their foremost representatives Han Fei and Li Si were his disciples. Xun Zi was the past master of the ancient Confucians who symbolized both the end of the classical age and the initiation of the mediaeval His deep-rooted realism cast away the deep-rooted tradition of unmitigated idealism professed by the early Confucians. Yet at the same time, he performed also as the hero of a great tragedy, because following him there emerged a momentous transition in the history of ideas. Since then the spirit of the classical thinkers in their thoroughgoing search for the truth of the world and of life vanished, and the vision of the philosophers was confined to speculation on practical politics. And thus political practice outweighed the transcendent values of humanity.

During the Warring States Period (5th-3rd century B.C.), statecraft constituted the predominant thinking of the day. Against a background of constant change, the scholarly preaching on morality reached an impasse. New schools sprang forth, each professing its pragmatic doctrines to meet the urgent need for a strong ruling power. Among them were the Strategists with Sun Bin and Wu Qi as their foremost representatives, who propounded the art of war as the means to achieve political hegemony. Along with the military Strategists were the Political Strategists (or Diplomats) who, like the *Realpolitik* school of World War II, specialized in political trickery and maneuvering. And by far the most important school was that of the Legalists. The emergence of such a current of thought was characteristic of the age. It gave rise to a radically new atmosphere in the sphere of learning and thinking. These new doctrines paid more attention

① *Book of Mencius*, "King Hui of Liang."

② *Book of Xun Zi*, "Tian Lun."

to the laws of the objective world, natural and human, and deviated far from the early Confucians' interest in moralizing. They worked hard to probe into the objective laws of human relationships never touched upon by their predecessors—a contribution deserving of high regard. Yet at the same time, they had lost sight of the humanist values and ideals. Such was the shortcoming in the theories of the Legalists.

On the eve of the great unification, only four among the "Seven Powers" were truly worthy of the name. Han, Zhao and Wei in the central area of the land were relatively weak, their geographical position rendering them incapable of self-sufficiency. The four powers then were Yan to the north, Qi in the east, Chu in the south and Qin to the west. Yan and Qi had been powerful for some time, but eventually the greatest two powers left were Qin and Chu, both enjoying a dominance in their geographical area. They each occupied a large territory with an enormous hinterland, while Yan was left only the uninhabitable deserts to her north and Qi the great sea to her east. In ancient China the most developed region was the "Central Region" in the middle and lower valley of the Yellow River, and both Qin and Chu were rather far from this developed area. Yet the Legalist ideas and practices in their mature phase appeared against the background of the competition for hegemony between Qin and Chu, with the eventual unification of the whole land under the reign of the Qin Dynasty.

The ideological trends of the Legalists might be roughly summarized under three headings: one stressed the importance of the political situation with Shen Dao as its representative, another stressed political craft with Shen Buhai as its representative, and the third stressed the rule of law, being represented by Shang Yang. In fact, the three schools had little difference between them, with only a slight shift in their respective emphases. Later it was Han Fei who synthesized them all into a mature system of Legalist doctrine. On Shen Dao and Shen Buhai there are few sources left to us, apart from excerpts from the writings of others. Han Fei once cited Shen Dao:

> The flying of a dragon depends on the clouds, the starting of a snake depends on the wandering mists. With the vanishing of the clouds and the mists, the dragon and the snake will be but the same as the worm and the ant, because then they have lost their support. A good man might be subdued by a bad one because he possessed less power and a lower position. And a bad fellow could overrule the wise because he possessed strong power and a high position. Yao the sage-king could not rule three men as a plain person, while Jie the tyrant could overrun the whole world as the emperor. By this I was led to acknowledge that it is the position that matters, and wisdom and intelligence are

not worthy of desire.[1]

Whoever once attains power will get hold of everything he wants. The only thing of greatest importance is power and thc position affiliated to it. One has to admit that the Legalists thus came very near to the essence of the political mechanism. During the Cultural Revolution, Lin Biao proclaimed that one could get hold of all he wanted as soon as one has power. Hence it is necessary to uphold "an absolute authority" and to never for a moment forget the watchword, "power." Following him, Jiang Qing and the "Gang of Four" vigorously professed the everlasting conflict between the Confucians and Legalists and assumed themselves the direct heirs to the Legalists. Thus arose the campaign of the "struggle between the Confucians and the Legalists" during the Cultural Revolution. Carried to the extreme, all political intrigue and trickery is justified in the obsessed pursuit of power. Alongside Shen Dao, another outstanding Legalist, Shen Buhai (b. ca. 400 B.C.), stressed the art of ruling. As Han Fei said of him:

Shen Buhai professed the art of ruling, whereas Gongsun Yang [i.e. Shang Yang] upheld the law. By the art of ruling, Shen Buhai meant the conferring of a post on an official and thereby exacting his deeds by his obligations, while the sovereign holds power over his life and death and scrupulously examines the ability of all officials. This is what a sovereign should grasp firmly in his own hand.[2]

That is to say, the art of ruling is only the sovereign's grasping of the power of life and death over his subordinates and ensuring that every official do his duty in correspondence with his post. Shen Buhai was a native of the kingdom of Zheng, and he later went to the kingdom of Han where he was appointed premier. Such a case was often found in ancient Greece, where the citizen of one country might serve other countries. It was recorded in ancient sources that Count Zhao of Han entrusted Shen Buhai "to regulate social and political order within and to deal with other countries abroad."

Shang Yang (c. 385-338 B.C.) has been generally acknowledged as the foremost representative of the Legalists. It was an age when "the rites were broken and the music collapsed"—rites and music being the symbols of social and political order. Thus the age was seen as fundamentally shattered and in urgent need of the establishment of a new coercive power to maintain social order. There was a call for an autocracy as replacement for the "rites and music"

---

① *Book of Han Fei Zi*, chap. 40.

② Ibid., chap. 43.

of antiquity. Duke Xiao of Qin entrusted Shang Yang to carry out a large-scale reform. According to Sima Qian's *Records of the Historian*, before his reform Shang Yang—fearing the people's distrust—placed a big log before the south gate of the city, proclaiming that whoever was able to move it to the north gate of the city would be paid ten pieces of gold. People wondered at his decree and dared not to move the log. Then Shang Yang declared that whoever was able to move it would be paid fifty pieces of gold. Someone finally moved the log and was paid that sum. This event showed his honesty, and his reform was carried out smoothly. Within ten years of his reform, the people of Qin were greatly pleased. There were no more thieves and bandits in the country, and no one would pick up for himself what others had lost. Every household was well-fed and people were ready to fight for the public cause but shunned personal strife. The whole country was well-ordered.①

His book as we now have it is probably not his own work, but it undoubtedly embodies much of his own thought. In one chapter he presents his view on the course of the development of human history, summed up in three stages.

> As the cosmos was created, people were born. At that time, people knew only who their mothers were but knew not who their fathers were.
>
> In the ancient times people loved only their family members and loved only what was private to them. In the more recent past, people honored the worthy and preached virtue. In modern times people admire the dignitary and venerate officialdom.②

Each of the three historical epochs had its own peculiarities. The ancient times were those under the rule of the hereditary nobles. In the middle past, the Mohists honored the worthy and the Confucians preached virtue. At this stage of history, the principle of sovereignty differed from that based on the heredity of the noble households and replaced it with the ability and virtue of outstanding individuals. By the modern times was meant the age of the Warring States, its characteristic being the veneration of the dignitaries and officialdom, the worship of power substituting the worship of virtue and talent. With the unification of the whole land by the First Emperor of Qin, one of his cardinal measures for ideological control was ordering the people to "take the officials as their teachers." "To admire the dignitary and to venerate the officialdom" was advocated, to steer the thoughts of the people; otherwise they would be likely to deviate from the official line of ideology. It was then that the royal officials replaced "the contending of the hundred schools" of former times. Under the rule of a despotic autocracy, there was always a pressing need for ideological

① Sima Qian, *Records of the Historian*, "Life of Shang Yang."

② *Book of Lord Shang*, chap. 7.

control. Thus the mediaeval ideological despotism stepped opportunely to the fore, in substitution of the hundred schools of the classical age. As a forerunner of the Legalists, Shang Yang provided a philosophy of history as the theoretical basis for a grand reformation. The main thrust of his idea was roughly thus: the social situation was always changing, and so the principle adopted to cope with it should also always change. In former days there had been various teachings, but which of them should be followed? And there were so many sovereigns, each unique in his own way—whom of them should we imitate? Surely there could be no invariable criterion, and hence no need to obey any of them absolutely. In the past, all kinds of legislation arose purely to meet the current circumstances, and all laws and rites were only expedient for the time being. Hence there could be no principle of government constant and invariable for all times. If we aim for the benefit of the country, we ought not to follow the ways of the ancients unvaryingly. Precisely this sentiment was later repeatedly amplified by Han Fei. What the Legalists so earnestly strove for was reform, or rather the overthrow of the laws of the hereditary nobility of the past. The nobles had proven a strong obstacle against the establishment of an autocracy, which could only be established at the expense of the privileges of the noble lords. This historic process realized by the Qin regime, there was witnessed the striking scene of "the abolition of feudalism and the institution of the local prefectures," similar to events in the West when royal despotism was established by diminishing the power of the noble lords.

Guan Zhong (d. 645 B.C.), or Guan Zi, the premier of the kingdom of Qi, was also generally considered a forerunner to the Legalists. Guan Zi lived even earlier than Confucius, whose *Analects* praised Guan Zi. Guan Zi left no writing of his own. The book by the name of *Guan Zi* was a work of later ages, but might be regarded as a reflection of some of his main ideas. In this book there reads,

> A wise sovereign is in a high position, and this very position enables him to exercise coercion, and to prevent his subordinates from doing wrong. What makes his subordinates dare not to make a fool of him is not that they care for him but that they are afraid of his power.
>
> The people hurry to serve him, not because they love him, but because they fear his authority.

Therefore, he concludes,

> An intelligent sovereign holds in his hand the power to guarantee his unchallengeable rule over a servile people, and occupies a position of supremacy from which to reign over his docile officials. [The result is that] his orders will be carried out and his prohi-

bitions will be strictly observed; the sovereign is in his high dignity, and his subjects are in their humility.①

The main ideas of the Legalists are summarized in these quotations.

The Legalist school was also an offspring of the Taoist school. In the *Book of Han Fei Zi* we read chapters such as "Commentary on Lao Zi" and "Explanation on Lao Zi", and Sima Qian's *Records of the Historian* gives a comprehensive biography covering Lao Zi, Zhuang Zi, Shen Buhai and Han Fei altogether. Indeed, one may find much intellectual relation between the Legalists and the Taoists, particularly Lao Zi. It has often been said that the *Book of Lao Zi* was a book on warfare. To be sure, *Book of Lao Zi* dealt with a lot of political strategy and might be fairly interpreted as discussing "the art of how to be a sovereign." In addition, some of the basic philosophical assumptions of the Legalists showed a strong Taoist vein. Of course, there was also an evident difference between the Legalists and the Taoists. Rejecting human effort, the Taoists upheld naturalistic non-activity—a return to nature in opposition to any artificial or volitional activity. Any human activity is in its essence unnatural and hence violates natural innocence.

Though the Taoists did not approve any social or political institution, there was nevertheless an intellectual link between the Taoists and the Legalists. For the Taoists the best social order is that which best conforms to the natural order. And the natural order is simply the obedience to natural law. A salient feature in the history of ideas in China is that the idea of natural law never attained a clear articulation. As such, the Taoists did not reach definitive conclusions on natural law; however, their work did carry some implications on it. Nature has its own law independent of any human will or effort, and this is natural law. According to the Taoist teaching, if people behaved in accordance with the natural law, they would lead the best possible lives. The Legalists stressed the notion of law, and one of its origins was derived from the Taoists. Yet the difference between them is also obvious. The Taoists proclaimed the natural to be the best, so that people should earnestly strive to return to nature and never rebel against nature, as echoed in the opening of Rousseau's *Emile*. Yan Fu's "Commentary on Lao Zi"—a work often neglected by the reading public—points out emphatically that Lao Zi's intended return to nature was the same as Rousseau's. And this comparison sounds quite reasonable. The Taoists Lao Zi and Zhuang Zi asked for a return to nature, but Xun Zi proposed controlling Heaven's mandate and making use of it to profit ourselves. This is not a simple return to nature, but a

① *Guan Zi*, "Ming Fa Jie."

conquest of nature for our own gain. Han Fei, as Xun Zi's foremost disciple, went even so far as to apply this idea to the sphere of political practice. He placed more emphasis on human effort. The essential impulse of his thought was to scrutinize the weakness and evil in human nature and to exploit it to enforce the ruling power of the sovereign. Truly, the Legalists are fully qualified to be known as the Machiavellians of historical China.

[II] Han Fei, Li Si and the Legalists' Tragedy

Of the historical records relating to the Legalists, the most important are the biographies in Sima Qian's *Records of the Historian*: "Li Si" and "Lao Zi, Zhuang Zi, Shen Buhai and Han Fei." Lao Zi's thought showed deep concern with the study of the art of ruling and frequently mentioned the term "sage." The "sage" in the *Book of Lao Zi* refers directly to the supreme sovereign. In this respect the Taoists were surely the predecessors of the Legalists. Sima Qian avowed that "the doctrine of Shen Buhai was derived from the learning of Huang Di [the legendary founder of Taoism] and Lao Zi with the rule of law and penalty at its core."① Han Fei and Li Si were the great synthesizers of the Legalist school—its greatest theorists as well as its greatest practitioners.

Han Fei "came from a house of nobility in the state of Han. He was fond of studying the rule of penalty and law and the art of governing, the main themes derived from the learning of Huang Di and Lao Zi." "Han Fei and Li Si were both followers of Xun Zi, but Li Si thought himself far inferior in comparison with Han Fei."② Thus there broke out a typical Legalist competition for power and position between the two. When the king of Qin (later the First Emperor of Qin) read the *Book of Han Fei Zi*, he was fascinated by it, sighing: "Alas, if only I could join with him together, I would fain die with no regret left at all."③ Later, when Han Fei was on a mission to the State of Qin, Li Si was jealous of him and attempted to persuade the king of Qin with these words: "'Han Fei is a dignitary of the noble house of Han. Now Your Majesty hopes to annex other principalities, but Han Fei would in the end not serve the cause of Qin. This is but a commonplace of humanity. If you do not have him in service and after a prolonged stay send him back, this is just to cause harm to yourself. It is better

① Sima Qian, *Records of the Historian*, "Biography of Book of Lao Zi, Zhuang Zi, Shen Buhai and Han Fei."

② Ibid.

③ Ibid.

to kill him under the exaction of law.'"[①] The King agreed with him, and Han Fei was compelled to commit suicide. Such was the tragedy of the Legalists. Sima Qian commented on this, "Han Fei drew up the rules to regulate all affairs by a clear clarification of the right and the wrong in the bitterest and most merciless way. All was derived from the Taoist idea of Tao and Virtue. So deep and penetrating was the influence of Lao Zi."[②] This comment on Han Fei is deep and penetrating too—people can learn a host of political maneuvers and tricks from Lao Zi.

Li Si (280-208 B.C.) was a native of the State of Chu. When he came to Qin, the king of Qin appreciated him so much that "Li was appointed by the king as his counselor-general, and the king adopted his proposal to send special envoys to persuade the princes of other countries by bribing them with precious articles and money. Those princes and dignitaries who were susceptible to bribes would be lavishly rewarded; while those who refused would be assassinated. Thus the seeds of discord were sowed between the sovereigns and their subordinates."[③] After the unification, Li was appointed prime minister, indeed the first in the history of the whole land. The institutions and structures of this unprecedented unified empire were designed by Li Si. He put to the emperor that the reason why the land had so long been in tumult and could not be settled under a single authority was that there existed too many different theories, each in its own fashion eulogizing the ancients while reproaching contemporary society, thus resulting in a great ideological confusion of the entire realm. Hence, for the great unification of the empire, a uniform ideology was absolutely necessary, in order "to differentiate the black from the white and to subjugate all under a sole rule." Down to the last century in China, under the rule of the KMT, there was still such a slogan: "All erroneous and confused ideas ought to be corrected." We can see how enduring this tradition of ideological despotism has been, ever since long ago. Han Fei in his book asserted, "The Confucian intellectuals disturb the rule of law by their learning and the knights-errant violate the prohibition with their martial strength."[④] Both proved a menace to the rule of the imperial sovereignty. If the people could not be brought under the rule of a single ideology, then "the power of the sovereign on high would decline while various interest groups would thrive from below."[⑤]

① Ibid.

② Ibid.

③ Ibid.

④ See also Sima Qian, *Records of the Historian*, "Lives of the Knights-Errant."

⑤ Sima Qian, *Records of the Historian*, "Biography of Li Si."

Thus he suggested to the emperor: "Let all literature, the *Book of Songs*, the *Book of History* and the sayings of the Hundred Schools be banned... What are to be left are the books of medicines, oracles and gardening. And let all scholars take the officials as their teachers."① This proposal was willingly adopted by the First Emperor, the result being the famous scene of "the burning of books and the burying of the Confucian [scholars]." One of the Qin policies was that "all those who denounce the present in the name of the ancients are to be sentenced to death together with all their families." That is, all those who dared to oppose the present (Qin) regime with the ancient doctrines, such as the Confucian and the Taoist, would be put to death together with their households. Such practices were continued repeatedly in later ages. One may readily cite many appalling instances of "literary inquisitions" in the Qing Dynasty. A notorious instance was the case of Lu Liuliang, a famous scholar whose corpse was whipped for blasphemy even after death.

Before the establishment of a unified empire, people followed different lines of teachings. "To take the officials as their teachers" as proposed by Li Si meant that people must rely on officialdom as their sole guide. Besides this, one was not allowed to hold his own ideas. A despotic regime required a universal ideology as its indispensable guarantee, without which it could have no sense of security. Bertrand Russell contended that no empire has ever been good. All great unified empires in history demanded a uniform ideology as their indispensable spiritual and intellectual support and hence impeded the free development of human minds. Of all the ages of intellectual flourishing, none appeared under such universal despotism. It has proved unprofitable for the progress of human culture. But Li Si contended that the strength and consolidation of the imperial authority lay nowhere else but in its absolute dominance. He claimed,

In order that a wise sovereign can be in a position to hold a dignified power for long and over the whole land, there can be no other way than his capacity to dictate, to supervise and to punish, so that no one in the world dares to go against him.②

In short, the only approach chosen by an intelligent sovereign is to exercise the absolute power he holds over his subjects. This is the typical language of the Legalists. Further, Li Si expounded, "An intelligent sovereign dictates over all others, so that the power dwells with the sovereign but not

① Ibid.

② Ibid.

with his subordinates."① A sovereign has to rule all by himself personally and the supreme power can never be shared with others. The traditional Chinese rendering of this reads: "the highest outline is to be dictated by the sovereign alone." This despotic polity has ever since been the major feature of the Chinese tradition. There was a couplet hanging on the wall of the main palace of the Emperor Qianlong to the effect: Only a single person should rule over the whole land, but never should the whole land serve a single person. The second half of the couplet is a mere play on words, and the crucial point is the former half. The central political system founded by the Qin Dynasty, with its related institutions and policies, has ever since constituted the main character of Chinese political culture for more than two thousand years. The saying of Tan Sitong—that the Chinese thought of two thousand years and more has been but the learning of Xun Zi and the Chinese polity of the same time has been but the polity of Qin—was in a certain sense well-grounded. After all, the Legalist tradition can be traced to nowhere else other than its earliest founder, Xun Zi.

The personal endings of the Legalists were generally bitter. Shang Yang, the earliest Legalist to carry out his grand-scale reform in Qin, later failed in a power struggle and was exiled. But in his exile no one dared to take him in, for—in accordance with the law that he himself had promulgated—hosting a refugee would receive severe punishment. So finally Shang Yang was arrested, and suffered the cruelest execution. This story led to a common proverb, "to execute oneself by one's own law." Han Fei, the greatest Legalist thinker, was killed by the intrigues of his Legalist colleague Li Si, who in turn later also became the victim of an appalling political intrigue. When the First Emperor of Qin died, Li Si and Zhao Gao (both being the favorites of Hu Hai, the second son of the First Emperor) contrived to fabricate an edict of the deceased emperor ordering the death of the legitimate successor, the Crown Prince Fu Su. With Hu Hai ascending to the throne there ensued a power struggle between Li Si and Zhao Gao. Li Si at last failed and suffered a miserable end, not unusual in such political contests. Such was the end of the most faithful follower and the deserved victim of the Legalist line. The Legalists were fond of the machinations of power, and were mostly caught in their own traps—Shang Yang, Han Fei, Li Si and others included. Just like the career of an athlete, no matter how excellent, the Legalists were doomed to end their careers in failure. One can never be an eternal victor in the arena.

Another reason for the fate of the Legalists is that the historical circumstances

① Ibid.

demanded they carry out their principles by launching a large-scale reform. Yet in any given society there is always a privileged class, and any attempt to alter the status quo will lead to an attack on the interests of the privileged. As a rule, the privileged class hold superior strength in their hands. In confrontation with it the new social forces usually suffer a defeat. In order to achieve the goals of their reforms, the reformist camp should be wise enough to find the path of least resistance. The best strategy seems to lie in bribing the privileged. Such an instance may readily be found in the case of Zhao Kuangyin, first emperor of the Song Dynasty, who successfully bribed his generals to give up their military powers at the price of providing them with wealthy and luxurious lives. In the case of the Bourbon kings Louis XIII and Louis XIV of France, Versailles was made a *palais sans souci* for entertaining the independent feudal lords, who would then no longer block a despotic king. It is a pity that the Legalists, keen as they were in their theoretical insights, were too engaged in the intrigues of *Realpolitik*. Hence their miserable fates.

The Legalists were not wholly unaware of their own fates. Han Fei in his book showed a deep bitterness in his presentiment:

> Wise scholars are certainly far-sighted and scrutinizing enough to search into the depth of others' privacy. Well-trained legalists are certainly strong-minded and honest enough to rectify foul play... Therefore once the wise legalists are in power, those already in high positions will surely be outlawed. Hence the wise legalists and those privileged people in power are in a life and death enmity.①

During the time of the Cultural Revolution (1966-1976), there was a high tide of the campaign of "the struggle between the Legalists and the Confucians." The leaders of that campaign supported the Legalists, and the campaign's outcome is already well-known to all. Hegel once remarked that historical events always happen twice, the first time as tragedy and the second as farce. The Legalists too appeared on the stage of China twice, the first time in the tragedy of the pre-Qin Legalists, the second time in the farce of the contemporary Legalists—the so-called Proletarian Revolutionaries. There is a popular proverb common to historians, "History never repeats." Yet there is still another proverb: "There is nothing new under the sun." Both are true. History never repeats, and what is past is past and cannot be repeated. Yet there are so many events that happen in the same way and that look nearly entirely the same. A concrete event is once forever, it cannot be repeated. But the rules governing it are eternal and never change.

The cardinal concern of the Legalists was how to obtain and strengthen

① *Book of Han Fei Zi*, chap.11.

absolute power, i.e. the basic rules of the movement of power. It seems strange that in the seventies of the last century, while the modern Legalists of China were so vehemently advertising the traditional Legalist school, they had lost sight of Machiavelli. Machiavelli (1469-1527) is surely the foremost Western Legalist. From a comparative study of Machiavelli and Han Fei, one may conclude that they shared the same basic line of reasoning. Machiavelli the Florentine was a typical Renaissance man, and it was not until the Renaissance that it was possible for a Machiavelli to come out. It was only then that "the awakening of man" unfolded. Before that time, the Western world was under the rule of theocracy; all was wrapped in the dress of theology and political issues were obliged to be understood in theological terms. In this respect, the Confucians were very similar. The Confucians deified the ancient sages in whose name were initiated all human institutions. Such also was the way of thinking in the mediaeval West. Under such an ideological monopoly, man was rendered incapable of observing human beings from a human point of view. Through the prism of theological indoctrination, reality was condemned to be a mere distorted picture. Marx valued Machiavelli as the first who observed men from a human point of view. In this way Machiavelli liberated the study of politics from the yoke of theological teleology, and reestablished it on the basis of the power struggle of the human world. The Confucians took the state to be a work of art designed by the sages; the mediaeval scholastics saw it as an embodiment of the will of God. It was Machiavelli who first located its center of gravity within the state itself, just like Newton found the law of universal gravitation in the natural world itself. The secret Machiavelli discovered was only this: all polities revolve around the center of power. Politics is nothing other than the power struggle of daily life. This is the great contribution of Machiavelli, and it is exactly the contribution that the Legalists made some 1700 years before Machiavelli. What Machiavelli discussed in his immortal work *The Prince* was the art of ruling, and this was precisely the concern of the Legalists. Thus, the late Prof. Xiao Gongchuan remarked,

> The Confucians confounded politics and morality as one with a strong overtone of the mentality of the ancients. But Han Fei studied political power by casting morality out of the sphere of politics and thus founded his political philosophy with a modern form.[①]

① Xiao Gongchuan, *A History of Chinese Political Thought,* chap. 7 (Shenyang: Liao Ning Educational Press, 1999).

[III] Human Nature and the Rule of Law

Both the Chinese Legalist Han Fei and the Occidental Legalist Machiavelli derived their theories from their ideas of human nature. Indeed, we may say that each of the classical schools derived their ideas from their specific theories of human nature. For instance, Mencius upheld goodness as inherent in human nature, containing the seeds of benevolence, duty, righteousness and intelligence, and the question lying only in how to nourish and develop them. The whole system of Mencius' theory of benevolent polity was derived from this. The theory of human nature was of vital significance both to the ancients and to the moderns. Smith's epochal *Wealth of Nations* also started from the supposition of his theory of human nature. If human nature were otherwise than he supposed, then his whole theoretical structure would fall to pieces.

Xun Zi asserted that man is evil by nature, and that good is a work of education. Han Fei went even further, to assert that the evil in man's nature is such that it is incapable for him to do any good. Han Fei stated his argument on the evilness of human nature with a piercing sharpness.

> An artisan makes a carriage in the hope that someone becoming wealthy and powerful may be in need of it; a carpenter makes a coffin in the hope that someone may die young. It is not that the artisan is benevolent and the carpenter evil. It is because the carriage would not be sold if no one is a dignitary, nor the coffin if no one dies. The carpenter does not hate any one, but his interest depends on the death of others.[①]

And again:

> When the parents beget a baby, they will congratulate each other if it be a male and smother it if it be a female. Either being a male or a female, it is begot from the bosom of the parents. Yet the male one would enjoy congratulations while the female would be smothered; it is entirely due to speculation about their later expediency, with a view to the profits in the long term. Therefore the parents treat their children from a speculative view of gain and loss. Then what is it like without the relationship of parents and children?[②]

Human interrelationship is but an expedient union of loss and gain, a mere game of calculated investment as shown in the relations between one and another, even between parents and children. All men are by nature concerned only with their own benefit, and yet have no reasonable knowledge of how to discern where their proper benefit lies.

---

① *Book of Han Fei Zi*, chap. 17.

② *Book of Han Fei Zi*, chap. 46.

Since human nature is born so cold-blooded but in possession of reason so insufficient, domination by an autocrat is the only solution. The autocrat with a full knowledge of human nature should make good use of human nature's weaknesses to strengthen his rule. Since human nature is extremely selfish, forever seeking gains and avoiding loss, a clever ruler should use his power to manipulate people to act in accordance with his will. He holds in his hand two things: carrot and stick. These two are enough to drive his subjects to submit to his will.

> What enables a wise sovereign to rule over his subjects are the two handles [of power], namely rewards and punishments. What is meant by rewards and punishments? Slaughter is punishment and honor is reward. All his subjects are afraid of being punished and desirous of being honored. Therefore when the sovereign independently and solely makes use of the means of punishing and rewarding, all his subjects fear his authority and follow the way of his preference.①

These two powers, "menacing and luring," are the concrete manifestations of the coercive force in the sovereign's hand. For Han Fei, in view of the basic laws of human nature, this is the most efficient means for ruling the subjects. Thus he asserted:

> To rule a nation, the sovereign has to act in accordance with the reality of human nature. Since human nature is endowed with its inclinations for what is preferable and what is not, so rewards and punishments are useful. Since rewards and punishments are effective, relevant prohibitions may be declared and thus the rule of the sovereign is accomplished. As the sovereign reigns on high with full power in his hands, his orders will prevail and his prohibitions will be observed. The leverage is the control over the life and death of the people, and power is the weapon to control the populace.②

Just because human nature ever tends toward profit and away from disadvantages, so these two instruments are the most effective means in handling the people. Through rewarding and punishing, a sovereign is in a position to master his subjects. This is the only valid measure for running the political mechanism. All thought and behavior of the people should be regulated and channeled to follow the decree from the highest royal power, and as a result the whole nation will be kept in uniformity under a sole supreme sovereignty. Such a great uniformity admits no exception whatsoever, whether in ideas or in actions, and only a thoroughly autocratic regime is capable of guaranteeing this. Eventually Han Fei was led to the conclusion: "In the reign of a wise sovereign, his decrees are the most heavy and his laws the most appropriate. There are no other words heavier than his decrees and there are no other orders more appropriate than his laws. His words are the sole dignity and his laws the sole validity. Hence all words and behaviors not in compliance with his decrees and orders have to be banned."③

---

① *Book of Han Fei Zi*, chap. 7.

② *Book of Han Fei Zi*, chap. 48.

③ *Book of Han Fei Zi*, chap. 41.

On this argument of his, a criticism suggests itself. The rule of law in its strictest, most absolute sense has never existed at any time or place in the history of mankind. Whenever and wherever there is the rule of law, there are exceptions to the law, i.e. the right of exception. After the Watergate incident, Nixon—as exacted by the rule of law—ought to have been tried by the court, but he was granted a special amnesty by his successor, President Ford. According to the general rule of expense accounts, one has to submit all expenses in detail to the treasurer. But Chen Ping, the chief assistant to Liu Bang (first emperor of the Han Dynasty) was never required to submit to the treasurer his expenditure on bribing his enemies and other covert activities. "Murderers ought to be put to death"—this was the first decree of the Convention of the Three Chapters proclaimed by Liu Bang on his triumphal entry into the capital. It was also general practice for later ages. But in all times there have been exceptions to this rule. In China's middle ages, a favored nobleman was often granted an iron sheet in vermilion letters, stipulating that as long as he did not commit high treason against the royal throne, he might be granted amnesty from capital punishment ten times. That is to say, he had the privilege to murder ten people without being punished, providing he did not rebel against the emperor. Henry Maine, the famous British historian and jurist of the 19th century, in his *Ancient Law* propounded an insightful view that every law at the moment of its very stipulation is destined to encounter its own violation. No law is nor can be everlasting, and no law in the world avoids change. Each law is in a constant process of its own transmutation. It is fated to gradual attenuation, before finally stepping off the stage and vanishing. Even the fundamental law of a country—its constitution—is no exception. Analogously, once a baby is born into this world, he immediately begins walking step by step toward death. Any rule of law has its exceptional cases, and hence there exists the right of exception. Those who enjoy this privilege are beyond the restraints of the law. When regarding the rule of law, we must acknowledge at its side the rule to the opposite effect, "Let politics take command." *Realpolitik* considerations always outweigh the universal prescription of the rule of the law.

The Legalists were realists, and their theories had to meet the immediate requirements of expediency rather than the eternal justice of law. It is there that they fell into their own trap. In all times there have existed privileged classes who enjoy extra-judicial rights unattainable by the common folk. Yet the Legalists failed to recognize this extra-judicial force, and longed naively for an all-powerful rule of law as a grand social panacea. The tragic end of the leading Legalists was the cruel consequence of this shortsightedness.

The world of real politics is an arena of power struggle far more complicated than they had dreamed, and they were caught in their own shortcomings. The Legalists preached the absolute power of the law while neglecting that those in power were above the power of the law. Wherever the majority of the people is subject to the rule of law, there surely also exists a privileged class with extra-judicial powers. The Legalists failed to realize that the rule of law could never be universally practicable, for there was always a part of the population who were over and above the law, and who were powerful enough to subject it to their own will. Every instance of the so-called rule of law is accompanied by the rule of extra-judicial power as its inevitable complement. Such is the same even in the spiritual world. The Neo-Confucians preached loudly what was called benevolence and morality, but meanwhile they supplemented much that ran contrary to benevolence and morality, not only in their actions but also in their hearts. The Neo-Confucians of the Song period, despite their sanctimonious bearing, were especially fond of writing passionate love poems. These sides of their personality supplemented each other and formed an integral whole. On the one hand the Legalists professed the strict rule of law and severe punishment, but on the other they were ignorant enough even to fail to recognize the natural laws of the movement of power. Did they really suppose that setting a perfect rule of law would suffice to meet the requirements of all problems? It is indeed a scholar's wishful thinking, but wishful thinking by no means converges with the cruel reality of real political life. On this, the Weimar Constitution of modern Germany furnishes us with a ready example. The Weimar Constitution following the end of World War I was generally acknowledged by most jurists and political scientists as the finest constitution to have ever appeared. But this finest constitution led eventually to the most disastrous regime in Nazism. Of course, one need not hold that the Hitler regime was the direct product of the Weimar Constitution, but it is undeniable that the Weimar Constitution did not prevent Hitler from usurping the highest power. It was after all only a sheet of paper. The unfortunate fate of the Legalists may be imputed to their failure to recognize that a mere document of law could not be carried out by itself. All enactments of laws are conditioned by the extra-judicial manipulation of power, which is destined to contradict the rule of law.

[IV] Statecrafts of the Legalists

For a sovereign, dependence on his dignified position and legal sanctions is still insufficient to guarantee the solidity and efficacy of his rule. The efficacy of different sovereigns, though each holding the same position and the same reins of power, might develop quite differently. The key lies in their different practices of political trickery. "If the sovereign does not have a good mastery of the arts of political skill, he will be but a fool on high; and if the high officials do not keep to the rule of law, tumult and disorder will ensue below. Both are indispensable for the rule of a sovereign."① The core of Han Fei's thought is to elaborate the art of ruling, and to devise a specific system of statecraft, very similar to what Machiavelli had so devoutly pursued in *The Prince*.

Just like Han Fei, Machiavelli identified human nature as extremely selfish and ungrateful. Both held the view that the web of inter-human relations consisted only in the pragmatic deliberations of advantages and disadvantages, without a trace of tender-heartedness. And such is the relationship between the sovereign and his officials. The liaison between them is formed for their respective gains and losses. Hence Han Fei claimed:

> Order and strength emanate from the rule of law. Weakness and tumult emanate from partiality. When a sovereign is conscious of this, his righteous rewards and punishments do not arise out of benevolence to his followers. Rewards are paid due to one's achievements and punishments due to one's faults. When his followers are conscious of this, their devotion until death does not arise out of their loyalty to the sovereign. When a sovereign does not identify himself with benevolence, nor his followers with loyalty, then he will really be a king.②

A sovereign should be good at utilizing his followers to serve his purpose, yet should see clearly that the interests of his followers are not always the same with his own. Hence the sovereign has always to keep alert towards his followers. "Those who are conscious that the interests of the sovereign differ from those of his followers will be kings indeed, and those who take both sides as one and the same will perish."③ In another paragraph, Han Fei sketched the typical relation between the upper and the lower parts of society: "The Yellow Emperor [Huang Di] once said, 'There are daily battles between the high and the low.' Those below hide their selfishness in testing their superiors, and those on high exploit their followers with the measures in their possession."④ And even the most sagacious Emperor Taizong of the Tang Dynasty remarked, "The sovereign possesses only one mind, but so many attack it." There is

① *Book of Han Fei Zi*, chap. 43.

② *Book of Han Fei Zi*, chap. 35.

③ *Book of Han Fei Zi*, chap. 48.

④ *Book of Han Fei Zi*, chap. 8.

an unceasing war between the sovereign and his followers. The sovereign is forever testing the loyalty of his followers, just as his followers are forever trying to test the pleasures and disgusts of the sovereign. Though the sovereign possesses the supreme position, it does not mean that he will always hold supreme power. Very probably his power will fall into the hands of others, and he will be usurped by some other. In his *Phenomenology of Mind*, Hegel makes a remark pertinent here. In the relationship between the master and his slave, the slave properly ought to serve his master, but such a relationship might turn to its opposite. The master has to rely on his slave for many things, and ultimately for everything. Thus then the situation is reversed. The slave becomes the master of his master, and the master becomes the slave of his slave. Once the slave has perfected the ways of living and thinking of his master, the case turns upside down, and the master submits to his slave.[①] This process has too often happened in the history of mankind. The relationship between the Emperor Xi zong of the Ming Dynasty and his favorite eunuch Wei Zhongxian is one of the most outstanding examples. Such transformations of relationship are only too frequent in life. For instance, men were obedient to the deities. When there was a drought, people would pray to the deities for rain. But when people learned the rule of the deities' actions, they found they could induce the deities to make rain by offering sacrifices to the deities. Thus the deities became obedient to the human beings. In the long course of China's history, many imperial eunuchs and court favorites dictated over the emperors, just because they had mastered the ways of their emperors. Hence the issue is how a ruler can hold his position of mastery over others without being mastered by others. This is the central point that Han Fei focused on.

The key to the art of ruling is the sovereign's maintenance of absolute authority. He must be skillful enough to drive his inferiors to do the duties he has entrusted to them. To preserve his absolute authority, first of all, he must hold tightly the "two handles" (of rewards and punishment) in his own grasp so that the highest power will not for a moment fall into the hands of others. Lao Zi had professed, "The realm's edged tools [i.e. the operations of the highest power] should not be shown to anybody."[②] Han Fei amplified Lao Zi's idea, "A sovereign ought to overpower his inferiors. Once his power is lost, it can never be regained." And further, "Rewards and punishments are the edged tools of a nation. When these are within the grasp of the sovereign, the sovereign

① Hegel, *Phenomenology of Mind*, chap. 4.

② *Book of Lao Zi*, chap. 36.

rules over his inferiors; and when these are within the grasp of his inferiors, the sovereign is ruled by his inferiors."[1] To gain a favorable position from which to rule others and not be ruled by others, a sovereign must not let his intentions be comprehended and mastered by others. This essential point of the art of ruling advocated by Han Fei is encapsulated in the traditional Chinese sayings: "The final decision is made by the sovereign alone," and "His favors and furies are inscrutable." For this purpose, the lord should be shrewd enough never to let his inferiors grasp his emotions and intentions, lest he fall prey to them.

The *Book of Han Fei Zi* deals minutely with different aspects of statecraft. Some writers even took it to be a perfect summation of the autocratic theory in ancient China.[2] In reality, the traditional political mechanism in China has been a combination of Confucianism and Legalism—or outwardly Confucian and inwardly Legalist; Confucianism on the surface and Legalism in the core. It seems the rulers of ancient China have been accustomed to preach benevolence and morality in Confucian language, but in reality what they practiced was the Legalist art of political trickery. One of the cardinal influences of the Legalists on China's political tradition was just this refined understanding of the cut and thrust of politics.

The Legalists concentrated on the continuation of the sovereign's absolute authority. Han Fei taught, "In possession of a great power you will be paid homage by others, while in possession of a feeble power you will pay homage to others. Hence an intelligent sovereign engages in the strengthening of his power."[3] If a nation is to maintain its own existence when surrounded by other powers without having to fear being conquered, the most urgent task is good preparation in farming and war. Thus the strengthening of military force became the primary concern of the Legalists. As for all other issues that do not serve this goal, an intelligent sovereign should discard them mercilessly. Han Fei had clearly pointed out, "Learned and wise as Confucius and Mo Zi were, if they neither farmed nor plowed, then what could they contribute to the nation? Devout and plain as Zeng Zi and Shi Yu were, if they did not engage in battle, of what use would they be to their nation?"[4] Everything should be subordinated to the urgent political needs. But the popular moral preaching of the Confucians was often incompatible with these basic political demands. Han Fei severely criticized all those who followed their own way and did not respond to the require-

① *Book of Han Fei Zi*, chap. 21.

② Xiao Gongchuan, *History of Political Thought in China*, chap. 7, 5.

③ *Book of Han Fei Zi*, chap. 50.

④ *Book of Han Fei Zi*, chap. 47.

ment of the political situation. For him, outside of the political sphere, no other realm of learning has independent worth. In contemporary terms, this is the injunction to "let (autocratic) politics take command," at the expense of all other principles and practices. All succumbs to the immediate need of politics. Such a mode of thinking has its advantages as well as its defects. For the purpose of accomplishing an immediate political goal, it would be the most effective way, for then everything is brought under the demand of a specific political aim. Yet at the same time it has its unavoidable shortcomings. Overemphasizing the political needs in an extremely utilitarian way would result in the sacrifice of many normal developments in the long run. Viewed from the angle of intellectual development, once the slogan of "Let politics take command" is overemphasized, it leads to an unhealthy state of mind, and our mode of thinking is greatly deformed. During the years of Cultural Revolution, "Let politics take command" was held supreme by the Gang of Four. They highly praised the Legalists and fabricated a myth of "the struggle between the Confucians and the Legalists," since the Legalist theory and practice came very near to their dogma of "let politics take command." Down to the present day, we are still in want of a searching and critical study of the "struggle between the Confucians and the Legalists." Such a study and criticism ought to include two aspects: (1) What are the relevant intellectual traditions and why were they revived just at that specific period known as the Cultural Revolution? (2) What was the relation between the political circumstances of that specific period and the intellectual campaign known as the struggle between Confucianism and Legalism? We are not yet very clear about all that. But considering the details, one may well accept the "struggle between Confucianism and Legalism" as an undoubtedly integral part of the ideology of the Cultural Revolution, and that the motto "Let politics take command" inherited the Legalist spirit, i.e. let everything be subject to the immediate political necessity.

The Legalists also shared certain similarities with the Mohists. The Mohists strongly advocated frugality and hard work, rebuking and discarding all luxury and even music. The result of such practices could only be a community of ants or bees, under the name of "civilization." The entire content of all members' lives in such a community would be nothing but hard labor. Since the Legalists stressed only farming and war, certain groups of society were inexorably down-trodden. One category was men of letters, since they were good at persuading people with their speeches and hence could be harmful to the community. Another was the dialecticians, i.e. the Logicians, because they fomented ideological chaos among the people. Naturally the Legalists were in opposition to those who preached the care of one's own life, i.e. the Taoists and the followers of Yang Zhu. The utopia longed for by the Legalists was a nation totally engaged in farming and war under the efficient rule of an able sovereign. Such an ideal reminds us of Sparta in ancient Greece, or modern militarist nations. We can recall the popular quotation from *Book of Han Fei Zi*: "The Confucian intellectuals disturb the rule of law by their learning and the knights-errant violate the prohibition with their martial strength."① This saying was later cited by Sima Qian in his *Records of the Historian*. The Confucian teaching always proved an obstacle to the Legalist ideal of the rule of law. For instance, the Confucian basis of moral norms on the family was often incompatible with the Legalist emphasis on the priority of current political necessity. In the *Analects* there is a paragraph on the nature of uprightness:

> The Duke of Ye informed Confucius, saying, "Among us here there are those who may be styled upright in their conduct. If their fathers have stolen a sheep, they will bear witness to the fact." Confucius said, "Among us, in our part of the country, those who are upright are different from this. The father conceals the misconduct of the son, and the son conceals the misconduct of the father. Uprightness is to be found in this."②

Against this Confucian view of uprightness, Han Fei protested,

> There was an upright man in Chu who went to the judge accusing his father of stealing a sheep. The judge sentenced him to death, condemning him for being upright as regards the sovereign but not upright as regards his father. He deserved this sentence. From this, it might be seen that an upright follower of the sovereign was a wicked son of his father. A man of Lu followed his sovereign to the battle, and was defeated successively three times in three campaigns. Confucius asked him for the reason. He replied, "I have an aged father, and if I die, he will have no support." Confucius took him as a filial son and recommended him for promotion. From this, it might be seen that a filial son of the father was an unfaithful follower of the sovereign.③

The phrase "the knights-errant violate the prohibition with their martial strength" likely referred to the Mohists. In a certain sense, the Mohists were the knights-errant (xia, i.e. the chivalrous persons) of China. They had very strict organization and often performed acts of chivalry. They were part of an age-long tradition in the culture of China. The Legalists promoted strongly the rule of law in governing a nation, but the actions of the knights-errant frequently came into conflict with the law promulgated by officialdom. The Legalists could not tolerate them, for the Legalists' ambition was to bring all under the exclusive dominion of political authority, the sole criterion for everything being political utility. Politics

① *Book of Han Fei Zi*, chap. 49.

② *Analects*, chap. 13.

③ *Book of Han Fei Zi*, chap. 49.

meant only the ruling power of the sovereign. All that was helpful to this end they would uphold, and all that was not would be prohibited. Like the Mohists, the Legalists were against music, for music seemed of no use to the strengthening of political power. This shows that the Legalists had lost sight of the humanistic value of the spiritual life, and had never come to realize that the arts might also serve political ends. Confucius had recommended that his disciples learn literature and music without which human life would be rough and uneven. The Legalists failed to see the value of human culture and the intrinsic value of a noble life. Their overemphasis on the practical utility of farming and warfare would result in undermining their ambition for increased power. Human life and the wider society are complex, and one cannot reach a certain goal by sticking to that goal alone and neglecting all other factors. The dissolution of the USSR is a relevant example. To a considerable extent, the USSR promoted labor and war in adherence to the Legalist theory, to the neglect of the common people's well-being. The result was its own dissolution. Myopic pursuit of armament and hegemony became the cause of the country's own ruin. To strive for a certain goal one-sidedly cannot bring what one wants. In a certain sense, the Legalists' ideal did come true. By carrying out the Legalist philosophy, the First Emperor of Qin did achieve the great unification of the entire land under his sole rule, and he intentionally ruled according to the Legalist line. But his dynasty soon collapsed, within only two decades. Of course, the causes for it were manifold, but the fundamental reason was their failure to recognize that the sound and solid development of a society had to rest on a balanced foundation. To one-sidedly stress military force or political control to the oblivion of a sound and broad basis could only lead to disaster. During the dissolution of the USSR, the greatest military force ever, the Red Army, did not play any role to prevent it. The military force of the Qin Dynasty was strong enough to smash the other six powers one by one, but a handful of rebels headed by Chen Sheng and Wu Guang destroyed it within a couple of years. The Legalists longed for a strong military power, but their ways and means did not and could not achieve their goals. No reasonable theory completely ignores utilitarian concerns, yet utilitarian speculations alone can not lead to utilitarian ends. At the back of any utilitarian motive, there always exists an extra-utilitarian element in the last analysis. Every means serves an end, but the end of all ends serves no end—the end of all ends is an end in itself. Thus Jesus Christ once taught, "For whosoever will save his life shall lose it; and whosoever will lose his life for my sake shall find it."[①] The value of life is an end in itself, and it can never be subject

① Matthew 16:25.

to any utilitarian end. Or as Kant had it, man himself is an end but never a means to serve some end. When one considers some practical utility, one has to consider the non-utilitarian composition in it and behind it. But all humanistic values and ideas had been abruptly repelled by the Legalists. With all their keen insights in the sphere of politics and power struggles, the Legalists were yet extremely blind and ignorant in their understanding of human nature.

[V] The Realist Spirit of the Legalists

Both the Confucians and the Taoists revered the ancient time, not the present, with a deep reverie of the happy life of bygone days. Contrary to them, the Legalists held a vivid view of the progress of human culture. As mentioned above, Shang Yang had already worked out a philosophy of history propounding a theory of the three stages in the progress of human history. Han Fei succeeded and developed further this theory of progress. This indeed is praiseworthy, for the ancients as a rule held the view of the retrogress of human history, that the days of the reign of the ancient sage-kings were the best, each subsequent reign deteriorating generation after generation. Both Confucius and Mencius effusively praised the legendary sage-kings of antiquity, and Lao Zi and Zhuang Zi exhorted people to return to archaic innocence. In sharp opposition to those wishing to go "back to the ancients," Han Fei proposed his distinct idea of the progress of history. He noted although the then prevailing teachings of Confucianism and Mohism both cited Yao and Shun as their models, the interpretations of the schools were actually quite different. After Confucius and Mo Zi, the Confucians split up into eight sects and the Mohists into three. Then who among them should be identified as the genuine disciple of their masters? If anyone purported to preach the way of the ancient sage-kings of two thousand years prior, he was certainly either an idiot or an imposter. Han Fei proceeded:

> The ancients engaged in being virtuous, those of the middle past contended with their intelligence and the moderns compete by force. The lives of the ancients were simple and plain, not complicated and refined, so that one could both plow and at the same time serve to drive the cart. The ancient population was very scarce and mutually intimate, their provisions abundant so that they cared little about their profits and took it light to profit others, Hence there were transfers of the royal thrones with perfect politeness.①
>
> That the ancients took their property so lightly was not due to their generosity but

① *Book of Han Fei Zi*, chap. 47.

due to their abundance. That the moderns engaged in fierce competition was not due to their vulgarity but due to their meagerness.①

In comparison, Confucius and Mencius were the idealists who stressed the moral cultivation of the inner life, while Xun Zi and the Legalists were the materialists who stressed the function of material lives. Xun Zi and the Legalists realized the difference between contemporary lives and those of the ancients. Since the material conditions of life changed, so people's ideas and behavior naturally changed correspondingly. In their view, we ought to follow not the ancient sages but the modern sages, i.e. the later kings. Han Fei declared that if the moderns still adored the ways of the ancient sage-kings, they ought to be ridiculed by the modern sages. The modern sages were much more intelligent than the ancient ones, and hence "the sage should not expect to follow the ancients or any unvarying way." There had never existed a constant way that ought to be followed to eternity. People should only observe the current world and make preparation accordingly, i.e. people should concentrate their minds on current affairs and on that basis work out their plans and projects. Han Fei cited a well-known fable. Once a peasant in the state of Song, while plowing in the field, saw a rabbit run past, before it hit a tree and died as a result. This man had got a rabbit without laboring. Since then he did not labor but just waited for the same lucky accident under the tree. Surely such luck would not reappear. Han Fei concluded, "All those who intend to rule over the people of today with the politics of the ancient kings are the same as those waiting for the rabbit under the tree."②

This shows that Han Fei's vision was directed forwards and not backwards, while the tradition of the Chinese had always been to direct their vision backwards, even the great reformer Kang Youwei at the end of the 19th century being no exception. The Legalist view of history, characteristic of their forward-looking attitude, broke up the pedantic and hypocritical preaching of the old-fashioned idealism, and thereby opened up a radically new phase in the intellectual history of China.

Another, more philosophical contribution of the Legalists involved the issue of whether there is an eternal and invariable Tao (Way) in the universe. This has forever been a problem in philosophy. Is there any eternal and invariable principle, law or rule, or are these principles themselves always changing? This perennial question concerns not only the human world but also

① *Book of Han Fei Zi*, chap. 49

② *Book of Han Fei Zi*, chap. 49.

the natural world. Is there eternal law in natural science? There was a time when people took the law of universal gravitation as eternal and unchanging. The foremost scientist of modern China, Li Shanlan (1810-1882), emphasized that this law of universal gravitation as forever invariable. Most scientists nowadays probably do not share the same view any longer. Our knowledge is always renewed in its progress, and we have witnessed scientific revolutions more than once in which the traditional system is completely overthrown and replaced by the new. The Ptolemaic system was replaced by the Copernican. The biological system of Cuvier was revolutionized in the mid-19th century by the Darwinian theory of evolution. Then is the Tao (the First Principle) forever unchanging? Or is it changeable, and always in change? To have proposed such a problem should be regarded as a valuable philosophical contribution by the Legalists. It must be noted that this does not mean that their answer is also correct. To have proposed a question sometimes is a contribution no less than to have afforded an answer to it. The Legalists' contribution to the history of ideas exists in having proposed this basic question of philosophy.

Just because the Legalists were infused with a realistic spirit, they were able to inquire into many issues never noticed by the idealists, and to propose many topics and arguments never touched upon by others. The following pronouncement on the problem of population affords a striking example:

> Nowadays it is but ordinary to have five sons in a household, and each of them in turn has five sons, and thereupon a grandfather has twenty-five grandsons while alive. This is why the inhabitants are too numerous while the wealth is too scarce and the labor is too hard while the provision is too trifling. This causes strife among the populace.①

The above-quoted lines of Han Fei's theory of population antedated Malthus' *Population* by about two thousand years. Malthus taught that the growth of population was in proportion with geometrical series, by far surpassing the growth of the means of living. This presents a great menace to mankind. Han Fei might be ranked as one of the earliest to touch on the problem maintaining the balance between population growth and the development of production, as well as with the natural environment itself. Prof. Lei Haizong, a renowned historian of the last century, propounded his opinion on the historical cycle in China in a similar way. There have occurred cycles of peace and war succeeding each other one by one. After the great turmoil of the Qin Dynasty, there was a reign of peace and prosperity in the early Han Dynasty; after the great turmoil of the Sui dynasty, there followed the peace and prosperity of the

① Ibid.

Tang Dynasty; and after the great turmoil of the Ming Dynasty there came the reign of peace and prosperity of the early Qing Dynasty. Prof. Lei explained such historical cycles as follows. The population was always increasing, especially in times of peace and prosperity. But when it reached a certain limit, the production would become incapable of supporting the population, and there would then burst forth an upheaval caused by the famine. It was only after a series of civil wars and agitations that the population would fall to the level of the peaceful days. Then and only then, as the land became again sufficient to support the population, would it regain its peace and prosperity. In this way, war and peace alternately succeed each other. The secret of such cycles of alternating peace and war is key to the history of China. We may find in Han Fei a forerunner of this interpretation of history, starting from the relation between land and population.

Again in another passage, Han Fei declared,

> Those who are indulgent and lazy will become poor, while those who are hard-working and thrifty will become rich. Now the government taxes the rich and hands out to the poor. This is just to exploit the hard-working and thrifty for the benefit of the lazy and indulgent. This cannot encourage people to work hard and be thrifty.①

More or less all governments have employed some sort of welfare policy. Its substance is to take from the rich and give to the poor. Han Fei stood against such a policy. It is noteworthy that he proposed such a theory more than two thousand years ago and stood in direct opposition to the prevailing view based on benevolent administration. Down to the present day, people still worry about the same problem. A society can hardly subsist without some kind of welfare policy. But too much welfare would tend to be harmful to a lively mechanism of competition and to the vitality of a vigorous development. This is a problem for modern societies, but the ancient Legalists had already encountered it and discussed it.

[VI] The Defects of the Legalists

The ancient philosophers were prone to criticize other philosophers in their writings, the examples of Zhuang Zi's "The World" and Xun Zi's "Refutations of the Twelve Philosophers" being widely known. Generally speaking, the shortcomings of most ancient philosophers consisted in the fact that, despite all their keen insights, they often fell short of seeing the world whole with a balanced

① *Book of Han Fei Zi*, chap. 50.

and all-round outlook. So was it also with the Legalists, who—though extremely deep and keen in their insight into the essence of human nature and human relationships—were often distorted in their mode of thinking by their partiality for the ugliness in life. This often led to erroneous judgments.

The application of a theory must be limited within its proper bounds. The law of universal gravitation holds, but only under certain conditions, without which it is nullified. The law of universal gravitation may be applied to explain the motions of the physical world, but not the tragic story of the heroine Lin Daiyu in the novel *A Dream of Red Mansions*. So this very law is invalidated in explaining the story of Ms. Lin. Each theory has its specific field of application beyond which it is of no avail. We may agree that wherever there are human beings there are class struggles, but we are not as justified to assert that the theory of class struggle can explain everything in the human world. In the same way, we are justified to assert that every movement in the physical world follows the law of universal gravitation, but we are not as justified to assert that every event in the physical world is governed by the law of universal gravitation. The Legalists took the struggle for power as the sole determinant in our political and social life. This is surely a too biased simplification of the human world. Out of its proper sphere, every theory is nullified.

So the Legalist theory (and especially that of Han Fei) ought to be restricted to the sphere of its validity. We can recall Pascal's "L'homme n'est ni ange ni bête."[①] The Confucians turned their sights only on the angelic side of human beings in constructing their theory. The Legalists were just the opposite and looked merely to the beastly side of human nature, and thus degraded human beings to the level of beasts. Both views were incomplete and failed to see human nature in its entirety. He possesses an evil side as well as a noble side. Taking only one side would fall short of a sound and comprehensive understanding of the true nature of humanity. Misguided by its partial view of man and his nature, the Legalist theory leads logically to the legitimation of despotic autocracy. And the art of ruling as formulated by the Legalists, i.e. "the two handles" theory, was nothing more than naked threatening and enticement. And indeed, the method of all rulers over their subjects through history has been none other than such threatening and enticement. In this respect, the Legalists appeared astonishingly naive. Their whole theory rested on the supposition of the inborn evilness of human nature. And their theory would work only when human nature conducted itself in such an evil manner. And when

① B. Pascal, *Pensées*, ed. Brunschvicg, 140.

it behaved otherwise, in a noble manner, their theory would be nullified. If all people in the street were sages (as Wang Yangming's disciples of the late Ming Dynasty asserted), or "all the Chinese were sages like Yao and Shun," then the Legalists' "two handles" doctrine would be of no use. In most cases, most people were afraid of death, but there were indeed cases in which "the people do not fear at all to die; what's gained therefore by threatening them with death?"① Many a time "the people are so hard to rule because of those who are above them, whose interference causes distress."② To be sure, the common people in certain cases are not afraid of death once their passions are inspired. This is the dialectic of history. There are ordinary cases as well as extraordinary ones. Most people in most cases are in a normal state, i.e. they are afraid of death and are easily enticed. But there are cases when people do not fear death. The fall of the Qin Dynasty (the typical representative of the Legalist regime) presents a good example. Under normal conditions people are afraid of death and subject to the threats of power. But there are those who prefer to die rather than to live under certain circumstances. Bo Yi and Shu Qi, refugees of the Shang Dynasty, willingly starved to death rather than live under the new regime of the Zhou Dynasty. There were too many such instances to be enumerated. Perhaps it is reasonable to say that the basic issue in the art and science of politics is how to find an optimal equilibrium between the individual and the authority, and how to keep a state well-balanced between the two. Both sides are interdependent within a unified community, the one always being conditioned by the other. The political authority tries to keep the people in obedience, and oftentimes the resort to dictatorial means of reward and punishment proves effective. Meanwhile, the people now and then use violent measures at risk of death. One of the fatal defects in any Legalist theory (Machiavelli's included) lies in this: they recognize in human nature the elements of humility, but never those of rebellion. They had mistaken that part of human nature for the entirety. They never reached a clear knowledge of the sphere of validity of their theory. In the end, the Legalists deserve to be honored as the earliest theorists of human nature along the line of objective and scientific research. It was left for later generations to probe this issue on a higher level.

The Legalists further developed Xun Zi's theory of the evilness of human nature by identifying human nature with cowardice and selfishness. Once a person has mastered this, he will be qualified to rule others competently. This

① *Book of Lao Zi*, chap. 74.

② Ibid., chap. 75.

should be admitted as both an advance and at the same time a step backward in the history of our understanding. In terms of progress, it deepened our understanding of human nature. Unlike the past philosophers who merely praised the goodness of human nature and professed the coming of a future society in a fictitious state of happiness and welfare, the Legalists came to realize that human nature was not at all so good, and has a predominantly evil ingredient in it. There was a great deal of evil and selfishness inherent in human nature. It ought to be acknowledged that this was a deeper awakening of the epistemology of human nature. Yet at the same time, it meant also a retrogress, because it did not see human nature in its entirety, and was only concerned with its dark side. If the Confucians may be regarded as tending toward hypocrisy, then the Legalists may be regarded as tending toward fascism. The Confucians might embrace an optimistic (though always illusory) view of the future, but the Legalists could never entertain a hope for an ever-progressive society. What engaged them was merely the strengthening of the political mechanism so as to ensure an ever-stronger ruling power. It was the Legalists who came forth to strip away the sacred robe of human nature that mankind had been adorned with by conventional beliefs. Ever since antiquity, people had held a deep-rooted belief that mankind could hope for a better world and a better life, provided the good qualities in human nature were given opportunity for expression. People were customarily not humble enough to confront other elements in human nature which might become disastrous under certain social circumstances. The Legalists brought to light the omissions of the intellectual background by revealing the truth lying hidden in human nature. This indeed constitutes an unprecedented enhancement of our thought. According to the wording in the *Bible*, the first step mankind took into civilization was a degeneration into sin. This description might properly be applied to the works of the Legalists. Their ideas deservedly represent a great step forward in the intellectual history of mankind, yet such progress was also a great step towards degeneration. They were concerned not with what was glorious but with what was dishonorable in our life. It was upon this starting point that the Legalists planned and carried out their political and social scheme.

Since the Legalists held only this view as their premise, their theory as an academic construction degenerated into a series of political strategies, or even scheming and intrigues, on which one can find only too many stories from historical sources. Overall, human nature shows its evil as well as its nobility at the same time. To maintain a regime merely by means of brutal force, but not simultaneously by improving the people's lives materially as well as spiritually, a regime could hardly last long. Jia Yi, the outstanding political theorist in the first years of the Han Dynasty immediately following the Qin Dynasty, remarked that as the Qin regime contravened all rites and righteousness and demolished all moralities, their customs and dynasty were in decline day by day. Jia Yi and Sima Qian were both of the early Han Dynasty, not long after the fall of Qin; and their criticisms of the Qin regime were based on their personal experiences. Sima Qian praised the achievements of the Legalist reforms, but severely criticized the Legalists' cruel practices which had led to a rule of brutal suppressions. As contemporaries of Stalin, we may well remember how he was blamed for having sowed distrust among the people under the pretext of encouraging alertness against the enemy. Social stability and universal fraternity are indispensable conditions for peace and prosperity, no less than the strict enactment of law and the rule of an absolute authority. The advantages and disadvantages are always concurrent and mutually dependent. Over-alertness leads to distrust among people with the effect that any normal and sound human relationship would be impossible. The Legalist teaching at length degenerated into a set of mere games of trickery, which was a double-edged sword. Those in power might employ it to deal with their inferiors, and their inferiors in turn might employ it to deal with them.

There was an old saying: mere law cannot be enacted by itself. Shang Yang had said, "There are laws in every country, but there is no law that can enact any law."[①] Law does not enact itself, but relies on people for enactment, and hence to a considerable degree depends on human intellectual consciousness. Rousseau held that the more laws there are, the less are the ruling powers of the nation. The force of law is embodied not in letters, but is inscribed on the hearts of people.[②] Herein lies the genuine relation of law and morality. If the social manners and behavior are good and sound, voluminous laws are unnecessary. The sound maintenance and development of a society never depends on the mere words of laws. Therefore the issue is how to find an ideal point of equilibrium between the Confucian rule of benevolence and the Legalist rule of law. It is a pity that all the despotic emperors found only the equilibrium known as "Confucian outwardly, Legalist inwardly," i.e. a medley of the two, benevolence in words and cruelty in deeds.

The transition from Confucianism to Legalism was namely a transformation from the culture of rites to the culture of laws. To use an expression from H.

① *Book of Lord Shang*, chap.18.

② Rousseau, *Social Contract*, bk. 2, chap. 12.

Maine, it may be compared with the transition "from status to contract." Rites meant the social norms corresponding with social status, not to be applied to the common folk, while law was—at least nominally—of universal validity for all and hence had something of the character of a contract. Viewed from this aspect, the struggle between the Confucians and the Legalists may be endowed with a new connotation. The Confucians preached the return to the ancients, while the Legalists propagated demand for reform. Therefore, the struggle between the two camps was imbued with a symbolic significance which persisted down to modern times. The Legalist school represented simultaneously both a progress and a retrogress. Its progressiveness dwelt in its scrutiny of what is the real in human nature, not the ideal as the Confucians so loudly propounded. Its retrogressiveness dwelt in its lack of a complete world-view (Weltanschauung) and life-view (Lebensanschauung). They had completely lost sight of what is elevating in spiritual life and what is valuable and ennobling among people and between man and nature. In fact, they represented the end of an old age and the beginning of a new one. They were preparing public opinion for the coming new epoch, that of a unified land under an absolute and supreme imperial power. The respective spiritual phases of the two epochs differed greatly, each representing a specific stage in the history of China, i.e. the ancient or classical, and the mediaeval or scholastic. The Qin Dynasty under the Legalist guidelines launched a political and cultural campaign which terminated the ancient time and initiated the mediaeval age. Its success and failure reflected the merits as well as the shortcomings of the Legalist doctrine. The Legalists played an overture proclaiming the coming of a new historic epoch. The spirits of the two succeeding epochs differed from each other as much as they differed in their respective historical characteristics. China underwent a great historical transformation during the rule of the Qin Dynasty. It was then that she stepped from her classical time into the mediaeval. The Qin Dynasty presented the scene of a historical experiment under the theoretical direction of the Legalists. The success and failure of the Qin Dynasty bore witness to the success and failure of the Legalists. As to the mediaeval scholastic thought in China that followed the classical times, it would require a new book.

Epilogue: The Traditional Mode of Thinking and Its Modernization

The cardinal turning point in the whole course of human civilization is its move from traditional society into modernization. There seems no ground to suppose that the traditional society is destined as a matter of course to embark on the road to modernization. But the historical facts show that once a society has stepped into the stage of modernization, all other civilizations follow its step both at the material level and correspondingly at the level of spiritual life. And it is impossible for them not to do so; it is as though they are duty-bound and cannot turn back.

The ancient classical civilization of China was among the foremost in human history. Yet following the 15th and the 16th century, after the Renaissance, the Age of Discovery and the Reformation formally drew back the curtain of modernization in the West, the Chinese civilization began to lag behind. Down to the 20th century her development had never caught up with the pace of the modernized West. The history of the last four centuries was for her the history of a series of set-backs, defeats and submissions. As the concluding remarks of the present book, let us from the angle of intellectual history attempt a brief inquiry into the reasons why China had so fallen short in stepping onto the main road of modernization.

Now, what is meant by modernization? Or, what constitutes the criterion or the concrete content of modernization? The answer might be roughly as follows. First of all, it includes modern science (distinguished from ancient science)[①] and its application (industry). Accompanying it are the corresponding socio-political, intellectual and ideological conditions without which modern science could not gain ground to grow and flourish. Or in terms plain and simple, its requirement *sine qua non* is an atmosphere of democracy.

① F. Engels, *The Dialectic of Nature*, "Introduction."

In ancient and mediaeval times, science in China held for many ages a leading place. Among the ancient nations perhaps only Greece might rival her, and in the Middle Ages only Arabia might qualify to be compared with her. But since the time of the Renaissance when the West made great strides in establishing the classical system of modern science, China was by comparison trailing behind year after year. The classical system of modern science was already firmly founded in the late 17th century, but down to the mid-19th century China still knew nothing of it at all. Why is it that science in China, having so long enjoyed a leading position in world history, began from the age of the Renaissance to fall behind? How is this phenomenon connected with the traditional Chinese way of thinking and how did they influence each other? Would it have been possible—if China had had no connection at all with the West—for China to go on along her own tradition and in her own way attain the height of modern science by herself?

[I] Previous Interpretations of the Absence of Modern Science

Comparing the different lines of their respective intellectual development, the most striking moment in history seems to be as follows. Since the Renaissance the West underwent a scientific revolution which brought about a fundamental transformation of the spirit, the understanding of their cultural tradition, and their mode of thinking, while throughout the history of China there was no such scientific revolution that her culture and mode of thinking could ever rid itself of its mediaeval tradition. In the last five centuries the theoretical systems in the West have mostly emerged under the strong intellectual influences of modern science, and many philosophers were themselves scientists, from Descartes, Pascal, Leibniz, Kant, Spencer, Poincaré, and Mach down to Bergson, Russell, Whitehead and Wittgenstein of the last century, which saw the rise of the modern analytical school. By contrast, Chinese thought down to the late 19th century proceeded unbroken within the framework of the mediaeval scholastic tradition, completely untouched by modern science and consequently never influenced by it in any way. Ruan Yuan (1764-1849), the leading sinologist of the early 19th century, was in his monumental work *Lives of the Mathematicians* still ignorant of the classical system of modern science. Faced with the debate between the heliocentric theory and the geocentric theory introduced by the West, he showed a sense of puzzlement, not knowing which one he should choose to follow. Though modern science in its classical form was eventually introduced into China by Li Shanlan, the foremost Chinese mathematician of the late 19th century, it was not until Yan Fu's translation of T. H. Huxley's *Evolution and Ethics* (the Chinese title translates as "The Theory of Evolution") in 1896 that Chinese intellectuals began to formally break up the scholastic framework, and to adopt a brand new way of viewing the world and mankind, as well as society and history. From then a brand new horizon was opened for Chinese thought.

Why is it that the modern scientific revolution occurred in the West rather than China? The reason has been explored in various ways by both Chinese and Western scholars. A simple answer so often quoted is this: modern science came to the fore with the development of the capitalist mode of production; and since capitalism did not appear in China, so there was naturally no scientific revolution in China. Such a thesis sounds logically incomplete, since it does not give a satisfactory answer to the question: why was there no capitalism in China? It is often argued that the reason that China had no capitalism was her antiquated relations of production, which hindered the development of the new productive forces. But a further question still arises. Why was science, as the most active factor in productive force, unable to burst out of the constraints of the outdated relations of production? This appears very puzzling and hard to answer. Because after all, it is the relations of production which ought to conform to the requirement of the productive forces, but not vice versa, i.e. the productive forces do not have to conform to the relation of production. Commodity economy, private ownership of productive means and the employment of labor etc.—all these factors can be found at almost all times the world over, and these alone do not mean the germination of capitalism. A germination should be followed by a flowering and a harvest of the fruit. If the germination lasted more than four centuries and yet did not bring about any flowering or fruit, then it is doubtful whether it is really a germination. Marx in his *Das Kapital* emphatically pointed out that the seeds of capitalism had already scattered across the Mediterranean cities during the last years of the 15th century, and the curtain was formally drawn back in the first three decades of the 16th century.[①] It is simply unimaginable that the stage of germination could last as long as several centuries. It seems that the thesis of "the restrictions of the relations of production" theory is just like the "germination of capitalism" thesis—it too falls into logical tautology. Such an approach may perhaps help Chopin in composing his waltz, watching the little dog trying to catch its own tail, but it surely offers no help in

---

① K. Marx, *Das Kapital*, vol. 1, chap. 24.

explaining how modern science, the foremost keynote in the history of mankind, and the modern ideas and cultures closely correlated with it, stepped forward onto the stage.

Another answer to the question is given in terms of the mode of thinking. It reduces the reason for the emergence of capitalism and modern science to the function of spiritual elements, taking them as an intricate whole. Max Weber, R. H. Tawney and Albert Schweitzer and others may be enlisted as its representatives. They integrated the historical scene with the spirit of Protestantism (and especially Calvinism). Such an answer starts from an unwarranted view that it is the human idea that determines the historical phase but not vice versa. Yet if human ideas are not regulated and determined by historical reality, then whence would they come forth? If a certain world-view determines the historical features of an epoch, then why can such an assertion not be reverted so as to affirm that it is the historical feature of that epoch which determines its specific world-view? Why was it the 16th and 17th centuries that produced this sort of thought, enabling capitalism and modern science to appear in the arena?

In connection with this approach there is another line, which attributes the reason for China's shortfall in developing modern science to the Chinese mind's affinity for practical application (e.g. the four great inventions: compass, gunpowder, printing and paper) rather than abstract thinking (e.g. geometry). In other words, theoretical speculations are too constrained by their national characteristics of practicality to thrive freely. The traditional imperial examination system and its focus on the exegesis of the sayings of the ancient sages had seriously constrained the rigorous growth of any scientific reasoning. By inference from this view, the difference between the Chinese and the Western is both one between the different nature of the two cultures and at the same time one between the ancients and the moderns. Some contemporary scholars (including Tawney and Feng Youlan) were inclined to stress the difference between the ancients and the moderns. In fact, as early as two centuries ago Hume had already mentioned the fact that the reason for China's lagging behind in science is the great unification in the political and cultural sphere that seriously impeded the liberty of thinking and speech. Without the freedom of thought, there would be no advancement of science (at least modern science). Hume's thesis may provide a keen insight; yet he did not make further scrutiny into the mode of thought in China and from there proceed to study the topic he had touched upon so wonderfully. In the last century H. G. Wells mentioned that the worship of tradition and the mentality of sticking to routine had prevented the Chinese mind from giving play to their independence and initiative, so necessary to any advancement in science and theoretical thought.

[II] Material Conditions of Modera Science

As regards the birth and development of modern science, it requires both its specific material as well as intellectual conditions. In its material conditions, it requires a specific social class whose interests are closely related with scientific knowledge, i.e. the interest of that class is in need of science. Such a material condition was conveniently provided by the bourgeoisie who were then rising to the fore and soon got hold of political power. But this very condition was absent in all other then existing nations. By that time this newly rising bourgeoisie in the West was in urgent need of various kinds of new knowledge from astronomy, geography, navigation, manufacturing, and artillery to world politics, economics, trade, social life and history. Such knowledge was closely bound up with their immediate interests, though it did not much concern the interests of the traditional ruling classes. As late as the first years of the last century the nobilities of the underdeveloped nations in Asia and Africa customarily sent their descendants to receive their education at Oxford and Cambridge. Yet when their boys came back to their native countries, instead of introducing the Western institutions and regimes into their countries, they preferred rather to keep on enjoying their former way of life with their inherited privileges. The secret of this lies in the fact that science brings about a collapsing effect in the social hierarchy. Under a strict hierarchy of status and privileges, people are unequal by their birth. Projected onto the material world, it imposes inequality on all material objects: some things are nobler while others humbler, the celestial nobler while the terrestrial humbler, the "heavenly principle" nobler while the human desires humbler, etc. But with the advent of modern science this world of hierarchy with its ranks and status was transubstantiated into a world of equality of all things; the mediaeval heterogeneous world-view gave way to the modern homogeneous one. All things (human beings included), no matter how great or how trifling, are of equal value before the tribunal of science. All must obey its iron law and thus are equally the objects of scientific research with no distinction of the nobler or the humbler, the higher or the lower. Even the Creator, as Descartes put it, has to obey the iron law of nature. By this line of reasoning, there is of course no distinction of rank or gradation among people. All people have to obey the same iron law of nature, no matter what status she or he may enjoy. Wherever the idea of status and the institution of social rank reigns, modern science can hardly appear and develop. To break out of such an intellectual constraint based on the idea of status and traditions, modern science and ideas had undergone a long and arduous way of strife. In China, this obstacle had never been broken. That was the reason why Lu Xun, the outstanding proponent of modern values, so strongly appealed for the use of science as the weapon to smash all kinds of nonsense.

In close correlation, another condition for the birth and advancement of science is its veneration and promotion by the existing social and political institutions, i.e. the existing social and political institutions have to be able to attract human talent to engage in scientific careers. Since the Renaissance the establishment of various kinds of scientific associations and learned academies has become a prevailing fashion. The strong impetus it has given to the development of scientific careers is already universally known. Yet such a current ran contrary to the traditional spirit in China. The Chinese traditional spirit longed to pass through the gate leading to virtue but not to knowledge. Faust, to satisfy his search for knowledge, even went so far as to sell his soul to Mephistopheles—such an action was never valued in Chinese culture. In the history of China it has been only virtue or morality that reigned over all else. Knowledge in itself has never had independent value whatsoever. The value of knowledge exists only in its service of some ethical end. The prospects of the life and career of an intellectual, along with his position, honor and interests, are all connected with his virtues (or rather his outward show) and not with his knowledge. Since the early Han Dynasty (2nd century B.C.) when Confucianism was officially elevated as the state orthodoxy by the emperor, the famous historian Ban Gu expressed his regret explicitly in his *History of Han* that the Confucian learning had already degenerated into a means for obtaining official positions and privileges. Later, through the imperial examination system with its scholastic studies in the middle ages, the imperial power further strengthened itself by extracting the elite of the learned people into its hierarchical structure. The reason that scientific knowledge was generally in oblivion was that it proved disadvantageous to the ruling order of the privileged hierarchy. In Socrates' celebrated dictum, knowledge is virtue. But in the tradition of China, knowledge itself is no virtue, but a mere means in service of virtue—an expression equivalent to the idea that "Science is the servant-maid of theology" in the mediaeval West. When Galileo (1564-1642) was founding the cornerstone of modern science in the West, his contemporary Song Yingxing (1587-1666), the encyclopedic scientist of China, was working on his book *The Exploitation of the Works of Nature* (*Tian Gong Kai Wu*), which he announced with regret was not relevant at all to obtaining official ranks and privileges. (It is a genuine pity that the book did not touch upon scientific theory.) Later, his book was lost for centuries in his native country, and not until modern times was it found in Japan and reintroduced into China. The only road for the Chinese intellectuals to take was that of the honors and privileges of officialdom, or in other words, to get high official positions and become wealthy. But success along this road requires no scientific knowledge—only one's noble blood lineage, one's social relationships, and one's skill in writing the stereotyped eight-part essay composition. This type of essay needs no innovation of scientific ideas but only hypocritical preachings following the official mode. What the satirical novelist Wu Jingzi in his *An Informal History of the Confucian Scholars* (*Ru Lin Wai Shi*) said through the mouth of his character Ma Chunshang hit the point exactly: "If you do not walk this road, who would be likely to confer on you a position in officialdom?" In the novel *A Dream of Red Mansions* of the early 18th century, the author Cao Xueqin vividly described such a mentality. When Jia Zhen, a dandy of the noble house, was informed that the younger generation of his family were not engaging in studies, he replied contemptuously: "There is no need for families like ours to engage in study." Those of noble blood relied on their privileges, and naturally had no need for scientific knowledge at all. On the contrary, more knowledge tended to become a potential or direct menace to the ruling class founded on hereditary status. In the main, this was the case in China's Middle Ages. Down to the late 19th century Chinese society was no yet mature for allowing the birth and growth of modern science and inducing the intelligence of the scholars to engage in modern scientific research. Just because the interests of the then ruling class had no need of scientific knowledge, science has always been servile to the social orthodoxy.

[III] Intellectual Couditions of Modern Science

The birth and growth of modern science also required its indispensable intellectual conditions.

Firstly, as stated above, it requires a world-view which takes the universally valid iron law as its presupposition—an iron law which decrees that all created things are equal without discrimination. Such a world-view and the world-view of distinction between the nobler and the humbler are mutually exclusive to their very roots. It was the world-view based on the discriminations between inborn qualities that made possible the reign of the Aristotelian-

Ptolemaic theory and stubbornly impeded the emergence of modern science and modern thought for centuries. In order to struggle for its own right to life, modern science had to reject such a world-view of the innate inequality of all things and reposition everything on the same ground, based on the premise that all is created equal. The differences among all things are merely quantitative instead of qualitative. Neither what is celestial is sacred, nor what is terrestrial is despicable. So it is with the natural world, so it is also with the human world. There is no definite line of demarcation between the Heavenly Principle and corporeal desire as so repeatedly preached by the later Neo-Confucians. This new world-view based on the idea of a universal law valid for all came onto the stage in modern history. Yet in the history of ideas in China there has never been such an idea of law applying equally to all creatures. The sages and the populace each had to follow their own way of life in order to meet the requirements of a hierarchical social order. Nevertheless, the idea of a universal law is an indispensable presupposition of modern science. The human world is also a part of the natural world—though a particular, even alienated part of it. So the specific law of the human world ought to be derived from the universal law of the natural world, and cannot be in contradiction with it. Yet the Chinese way of thinking had reversed the order by putting the ethical obligation first and then plumping it up into the universal law governing the natural world. The whole universe was thus transformed into an ethical hierarchy.

Secondly, scientific knowledge ought to be the result of our investigations and experiments carried out consciously, systematically and purposefully, and hence its criterion is not any ethical belief or dogma but the facts of our experiences. Aristotle pronounced that a heavy body must fall down faster than a lighter one. But the dogma professed by any sage does not matter in the kingdom of science. The truth has to be tested by the experiment of two bodies falling from the leaning tower of Pisa. (This often-quoted story about Galileo is only legendary, and is cited here as a mere illustration). The starting point of modern science is not any sacred dogma but our observation and experiment. Nevertheless, it has to be admitted that although in the Middle Ages of China there were no systematic theorists like Francis Bacon or Descartes, we may still find some germs of scientific observations and experiments. As early as the Song period, Shen Kuo (1030-1095), the foremost scientist of his age, recorded a multitude of natural phenomena in minute detail, and his marvelously keen insights ought to be ranked among the foremost in the history of science worldwide. Later in the Ming Dynasty, Xu Guangqi (1562-1633) engaged in agricultural experiments for a considerable time, and the scale and spirit of his experimental work was comparable with that of his contemporary Galileo. But on the whole the scientific research at that time in China was still in a state of fragmentary spontaneity and had not yet attained the height of a conscious and persistent current under the guidance of a strict universal discipline. These isolated cases were still insufficient to promote the emergence of modern science.

Thirdly, the data from observation and experiment have to be formulated into a mathematical model, without which there can be no theoretical system of science (its classical form was provided by the work of Newton as shown in his *Mathematical Principles of Natural Philosophy*), nor any advancement towards a persistent progress in the depth and breadth of science (as expounded in the philosophical principles in the last part of the same book). The formulation into a mathematical principle means a quantitative derivation of the acquired data, and such a process is properly an integral part of a quantitative world-view. In pre-modern times, some thinkers and scholars in China made significant efforts along this direction with a vivid modern tint. Among them were Xu Guangqi of the Ming Dynasty (16th-17th centuries) and Jiao Xun of the Qing Dynasty (18th century). Xu had resolutely aspired to summarize all knowledge into a mathematical matrix which and only which was qualified to serve as the end of all scientific knowledge. It is a pity that he fell short of undertaking the mathematically-oriented mechanical experiments like his contemporary Galileo. And the long series of his agricultural experiments by their very nature were even further from a mathematical orientation. All in all, he has to be counted the first in China to try consciously to reduce natural science to a mathematical system. As to the line Jiao Xun took, it was not exactly experimental science in its modern sense. His central idea is rather that mathematics is the transcendental legislator of the universe, or as Sir James Jeans would have it, the Creator is a mathematician who created the universe after the mathematical pattern. Though Jiao's idea was not quite in the same line as modern science, still it had something in common or in correspondence with it. Anyhow, the Chinese scholars had already embraced some definite sense that science needed to undergo a process of mathematization, although this idea had not yet formed a major current in academic circles.

[IV] Characteristics of Chinese Culture and Modern Science

What led modern science to emerge in the West instead of in China may also be retraced to their different cultural backgrounds. In contrast to China, the

Occidental culture has been more inclined to intellectualism. As earlier noted, "philosophy" etymologically means "the love (philo) of wisdom (sophia)"; hence this very term was translated by the Jesuit missionaries coming to China in the 16th and 17th centuries as "the learning of the love of knowledge." Even the most virtue-oriented philosopher Socrates affirmed emphatically that "knowledge is virtue." By contrast, the main current of thoughts in China has always been virtue-oriented rather than intellect-oriented, that is, knowledge is forever in service of virtue and possesses no value in itself. Therefore, above all, the pursuit of knowledge in China has existed to serve the fulfillment of an obligation of virtue but never for the sake of knowledge or understanding itself. It was not only the Confucians who held virtue in the primary place, for the Taoists also asked people to "get rid of wisdom," "cast away the intellect"[①] and "Be done with learning."[②] Knowledge itself is never worthy of being longed for. The ideas of the West have always possessed a strong mien of intellectualism. Even in the theological arguments among the mediaeval scholastics, and their religious beliefs often drew on logical inference such as the ontological proof of the existence of God—a sharp contrast to the philosophical discourses of the Chinese, who were more accustomed to employ metaphors or analogies. It seems that, for the Chinese, virtue is the truth of a higher level and cannot be proved or guaranteed by pure intellectual knowledge. For them, the value of life exists not in the search for the secret of the world but in the realization of ethical obligations. Throughout China's history, the sacrifices of their heroic figures or eminent personages have all been dedicated to the cause of some ethical duty rather than to something within the sphere of pure intellect (such as the case of Galileo's persecution for the sake of his research into some truth of pure science). What the Chinese sought was the fulfillment of virtue, and never that of scientific truth or of beauty, arts, etc. In a certain sense, the contrast between the Chinese and the Occidental way of thinking may be identified as that between virtue and knowledge. Essentially it is what we have discussed in the preceding chapters, i.e., the ethico-politico-centric cultural characteristic of the Chinese people blended with their specific spirit of practicality. The very term "science" originated from the Latin word "scientia," meaning knowledge. Marx professed that his theory was scientific socialism. This showed that he put science above everything else and elaborated his socialism in contradistinction to others as the conclusion of science; but in China it is stressed that science

① *Book of Lao Zi*, chap. 20.

② Ibid., chap. 21.

serves socialist politics, such that the ethico-political interest reigns supreme.

It is likely just because of the Chinese emphasis on ethical supremacy that in China there has been no religion in the Occidental sense of the word. Knowledge relates to the individual but ethics relates to the community; yet the individual was given no independence of his own, and has been always merely a part of the community. If the individual be the final entity, he must resort to some reliable knowledge as his ultimate support. But when one is subordinated to the community, then the community and inter-human relationships assume the role of an ultimate support, instead of any knowledge. Religion in the West may be said to contain such a duplicity: in the respect of the dogmatism in its doctrine, it is contradictory to the pure reason of scientific knowledge, but in its ever-insatiate longing for the infinity, it is largely concordant with science in their shared pursuit of the infinite. In close connection with this, the most significant phenomenon in Chinese intellectual history is the absence of any atomism in the style of ancient Greece or of mechanism in the style of the modern West. Those two lines of thought successively framed the most fundamental and decisive factors in the formation and development of modern science and scientific thought. In the late ancient times, the great migrations of peoples in the West led to the dissolution of the blood-lineage system of the traditional clans. The starting point of individualism is the face-to-face confrontation between the individual and the bondage of mediaeval hierarchy. The reason why China had no modern science is precisely the reason why China had no individualism or mechanistic atomism. In China blood-lineage has never been dissolved, and so the individual has always been confined within a social web of interpersonal relationships in which everyone is regulated and controlled by his status in that web. As Henry Maine wrote, "The movement of the progressive societies has hitherto been from status to contract."① From this perspective, the traditional society of China has always remained in a state of status rather than one of contract. The individual has never enjoyed independent existence as a monad. The individual exists only for the sake of the ethical relationship and hence has to dedicate all that is his to the cause of the supra-individual community. He has no right to his own choice, but has to give up everything of his to the community. Besides this, he has no value of his own as an independent individual. His vocation exists only in fulfilling the demands of interpersonal relationships to his utmost.

By the same token, the value of an individual life exists entirely in his

① H. Maine, *Ancient Law*, chap. 6.

contribution to the ethical demands of the community in spite of himself. Knowledge and truth, beauty and art, romantic love and all such things can possess no intrinsic value of their own. One is not to seek knowledge for the sake of knowing (the Aristotelian disinterested contemplation) but to realize one's ethical obligation to the cause of the community. Neither knowledge nor the individual life has any value of its own, except as a mere means for the sake of certain ethico-political ends, fictitious or real. When an individual is assumed as an ultimate entity, he has to resort to some knowledge, certain and reliable, as his ultimate spiritual support. But when the individual is subordinate to human relationships, then the human relationship replaces all knowledge as his last resort. The Christianity of the West also possessed its own dual character. In its emphasis on religious dogma, it was by nature repellent to pure reason. Yet in its ceaseless and unquenchable pursuit of infinity, there was something in it similar to the scientific longing for the ultimate truth.

In China, the individual has been forever interwoven into a web of blood-bond relationships within which every member is bound to be regulated and controlled by his position or location in this web. This ethico-political bondage reigns over the individual in his entirety, all his ideas and behaviors included. All of one's ideas and behaviors have to conform to his status as exacted by this specific field, whether by satisfying loyalty to the sovereign, filial piety to the family, or whichever other demand may ensue. Without all this, life is regarded as meaningless. Such an intellectual and cultural background may serve to explain why there has been neither atomism nor the related mechanism, so essential for the formation of modern science.

Atomism and mechanism hand in hand with individualism and the idea of universal law are the theoretical presuppositions from which modern science took its start. Some have argued that in ancient China Mo Zi's works embraced certain elements of atomism, while others thought that in Zhuang Zi's chapter 'The World" there can be found a hint of the concept of the atom. One may interpret them as one wishes, but there is no evidence that the Chinese had already took on the idea of atomism as a definite theoretical construct. As to precursors that might have anticipated it, this depends largely on how we define the term "germination," as discussed above. Anyhow it is beyond doubt that in the pre-modern times we can find no systematic exposition of atomism and mechanism in China, just as we can find no capitalism in China. Thus it is but natural that modern science did not appear in China. And the question of why atomism and mechanism did not appear in China is closely correlated with the fact that the individual was never a final independent entity and that the natural world was but an outward projection of the ethical fiction. Just as there was no individualism in the ethical world of the Chinese, so there was no atomism nor mechanism in their world of nature. Modernization depends on modern science. The secret behind the lingering steps of modern science in China ought to be identified in the depths of her cultural and intellectual heritage.

In the main, the Chinese thinkers were used to seeing the individual only in the light of the community but never in the light of an isolated and independent self-existence *per se*. Their world-view was holistic and organic rather than atomic and mechanic. Such a deep-rooted world-view has led them never to orientate their thinking from the standpoint of the individual or individualism. An all-embracing web of interpersonal relationships had swallowed up all that was individual or individualistic in nature for countless ages.

Since modern science trod its way via atomism and mechanism, could it have been possible for the traditional Chinese way of thinking—which had had no engagement with either atomism or mechanism—to step into the palace of modern science all by herself with no contact from the West? On this issue, Joseph Needham professed that the route that science in China took was the naturalistic approach of the Taoists, i.e. a synthetic, organismal model—an approach which is not only capable of reaching the height of modern science but also represents the orientation for further development of science in the future. According to him, science in the West will too turn from the analytic road of mechanism to the synthetic road of organism.

[V] Afterwords

As a matter of course, historical study should be permitted to make rational suppositions, which are however incapable of testing by experiment. The above-mentioned viewpoint of Needham merely expressed his personal preference and expectation. Perhaps we are forever unable to verify or falsify whether the route modern science has traveled in the West is the only one universally valid for all peoples. If China had never had any contact with the West, could her traditional culture and ideas independently match the height of modern science without taking the analytic way of atomism and mechanism in the style of the West? This question may depend on a still larger one. Is there a universal law of the development of human culture valid for all peoples with no exception, or is every people only following her own way of development, or are both true simultaneously, i.e. while it follows the universal law, it adopts at the same time a way of her own? If both are valid at the same time, the universal law should reign over the particular. What is particular cannot outrun the universal, and this holds too in the field of the history of ideas. In researching the singularity of each culture, one ought to consider first what is common to all cultures. This does not mean any devaluation or even complete elimination of the intellectual peculiarities of different peoples. On the contrary, it is exactly the specific contributions of each and every people that form the variegated blossom of the sum of the civilization of mankind.

I am of the opinion that the future development of scientific ideas may prove a turning away from the channel of the mechanic and the analytic to that of the organic and the synthetic as Needham predicted. Be it the case, then the mode of thinking in classical China will assuredly and decidedly be able to provide significant contributions. Nevertheless, the mechanical and analytical mode of thinking is ultimately both an indispensable and insurmountable step leading to the palace of modern science. It looks impossible to reach the next step by abruptly jumping over the immediate step. The dictum "natura non saltum facit" is probably not correct for natural history, but "scientia non saltum facit"[①] is very likely a correct universal law of our thought and knowledge. After all, the process of isolated analysis precedes that of an overall synthesis. A Galileo has to precede a Whitehead—to use the name of a figure whom Needham was so fond of citing. The traditional way of thinking in China, whether the Confucian or the Taoist, directly resorts to a grasp of the totality of the Tao (Way) while discarding all mechanical analysis to total oblivion. Perhaps this is the reason why China did not tread the way leading to the hall of modern science all by herself.

Philosophy furnishes us not only with knowledge, but also—what is more important—wisdom. Although the ancient philosophy in China did not lead directly to modern science, the wisdom offered by its particular way of thinking would undoubtedly help to enrich the depth and breadth of modern thinking.

① "Nature does not make leaps," and "science does not make leaps."

Index

图书在版编目（CIP）数据

中国古代哲学批评史 = A Critical History of Classical Chinese Philosophy：英文／何兆武，彭刚著．
北京：新世界出版社，2009.9
ISBN 978-7-5104-0537-2

I. 中… Ⅱ. ①何…②彭… Ⅲ. 哲学史－中国－古代－英文 Ⅳ.B21

中国版本图书馆 CIP 数据核字（2009）第 156830 号

中国古代哲学批评史（英）

作　　者：何兆武　彭刚
责任编辑：李淑娟　许靖国
英文审定：Ricky Jeffrey
封面设计：贺玉婷
版式设计：清鑫工作室
责任印制：李一鸣　黄厚清
出版发行：新世界出版社
社　　址：北京市西城区百万庄大街 24 号（100037）
总编室电话：+ 86 10 6899 5424　　68326679（传真）
发行部电话：+ 86 10 6899 5968　　68998705（传真）
本社中文网址：http://www.nwp.cn
本社英文网址：http://www.newworld-press.com
版权部电子信箱：frank@nwp.com.cn
版权部电话：+ 86 10 6899 6306
印刷：保定天德印务有限公司
经销：新华书店
开本：787 × 1092　　1/16
字数：200 千字　　印张：20.25
版次：2009 年 10 月第 1 版　　2009 年 10 月第 1 次印刷
书号：ISBN　978-7-5104-0537-2
定价：38.00 元
